Business Plan Business Reality

Starting and Managing Your Own Business in Canada

James R. Skinner

Humber Institute of Technology
and Advanced Learning

Second Edition

PEARSON

Prentice
Hall

Toronto

Library and Archives Canada Cataloguing in Publication

Skinner, James R. (James Ross), 1950–
    Business plan, business reality: starting and managing your own
business in Canada / James R. Skinner.—2nd ed.

Includes index.
First ed. published 2003 under title: Business plan to business reality:
    the practical guide to working for yourself.

ISBN-13: 978-0-13-199763-9
ISBN-10: 0-13-199763-7

1. New business enterprises—Canada. 2. Self-employed—Canada.
3. Small business—Canada—Management. I. Skinner, James R. (James Ross),
1950–. Business plan to business reality. II. Title.

HD62.5.S574 2007   658.1'1410971   C2006-904779-0

ISBN-13: 978-0-13-199763-9
ISBN-10: 0-13-199763-7

Editor-in-Chief: Gary Bennett
Acquisitions Editor: Karen Elliott
Marketing Manager: Eileen Lasswell
Associate Editor: Rema Celio
Production Editor: Jen Handel
Copy Editor: Integra
Proofreader: Kelli Howey
Production Coordinator: Christine Kwan
Composition: Integra
Art Director: Julia Hall
Interior/Cover Design: Chris Tsinziras
Cover Image: Getty Images/Eric O'Connell

1 2 3 4 5   12 11 10 09 08

Printed and bound in Canada.

Brief Contents

Contents

Preface

To the Student and the Aspiring Entrepreneur

DON'T YOU DARE SKIP THIS PART!

Most people skip over the preface, in a hurry to get to the stuff that they want to know. By reading the preface, however, you are more likely to understand the context and organization of the material. As a result, the material will be faster and easier to learn. So please read it.

The purpose of this text is to provide you with the basic knowledge required to plan, start, and manage a small business or some form of self-employment. The text is designed for post-secondary-level courses and workshops. It can also be used by anyone who wants a "do-it-yourself" plan for self-employment (actors, animal wranglers, bodyguards, bush pilots, choreographers, decorators, fashion designers, landscapers, private investigators, researchers, singers, sound mixers, writers . . .) as well as those who will start more traditional small businesses (appliance repair centres, clothing stores, consulting firms, computer services, machine shops, paralegal offices, photography studios, publishing companies, restaurants . . .). The list is endless and likely to include your own business idea.

You probably do have some kind of moneymaking idea kicking around in your head, but that's all it is: an idea. The idea itself has little value, since, like most people, you're not likely to act on it. But the minute you write your idea down it starts to become a *plan*. That is the first step toward working for yourself; writing a business plan.

So, Part 1 of the text is organized the same way a business plan is organized. Chapters 1–5 correspond to the sections of the basic start-up business plan. Part 2 of the text, Chapters 6–8, is about alternative methods of starting into business: franchising, buying a business, or taking over the family firm. And Part 3, Chapters 9–11, covers the long-term management of the business as well as the development of the entrepreneur. Some courses or individuals will use only the first five chapters, some will use all of them, and some will use various other selections of chapters.

The style of this text is intended to:
- *Show you where to get help.* You don't have to know everything there is to know about business to make money. Few self-employed people are capable of doing it all themselves, and the emphasis will be on getting professional help for the hard stuff. Look for the *Get Help* items for sources of assistance.
- *Use your learning time efficiently.* A series of *Test Yourself* true/false questions have been sprinkled through the text as an easy way of checking whether you are absorbing the information. When you encounter a question where you really don't know the answer, either take a break or skip back a few pages and start re-reading.

You probably have some kind of moneymaking idea kicking around in your head, but that's all it is: an idea. The idea itself has little value, since, like most people, you're not likely to act on it. But the minute you write your idea down it starts to become a plan.

- *Use your existing knowledge.* We all learn better and faster when new concepts are attached to our own ideas and existing knowledge. For this reason, you will be prompted to *Ask yourself* about your own personal experiences, observations, conclusions, and decisions throughout the text.
- *Get you moving.* Simple *Head Start* exercises provide a relatively painless way to create parts of your business plan. Alternatively, these exercises may be used by your instructor as short assignments.

Throughout the text, examples from a wide variety of businesses are used. For some readers, this may at first seem distracting. For example, if you are thinking about starting a restaurant, you really only want restaurant examples; you don't want to read about a garage or a sound equipment rental firm. If you are studying aviation management, you want to see examples from your own industry. But this prejudice comes from failing to recognize a simple truth: business is business. There clearly are some differences between how independent film producers and owners of plumbing companies do their work, but not in how they *make money*. They both make money by applying the same principles of business.

Many talented artists and skilled technicians profess little interest in *business*. They make the critical mistake of believing that financial success will automatically come as the result of their skills or talents. But *Ask yourself: How many great artists have died penniless? Know of any third-rate musicians that nevertheless make lots of money?* Skill and talent are only a small part of the route to financial success. The rest is business. Once you see yourself as a businessperson, every time you fill your gas tank, go to the bank, or eat in a restaurant, you'll be learning a little more about how to make money in your own field. You'll truly be *in business*.

To the Professor

There are few teaching experiences more satisfying than seeing students learn something that they will actually use throughout their working lives. Courses in starting and managing small businesses provide knowledge and skills that have many practical applications for both employment situations and personal financial management. So even though (for most of us teaching entrepreneurship) only a minority of our graduates go on to be successful business owners, our courses are among the most influential for all the students who take them.

The text and support materials are designed for a range of post-secondary levels covering courses that focus on *new business start-up* as well as those emphasizing the on-going *management of small enterprises*. To accommodate this variety, the text is divided into three parts:
- Part 1 (Chapters 1–5) covers the basic start-up business plan.
- Part 2 (Chapters 6–8) examines alternative methods of starting into business: buying a franchise, buying an existing business, or taking over a family firm.
- Part 3 (Chapters 9–11) explores the long-term management of the business as well as the development of the entrepreneur.

Each chapter is followed by a workbook template for completing that particular portion of a business plan. This text is intended for use by:
- *Business students*, typically in undergraduate diploma and degree programs that usually include one or two required courses in entrepreneurship.
- *Non–business students*, including a huge array of arts, technology, and applied science programs that may lead to some form of self-employment for the graduate.

- *Start-up entrepreneurs*, typically in continuing education classes, short courses, and work-shops leading directly to self-employment or small business ownership.

The Course Application Chart shows typical chapter selections for different levels of courses. For those developing new courses in entrepreneurship, the Instructor's Resource Manual contains valuable design assistance. (See below.)

This edition has been specifically prepared for the current realities of post-secondary teaching: fewer classroom contact hours, larger class sizes, reduced marking or evaluation time, greater reliance on part-time/occasional faculty (who often have minimal preparation time), and higher expectations from administrators and advisory boards for generic skills, currency of material, and student satisfaction. With all of this in mind, the comprehensive Instructor's Resource CD-ROM (ISBN: 0-13-233213-2) includes the following resources:

- *Instructor's Resource Manual.* This comprehensive guide includes the following resources:
  - *Lesson Notes.* The notes are in the form of questions that instructors can ask leading to the development of the lesson or mini-lecture.
  - *Exercises/Project Assignments.* Short in-class and homework *Learning Tasks* are provided for each chapter. In addition, a detailed outline is provided for a major project

COURSE APPLICATION CHART

Program Type	Chapters (Typical)	Example Course Titles
- Practical non-credit start-up workshops - 2–3-year business diploma (as introductory course) - 2–4-year non-business degree or diploma	1–5	- Writing a Business Plan - Developing a Business Plan - Planning a New Business - Introduction to Entrepreneurship - Starting a Small Business
- 3-year business diploma - 3–4-year non-business degree or diploma (as advanced course) - 4-year business degree (as introductory course)	1–7 or 1–8	- Introduction to Business Ownership - Independent Business - Small Business Ownership - Organizing a New Business
- 3-year business diploma (as advanced course) - 4-year business degree	1–5 & 9–10 or 1–5 & 9–11	- Small Business and Entrepreneurship - New-Venture Development - Small Business Management
- 4-year business degree (as advanced course)	1–11	- Managing Business Growth - Small, Medium Enterprise Management - Building an Independent Business - Entrepreneurship and Management - Strategic Entrepreneurship - Advanced Entrepreneurship

that involves reporting on an existing small business. (This is especially valuable for independent or distance-learning courses.)

- *Generic and Customized Case Studies.* A series of 22 short case studies are available to illustrate specific concepts from the text. For business programs, these use examples from a wide selection of industries. But, for various non-business programs, the cases have been customized and are available as a package specifically for Internet management, photography, paralegal, electrical control, hospitality, golf, and other programs. (Check with your Pearson sales representative on availability for your specific program.)
- *Test Bank.* Multiple choice, true/false, fill-in-the-blank, short answer, and essay questions are provided for each chapter of the text. As well, an example comprehensive final exam is included. This can also be used as a comprehensive challenge test.
- *Marking Notes.* Correct answers for objective test questions are provided as well as suggested marking schemes for short answer and essay questions and for business plan submissions.
- *Course Design Notes.* A formula to assist with identifying the appropriate course level for your students is provided along with example course outlines for different levels of entrepreneurship courses.
- *PowerPoint® Presentations.* Lesson topics are provided as PowerPoint slides for each of the chapters.

This edition also includes a Text Enrichment Site for students at **www.pearsoned.ca/text/skinner**. This site provides updates, weblinks, study tips, and errata material for instructors and students alike.

Acknowledgments

The author would like to thank the wonderful team at Pearson who worked tirelessly on this project: Acquisitions Editor, Karen Elliott; Marketing Manager, Cas Shields; Associate Editor, Rema Celio; Production Editor, Jen Handel; Production Coordinator, Christine Kwan; Copy Editor, Integra (Murugaraj); Proofreader, Kelli Howey; Cold Reader, Gilda Mekler.

A special thanks to the reviewers of this second edition who will each be able to see their contributions here: Terri Champion, Niagara College; Paul F. Dunne, College of the North Atlantic; Michael A. Malazdrewicz, Brandon University; Paul Myers, St. Clair College; Kayrod Niamir, Dawson College; Robert Salomons, Southern Alberta Institute of Technology.

Finally, thanks to Michael Hatton (who started this project rolling at Humber) and all those whose support and assistance made this book possible: Adrienne Armstrong, Edmund Bauman, Jim Beatty, Doug Campbell, Alvina Cassianni, Ray Chateau, Chris Chown, James Cullin, John Currie, Rick Embree, Andrea Falkenberg, Toby Fletcher, Jane Forbes, Keith Hebblewhite, Sandie Heirwegh, Susan Lieberman, Karen Low, Peter Madott, John McColl, Richard Michel, Dave Nugent, William E. Rowberry, David Ross, Tracy Ryder, Ryke Simon, Ramesh Srinivasan, Laurie Turner, Barb Watts, and Pam Welsh.

The author also wishes to thank all those who have adopted this text and welcomes any comments at **jim.skinner@humber.ca**.

chapter 1

The Concept:
What Business Will I Be In?

LEARNING OBJECTIVES

On completion of this chapter, you should be able to:

- *Discuss the definition and role of "small business."*
- *Outline the characteristics of successful entrepreneurs.*
- *Assess your own potential as an entrepreneur.*
- *Identify advantages and disadvantages of an entrepreneurial lifestyle.*
- *Discuss the difference in skills required for entrepreneurship vs. employment.*
- *Define a new business in terms of what it will sell and to whom.*
- *Compare the various legal forms of business.*
- *Identify sources of help to prepare a business plan.*
- *Prepare the Concept and Summary portion of a business plan.*

What Does It Mean to "Be in Business"?

SMALL BUSINESS AND ENTREPRENEURSHIP This book is about starting a **small business,** and most of us hold a pretty clear picture in our minds of what a small business is. But most of us are wrong; at least according to the experts. *Ask yourself: How many employees can a business have and still be considered small?* There is no standard definition of *business size.* But many of the academics and researchers who study these matters tend to define a *small business* as a company having fewer than 500 employees, sometimes more.[1] Now that's a lot bigger than most of us picture small businesses to be, but there is some logic behind this definition. Strategically, how you plan and run a business of 1 person—or 3 people or 40 people—is not terribly different from the strategy used in firms of up to 500 people.

✓ **Test Yourself 1.1**
True or False? An idea starts to become a plan when it is written down. (*Hint:* If you aren't sure about the book's answer to this question, go back and re-read the Preface.)

small business An independently owned organization that exists to make a profit for its owner(s), often measured as having fewer than 500 employees.

micro-enterprise A very small business, usually measured as having fewer than five employees.

self-employment Working either as a freelancer or as a short-term contract worker—not a permanent employee of any firm, but not technically a business owner (not having employees or any significant business assets); still an entrepreneur, requiring a business plan.

Canada Revenue Agency A department of the federal government that acts as Canada's tax collector.

freelance An independent service provider, not employed by any one company, and sometimes producing work before it has been sold.

entrepreneur Someone who risks money (or their own time and effort) to make a profit. All business owners, freelancers, and otherwise self-employed people are entrepreneurs.

✓ **Test Yourself 1.2**
True or False? A business could have up to 500 employees and still be considered a "small business."

✓ **Test Yourself 1.3**
True or False? A freelance journalist is generally considered to be a business owner.

✓ **Test Yourself 1.4**
True or False? A freelance journalist should be working with a business plan.

✓ **Test Yourself 1.5**
True or False? A freelance journalist is an entrepreneur.

The lesson here is that organizing and running a business of any size is a complex activity that takes thought and planning. Realistically, over 90 percent of the small businesses in Canada have fewer than five employees.[2] This is a category that many researchers would call **micro-enterprise**: operations, often family-based firms, which typically have just one or two people.

And what about the one-person business? **Self-employment** is a term used to describe individuals who work on their own, often out of their homes, and often on a contract basis for various companies. Some of these people may not be classified as business "owners," but rather as "contract employees." In fact, **Canada Revenue Agency** treats many of these people as employees even when they consider themselves to be in their own business. This raises the question, "What is a business?"

Generally, a business must have some value of its own, apart from its owner. The question to ask yourself is this: *Could I sell the business?* If you're a one-person plumbing company, the answer is probably yes, in that selling the business would mean selling the truck, the tools, the company name, and maybe some contracts. If you're a **freelance** speechwriter, however, the answer is probably no. In this case, the entire existence of the business would depend on you, the owner, without whom there would be nothing to sell.

Ask yourself: Does this mean that freelancers who earn their living by selling their personal services are not "in business" and do not need a business plan? IT DOES NOT! Even though lenders tend not to treat freelancers as businesses, they still have to plan and carry out most of the same business activities as those who have a business that they could sell. Freelancers, to be successful, should still use a business plan.

Although freelancers may not always be considered business owners, they do practise *entrepreneurship*. They risk their time, labour, and money in order to make *profit*. This is the essence of entrepreneurship. So even though not all **entrepreneurs** are official business owners, certainly all business owners are entrepreneurs. *Ask yourself: Am I clear on the definitions of entrepreneurship, small business, self-employment, freelance?*

Despite the fact that the above terms have precise meanings, they will be used interchangeably in many instances in this text. That's because all entrepreneurs—small business owners, freelancers, and self-employed people—need business plans. And the business plan is what this book is all about.

This first component of the business plan demonstrates that you have given some thought as to whether you are the right kind of person to start a business. It demonstrates that you have the right training and experience and that you know what you are getting into. It also clearly states the nature of your business and the legal set-up, describing any partner or investor relationships.

Should I Be Working for Myself?

Entrepreneurship is a great equalizer. It has long been a way to overcome barriers against ethnicity, age, and gender. True, some ethnic and cultural groups are more likely to have a tradition of entrepreneurship, but this is usually because of historical discrimination barring them from trades or professions in many parts of the world. In Canada, for some aboriginal groups who traditionally lacked access to business capital, entrepreneurship has become a route to self-sufficiency. For the young in Canada, entrepreneurship is now highly encouraged, with many government support programs and non-profit organizations. And the growth in entrepreneurship by women in the last few years has been explosive. Forty-seven percent of Canadian businesses are now at least partly owned by women, who have access to borrowing money equivalent to that of their male counterparts.[3]

THE ENTREPRENEURIAL PERSONALITY   *Ask yourself: What kind of personalities do successful entrepreneurs have?* Do you think of terms like aggressive, outgoing, intelligent, dedicated, self-motivated, ruthless, single-minded, charismatic, scheming, and so on? This is how many of us picture entrepreneurs. But take a moment and think about some real-life entrepreneurs you may have met, not the ideal entrepreneurs of popular culture. Think of someone who is, perhaps, the owner of the dry cleaner near your home, the owner of the drug store where you work part time, or the owner of the garage that fixes your car. These are people who make a living by running their own business; in other words, successful entrepreneurs who, for the most part, are not the perfect heroes of modern mythology. In fact, they tend to be pretty ordinary people: some of them kind, some shy, some lazy—not the movie image of the successful entrepreneur.

Complete the following "trait test."

 Get Help 1.1
Links to many resources for young entrepreneurs (under 35) can be found on the website of the Victoria-based *Young Entrepreneurs Association*: ***www.yea.ca***.

Get Help 1.2
For information about assistance to aboriginal businesses, start with the Aboriginal Canada Portal (***www.aboriginalcanada.gc.ca***) and click on *economic development and business*.

Get Help 1.3
Women Entrepreneurs of Canada is a non-profit organization that champions women's entrepreneurship. Their website is ***www.wec.ca***.

Trait Test[4]
Score each of the following statements according to how true it is of you. Calculate a total at the bottom.

> 0 = never true of you
> 1 = occasionally true of you
> 2 = usually true of you
> 3 = always true of you

I am confident in my ability to influence others. _____
I work harder than most others I know. _____
I have a clear picture of my future. _____
I spend more time attending to responsibilities than most people do. _____
I have specific long-term goals. _____
I spend time each week planning my future. _____
Compared to most people, I take work or school seriously. _____
I do a thorough job in completing my tasks. _____
The steps to success are obvious to me. _____
I believe in my own ability to succeed. _____
I work more hours per day than the average person. _____
I see myself as controlling my own destiny. _____
Compared to others, I am more likely to exercise self-control. _____
I make the major decisions that affect my life. _____
I know what I want to achieve. _____
TOTAL _____

Many small business texts start out with a self-assessment test of some sort, something to see if you're the right kind of person to run your own business. So, what characteristics are these entrepreneurial tests typically looking for?

Most of these tests are looking for the same characteristics that are *popularly believed* to be true of entrepreneurs. They are typically based on some form of research, but for the most part, this research lacks validity. In fact, much of it is "**junk research**"—looking at characteristics of people who are already successful business owners, instead of looking at the traits that entrepreneurs had *before* they became successful business owners. There are a few rigorous studies of the traits that help people to *become* successful entrepreneurs, and the results of these show that *most people have the potential to start and run a business.*[5]

junk research Studies that are based on flawed logic or poor application of scientific methods.

SELF-ANALYSIS   Generally, but not universally, successful entrepreneurs tend to be a little more hard-working than the rest of the population; they tend to be more goal-oriented; and they tend to have more confidence in their own ability to influence their futures. These are the characteristics that the self-scored test above is looking for.

Scores

Above 38	well above average
34–38	above average
26–34	average
22–26	below average
Below 22	well below average

If you didn't get the score you wanted, don't worry about it. Remember, with self-assessment tests like this there are always questions of validity and reliability—if you were to have something different for breakfast tomorrow, and were to rewrite the test, you might get a different score. There is little evidence that these tests can actually predict entrepreneurial accomplishment. Besides, the real value in tests like the one above is that they make you ask yourself about yourself. *Ask yourself: Am I the kind of person who can start and run a business?*

There is little doubt that a certain combination of personality, skills, and desire produces the ideal entrepreneur. But some of us have no inclination to run our own business, regardless of our talents in these areas. Circumstances, however, make some people believe that self-employment, though not their first choice, is the only option available to them: the graduate with a diploma but no job prospects, the aging "downsized" middle manager, the new immigrant with no Canadian work history, the mature homemaker who has been out of the workforce for many years and can't find employment. These people are often categorized as "reluctant" entrepreneurs. **Reluctant entrepreneurs** are less likely to be committed to the business and often will abandon the process of starting their own firm as soon as a suitable job becomes available to them.

reluctant entrepreneur Someone who would rather work for an employer but is forced into self-employment because they cannot find a suitable job in their chosen field.

✓ **Test Yourself 1.6**
True or False? Most of the "entrepreneurial ability" tests are accurate predictors of one's ability to start a business.

The question of *desire* to start one's own business is perhaps much more important than ability. This desire is certainly influenced by a person's concept of "being in business." Many consider it a lot more prestigious to be president of a five-person company than to be manager of a 500-employee division of a giant organization. Most entrepreneurs have strong feelings about the importance of business ownership—they really want to do it. *Ask yourself: Do I really want to do it?*

What Sort of Lifestyle Can I Expect?

PERSONAL DEMANDS   There is a strong emotional component to entrepreneurship. It is the passion that an owner has about his or her business that provides the tremendous amount of energy required to start a new venture. Right now, you probably spend too much time watching TV. If you go into business for yourself, that won't be a problem. Surveys show that business owners, especially at start-up, may work many more hours than the average employed person works. One Canadian study shows that entrepreneurs work about one-third more hours than salaried employees.[6] About a third of entrepreneurs routinely work more than 50 hours per week.[7] This lifestyle is demanding: it's not for the dabbler, the hobbyist, or the part-timer. Furthermore, you have to know what you're doing. This is why *having worked for someone else in the same industry is one of the stronger predictors of new-business success.*[8] Unfortunately, many people go into a business where they have no experience. Lack of experience and not understanding the time demands—these are among the main reasons that the majority of new businesses fail. In fact, two-thirds of new micro-enterprises don't last 5 years[9] and only 20 percent make it to the 10-year mark.[10]

With all that extra work and all the responsibility and risk of running a business, the stress can be significant. Nevertheless, the research is still unclear on whether it's more stressful to be an employee or to be the boss. But if you've got a job, *Ask yourself: Of all the people in my life, who gives me the greatest amount of stress?* If your answer is "my boss," you're in the same boat as most employed people. The great irony is that by becoming the boss yourself, in owning the company, you may work as though you were a slave to the business. Despite that, the majority of successful entrepreneurs report that they love the independence. *Ask yourself again: Do I really want to be my own boss? How badly?*

FAMILY ISSUES   If you're involved in a committed relationship, the decision to go into business cannot be yours alone. Because of the time and financial demands (even for successful firms, it usually takes a good while to start making money), it is important that you have the total support of your life partner. Without this support, you may find your spouse and the business competing for your attention: one of them will have to lose.

Some couples resolve this by going into business in partnership, an arrangement that has its own set of advantages and disadvantages. When your life partner and your business partner are one and the same, you could end up together 24 hours a day, seven days a week. This kind of closeness works well for some pairs, but for others absence makes the heart grow fonder. *Ask yourself: How will starting a business affect my relationship with my life partner, spouse, or fiancé?*

Similar issues arise when you have children. Obviously, when starting a new business, you will have less time to devote to your kids than if you were employed or a stay-at-home parent. Home-based businesses may seem like a solution, but picture yourself on the phone with a demanding customer while a determined three-year-old tries to get your attention. (See "Home-Based Businesses" in Chapter 2.) When the kids are older, however, one of the big advantages of owning your own firm is that it can provide employment for family members. As children mature, the tendency to socialize less and less with parents can be offset by the closeness of working together. *Ask yourself: How will owning my own business affect my relationships with my children?*

> **? Get Help 1.4**
>
> If you are unsure about your own suitability to run a business, arrange an interview with an employment or career counsellor through your local community college or check with your local Service Canada office (1-800-O-Canada) for any programs near you.

SMALL BUSINESS PROFILE 1.1

Rocky River Sign Co. Inc.

Cameron Mahy was working for Canada's largest sign company in 1994 when he got notice that he was being let go. Essentially, he and others were being replaced by new technologies. But Cam had no regrets since the company and its artists from all over the world had trained him in the classic art of sign painting. The path ahead was clear to Cam because he had been an entrepreneur for most of his life. As a kid, starting with a paper route, Cam had progressed to a lawn maintenance business by age 12, and even as a full-time employee he was painting signs on trucks for his own clients. So when he lost his job, Cam immediately signed up for a federally sponsored business start-up program, where he learned to write a business plan. Thus the *Rocky River Sign Company Inc.* was born.

In the first two years, the business was growing, but there were many problems. Cam was a great designer and artist and good with the customers, but details like billing and accounting were not getting attended to. Then, in 1996, Cam's wife Robin joined the company and, with her background in banking and administration, she organized the operation to run smoothly and efficiently. Interestingly, over the years Robin has picked up more involvement in the design end of things, showing her own creativity with banner, vehicle, and even apparel designs.

These days, *Rocky River Sign Co.* targets primarily small local firms, providing them with a complete range of signs from illuminated storefront and rooftop signs to decals, window signs, billboards, vehicle signage, and even custom embroidery that lets customers wear their signs. Cam is recognized for some of his more visible work that includes murals on major buildings and even painting the logos on the Astroturf field for the Grey Cup.

Typically, Robin works the five-day, nine-to-five workweek while Cam can put in 70–80 hours as the business goes through a growth spurt. The company has three employees now, but Cam expects it to grow to five over the next couple of years. Cam sees no disadvantage to working with his wife, whom he describes as "definitely my best friend."

Get Help 1.5
To read about recent Canadian small business success stories go to **http://sbinfocanada.about.com/od/successstories/**.

underground economy All of the illegally unreported business and consumer transactions conducted for cash or barter on which taxes are not paid.

EMPLOYEE VS. ENTREPRENEUR There is lots of good news about being in business for yourself, including the money. Small businesses that are successful can provide their owners with incomes far above the average for employed people. The statistics don't always reflect this clearly, but still show entrepreneurs as making somewhat more than the average.[11] The statistics, however, can be misleading. When small-business incomes are reported, they tend to include the failing companies (with little or no personal income for the owner) and they do not include the **underground economy** (the billions of dollars in unreported income that is funnelled through small companies each year).[12] When working for an employer, there are many factors that limit the employee's income including what society thinks is fair pay for a particular job and the labour market itself. *Ask yourself: Why would an employer pay any more for help than is necessary?* But when working for yourself, you can take home as much money as the business can produce. The sky's the limit. Every one of Canada's billionaires got that way by owning businesses, not by working for the government or big companies. If becoming wealthy is your goal in life, your single best chance for it is through entrepreneurship.

For a number of years, educators and employers in Canada have been co-operating to help foster **employability skills** in today's graduates. These include skills in

- oral and written communications
- mathematics
- time management
- teamwork
- computer literacy.

employability skills The general knowledge and abilities that employers seek in prospective employees. Examples are literacy, computer literacy, numeracy, time management, and teamwork skills.

Certainly, all of the above could be advantageous, not just in employees, but to the small business owner personally. In addition, however, the entrepreneur needs some skills in the following areas:

- *Financial planning.* A huge number of *potentially profitable* firms go bankrupt each year simply because of the entrepreneur's inability to understand and plan "cash flow."
- *Sales/negotiation.* The entire profit-making process starts with convincing someone to buy your product or service. Profit can also depend on an entrepreneur's ability to make deals with suppliers, regulators, and even employees.
- *People management.* While not necessarily important at start-up, the eventual growth of a business is going to depend on employees, which the entrepreneur will have to recruit, train, and motivate.

These are **entrepreneurial skills.**

To be a successful entrepreneur, however, *you don't have to do it all on your own!* While employees may be judged on their personal skills, entrepreneurs are not. Entrepreneurs are judged solely on their ability to make profit. An entrepreneur who lacks financial skills can rely on an accountant for help in this area. A poor negotiator can partner up with a strong negotiator. It is also possible to start a business by buying a franchise where all of the management systems and training are provided. So, the real skill of the successful entrepreneur becomes the ability to assess himself or herself and seek help in any weak areas. *Ask yourself: What entrepreneurial skills do I have? Which do I need help with?*

entrepreneurial skills The knowledge and abilities necessary to make profit in business. These include financial, negotiation, and people skills.

✓ **Test Yourself 1.7**
True or False? Computer literacy would be classified as an entrepreneurial skill.

Head Start Exercise

1.1   Prepare a brief résumé of your education and work experience. Then, in three or four brief sentences, explain why a career as an entrepreneur would be appropriate for you. ($1\frac{1}{4}$ page maximum.)

What Is My Business Idea?

CAUSES OF DEMAND   Every change produces a business opportunity, sometimes called a **gap**. The kind of change doesn't matter: political, economic, social, cultural, environmental, technological. A growth in the number of school-aged children means a need for more photographers taking class and graduation pictures. An increase in purchasing via the Internet means a need for more web-page designers targeting businesses. More online magazines means a need for more freelance journalists.

gap An unsatisfied need or opportunity in the marketplace, produced by some kind of change that has taken place.

Why is now a good time to start a business of the sort you are proposing? This is a natural question from lenders or prospective investors when approached by someone starting a business. The best way to answer this question is by pointing out some sort of change that has given rise to this business opportunity. For example: "There has recently been a big increase in home schooling, so I am starting an online service to sell teaching aids to parents who teach their kids at home." *Ask yourself: What was the change that produced an opportunity for my favourite band? My favourite restaurant?*

SPECIALIZATION   The highest-paid medical doctors are the superspecialists—those who treat only a certain organ or fight a particular group of diseases. When something is wrong with your heart, you want only a cardiologist. Even though a family physician may be well enough trained to diagnose and treat you, if it's your heart you probably want to see a cardiologist. If you are accused of tax evasion, the lawyer who handled your will or real estate transaction may be perfectly competent to handle the problem. But you would rather have a specialized tax lawyer, even though you know it will cost you more.

It works pretty much the same for other small businesses: generally, those that specialize make the most money. This isn't always an easy concept to accept. It might seem that the greater the variety of goods or services you sell, the more opportunity you will have to make money. But that's wrong. An electronics store that specializes in audio equipment does not have the overhead of a store that has to carry TVs, DVDs, cameras, computer equipment, burglar alarms, and so on. And the true audiophile shopping for those special speakers wants to buy them (and will willingly pay more) from a specialist.

There is also the issue of efficiency from specialization. If you're a freelance writer who specializes in speech writing, you can generate speeches more quickly and of better quality than the writer who does a magazine article one day, an instruction manual the next, and a promotional pamphlet the day after. Each of these writing styles has a time-consuming learning curve associated with it. Furthermore, you, as the specialist, have the further advantage of being perceived as a monopoly: the right one (the only one) to deal with.

Head Start Exercise

1.2   Make some notes explaining how you will make money by specializing in particular products or services ($\frac{1}{4}$ page maximum).

For small businesses, it is generally more profitable to specialize in a narrow range of products or services. But there is another way that a business can and should specialize: in the types of customers that it aims to capture. This is called **targeting** and, generally, small businesses that target narrow groups of customers are more profitable than businesses that tend to see themselves as being for everyone.

targeting Specializing in a particular group (or groups) of potential customers.

TARGETING   This is often a difficult concept for new business owners to accept, since the narrower the target that a business pursues the fewer the potential customers that are available.

Let's say you own a CD store and you have never met anyone who didn't like music. So your store could be for "everyone." However, if your store targets a particular age group—say, 18 to 35—there will be fewer potential customers than if you target "everyone," but your business will likely make more profit. And if your business narrows its focus to people in a particular geographic area—say, uptown neighbourhoods—there will be even fewer potential customers but your business will likely make even more money. And if your business narrows its focus even more—say, to people in a particular economic group—it will likely make even more profit. It may seem strange since each narrowing of the target group leaves fewer potential customers, but it's true! You'll make more profit.

If your store is targeting people who are all the same age, all live in the same area, all have the same incomes, the same education, the same attitudes, you can be fairly sure they will all listen to basically the same music. A business such as this can carry everything that its customers want without having the big expensive inventory needed to satisfy "everyone." In addition, advertising to this target group will be a lot cheaper than advertising to everyone (because they all live in the same small area). This saves you money, allowing for more profit.

✓ **Test Yourself 1.8**
True or False? Specialization in fewer products or services generally means more profit for a small business.

✓ **Test Yourself 1.9**
True or False? Specializing in a particular product or service is called "targeting."

Head Start Exercise

1.3 Make a list of particular customer groups you could target and note why each might be a good idea ($\frac{1}{4}$ page maximum).

DEFINING THE BUSINESS   Agreeing with the principle of specialization is one thing, but actually deciding how your company is going to do it is another. Let's say you have training in graphic arts and you worked for a sign manufacturing company; there is an *opportunity* in the sign industry based on recent technological changes allowing for inexpensive computer-based design and colour printing; there is a store for rent on the main street of your hometown and you see it as an opportunity to start a "quick-sign" store. The two specialization questions you must ask yourself are:

- *What am I selling?*
- *To whom am I selling?*

The easy answer is "*I am selling signs to anybody who wants to buy them.*" Unfortunately, this is also the wrong answer. If Shell Oil wants to buy 11,000 high-tech illuminated signs for its gas stations in Europe and North Africa, your small business obviously cannot supply them. In fact, the business you can afford to set up involves a single graphics computer with one printer that can print only on fibreboard, plastic, or paper surfaces to a maximum size of one square metre. (That is, no large illuminated signs like Shell needs.) You are already specialized by the limitations of your company. So what you expect to be selling can now be defined as *small non-illuminated signs*.

Defining *what you're selling* also helps to define who the potential customers will be. Who is able and likely to buy the type of signs you are selling? Independent gas stations offering tune-up specials, real estate agents needing "for-sale" signs, pizza parlours pushing two-for-one deals, car dealers with finance rate discounts—these are all small retail and service businesses. Logic tells us that small companies such as these are not going to chase

✓ **Test Yourself 1.10**
True or False? A business should try to have as wide a variety of potential customers as possible.
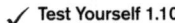

halfway across the country to buy signs: they will shop in their own geographic area. So maybe your market now becomes *small retail and service businesses within the town (or neighbourhood) where you are located.*

We are getting closer to a definition of the business. But remember: writing the business plan is really a process of rewriting, and the thing we are going to rewrite the most is the definition of the business. So, defining the business is often a process of *redefining* the business, many times. Therefore, our current definition is only a working definition, and we can expect it to be modified and refined when we look into issues of market research, sales strategy, location, competition, and so on.

◇ **Get Help 1.6**
After you write out the definition of your business as completely as you can, show it to a journalism student, marketing teacher, or the best writer you know. Ask them to summarize what you've written. Repeat this process several times. Try to remember that you are only getting editing help, and that the actual business concept must be your definition.

Head Start Exercise

1.4   Take a few minutes right now and write out the first few lines of the plan for your business idea. Briefly indicate what you will be selling and to whom you plan on selling it. ($\frac{1}{8}$ page maximum.)

Do I Need a Partner?

The "business opportunities" column of the newspaper lists many people looking for business partners. Typically, these are *people with ideas* looking for *partners with money.* There are few legitimate ads from people with lots of cash but fresh out of ideas. People can and do find partners, but it's usually from less formal sources than newspapers. Relatives, fellow employees, classmates, friends . . . these are the people one is most likely to partner up with in a new business. In many cases, the partnership is formed before the concept for the business is clear and before anyone has asked whether they really need a partner. *Ask yourself: Do I really need a partner? Why?*

There are lots of legitimate reasons for having a partner: sharing the risk, increasing financial resources, personality reasons, reasons of expertise, and so on, but the fact that someone is your cousin or long-time friend is not, by itself, reason enough to include them in the business. You should not form partnerships because of past obligations, but rather for mutual future benefit.

PARTNER PERSONALITIES   You may well need a partner—sometimes more than one. The question then becomes what personality traits and skills do you want in your partners to complement your own personality and skills. Ideally, your weaknesses will be their strengths and vice versa. Also keep in mind the extraordinary number of hours that you will be working with your partners. At the very least you want people you will get along with.

Don't forget that starting a new business is an emotional undertaking and your relationship with any partner will be emotionally charged—that means conflict, even fighting. But the purpose of a partnership is to spend your time making profit, not war. Partnership conflict is inevitable and not totally counterproductive. It can often help to look at problems from more than one perspective, but protracted fights among partners are just bad for business. *Ask yourself: Am I likely to fight longer with someone who is just like me, or with someone who is my opposite?*

As with most human conflicts, the battle is likely to be over quickly if one of the partners is dominant. Forget about trying to find a partner with whom you are perfectly evenly matched. Having one of the partners dominate could well be to the advantage of both. And when partners cannot resolve conflict themselves, it is worthwhile to seek the help of a professional mediator.[13] If **mediation** is not successful, partners can then turn to **arbitration** so that the conflict can be settled and they can get on with making some money. Over the past few years there has been a tremendous growth in Alternative Dispute Resolution (ADR), and professionally designated mediators (Chartered Mediator—C. Med.) and arbitrators (Chartered Arbitrator—C. Arb.) are easy to find.

PARTNERSHIP AGREEMENTS   We know that it is important to reduce conflict between partners, and one of the most effective ways to do this is with a detailed **partnership agreement**.[14] *Ask yourself: What kinds of issues are likely to be covered in a partnership agreement?*

The basic questions to be answered by a partnership agreement are:

- Who puts in how much of the capital?
- Who gets what portion of any profit?
- Who has authority over which decisions?
- What are the responsibilities of each partner?
- How can disputes among the partners be settled?
- How can the partnership be changed?
- How can the partnership be ended?

These issues seem pretty simple, but simple issues become enormously complex if they are not clarified at the beginning of the relationship. What if you were to start a partnership with your friend? You agree that the friend will invest 60 percent of the capital to start the business and he will have 60-percent ownership. You will invest 40 percent, but you will have to borrow your initial investment from the friend. The friend will receive both his and your share of the profits until the borrowed amount is paid back. But what if there are no profits? Do you still owe the money to your friend?

Let's say you enter into partnership with two friends of yours who happen to be cousins to each other. At some point, the cousins decide that they would like to bring in a fourth partner, another of their cousins. You don't know the new cousin and are against the idea. What happens now? Can they outvote you? Do you have a veto?

You and a friend each invest $5,000 to start a partnership. A few weeks into the business, your friend tells you that he has changed his mind and wants out. You say, "Okay, you're out." The friend says, "Good, now give me back my $5,000." You explain that the money has been spent on equipment, but when the business starts to make money you will pay him the $5000. Your friend wants his money immediately and insists that the equipment be sold and that he get his share. You refuse. Who is right?

mediation The use of a neutral third party to settle a dispute by assisting the disputing sides to come to a voluntary agreement.

arbitration The use of a neutral third party to settle a dispute by examining the arguments of the disputing parties and then imposing a binding decision on the parties.

Get Help 1.7
The website of the ADR Institute of Canada provides information on Alternative Dispute Resolution and has a service to help you find appropriate mediators and arbitrators. Visit **www.amic.org**.

Test Yourself 1.11
True or False? The definition of a business may change a number of times during the writing of the business plan.

partnership agreement The contract between two or more people who are entering business ownership together.

Test Yourself 1.12
True or False? In a good business partnership, no one partner should ever be dominant.

Test Yourself 1.13
True or False? The decision of an arbitrator must be adhered to by the disputing parties.

Test Yourself 1.14
True or False? The decision of a mediator must be adhered to by the disputing parties.

Get Help 1.8
If you're planning to have your life partner as your business partner, you may want to look at *Partners at Home and at Work*, by Annette O'Shea and Sieglinde Malmberg, published by the Self-Counsel Press. Out of print now, but available in many libraries, it offers techniques for dealing with specific problems of a double-partnership arrangement.

Get Help 1.9
You can get a do-it-yourself partnership agreement from a business supplies store, or log on to **www.lawdepot.ca** and view the templates. Partnership agreements are an area where paying for some legal advice can be a great investment.

sole proprietorship A legal form of business where only one person owns and has the legal right to operate the company. The sole proprietor has unlimited liability for the company's debts.

unlimited liability Total personal responsibility for the debts of a business.

If the above eventualities are not covered in the partnership agreement, they might have to be settled by a court and involve the expense of lawyers. Better to pay the lawyer less upfront to have a proper partnership agreement drafted that all of the partners fully understand. *Ask yourself: What happens to the friendships in the above three examples?*

Head Start Exercise

1.5   Draft a brief list of provisions you would demand in any partnership contract (1 page maximum).

Don't be scared away from the whole idea of partnerships just because of some potential problems. Many of Canada's most successful businesses were started as partnerships. Just be sure that you "partner up" really carefully.

What Will My Business Mean Legally?

One of the early decisions to be made in starting up a business is the selection of a legal form. Like other early decisions, you might change this one by the time you complete the business plan, or even at some point after the business is up and running. For the majority of new businesses, the choice of legal form is a simple decision of whether or not to incorporate. Nevertheless, you should know that more than two choices are available and understand the advantages and disadvantages of each.

SOLE PROPRIETORSHIP   This is the simplest, cheapest, and most common form of business. It is a business owned and operated by one person. It doesn't mean that the company has only one employee—it can have any number of employees. It just means that only one person has the inherent right to control the business. If you have a **sole proprietorship**, you and the business are one and the same as far as the law is concerned.

Let's say the owner of a sole proprietorship arts-supply store passes away. The owner no longer exists and, legally, the business no longer exists. Members of the owner's family will inherit the assets (that is, the property) of the business (the sign, the art supplies, the cash register) just as they will inherit the owner's other personal assets: cash, clothing, broken guitar. The family may decide to keep the business going. But what they are doing in a legal sense is taking the inherited assets (the sign, the supplies, the cash register) and investing them into a brand-new business. The assets of the business are the personal assets of the owner.

And just as the owner *personally* owns the assets of the firm, so does he or she *personally* own the debts of the firm. This is what is meant by the expression **unlimited liability**: there is no limit to how much the owner is personally responsible for the debts of the business. If a sole proprietorship is closed down because it cannot pay its debts, the owner is still responsible for them; the owner must use personal assets to pay the debts.

Each province and territory has its own business registration rules. Generally registration is required if you are operating a business under any name other than your own exact first and last name. Even then, it is a good idea to register because you may need the registration certificate to get other business documents and it's not expensive. If you do carry on a one-owner business without registering, you will be considered to have a sole proprietorship. If you carry on a business that has more than one owner and fail to otherwise register the business, you will be considered to have a **general partnership.**

GENERAL PARTNERSHIP   The general partnership legal form is similar to sole proprietorship, but it applies to a business that has two or more owners, each of whom has the right to make decisions about the business and each of whom has *unlimited liability*.

This is the single most important issue to be aware of when entering into a general partnership. It means that each partner has 100-percent responsibility for the debts of the business: not just responsibility for their own share, but responsibility for the entire amount of debt. It means that you can personally be liable for any mistakes your partners make as far as the business is concerned. The implication here is that you must be prepared to have considerable trust in your partners and should know as much as possible about their financial circumstances as well as any agreements they might make on behalf of the business.

Despite some of the obvious inherent dangers, a general partnership is inexpensive to register and may offer significant tax advantages at start-up.

CORPORATION   People talk about the "big corporations," but size has nothing to do with legal form: a one-person company can be a **corporation**. The owners of a corporation are referred to as *shareholders*. Generally, for small corporations, owning 51 percent (or more) of the shares gives someone the power to decide who will run the company. Also, in most cases the percentage of shares a person owns reflects the percentage of any dividend (profit that the company decides to pay to shareholders) that the person will receive.

The owners of a corporation, however, unlike the above forms, do not personally own the assets of the company. When a business is incorporated, the law recognizes the company as an "*artificial person*," and it is this artificial person who owns the assets.

It is also the artificial person who is responsible for the debts, and this is what we mean by **limited liability**: the owner's responsibility for the debts of the business is limited to however much he or she has invested in the firm—the owner's personal assets are not at risk if the business has failed.

Compared to a sole proprietorship or general partnership, it is considerably more expensive to form a corporation, ranging from several hundred dollars for "do it yourself" to several thousand dollars for having one of the more expensive law firms handle the incorporation.

OTHER LEGAL FORMS   The vast majority of new small enterprises are registered as one of the above three forms. There are, however, other forms you should know about.

general partnership A business where two or more people own and have the right to manage the company. Each owner in a general partnership has unlimited liability for all the debts of the company.

✓ **Test Yourself 1.15**
True or False? In a sole proprietorship, the owner of the business has unlimited liability for company debts.

❓ **Get Help 1.10**
Check with your provincial business registrations office for the cost of registering a sole proprietorship or general partnership. For online information, log on to ***www.cbsc.org***. Click on *Starting a Business,* then choose the *Business Start-up Assistant.* Find your province or territory and click on *Registering Your Business.*

✓ **Test Yourself 1.16**
True or False? In a general partnership each of the partners can be held personally responsible for all of the company's debts.

corporation A legal form of business that exists separately from its owners (shareholders), who have limited liability for the company's debts.

limited liability A situation in which company owners do not have any personal responsibility for the debts of their company. The personal assets of the owners are protected.

limited partnership A legal form
of business with some partners (at
least one) having unlimited liability
and some having limited liability.

limited liability partnership
A legal form of business available
to professional firms that provides
partial liability protection to the
partners.

worker co-operative A legal
form of business where the
employees (at least a majority
of them) are the owners of the
company. Each owner has one
equal vote in selecting management and directing the company.

◇ **Get Help 1.11**
If you would like to find out
more about co-operatives,
you will find good links at
www.agr.ca/policy/coop.

◇ **Get Help 1.12**
The Canada Business website is a
good place for information on legal
forms: **www.cbsc.org**. Be cautious of U.S. sites in this area (their
rules are a little different) and be
cautious of advice from small-business owners, since many of them
are unclear on what legal form they
have: some think this is strictly a
concern for their accountants. If
you have any doubts before deciding on a legal form, call a lawyer's
office and start by asking how
much they will charge you for an
initial consultation.

✓ **Test Yourself 1.17**
True or False? In a limited partnership, all of the partners have
limited liability.

✓ **Test Yourself 1.18**
True or False? An individual may
be the only owner of a corporation.

✓ **Test Yourself 1.19**
True or False? An individual may
be the only owner of a general
partnership.

The three most common options are limited partnership, limited liability partnership, and co-operative.

Limited partnership is a form rarely used by new small businesses and it can be more expensive to set up than a corporation. It requires one or more limited partners who will have limited liability (just like investors in a corporation) but will have the same tax advantages as general partners. Unlike corporate shareholders, however, limited partners may not participate in the management of the company. In this form, there must be at least one general partner (there can be any number) who will have unlimited liability.

Limited liability partnership (LLP) is an increasingly popular form that applies to firms in self-governed professions (like lawyers and accountants). Be careful about confusing LLPs (as they are usually designated) with the limited partnership form. These kinds of firms are not permitted to incorporate, but the LLP form allows limited liability for the partners provided that they carry insurance at sufficient levels to meet potential liabilities. The LLP protects you from being liable for the mistakes or wrongdoing of your partners in the firm only, not against liability for your own mistakes or wrongdoing. LLP is not available in all Canadian jurisdictions at the time of writing, but most have it at least under consideration.

Worker co-operatives exist largely to provide employment for their members. The employees of the company are the shareholders and they have the limited liability protection of corporations. Unlike corporations, however, where the number of shares owned can mean the number of votes in running the company, in co-operatives each member (owner) gets only one vote regardless of how many shares he or she owns. In this sense, co-operatives are governed democratically. This form of business has been used successfully in things like artisan-based, food production, and forestry companies, and it could be applied in many emerging industries. For example, an information technology–based firm owned by a group of talented programmers could work as a co-operative.

The decision of legal form is usually influenced by:
- initial cost
- liability
- tax considerations
- the image the entrepreneur wishes to project
- the number of investors and their financial circumstances.

Choosing a legal form is one of the more complex planning decisions and often requires the advice of a lawyer, an accountant, or a marketing adviser. Nevertheless, a preliminary decision on legal form should be made in the early parts of the business plan.

Head Start Exercise

1.6   Choose a legal form for your business and make up a list of reasons explaining why this is the most appropriate form for you ($\frac{1}{2}$ page maximum).

How and Why Do I Write a Business Plan?

Most new businesses are started without the owner ever having written a formal business plan. But then, most new businesses fail within a year or two.

Pretty much every human activity is more likely to have a successful outcome if it is planned. This includes a chess game, an athletic contest, a vacation, asking someone for a date, and so on. Sure, people remember that spontaneous party which was so great, but it was memorable because it was a fluke. A good party is almost always planned. The plan isn't always written out, but it does exist. A business, however, is much more complex than a chess game or a party. No reasonable person would attempt to build a house or a radio or a vehicle or anything else that complicated without a written plan. So it only makes sense to use a written plan in building a business. Having a written business plan will improve your chances of survival.[15]

PURPOSE   Formal business lenders and investors require a written business plan. It's simple: if you want to borrow money from a bank or sell part of the business to investors (other than your grandparents), you have to have a written business plan. However, the reasons for having a business plan go far beyond this simple necessity. They include:

- *Compiling a business checklist.* By writing the plan down, the entrepreneur is forced to focus on all the elements of a business and all the problems that must be overcome, rather than those that most easily come to mind. It keeps the process of starting a business organized.
- *Communicating the plan.* Something as complex as a business cannot be explained orally. It would be like trying to explain the wiring in a TV without using a diagram. For lenders, investors, partners, advisers, and even potential employees, the only way to really understand the workings of a new business is to see them on paper.
- *Making the idea real.* Writing down the idea is the first step in actually starting a business. This makes the idea tangible: there is an actual, physical document that represents the business. This accomplishment stands as proof to the entrepreneur that he or she will be able to complete the process—it is a motivator.

Ask yourself: What other reasons might I have for needing a business plan?

FORMATS   For formal investors and lenders, the length and detail of the business plan varies with the requirements of the particular money source. In many cases, for a government-guaranteed small loan to a new business, the plan is little more than 10 pages, often completed on a fill-in-the-blanks form. For a venture capital firm investing in excess of a million dollars in a growing company, the plan could easily exceed 50 detailed pages plus appendices.

There is no standard format for a business plan. The format used here is one of the simplest and shortest and is in keeping with the recent trend of lenders to demand shorter, more concise plans. Most business plan templates start with an *executive summary*, containing information that is repeated in the introduction and often again in the body of the plan. The format used here combines the executive summary and introduction into a single element, *The Summary and Concept*, to minimize repetition.

Libraries and bookstores abound with business plan templates, and many banks offer free CDs, downloads, or booklets, each with its own outline for a business plan.

Keep in mind when using a business plan template that the amount of space indicated for any one topic is only a guideline. Each plan is unique. The amount of space needed is however much it takes to concisely explain that particular business.

✓ **Test Yourself 1.20**
True or False? There is no single standard format for the business plan.

✓ **Test Yourself 1.21**
True or False? A reasonable business plan should be a minimum of 50 pages in length.

GETTING STARTED   The business plan must be the work of you, the entrepreneur. There is little point in hiring a high-priced consultant to write a plan that is not made up of your ideas; you just won't follow it. That doesn't mean you can't get help for the process. Throughout this book there are tips on who and what can help you in preparing the plan. And if writing is just not your strength, there are lots of professional writers willing to proofread for you and fix up your grammar and spelling. But the ideas must be yours because your real purpose in writing a business plan is not just to end up with the document. Rather it is the process that's important. By having to prepare each element of the business plan, you are forced to think through all of the critical decisions involved in starting a business in a logical order—an order that will let you see contradictions and areas where your plan does not make sense. Writing it down forces you to make a better plan.

On the principle that it is easier to fix up a bad plan than it is to write a great plan from scratch, start by writing something that is less than perfect—or even fairly bad. Just get something down on paper or into a computer. It can always be fixed up later. Remember: Most of the work of writing a business plan is in rewriting.

Ask yourself: What will be the most difficult part of writing a business plan? What will be the easiest? The biggest problem with writing a business plan is the same problem encountered in any type of writing: overcoming procrastination. It is amazing how creative people can be in finding critical things to do instead of writing the plan: looking at locations, calling suppliers, shopping the competition—but the writing has to be done, so *just do it!*

✓Answers to Test Yourself Questions

1.1 An idea starts to become a plan when it is written down. *True*

1.2 A business could have up to 500 employees and still be considered a "small business." *True*

1.3 A freelance journalist is generally considered to be a business owner. *False*

1.4 A freelance journalist should be working with a business plan. *True*

1.5 A freelance journalist is an entrepreneur. *True*

1.6 Most of the "entrepreneurial ability" tests are accurate predictors of one's ability to start a business. *False*

1.7 Computer literacy would be classified as an entrepreneurial skill. *False*

1.8 Specialization in fewer products or services generally means more profit for a small business. *True*

1.9 Specializing in a particular product or service is called "targeting." *False*

1.10 A business should try to have as wide a variety of potential customers as possible. *False*

1.11 The definition of a business may change a number of times during the writing of the business plan. *True*

1.12 In a good business partnership, no one partner should ever be dominant. *False*

1.13 The decision of an arbitrator must be adhered to by the disputing parties. *True*

1.14 The decision of a mediator must be adhered to by the disputing parties. *False*

1.15 In a sole proprietorship, the owner of the business has unlimited liability for company debts. *True*

1.16 In a general partnership each of the partners can be held personally responsible for all of the company's debts. *True*

1.17 In a limited partnership, all of the partners have limited liability. *False*

1.18 An individual may be the only owner of a corporation. *True*

1.19 An individual may be the only owner of a general partnership. *False*

1.20 There is no single standard format for the business plan. *True*

1.21 A reasonable business plan should be a minimum of 50 pages in length. *False*

Questions for Discussion

1. Identify a movie where the main character is a successful entrepreneur (for example, *The Aviator*) and discuss whether the portrayal of the character is realistic or artificial.

2. Debate this proposition: "Canadian colleges and universities are in the business of training employees, not entrepreneurs."

3. Make a list of the major changes (political, social, economic, cultural, technological, etc.) currently underway in our society. Identify at least one entrepreneurial opportunity that each of these changes will create.

4. Discuss the advantages and disadvantages of being married to your business partner.

5. Discuss how incorporation (vs. sole proprietorship or partnership) changes the image of a company. When would it be a disadvantage to have a corporate image?

Recommended Reading

Good, Walter S. *Building a Dream: A Canadian Guide to Starting Your Own Business,* 5th ed. Toronto: McGraw-Hill Ryerson, 2003.

James, Jack D. *Starting a Successful Business in Canada.* Vancouver: Self-Counsel Press, 2004.

Magos, Alice H., and Steve Crowe. *Business Plans That Work for Your Small Business,* 2nd ed. Chicago: CCH Incorporated, 2003.

O'Shea, Annette, and Sieglinde Malmberg. *Partners at Home and at Work.* Vancouver: Self-Counsel Press, 1994.

The Business Plan, Section 1:
The Summary and Concept

SUMMARY

Note: The Summary is prepared only after all other portions of the business plan have been completed. Start writing your business plan with the Introduction below.

- Using information from section one of the business plan, briefly state what the business will be selling, the sorts of customers it will have, why there is an opportunity for this now, and why the owners are the right people to run this business.
- Using information from section two of the business plan, briefly identify the location and site, the direct competition, and the expected revenue in the first three years.
- Using information from section three of the business plan, briefly explain the firm's image or position in terms of product and price, as well as where the company will fit in the distribution chain.
- Using information from section four of the business plan, briefly outline the capital investment required, the roles the owner(s) will play in the firm, and the roles of any other employees.
- Using information from section five of the business plan, briefly outline the amount and sources of financing and collateral for the business and when the business is expected to start making a profit as well as how much profit is expected.

_____

_____

_____

_____

_____

_____

_____

_____

_____

INTRODUCTION

1. Describe the general nature of the business, the location, and identify any important or unusual features.

_____

_____

_____

_____

_____

_____

_____

_____

PRODUCTS AND SERVICES

2. Explain how your business will be specialized in terms of the products and/or services you will offer.

_____

_____

_____

_____

_____

_____

_____

_____

THE CUSTOMERS

3. Explain how your business will be specialized in terms of the customer groups you will be targeting.

_____

_____

_____

_____

_____

_____

_____

_____

THE OPPORTUNITY

4. Identify any circumstances or events that have led to a need that your business intends to satisfy. Be clear on why _now_ is a good time to start a business such as this.

_____

_____

_____

_____

_____

_____

_____

THE OWNER(S)

5. Name and give a brief background for each of the owners. Explain why this history is appropriate for running a business such as this one. Attach a résumé for each of the owners as an appendix.

    _____
    _____
    _____
    _____
    _____
    _____
    _____
    _____
    _____

6. Identify any entrepreneurial abilities of the owner(s), and if there is more than one owner, clarify the "complementary" nature of the relationship. Explain any personal motivation for going into business now.

    _____
    _____
    _____
    _____
    _____
    _____
    _____
    _____
    _____

7. Briefly estimate the minimum amount of money you (and any partners) will have to withdraw from the business each month in order to survive (or how long you can survive without relying on the business for income).

    _____
    _____
    _____
    _____
    _____
    _____

THE LEGAL ORGANIZATION

8. Identify the legal form of the business and clearly state *who* owns *how much* of the company. Explain your reasons for this legal set-up.

    _____

    _____

    _____

    _____

    _____

    _____

    _____

    _____

    _____

    _____

9. If there is more than one owner, explain who will be actively participating in the business and how. If there is a partnership agreement, identify the major provisions and attach a copy of the agreement as an appendix.

    _____

    _____

    _____

    _____

    _____

    _____

    _____

    _____

    _____

    _____

chapter 2

Feasibility:
How Do I Know It Will Work?

LEARNING OBJECTIVES

On completion of this chapter, you should be able to:

- *Explain the major considerations for the general location of a business.*
- *Explain the major considerations in selecting a particular site.*
- *Identify advantages and disadvantages of working from home.*
- *Discuss various issues/clauses of lease agreements.*
- *Define market potential.*
- *Identify several techniques for calculating market potential.*
- *Differentiate between direct and indirect competition.*
- *Identify several techniques for estimating future sales.*
- *Discuss methods of protecting against business loss.*
- *Distinguish among methods of protecting intellectual property.*
- *Prepare the feasibility portion of a business plan.*

You never really know for sure that your business idea is feasible until you actually try it. *It may not work*—and that's the risk-taking element of entrepreneurship. But remember, true entrepreneurs take only reasonable, calculated risks. So before getting into business, it's a good idea to look for *indicators* that the idea is feasible: that the business will be profitable. This isn't just for your personal benefit. Lenders or potential investors also want some kind of evidence that the business will fly before they hand over any cash. But as you examine the feasibility of your business idea, what if it starts to look as though it's *not* going to work? That just means that you should go back to Section 1 of the business plan and start modifying either *what* you will sell or *to whom* you will sell. Then you can check the feasibility of your *modified* business idea. If you can't find evidence that the modified idea will work, go back to Section 1 and modify again. Keep on modifying until you have a clear business idea that you can demonstrate is feasible.

In Section 2 of the business plan, you have to answer the question: "How do I know it will work?" This will include demonstrating that:

- The business is in the right place.
- There is enough trade to make pursuing it worthwhile.
- You have analyzed your competition.
- You can achieve some particular level of sales.
- There are ways you can protect your business.

Where Will I Locate My Business?

Ask yourself: How important is the location to the success of my business? Is there a difference between "location" and "site"? Where you put the business, in a general sense, is what we mean by **location:** a certain city, a certain region, or a certain neighbourhood. When we talk about **site,** we are being much more precise: a particular corner, an exact address, or even a specific part of a building.

location The general geographic area where a business can be found, expressed as a neighbourhood or municipality or even a region of the country.

site A specific place where business is conducted, expressed as a particular block, address, suite, or part of a building.

? Get Help 2.1

Call the chamber of commerce where you plan on locating. They will likely be able to advise you on the population base as well as the makeup of industry in the area. Many municipalities have a business development office that can supply similar information.

GENERAL LOCATION ISSUES   For most businesses, the feasibility of the company depends to some extent on where it is located. Of course, just how critical the location is depends on *what* you're selling and *to whom* you're selling. The main considerations for location are usually closeness to customers, transportation, suppliers, and various services.

Generally, but not always, the rule is to be as close as possible to your potential customers, regardless of whether they will be coming to you or you will be going to them.[1] But if you are starting some form of *online business* (where you deliver your service via the Internet), the actual physical location of your office may not matter at all. You will be as close to your customers as their own computers.

If you are locating to be close to customers, at a very minimum you must be able to demonstrate that there are sufficient numbers of potential customers in your area to support the business. There is no point in starting a wedding photography studio in a retirement community of 500 households. There is no point in being an investment consultant in a low-income community where no one has money to invest.

Some businesses depend on providing quick delivery to customers. If you are selling to a national or international market, this could require being close to the airport. But if you open a custom T-shirt store where most of your customers will be lower-income high-school students (with no cars), your transportation issue becomes the availability of public transit—so that your customers can come to you.

In most businesses the suppliers come to you, so you don't really care where they are located as long as they deliver on time. But, let's say you're starting a business that provides in-house publications to medium-sized companies. You'll do the writing, design, and layout, but will contract out the actual printing. For your business, it may be critical that you are located close to your printer for the frequent checking of proofs that will be required. (For manufacturing businesses, being close to your sources of supply is often the number-one priority.)

Banks, libraries, hospitals, swimming pools, courthouses, or universities are all services that your business may need to be close to. For example, you might start a highly specialized technology-based firm where you need to consult with top experts in your field. Proximity to a university where these experts likely work as researchers could be a competitive advantage.[2]

Head Start Exercise

2.1   Write a brief description of the location for your proposed business and note one or two advantages of this selection ($\frac{1}{4}$ page maximum).

SITE ISSUES   If your customers will be coming to you, then the site becomes a critical issue. The main considerations relating to site are traffic, visibility, parking, and neighbouring businesses. *Ask yourself: When might too much traffic be bad for business?*

Traffic can be of either the automobile or pedestrian varieties. If you are selling a frequently purchased product (*what*) to a broad consumer market (*whom*), then the trick is to find a site where lots of potential buyers[3] will be walking or driving by—lots of traffic. This is especially true for businesses like convenience stores and restaurants. If your customers are more likely to make a special trip to your place of business, then traffic is less of an issue. This would be the case if you have a roofing supplies warehouse or a hypnotherapy clinic.

In analyzing your traffic, the question you want to answer is: "How many potential customers pass by my place of business during times when they are likely to buy?" Even if thousands pass by your music store on the way to work at 7:00 a.m., it doesn't do you much good. People are more likely to buy on the way back home from work, at lunchtime, on Saturdays, or other obvious shopping times.

Information about *who* will come by and *when* they will come can be easy to get if you are leasing space in a major mall (the mall owners will likely have the information already). But for just about any place else, it means going out and doing some kind of measurement. This could involve renting an automobile traffic counter (easily available). Or it could mean getting a clipboard and lawn chair, sitting at the site, and counting how often the type of person you're looking for comes by, and at what times. If you can compare the traffic at your proposed site to the traffic at a similar business that you know to be successful, you have a strong argument for the success of your business.

Will passersby be able to identify your place of business for what it is? Will the sign be noticeable and readable from the stream of traffic? Can delivery people identify the address? Will the entrance be obvious? These questions are all concerns of visibility. A good lesson here comes from the experts. The key consideration for a U.S. sign company franchisor, in selecting their own sites, is the amount of traffic to which their sign will be visible.[4]

Visibility includes the ability to see into your place of business. If you rely on high traffic volume to provide your customers, you still have to get them out of the traffic and into your business. That's where your store window comes in. Potential customers have to be able to see what you've got before they will come in. And that's not just for retail businesses.

? Get Help 2.2

Counting traffic can be labour-intensive, so volunteer help from friends and family can come in handy. If more sophisticated help is required, you may want to contact a business teacher or marketing student to help you design a traffic study.

✓ Test Yourself 2.1

True or False? It is always important to have a location close to your customers.

✓ Test Yourself 2.2

True or False? Traffic analysis is very important for retail businesses.

✓ Test Yourself 2.3

True or False? Traffic analysis is very important for businesses that are industrial services.

The need for customers to see in can be important even for dental clinics or restaurants or accounting offices. New customers are more likely to come in if they can see inside.

Ask yourself: What parking problems bother you the most? The first question around parking is: "Is there enough of it?" Imagine you are planning to open an insta-print business in a small strip mall. If you go and look at the premises at 10:00 on a Monday morning, the parking may appear more than ample. But on Friday evening around 5:30, when everyone is picking up their baked goods and dry cleaning, your customers may have no place to park. So the real question is: Is there enough parking for *peak times*?

The parking must also be accessible. This means that the entrance will be wide enough, that there will be room to turn around, and that medians or islands will not obstruct traffic from the opposite side of the road. Don't lease a place with parking problems thinking that you can get them fixed later—it's just too difficult and time-consuming for the owner of a new firm to deal with landlords and City Hall on this kind of issue.

◇? Get Help 2.3

Check with the clerk's office at City Hall to find out about municipal parking permits and restrictions.

If parking is not available on the premises, what arrangements are there for customer parking? Will customers have to use on-street metered parking? Will you have a deal with a local lot that lets your customers park for free and charges the fee to you? How will this be administered? These issues have to be worked out in advance and explained in the business plan.

complementary business

A company that sells products or services different from yours, but to the same potential customers.

An advantageous site is one right next to a **complementary business:** a company that chases the same customers you chase, but sells them something different. For example, if you are opening a store that specializes in bar supplies and mixers, you couldn't do better than being next to a busy liquor store—unless, of course, the liquor store caters mostly to patrons who will be consuming directly from the purchase container. (These folks don't buy mixers.)

◇? Get Help 2.4

Check with the municipal planning department to see what other types of businesses are permitted in the area around your site.

Whether you put your new tattoo parlour next to a Harley-Davidson dealer or next to a high-priced beauty salon depends on the market segment you are pursuing.

And what if the neighbouring businesses happen to be in competition with you? *Ask yourself: Do you want to be close to your competitors or as far away as possible?* The answer, like just about everything else in the business plan, depends on *what* you're selling and *to whom* you're selling it. If you are selling something like office supplies to people who won't compare prices and quality before they buy (they just want convenience), then you don't want to be anywhere near your competitors. Otherwise, you'll just be splitting the available business with the competitors.

✓ Test Yourself 2.4

True or False? For the purposes of the business plan, the terms *location* and *site* are totally interchangeable.

On the other hand, if your customers are likely to shop around before they buy, then make it easy for them by being as close to the competition as possible. If you are opening a designer footwear store, make sure you are right beside other expensive shoe stores. If you are selling high-end photographic equipment, do it next door to other camera stores. When the customers are going to shop anyway, situate your business where they will go shopping. The challenge then becomes to specialize in ways that will make you slightly different from your competitors. (This is what you'll do in the marketing section of the business plan.)

Head Start Exercise

2.2   Identify the site of your proposed business and note one or two advantages of this selection ($\frac{1}{4}$ page maximum).

The Silk Weaving Studio

After textile school, Diana Sanderson's love of silk weaving led her into creating scarves, shawls, and other garments that she started selling at craft fairs. Her clientele grew steadily until 1986 when she was able to open a studio on Vancouver's trendy Granville Island. Today she is recognized as an established silk weaver and clothing designer.

Although the location is geared for the well-heeled tourist traffic, a large portion of Diana's business comes from her own Vancouver-area clientele. To support the area as an important tourist location, businesses on parts of the island receive rent subsidies. But this is not the case for the Silk Weaving Studio, which is in a more secluded, privately owned section of the island. Diana, however, is able to control her costs by sharing her studio space with up to five other weavers. Even though Diana is the lessee, decisions about the premises are generally made co-operatively by all the artists. Visitors can watch the weaving process while the artists work in the studio.

As is more typical of arts-based enterprises than other categories of business, Diana explains that the various artists tend to be "complementary to each other, rather than competitive." Working in different styles, they produce different products but all appeal to the same upscale clientele seeking a less trendy, more classic look in their wardrobes. "One of the most exciting things for me," says Diana, "is when a client comes in wearing something they bought 15 years ago and it still looks great."

Diana admits to being influenced by the tastes of her clients but would never produce something (and has even turned down requests to do so) just because it's trendy. She feels that the challenge for her is finding the right balance between business and art. For example, the business does not do typical retail promotion, other than her tasteful sign and website. The quality and style of Diana's products can be seen on her website: **www.silkweavingstudio.com**.

HOME-BASED BUSINESSES   For some companies, the site of the business is the owner's car, or a cell phone, or the back part of the basement. These are "home-based" businesses. Home-based businesses exist most commonly when you either don't meet the customer face-to-face (for example, mail-order or online businesses), or when meetings usually take place at the customer's premises (you go to them). The number of home-based full- and part-time businesses is growing rapidly as a result of new technologies and the increased contracting-out of work.

 Get Help 2.5
Check the Canada Revenue Agency website at **www.cra-arc.gc.ca** and search for *work-space-in-the-home expenses*. That page will explain which expenses are allowable for a home-based company.

The idea of working out of your home may be very appealing to you (work all day in your pyjamas and be able to fix lunch for the kids). However, the decision to work from home should always be based on *what* you're selling and *to whom* you're selling it. If your business is booking DJs for small local bars, working out of your basement is great since your customers (the bar owners) believe this will help provide lower prices for them. But if you want to be a talent agent for high-priced models and actors, then producers will expect you to have an office in the business or arts district of the city: it's an issue of credibility.

If you use part of your home for business purposes, some of your rent (or mortgage interest), maintenance, insurance, and utilities costs become a business expense. There are some restrictions, however, when you report these expenses on your tax return. Also, beware of possible limitations on working from home as a result of a lease you may have or municipal zoning restrictions.

If you decide to work from home, you must be able to explain the decision in the business plan, in terms of—you guessed it!—*what* you are selling and *to whom* you are selling it. In other words, you should be able to show that being home-based will be right for the business, not just good for your personal convenience.

LEASING THE PREMISES   Unless your business is home-based, for a new company it is usually not a good idea to buy the business premises, even if you can afford it. Owning the place can be too confining for a new business. If you own, there is too much of a tendency to plan your business around the limitations of the premises, rather than the needs of your customers. If you lease, however, you are more willing to move, or make demands of the landlord, to meet changes in the market.

Besides, property management is a whole different business from what you plan on doing. Stick to what you will specialize in and let someone else (the landlord) specialize in property management.

When it comes to leases, everything is negotiable. But the landlord is in the business of negotiating leases (you'll only do it once every few years), and so you are at a disadvantage. You can improve the odds, however, by knowing your prices before you start negotiating. Shop around and ask lots of questions.

The issues to be negotiated in a lease can include:

- *Basic rent.* There is usually a going market value of **basic rent** for retail space within a particular neighbourhood, expressed as a certain number of dollars per square foot per year. (The figure is usually based on the average sales per square foot of retailers in the area.) Calculate the number of square feet of the place and multiply by the annual rent figure, then divide by 12 to ballpark the monthly rent. For a new business, you can always try to negotiate a break on the basic rent—sometimes even a rent-free period to help the business get going.
- *Percentage of sales.* Many landlords will want a percentage of your retail sales on top of the basic rent so they can share in the success of the business. This is a major negotiating point, since the more they share in your profits, the more they should be willing to risk in terms of lowering the basic rent or providing a rent-free period.
- *Maintenance and other expenses.* Aside from utilities that you will have to pay directly, your property may have other expenses associated with it, such as your share of garbage pickup or snow removal, or gardening. You want to make sure that you are not responsible for these expenses while the landlord retains total control over the amount to be spent and the choice of contractors. These issues, too, are negotiable.
- *Length of lease.* The more the success of your business depends on the particular site, the longer you want the lease to run. The length of the lease can also be important if you plan to eventually bring in other investors or maybe sell the whole business. The more doubtful you are about the site, however, the shorter the term you want to commit to, since you can always negotiate an extension.
- *Lease renewal.* If your business is successful you want to be able to extend or renew your lease, but not under conditions where the landlord can change the terms to take the lion's share of your profits. So you want to have some pre-set conditions that you will be able to

basic rent The minimum rent charged by a landlord for commercial space, on top of which may be charged a percentage of sales, maintenance fees, and other expenses.

renew—maybe not at the same rent, but at some amount indexed to your improved sales and profits. In addition, you would like to negotiate a clause that allows you to terminate the lease if there is some substantial change in the conditions of the property, such as the closing of a road or the loss of pedestrian traffic.

- *Leasehold improvements.* The landlord will argue that any **leasehold improvements**— renovations, modifications, new fixtures, and so on—are to the benefit of your business and should be paid by you. If you can demonstrate, however, that any of your changes will increase the value of the property and would also benefit any future tenants, you may be able to convince the landlord to share in these costs.

There will be other issues in the lease, including the landlord's requirement for you to carry insurance on your business. (The landlord's own insurance on the property may require this.) Most issues, however, will be negotiable to some extent.

leasehold improvements
Modifications to the structure or décor of a commercial property that will remain the property of the landlord, even though they may have been paid for by the lessee.

Head Start Exercise

2.3 Find several vacant office, retail, or industrial sites that would suit your business (see Get Help 2.6). Contact the landlords or real estate agents and explain that you are in the process of writing a draft business plan and need rent figures on a site. Ask about terms such as the length of the lease, maintenance, and other expenses. For one site, create a list of the major lease issues and estimate how much each would cost your business on a monthly basis. (1 page maximum.)

How Much of My Kind of Business Is Out There?

MARKET POTENTIAL   Imagine that you are a banker and someone comes to borrow money to start a piano-tuning business (the *what* they are selling) for people who live in the Village of Parkside (the *to whom* they are selling it). *Ask yourself: What is the first question I would want to ask the borrower?* For most bankers, it would be "How much piano-tuning business is there in Parkside?"

What if a friend asks you to become her partner in a business that will paint new names on boats (*what*) for boat dealers in the Big Bay area (*whom*)? Wouldn't you wonder "Exactly how much do Big Bay boat dealers spend on name-painting? Enough to support two people? Enough for a business that could grow?"

The thing we want to know about here is called *market potential*: How much money a group of potential customers (*whom*) will spend on a particular product or service (*what*). **Market potential** isn't just how much a customer group will buy from your business; it is how much they will buy of the product or service in total, including from all your competition. (Note that the "customers" don't have to be people: they could be businesses or government agencies or senior citizens' clubs.)

✓ Test Yourself 2.5
True or False? For most kinds of business, it is better to buy rather than lease the property where the business is situated.

◇ Get Help 2.6
Real estate agents are always looking for prospective customers. Find an agent in the general location you are interested in, but be honest about it if you are only doing background shopping so you won't use too much of their time under false pretenses. Most agents will be happy to let you browse through the multiple listings and give you an idea of the kind of terms you can negotiate. Alternatively, check the online Multiple Listing Service at ***www.icx.ca***, where you can perform an industrial and commercial property search by geographic area.

◇ Get Help 2.7
Before arranging a lease, you may want to look at *Negotiate Your Commercial Lease*, by Dale R. Willerton, published by the Self-Counsel Press.

market potential How much money a group of potential customers will spend on a particular product or service.

If your business concept is to sell children's photographic portraits to wealthy people living in the downtown area, then the *market potential* would be "how much money all the wealthy people in the downtown area, *together*, spend on getting pictures taken of their kids." If you are starting a business selling something to lots of different customer groups, you will want to know the market potential for *each* of these groups.

Head Start Exercise

2.4   Go back to Section 1 of your business plan and look at how you have defined your business. Now, write a single sentence explaining the market potential you should be interested in; in other words: "I must find out how much money (the customer group you are selling to) will spend annually on (the product or service you will sell)." (1 sentence maximum.)

RELEVANCE   *Ask yourself: Why would I want to know the market potential?* Knowing *how much* business is out there is important at start-up because it helps you focus better on *to whom* you're selling. Later on, when your business is established, it helps you with the *long-range planning* for your business.

Maybe you'd like to start a company that installs burglar alarms in your hometown. You see your customers as being homeowners, small businesses, and local government offices—three separate customer groups requiring three different estimates of market potential. When you start your research, you may find that all of the small businesses already have alarms (so they won't be spending anything), and the government offices subcontract their security to large firms that handle the alarms. But it may turn out that most of the homeowners don't have alarms, although they intend on getting them. If that's the case, why waste your time chasing business in the other two groups? You can specialize in the single customer target. And remember: the more you specialize in a particular target group, the more money you are likely to make (as long as the group has enough market potential to support you).

Of course, a decision to narrow your focus like this means going back to Section 1 of the business plan and rewriting the concept.

Knowing the market potential helps you plan the long-range strategy for your business. First, having this estimate of the total amount of business going on in your field in your target area helps you predict your sales. (You're going to do that soon.)

It also helps with issues like planning for expansion. If the market potential is growing, either you have to grow or your competitors will.

Ask yourself: Is a bigger market potential better? In some cases, a really large market potential means that this particular customer group will attract competitors that are so much larger and better financed than you that you will not be able to compete. For example, you may want to start a computer repair business aimed at consumers in the northwest area of the city. Your research may show that with the growth of home computers, the repair business in your target area alone is worth millions of dollars. But if a national franchise operation like The Source

---

◇? Get Help 2.8

If you are having trouble expressing market potential for your kind of business, language might well be an issue. In this case, take your textbook and Section 1 of your business plan to a language instructor or language remediation centre for help.

✓ Test Yourself 2.6

True or False? Market potential includes your firm's sales of a product or service, as well as the sales of your competitors for that product or service.

✓ Test Yourself 2.7

True or False? You need to know the market potential for planning long-range strategy.

✓ Test Yourself 2.8

True or False? A separate estimate of market potential is required for each different customer group a business is targeting.

decides to go after home computer repair right across the country, this will include your "northwest corner of the city," and their advertising power will be difficult to overcome.

So you may decide to go after a different target; maybe working on contract, repairing class-room computers for school boards in your area. Of course, this means going back and rewriting the concept for your business plan.

MARKETING RESEARCH   Finding out the market potential is a type of **marketing research.** However, marketing research can include a lot of other things. Finding out the annual incomes of your customers, finding out who in the family does the shopping, finding out whether your customers prefer blue packages or red packages, all of these things are forms of marketing research and all of them might be nice to know. But new business owners can rarely afford to spend money, time, or energy on things that are simply "nice to know."

For a new business, the marketing research priorities are to find out how much business is out there (market potential) and how much of that your company is expected to get (sales forecast).

Beware of marketing research consultants who want to do an expensive survey for you that will be all packaged up in a glossy report but gives you only the "nice-to-knows." If you are going to pay anyone to help with marketing research, make sure that they explain what they are charging for and how it helps estimate your market potential as well as your sales forecast.

Ask yourself: How much time and effort should I put into estimating market potential? If you are borrowing money to start your business, the amount of market potential data required by the lender will depend on how much you want to borrow. If it is a small, government-guaranteed loan, the requirements will be modest: merely some evidence that there is an opportunity to make money—information you could gather yourself using a library, a tele-phone, and the Internet.

The greater the loan, however, the greater the amount of market data that will be required by the lender. Really substantial loans are more likely to be approved if they are supported by professional research completed by a third party—and that gets expensive.

Be realistic! There is no point in spending $20,000 on a feasibility study for a business that will cost $10,000 to start. Better just to risk the $10,000 and see if the business works. Trying out the business is itself the feasibility study: if the business fails, it likely wasn't feasible. On the other hand, if you risk your life savings to go into business, it would be reasonable to spend at least a few days analyzing the market potential. And there are lots of ways to go about this on your own. *Ask yourself: How can I go about estimating market potential?*

INFORMATION SOURCES   In any kind of research, it is always easier and cheaper to use information that has already been gathered by others; the kind of information you find in government publications, magazines, **trade journals**, business directories, and so on. This is called **secondary research** information. **Primary research** is actually having to measure things yourself. This is much more expensive and time-consuming, so always go to the "secondary" sources first—and be prepared to spend some time in a library.

---

marketing research Gathering and organizing information about groups of potential customers and issues of supplying them with products and services.

◇ Get Help 2.9
Trade journals will sometimes do research into how many customers it takes to support their own particular kinds of businesses. For example, you may find data on how many consumers it takes to support a single dental office or funeral home or decorating business. Find out if there is a journal for the kind of business you are starting and check all the back issues. (An index or journal search engine will cut down on your work.)

trade journals Magazines written for people involved in specific industries: for example, commercial fishing publications or professional teachers' magazines.

secondary research Using information that has already been gathered and published.

primary research Gathering new information from original sources.

Government statistics: Many government ministries, departments, and agencies (federal, provincial, and municipal) publish information about the production and purchase of all kinds of goods and services by consumers, businesses, governments, and other organizations.

? Get Help 2.10

For Statistics Canada publications, check a major library. You can get an idea of what is available from the StatsCan website: *www.statscan.ca*.

In Canada, the best place to start is usually with *Statistics Canada,* even if your target customers are not all across the country. Much of the "StatsCan" info is broken down into relatively small geographic areas. In addition to broad census information, StatsCan also publishes data on manufacturing and specialized pamphlets with statistics on a variety of industries and provides links to small business profiles with national and provincial data on more than a hundred categories of small business.

? Get Help 2.11

For a broad range of government websites, start with the Strategis website from Industry Canada at *www.strategis.ic.gc.ca*, or with the Services for Canadian Business site at *www.businessgateway.ca*. Excellent analysis of economic and industry trends can be found at *www.canadianeconomy.gc.ca*.

Federal and provincial government ministries publish data on industries and organizations important to the ministry. For example, ministries of agriculture will have extensive information on the operation of dairy farms, and ministries of education will have lots of information on how school boards spend their money.

Municipal governments will also publish information about the population and industries in their communities. For example, your City Hall will likely have data on the number and types of manufacturers in the city as well as the number and types of people these industries employ.

✓ Test Yourself 2.9

True or False? Trade journals are primarily magazines where different kinds of businesses can swap their goods and services with each other.

Business publications: Many publications go out and do primary marketing research on consumer and business expenditures and provide the information in the form of journals and handbooks. For example, *Sales and Marketing Management* magazine and the *National Post*'s *Financial Post* both produce handbooks on consumer buying behaviour.

business publications A huge variety of business directories are published, ranging from the phone company Yellow Pages to detailed corporate directories giving financial and employee details of particular companies.

Trade associations and journals: Most municipalities have active chambers of commerce, merchant associations, boards of trade, or industrial associations. Their main purpose is to benefit members by encouraging business and economic growth in their communities. For example, if you are thinking of opening a fast-food restaurant in a tourist town, the local chamber of commerce may well have detailed information on how much both tourists and locals spend on fast food (that is, the market potential), broken down by food category and time of year.

? Get Help 2.12

There are so many thousands of publications with market data you may wish to start with a directory of business publications: For example, *Where to Find Business Information*, published by John Wiley & and Sons Inc.

Many industries have associations set up to provide information and services to their member companies. These associations will often research the market potential for particular segments that their industries service, and publish the information in the industry's trade journals. The reference section of your library will likely have a directory of associations and an index of periodicals. Most associations now have a website, and many trade journals can be accessed via the Internet.

? Get Help 2.13

The website for the Canadian Chamber of Commerce, *www.chamber.ca*, offers a directory of its many local organizations.

When all else fails, go and ask: Gathering new information on your own (primary data) is expensive and time-consuming but at times necessary. This usually means administering some kind of questionnaire by face-to-face interview, telephone, or mail-in response. Most of us can do the labour associated with this kind of research but may need professional help in two areas: *questionnaire design* and *sample selection*.

? Get Help 2.14

Find a professor or senior student of marketing to advise you on questionnaire design and the validity of your sample size.

Ask yourself: How do you get people to tell you how much they (or their companies) spend on a product or service? Wording the questions properly can be tricky. If you can't afford to hire an expert, at the very least have your questionnaire looked over by as many volunteers as possible.

You don't have to survey every member of a market to get an idea about its potential. But *Ask yourself: How many people do you have to survey for your conclusions about a market to be valid?* Obviously, the bigger your sample, the more valid your conclusions about the whole market will be. A professional researcher can generate statistics about the probability of your conclusions being accurate. But if you're working on your own and have no research background, the best you can do is try to make sure that the sample you survey is somehow *representative* of the entire market. For example, you could ensure that you interview potential customers from all geographic portions of your market. Or you could demonstrate that your interview sample is similar to your entire market on some dimension you have found in secondary sources: the same average number of employees, the same average house size, the same average age, and so on.

It won't be easy to get primary information, but that doesn't mean you shouldn't try. Any data you do gather will be better than no data at all.

APPLYING THE DATA   It is easy to gather "facts" from secondary sources or even interviews and questionnaires, but the trick is to look for information that will be relevant to calculating the market potential.

Much of the secondary data for market potential is for large regional and national areas, but new small businesses tend to specialize in small target areas. So some form of *extrapolation* (making a prediction based on known facts) is usually involved in calculating the market potential.

For example, you may be starting a community newspaper in a town that doesn't have a paper of its own. You may be able to find out the total value of community newspaper sales for the entire country, but the market potential you are interested in is only for the one town. Well, you can easily figure out the population of the whole town and calculate this as a percentage of the whole country's population. Then, multiply that same percentage by the national market potential and it will give you some estimate of the market potential in the town.

In the business plan, you must be able to explain the logic behind any inferences you may make about the market potential, so always try to have someone knowledgeable check over your work.

Who Is My Competition?

Your business will have competitors—even if you are offering some kind of brand-new service that no one has ever offered before. If your service makes lots of money, you will quickly have lots of competition. Competitors fit into two broad categories: *direct* and *indirect.*

DIRECT COMPETITION   **Direct competitors** are firms similar to your own in terms of size, location, and the services they offer, and they pursue the same groups of customers that you are trying to get. If you have an auto-glass replacement shop, your direct competitors are the other auto-glass shops in your area. If you sell water-softening systems to homes in the western suburbs, your direct competitors are other small firms that sell water-softening systems in the same area.

◇ Get Help 2.15
Various provincial and federal agencies offer mentoring or counselling services for new entrepreneurs at little or no cost. Start with the phone book's blue pages, but have a draft of your business plan written out before you go for help—it gives the adviser something tangible to work with. Also, find out if there is a "small business enterprise centre" in your community. These centres usually have multiple sponsors that can include municipal governments, banks, and private industry. These centres normally offer coaching and referral services for the preparation of business plans.

✓ Test Yourself 2.10
True or False? Secondary research usually requires the use of questionnaires and samples of the market.

✓ Test Yourself 2.11
True or False? The majority of people going into business for themselves will require some kind of help in estimating market potential.

direct competition Businesses similar to your own that provide products or services similar to yours and that pursue the same potential customers you are pursuing.

Let's say you have a background in public relations and decide to start a conference management business to service major business associations in your city. Most of these associations sponsor an annual conference and you will contract for the design, promotion, and logistics of these meetings. You would easily be able to identify a number of established small conference management firms that rely precisely on this type of business. These companies would make up your direct competition.

INDIRECT COMPETITION   Continuing with our example above, keep in mind that associations are not *obligated* to use conference management firms to handle their annual meetings. Some of them will turn to large consulting firms, which—although it is not their primary business—will handle conference management, especially for established clients. Other associations will turn to local colleges or universities that handle this kind of business as a sideline to education and are also interested in renting out their own facilities for such meetings. Both of these suppliers would form **indirect competition** for your firm.

Indirect competitors are not primarily in the same business as your firm but are a source of supply for your customers. In some cases, customers themselves can be a form of indirect competition. In the conference example, some associations would choose to manage their conferences entirely with their own permanent staff. *Ask yourself: Where else will my customers be able to get the products or services I offer?*

ASSESSING COMPETITORS   In your business plan you must demonstrate that you have at least identified your competitors and, ideally, that you know their sales volume and their strengths and weaknesses. Typically, this information will come from:

- *Experience.* You may well have worked for one or more of your competitors or have extensive knowledge about the industry.
- *Primary research.* You may try to interview those who are knowledgeable about the competition, including employees, customers, or suppliers. You may even just observe your competitors (perhaps by unobtrusively hanging around the cash register), trying to keep track of sales.
- *Secondary research.* Published information about individual small businesses is rare; when it does exist, it is most likely to be found in business directories. Your indirect competition might consist of public corporations. These firms produce annual reports, often outlining the volume and sources of their business.

It can be important to note in the business plan any weaknesses you can identify in your future competition, but it is also important not to rely on these weaknesses because they cannot be considered permanent. As soon as you open up and start to take some of their business, competitors can be expected to clean up their act to defend themselves against you.

indirect competition Sources of supply that are not similar to your business but that are an alternative way for your potential customers to satisfy their needs.

✓ **Test Yourself 2.12**
True or False? A direct competitor is anyone selling the same thing that you sell.

◇ **Get Help 2.16**
Again, try your local library and ask a reference librarian to help you find business or corporate directories and relevant corporate annual reports. Be sure to explain your purpose to the librarian so he or she can help you get the most relevant information.

✓ **Test Yourself 2.13**
True or False? Your customers themselves may be a form of indirect competition.

Head Start Exercise

2.5 Make a list of your direct and indirect competitors, noting the strengths and weaknesses of each. List sources where you think you may be able to find information about the sales of these competitors. ($\frac{3}{4}$ page maximum.)

How Much Business Will My Firm Get?

The answer to this question is your **sales forecast**, a critical component of the business plan. This will show how much money you can reasonably expect your business to generate each year.

The forecast is necessary because so many of your business decisions will be based on how much money is coming in. Other parts of the business plan will determine your costs and expenses (the money going out); the difference between these (money in and money out) over the long term will show whether you can make a profit—even if you did not calculate the market potential.

For established companies, sales forecasting is fairly reliable because it is primarily based on their own past sales. But a brand-new business has no past sales. Despite this, sales forecasting must be undertaken not only for the sake of your own planning but also to satisfy the requirements of potential lenders or investors. Most business plans will show sales forecasts for a period of at least three years, even though the longer the forecast is, the less accurate it will be. However, the forecasts will be revised once the business is in operation and actual sales data become available.

Ask yourself: What will I base the sales forecast on? Your sales forecast should come from a variety of different sources that will be used to generate several different estimates of the sales you can expect. These different dollar values can be shown as a range of possible sales. But for the purposes of your business plan, you will still have to identify a single working forecast from the more conservative end of the range. The process of developing your sales forecast will be closely associated with the work to determine market potential and should follow the same principle of using secondary sources first.

In general, the more sources of information you use in preparing your sales forecast, the more accurate your forecast will be.[5] In addition, many sources will give you ideas for developing your own logical techniques to predict your sales. Nevertheless, it would be unlikely that you could use all of the following sources:

- industry statistics
- customer buying intentions
- how long it takes to get new customers
- expert opinion
- how much business the competition gets
- all the business out there
- the amount of business the firm can handle.

INDUSTRY STATISTICS   Much of the same library information on specific industries that is used to determine market potential can be used to look at **correlations of sales** within that industry. For example, you may find information showing how many dollars in sales travel agencies produce in total and also how many people are employed in travel agencies in total. This gives you the correlation of how many dollars, on average, are produced per person working in travel agencies. If you were starting a small travel agency and you expect to employ three people (including yourself), you could multiply the *industry average dollars per person* by *your three people* as one measure of what you can expect your agency

sales forecast An estimate of how much money a business will bring in over a given period. Typically, a business plan includes at least three years of annual sales forecasts.

correlations of sales Known facts about an industry that can be expressed as a ratio of the industry's sales.

✓ **Test Yourself 2.14**
True or False? A business plan will usually show sales forecasts for a period of at least three years.

◇ **Get Help 2.17**
Performance Plus, at **www.sme.ic.gc.ca**, is Industry Canada's small-business database of financial and other information. You can also find financial ratios data classified by industry in various Statistics Canada publications.

to sell. Also, industry averages of *sales to assets* can be multiplied by the value of all the things you need to start your business (your *business assets*). For example, industry averages of sales per square foot of retail space can be multiplied by the size of your prospective store.

CUSTOMER BUYING INTENTIONS   If you are already doing a questionnaire for the market potential you might as well also find out about *intentions to buy*. This basically means asking a sample of potential customers whether they would buy if you were to offer them your services at a particular price. Simply multiply the results from your sample by the number of potential customers in your entire segment. Keep in mind that some of your respondents could be lying in their answers, so get help in phrasing your questions to minimize this problem.

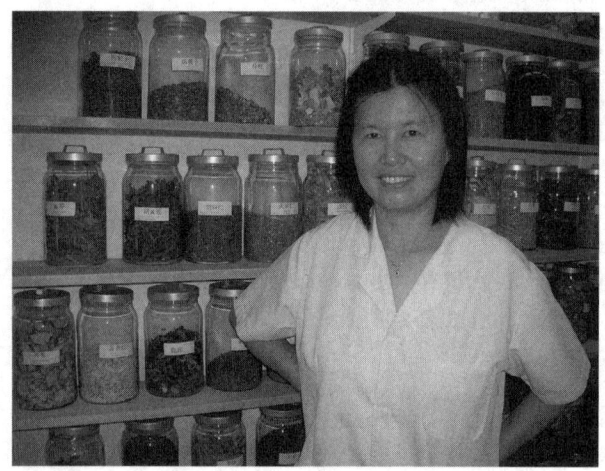

SMALL BUSINESS PROFILE 2.2
Herb Fragrance Oriental Healing Centre

Yuxiang Wang is a Doctor of Traditional Chinese Medicine (TCM). After studying and gaining certification in China, Yuxiang practised for 13 years before moving to Canada. Here, she worked in TCM clinics in Toronto's Asian communities for another six years. Finally, she was able to open her own business, as a sole practitioner, in 2005, in a rather surprising location.

Traditional Chinese medicine differs from Western medicine (which is also practised in China) in that TCM is as much about philosophy as it is about science. TCM is concerned about maintaining balances within the body, equating good health with a harmonious balance among various competing physical and spiritual forces. In this way it is focused on preventive medicine, rather than dealing with advanced disease processes. This form of medicine has evolved through a tradition of over 2000 years. The main treatment techniques offered by Yuxiang include:

• *Acupuncture*—which is gaining broader acceptance in the West.

• *Herbal remedies*—Yuxiang's store contains hundred of containers of dried herbs, roots, and other preparations.

• *Tuina massage*—a particular form of massage that concentrates on specific pain sites and acupressure points.

The city of Toronto has several large concentrations of Asian immigrant and Asian-descent populations. And most of the city's TCM clinics are found in these areas. This is not the case for Herb Fragrance Oriental Healing Centre. Rather, it is located in the Lakeshore West area, only blocks from the Polish consulate in a neighbourhood dominated by Polish and other Eastern European immigrant populations. The choice, Yuxiang admits, was largely one of lifestyle, as the site is only a few minutes' walk from her home. No formal research was done prior to start-up, but Yuxiang was banking on the growing acceptance of TCM in European and Canadian populations, the lack of competition, and the high volume of pedestrian and auto traffic. So far, the gamble seems to be paying off. Although most of the income comes from referrals (existing patients, other health care professionals) and former patients who travel some distance, there is still an important walk-in portion to the business.

Despite the risk of the location, Yuxiang's approach to her start-up was extremely cautious, with her main concerns being controlling costs (her husband provided the labour for the leasehold improvements) and securing comprehensive insurance.

HOW LONG IT TAKES TO GET NEW CUSTOMERS   If you are starting a business where you will have to go out and sell your service, at first you will spend more time acquiring new customers than you will spend servicing existing customers. (As the business matures, this ratio will change.) But if you know how many hours of selling or how many calls it takes to generate a single new customer, you can estimate your sales based on your selling hours available. Depending on your experience in the industry, you may already have a reasonable estimate of how many hours of calling on customers it takes to produce each sale. Alternatively, you may want to find this out by starting your business on a very small scale and selling your service to a limited number of customers. This is actually the process of **test marketing**. For a new business, of course, this can be done only in fields that do not require major investment for materials, site, or equipment.

Get Help 2.18
An introductory marketing research textbook or senior marketing student may be sources of help with the validity of your sample size and the phrasing of your survey questions.

test marketing Trying to sell your product or service to a limited number of customers and carefully measuring factors like customer feedback and how long it takes to make a sale.

Head Start Exercise

2.6   If you will be making sales calls, estimate, based on your experience, how many hours of your work it will take to get a new customer. If you lack experience, make a list of sources where you might get this information. ($\frac{1}{4}$ page maximum.)

✓ Test Yourself 2.15
True or False? The terms *market potential* and *sales forecast* mean approximately the same thing.

The question of how long it takes to get new customers also concerns the growth of your business, and will be used to modify your other estimates of sales. This is because most of the other estimates assume that your business will be operating at *full speed*, like an established firm. But it takes more work to get a new customer than to serve an existing one—and at the beginning all your customers will be new. This factor must be considered (and discussed in your business plan) when estimating your sales.

EXPERT OPINION   This method means interviewing several people who have expertise in your particular industry. These experts could include retirees, former employers, competitors, teachers, or people in the same business as you but in geographic areas away from your market area. In its simplest form, this method means first telling each expert about your business. Then ask the experts how much business (in dollars) they think you will be able to do. You are really just asking for their "best guess" given their limited knowledge of your business. The idea is to then average these expert guesses as an estimate of your forecast. You may find that the more expertise your experts have, the more reluctant they will be to give you a particular sales number. If this is the case, ask them for a reasonable range. Then, for your calculations, just pick the midpoint in the range. If you can get their "best guess" in writing, be sure to quote them in the business plan. Don't forget to include your own expert opinion (provided that you have sufficient knowledge and experience in the field).

Head Start Exercise

2.7   Make up a list of individuals whom you consider to have the best expertise available in the kind of business you plan on opening ($\frac{1}{4}$ page maximum).

? Get Help 2.19

Business credit agencies, like Dun & Bradstreet, provide financial and other data for many specific businesses. In fact, it is possible to order (at reasonable cost) a company report over the Internet. This will include information on the number of employees, the sales, and the financial position of the firm. See **www.dnb.ca**.

✓ Test Yourself 2.16

True or False? Your sales forecast will likely represent only a portion of the market potential.

HOW MUCH BUSINESS THE COMPETITION GETS   This is another form of correlation analysis—it's like looking at the industry statistics, but instead you are looking at individual direct competitors: businesses similar to your own that are going after the same kinds of customers. The idea is to estimate the sales of a specific competitor (by observation, interview, personal experience, or, in some cases, published financial information) and compare this to some other factor about the firm, such as traffic volume, amount of advertising, number of salespeople, and so on.

For example, you might be opening a translation service for a particular group of new immigrants in your city. You estimate the sales of your existing competitor (you had a summer job with them) at $400,000. You also know that they run daily ads in the business-personals column of the ethnic newspaper and all of their new business comes from that source. You decide that you also will run a daily ad in the same column. Obviously, that does not mean you will have sales of $400,000—you will be splitting the market with the competitor and some of their sales comes from repeat business, which you won't have at first—but it is another indicator of how much business you can do.

ALL THE BUSINESS OUT THERE   The market potential—all the business in your market area—can itself provide an estimate of sales when the competition is taken into consideration. For example, if you and three competitors are chasing the same business, with a market potential of $400,000, you might expect that each competitor (yourself included) would be entitled to a share of one-fourth, or a sales forecast of $100,000. The newer the product/service and the newer the market, the more valid this kind of estimate will be. In other words, if all the competitors are just starting up, like you, then this is a legitimate estimate. However, if you are competing against firms that have been around for 20 years, it won't mean much.

THE AMOUNT OF BUSINESS THE FIRM CAN HANDLE   Let's say you want to start a business maintaining swimming pools for condominium buildings in the east end of the city. You know it will take you half a day, once a week for each pool to keep them fully maintained. That means that the highest number of pools you could service (assuming you were to work 6 days a week) would be 12. If your average year-long maintenance contract were to be priced at about $6000, the highest possible sales forecast you could have would be $12 \times \$6,000 = \$72,000$.

It would be extremely unusual for a brand-new business to be operating at 100-percent capacity right from the start, but it is possible in a market where demand far exceeds supply. Nevertheless, this number, the most business you could handle (100 percent of your capacity) helps keep other estimates of your sales forecast in perspective. Furthermore, for some industries like hotels, manufacturers, and restaurants, the average operating level (what percentage of capacity) can be found by digging through the industry statistics.

The sample business plan following Chapter 5 shows estimates for market potential as well as a sales forecast for a fast-food business. Figure 2.1 on page 39 is another example of a professionally written sales forecast. This is from a business plan for a machine shop. Note how it uses multiple methods to produce conservative estimates and gives the source for each. *Ask yourself: Will I really need to prepare a sales forecast that is this detailed?*

Figure 2.1   **SALES FORECAST | Machine Shop**

1. Personal first year estimate of contracted sales agent   = $ 380,000

2. Average annual sales per machine shop production employee
($171,263)[1] × 3 production employees in this company   =   513,790

3. Average annual sales per machine shop employee (all types)
($133,717)[2] × 4 employees in total for this business   =   534,868

4. Average personal estimate of shop owner, shop machinist,
and two retired machinists   =   533,000

5. Average machine shop sales per dollar of fixed assets ($3.02)[3] ×
value of fixed assets for this company ($141,896)   =   428,525

6. Estimate of 100% capacity, if all machines were running full-time,
($988,000)[4] × average industry operating level of 80%   =   788,400

7. Market potential (as previously defined)   = $24,000,000

Method 1 is disproportionately low since it represents the estimate of the sales agent who has offered to work only half time (on straight commission of 10 percent) and promises to provide contracts at least in this $380,000 range in the first year. The owner, however, would also be selling part time and his contribution is not included here. Method 2 does not include the part-time production contribution of the owner. Method 3 does not include the part-time sales agent. Method 6 is included only to demonstrate the sales of the business operating at industry capacity levels, and Method 7 shows the entire value of the market. Leaving these last two out of the calculation, the mean average forecast is $478,000.

However, we will use an even more conservative forecast of $410,000 for the second year and allow for a 10-percent increase for the third year. Allowing a full six months to build up to the second-year sales rate, starting from zero sales, would mean a first-year forecast of ($410,000 × 75%) = $308,000, which is still below the sales agent's personal guarantee.

SALES FORECAST

Year 1	$308,000
Year 2	$410,000
Year 3	$451,000

1. Statistics Canada, Principal Statistics for Manufacturing Industries of Canada (Table 301-006), Annual Survey of Manufacturers, 2004.
2. Statistics Canada, Principal Statistics for Manufacturing Industries of Canada (Table 301-006), Annual Survey of Manufacturers, 2004.
3. Industry Canada/Statistics Canada, Small Business Profiles, Machine Shops (NAICS #3327) 2002.
4. Assumes 50 production hours per week and shop contracts of $380 per hour.

LEVEL OF DETAIL   Whether your sales forecast has to be as detailed as the one shown in Figure 2.1 depends. If you plan on borrowing $50,000 to start your business, the answer is a clear yes. If you want to risk $300 on a part-time venture, the answer is "forget it—too much work." But even then, you will need some kind of indicators of how much money will come into your business; otherwise, you can't do any kind of financial planning.

You may not yet know some of the information involved in preparing the sales forecast: exactly how many people will be working in the business, how many dollars in assets the business will have, how many square feet of space your business will use, and so on. Nevertheless, this does not let you get out of forecasting. You can and must prepare some type of sales forecast at this point, even without all the available information. But don't panic! Right now, your sales forecast is only a draft. So, for information you can't yet know, or decisions you haven't yet made, just use your best guess. When you get to the end of the business plan and have all the missing information, you can come back and redo the sales forecast—maybe several times—because writing a business plan is really *rewriting* a business plan. (You already know that.)

A word of caution: Throughout this text you are advised to "Get Help" from a variety of professors, and textbooks written by academics. But ask any professor for advice on a particular business decision and the answer is usually a variation on: "You need more information . . . then, the decision can be made using the new data." Academics tend to think in terms of perfect data. But real-life entrepreneurs don't work with perfect data. Entrepreneurs must strike a sensible balance between reducing risk and the cost of getting information. You are trying to get reasonable indicators of how much business is out there and how much business you can get. You need just enough information to satisfy yourself and your lenders or investors—but probably not enough for the academics.

Head Start Exercise

2.8   Quickly go back over the above sources of information for the sales forecast and note which ones will likely help you in predicting your sales. Think of some other methods you could use. Briefly outline how you will go about preparing your sales forecast. ($\frac{1}{3}$ page maximum.)

How Can I Protect the Business?

As you well know by now, all entrepreneurs are taking a risk. At the very least, when working for yourself you risk your time and effort. But when you or your business owns assets, these also are at risk from a variety of dangers, which you would like to be protected against. There is no such thing, however, as 100-percent protection against risk. The trick is to understand the risk and then try to reduce it in an economical way. Reducing risk, of course, is also an important issue for lenders or investors who wish to clearly see in the business plan how their capital will be protected.

SMALL BUSINESS INSURANCE   According to the Canadian Federation of Independent business, the vast majority of small business owners worry about the high cost of insurance.[6] New entrepreneurs often try to avoid insurance as an unnecessary expense. But as soon as your business, or you personally, have any significant assets, you must consider the protection of insurance.

It's possible to get just about any kind of insurance imaginable, at a price. But the types you choose will depend on the nature of your business. For example, as a literary agent you would likely want *errors and omissions insurance* to protect against the possibility of a problematic contract. As a workplace massage therapist for computer users, you would want *malpractice insurance* in case a client becomes injured. As a bookstore owner, you would be particularly concerned about *fire insurance.*

If you started an engineering firm to monitor office air quality, your people would constantly be going in and out of other people's businesses. In such a case, you would use a *fidelity bond* to protect customers against any illegal actions of someone you might hire. If you were in the office renovation business you might use *surety* or *performance bonds* to protect your customers in case you were unable to complete the work within the contracted time.

As an entertainer with your own band, you would consider *disability insurance* in case you were to get severe arthritis, leaving you unable to play your instrument. You might also have *life insurance* on other members of the band, acting as each other's beneficiaries (this is often done among business partners).

Almost everyone in business these days needs *automobile insurance.* This should include enough vehicle liability coverage to make it unnecessary for anyone to sue the business over and above any insurance settlement. In addition, *general liability* coverage is common (in case someone gets hurt at your place of business, or you are responsible for some form of injury or loss). And, for those working from home, many insurance companies offer *home office* packages that are in addition to regular house/apartment insurance. *Ask yourself: What will my insurance priorities be?*

Insurance is usually purchased through a *broker.* The independent **insurance broker** represents a variety of large insurance companies that the broker can "shop" on your behalf for the policy that best suits your needs and budget. *Ask yourself: What's the best way to get a good insurance broker?*

insurance broker An independent intermediary who sells insurance policies on behalf of a variety of large insurance companies.

There is always the Yellow Pages, which makes it easy to find someone in your neighbourhood—but do you really know the kind of person you'll be dealing with? Business texts often recommend finding an insurance provider by referral from someone you trust: a friend, lawyer, accountant—although it isn't always comfortable if you have to go back and tell your friend that you decided against his or her insurance broker.

Get Help 2.20
Search the Internet using the keywords "small business insurance" to find brokers who will provide quotes online for the coverage and type of insurance you want.

However you find one, the main thing to remember about insurance brokers is that they are primarily "suppliers" as opposed to "advisers." Even the best-intentioned, most ethical brokers cannot be objective about the amount of coverage you need, since they are paid by commission—the more insurance you buy, the more they get paid. You have to decide for yourself, based on your experience and research, how much insurance to buy. Once you've made that decision, you can be sure to get a good price by shopping around. If you are in a business with unusually or particularly high risks or you just need independent professional advice about insurance, you can hire a **risk management consultant.** These are professional advisers on risk and insurance requirements that neither sell insurance themselves nor are they associated with insurance providers. Licensing or registration requirements for risk management consultants vary from province to province.

risk management consultant An independent (usually licensed) adviser on property and casualty insurance risks and coverages.

SECURITY AND LOSS PREVENTION   You can lose your assets not just by being sued—assets are also at risk from those who would wish to steal them. No one likes to get ripped off, and good entrepreneurs plan to reduce risk from the more obvious methods of theft:

- *Pilfering:* This is the theft of small amounts of materials, usually by employees, suppliers, or transport people. It is a bigger problem in retail and wholesale businesses, but even in small offices the office supplies can disappear at an alarming rate. The primary defences against **pilfering** are tight inventory control (perhaps by having employees sign for supplies) and employee training (awareness of the costs and consequences of pilfering).[7]

- *Shoplifting:* If you plan on having a retail store that sells anything smaller than refrigerators, plan on encountering those who will try to walk off with inventory. The greatest number of perpetrators are juveniles,[8] but the hardest to protect against are the professionals. The more economical defences against **shoplifting** include a highly visible store layout, trained employees (who know what to watch for and how to respond), mirrors, and even security cameras (which have dropped in price over the past few years).

- *Embezzlement:* This happens when someone is entrusted with your (or your company's) money, but puts that money to their own use. Embezzlers can be professional service providers such as lawyers or accountants, or employees such as bookkeepers or cashiers. Protections against **embezzlement** include using only bonded or insured professionals and implementing strict cash handling and auditing procedures.

- *Burglary:* This is when your place of business is broken into either by vandals or by professional thieves. Defences against **burglary** start with a good set of locks and can include alarm systems, dogs, window bars, or security services. Obviously, the level of burglary protection will vary widely from the simple "no valuables" office to the high-end jewellery store.

- *Robbery:* Certain specific types of businesses are much more prone to **robbery** (all-night gas stations and convenience stores, retail jewellers, businesses with lots of cash on hand). Visibility, security cameras, "no-cash" signs, and a non-confrontational plan for dealing with would-be robbers are your best bets.

- *Fraud:* You are more likely to be defrauded when participating in something slightly shady, or high-risk, with the apparent potential to win big. For example, you might be offered twice your usual rate for a very large contract or order, but on the condition that you give extended payment terms. When it sounds this tempting, be suspicious: go by the book, get it in writing, check up on customers and suppliers. These are your major defences against **fraud.**

pilfering Theft of small quantities committed by employees.

shoplifting Retail theft by stealth, committed while the store is open for business.

embezzlement Theft by a person entrusted with handling a company's cash or other assets.

burglary Theft by breaking into a business at a time when it is closed.

robbery Theft by force or threats of violence.

fraud Theft by deceit or trickery.

Head Start Exercise

2.9   Write down the type of theft that would be most likely to affect you or your business. Identify the ways you will protect against this. List any start-up or ongoing expenses involved. ($\frac{1}{3}$ page maximum.)

INTELLECTUAL PROPERTY   Intellectual property laws are designed to protect your work in areas of the arts, communication, design, or applied research, but the actual enforcement of these laws is left to you. If someone steals your work in these areas, you have to take them to court and you have to prove that the work was yours. Registering your work with the appropriate government office is, of course, your best—and in some cases, only—acceptable proof.

You can protect yourself only in the areas specifically covered by the intellectual property laws: patent, copyright, trademark, industrial design, and microchip design. *Ask yourself: How do these forms of protection differ?* You may have a great idea, but even if you're the one who thought of it first, anyone is entitled to "steal" it from you if it doesn't fit into one of these categories. You can't protect just an idea.

Patent protection is for an **invention.** Let's say you invent a new kind of light bulb that uses salt crystals to produce light. (Hey, it could happen!) This would be a new technology, and if you applied for a Canadian patent you would be granted exclusive rights to your invention for 20 years in Canada only. Later, if you invented a way to use your salt-light as an electronic switch, this would be a new application of your technology and a second patent could be granted. You can use your Canadian patent application to file for patents in over 100 other countries through the Patent Cooperation Treaty, of which Canada is a member. Protecting foreign patents can be expensive and complex, but you can get help in this area from a **patent agent.**

Copyright protection covers software and works of art including writing, music, and visual arts. The creator of a work (or an employer who contracts the work) automatically owns the copyright. No registration is legally required, but you can register a work for additional protection. It is also a good idea to indicate your ownership of copyright on creative works as a warning to others that they may not possess, use, or copy the material without your permission. (Check the warnings on this text and make sure you don't violate the copyright.) Coverage is worldwide and normally extends for the life of the creator plus an additional 50 years.

A **trademark** protects a word, phrase, or symbol that identifies your company and its products. Trademarks are registered by country, and in Canada provide protection for 15 years, but this protection is renewable indefinitely. Large companies depend heavily on their trademarks (the Coca-Cola name, the Nike "swoosh," the McDonald's Golden Arches) and these companies rigorously enforce against anyone else infringing on them. So be careful not to violate their trademarks or you could find yourself in court—at a great disadvantage against such large firms.

Industrial design protection applies to a pattern, a shape, or an ornamental design of mass-produced manufactured products. Examples would include the shape of a spoon handle or the ornamentation on a table leg. Protection must be applied for and lasts for ten years, although a renewal fee must be paid at the five-year mark.

Microchip design is the only other kind of intellectual property specifically protected by law. Technically, it's called **"integrated circuit topography" (ICT)** and, unless you're in the business of designing microchips, you don't really need to know about it. If you do need to know: registration of a chip design is done on a country-by-country basis, although Canada now has reciprocal agreements with many other countries (20 at the time of writing). In Canada, protection lasts for 10 years. The designer of the microcircuits or the employer of the designer may apply for this protection.

✓ **Test Yourself 2.17**
True or False? Burglary and robbery are interchangeable terms.

patent Exclusive rights to a useful invention, granted by a government for a specified period of time.

invention A new technology or a new application of an existing technology.

patent agent Someone trained in engineering and law and registered with the federal Commissioner of Patents. Patent agents can assess inventions and assist with the patent application process. For more information, the largest association for patent agents, the Intellectual Property Institute of Canada, has a website at **www.ipic.ca**.

copyright Protection against anyone (other than the creator, or someone authorized by the creator) reproducing a creative work such as a drawing, piece of writing, audiovisual production, and so on.

? **Get Help 2.21**
The Inventive Women website has lots of examples of successful women inventors as well as information on intellectual property, mentoring, and even promotional assistance for women inventors. See **www.inventivewomen.com**.

trademark A word, phrase, or visual symbol that identifies the products or services of a company.

industrial design Registered rights to the original, visually aesthetic elements of a manufactured product.

ICT Integrated circuit topography; the design of a microchip, which can be registered for protection of exclusive rights for up to ten years.

Get Help 2.22

For information on patent, copyright, trademark, industrial design, or ICT, contact the Canadian Intellectual Property Office: Place du Portage Phase 1, 50 Victoria Street, Hull, Quebec K1A 0C9; phone (900) 565–2476. *Note*: there is a charge per call. Website: *cipo.gc.ca*.

There are other forms of intellectual property not clearly protected by specific laws, such as the details in your business plan or the secret recipes for your restaurant's cocktails. These are called *trade secrets* and attempts to protect them generally include non-disclosure agreements and reliance on the trust responsibilities of professional advisers who would see your confidential information. Even though employees have some responsibility to an employer,[9] rights to trade secrets are certainly more difficult to enforce in court than protected forms of intellectual property.

CREDIT AND COLLECTIONS   You could have a business where your sales are high and your costs and expenses are low, and that means lots of profit. Now, a profit "on paper" is great—but at some point you have to get your hands on the cash, and generally the sooner the better. Unfortunately, some clients are slow or reluctant to part with money, even when it is properly owed to suppliers. This is a danger against which you must try to protect yourself.

If your business sells to ordinary consumers, payment isn't much of a problem since you will likely use cash, cheques (guaranteed by phone, using companies such as Telecredit), debit cards, credit cards, or other third-party credit. For example, you could sell furniture from your antique store, arranging finance contracts (you do the paperwork) with a local bank or finance company. The finance deal, however, remains between your customer and the finance company and you will get the cash. Rarely can small retailers afford to get into the business of extending their own credit to customers.

But let's say you start an executive limousine service where you work on contract for large corporations. They expect to be billed on a monthly basis for your service. This puts you in the business of granting credit. Even if your monthly invoice says "payable on receipt," you have already allowed up to a month's worth of delayed payment. Furthermore, many companies will ask for another 30 days from receiving the invoice because of their internal payment systems. Now you could be waiting as long as 60 days to get paid. And what happens when their system breaks down and you have to wait still another month? What if payment is more than three months overdue?

Test Yourself 2.18

True or False? Copyright protection is "automatic" in that it does not legally require registration.

Test Yourself 2.19

True or False? A visual symbol can be protected by trademark.

You can't wait forever to take action. Instead, you should have a series of increasingly serious steps planned for dealing with delinquent accounts. The steps should be appropriate to the nature of your industry. For example, you may take your first action when an account is 7 days overdue. Figure 2.2 shows one kind of collections policy you might implement.

Ask yourself: What happens if a client who owes me money gets into financial trouble and might be going bankrupt? This is one of those cases where an ounce of prevention is worth a ton of cure. Small creditors of a bankrupt business rarely get much of the money they are owed— and the little they do get, they have to wait for.

The only real defence here is to try to avoid getting into this problem in the first place. Before extending credit, get credit reports. (These come from credit reporting agencies such as Dun & Bradstreet or Equifax/Creditel. They include information such as the sales of the firm, the amount of assets and debts it carries, and the speed at which it usually pays its bills.) Set limits of credit for individual customers and stick to these limits, regularly checking to see who owes you and how much.

Figure 2.2

EXAMPLE COLLECTIONS POLICY

Time overdue	Action
7 days	-a reminder phone call.
14 days	-a reminder phone call and -a follow-up letter.
30–45 days	-a visit to the company to discuss the problem and -a follow-up letter.
45–60 days	-stop supplying the company and -a phone call offering to pick up a cheque for outstanding payments.
75 days	-formal letter from a lawyer demanding payment, threatening legal action and -a phone call offering to pick up a cheque.
90 days	-sell the debt to a collection agency or -commence legal action.

✓Answers to Test Yourself Questions

2.1 It is always important to have a location close to your customers. *False*

2.2 Traffic analysis is very important for retail businesses. *True*

2.3 Traffic analysis is very important for businesses that are industrial services. *False*

2.4 For the purposes of the business plan, the terms *location* and *site* are totally interchangeable. *False*

2.5 For most kinds of business, it is better to buy rather than lease the property where the business is situated. *False*

2.6 Market potential includes your firm's sales of a product or service, as well as the sales of your competitors for that product or service. *True*

2.7 You need to know the market potential for planning long-range strategy. *True*

2.8 A separate estimate of market potential is required for each different customer group a business is targeting. *True*

2.9 Trade journals are primarily magazines where different kinds of businesses can swap their goods and services with each other. *False*

2.10 Secondary research usually requires the use of questionnaires and samples of the market. *False*

2.11 The majority of people going into business for themselves will require some kind of help in estimating market potential. *True*

2.12 A direct competitor is anyone selling the same thing that you sell. *False*

2.13 Your customers themselves may be a form of indirect competition. *True*

2.14 A business plan will usually show sales forecasts for a period of at least three years. *True*

2.15 The terms *market potential* and *sales forecast* mean approximately the same thing. *False*

2.16 Your sales forecast will likely represent only a portion of the market potential. *True*

2.17 Burglary and robbery are interchangeable terms. *False*

2.18 Copyright protection is "automatic" in that it does not legally require registration. *True*

2.19 A visual symbol can be protected by trademark. *True*

Questions for Discussion

1. Compare the province or territory you are in with the closest U.S. state as potential locations for opening a new small business in an industry like plastic moulding. Which location has the most advantages? What if the industry were TV animation? Specialty chocolate manufacturing? Used computer refurbishing?

2. Identify a highly successful consumer retail or service business in your area. What are the advantages of this firm's physical site? What could be improved?

3. Try to identify several popular songs that sound closely alike. Discuss why so many cases of copyright infringement in the music industry end up in court.

4. Why is it that, historically, so many inventors ended up penniless? Who makes money from their inventions? Discuss the fairness of this.

5. Discuss the idea that insurance is really "betting against your own success." Is insurance an investment?

Recommended Reading

Doman, Don, Dell Dennison, and Margaret Doman. *Market Research Made Easy*. North Vancouver: Self-Counsel Press, 2005.

Hair, Joseph Jr., Robert Bush, and David Ortinau. *Marketing Research*. Boston: McGraw-Hill Higher Education, 2006.

Hovey, Craig. *The Patent Process: A Guide to Intellectual Property for the Information Age*. Toronto: John Wiley and Sons Canada, 2002.

Jassin, Lloyd J., and Steven C. Schechter. *The Copyright Permission and Libel Handbook*. Toronto: John Wiley & Sons Inc., 1998.

Schelling, Jeffrey M. *Cyberlaw Canada*. North Vancouver: Self-Counsel Press, 1998.

Willerton, Dale R. *Negotiate Your Commercial Lease*. North Vancouver: Self-Counsel Press, 2003.

The Business Plan, Section 2: Feasibility

LOCATION

1. Explain the general area where your business will be located, describing the surrounding population of potential customers (provide numbers).

_____

_____

_____

_____

_____

_____

_____

_____

2. Describe any other factors in your choice of location, such as your proximity to transportation, suppliers, or relevant services.

_____

_____

_____

_____

_____

_____

_____

SITE

3. Describe the site of your business, including any relevant details such as parking, neighbouring firms, visibility, and traffic (provide numbers).

_____

_____

_____

_____

_____

_____

_____

4. Explain why this choice of a site is appropriate for *what* you are selling and appropriate for the customer groups *to whom* you are selling.

_____

SITE EXPENSES

5. If you are leasing your business premises, outline the major provisions of the lease including all rental and maintenance fees and renewal terms.

Or

If your business is home-based, calculate what percentage of the home (square footage) will be used exclusively for business purposes. Explain the ownership or leasing arrangements of the home.

_____

MARKET POTENTIAL

6. Clearly define the market potential that you will be estimating. In other words, you will be calculating the annual expenditures of which group of potential customers (*who*) on *what* product or service?

_____

7. List all the relevant data that you have gathered, indicating the sources. (If the information is extensive, attach the list of sources as an appendix.)

_____

_____

_____

_____

_____

_____

_____

_____

_____

_____

8. Clearly explain any calculations or logic involved in estimating the market potential, and indicate the dollar value of your estimate.

_____

_____

_____

_____

_____

_____

_____

_____

_____

_____

COMPETITION

9. Name, locate, and briefly describe any direct competitors that you will have to deal with. Provide an estimate of the sales of each, explaining your sources of information.

_____

_____

_____

_____

_____

_____

_____

_____

_____

10. Name, locate, and briefly describe any indirect competition that you will have to deal with.

_____

_____

_____

_____

_____

_____

_____

_____

11. Describe any advantages that you will have over the competition.

_____

_____

_____

_____

_____

_____

_____

_____

_____

SALES FORECAST

12. Make as many sales forecast estimates as you can, using different methods. Rank the different estimates to show the range of sales you might expect.

_____

_____

_____

_____

_____

_____

_____

_____

_____

13. From the information above, choose or calculate a single conservative estimate of sales that you will use for planning your business. Explain your choice.

_____

_____

_____

_____

_____

_____

_____

_____

_____

PROTECTING THE BUSINESS

14. Briefly describe any business insurance you will carry, explaining the coverage, the premiums, and the payment schedule.

_____

_____

_____

_____

_____

_____

_____

_____

_____

_____

15. Explain any techniques that you will use for protection against theft or other dangers to which the business could be subject (for example, security systems or operating policies).

_____

_____

_____

_____

_____

_____

_____

_____

_____

16. Describe any intellectual property of the business and how this will be protected.

_____

_____

_____

_____

_____

_____

_____

_____

_____

17. Describe any policies or procedures you will use before extending credit, and methods you will use for collecting outstanding accounts.

_____

_____

_____

_____

_____

_____

_____

_____

_____

Marketing:
How Will I Get Customers?

LEARNING OBJECTIVES

On completion of this chapter, you should be able to:

* *Discuss factors relevant to business image.*
* *Name and define the elements of the marketing mix.*
* *Compare service/product strategies among businesses.*
* *Compare the three basic pricing strategies.*
* *Identify various distribution options.*
* *Describe and compare various small business promotion options.*
* *Identify methods of developing selling skills.*
* *Discuss the interaction of the marketing mix elements.*
* *Prepare the marketing portion of a business plan.*

How Will I Become a Specialist?

So far, your business plan has explained exactly:

* Who you are.
* What your business will mean legally.
* Where you plan on doing business.
* What you will sell and to whom you plan on selling it.
* How much of your kind of business is out there (market potential) and
* How much of that total market you can reasonably expect to get for your own firm.

Now it's time to explain, in detail, how you plan on getting your customers. Not just the selling or advertising involved—**marketing** means more than that. You will be explaining how you will specialize your business for the particular groups of customers you are targeting.

The first step is to decide on your *image*.

IMAGE   Your company will have an image. This is the perception people will have about what your business is like. Of course, if you personally *are* the business, then we're talking about your personal image. You are going to have an image whether you intend to or not. So, obviously, it's better that your business image is one that you intend—one that is appropriate for *what* you are selling and *to whom* you're selling it.

To be more precise, your company will have two images: a **projected image** and an **expected image**. The projected image will be the impression of your firm, which is given by everything you do: how you or your employees dress, talk, act; what your place of business looks like, where it is situated, how it is decorated; where and how you advertise; whether you call people by their first name. All of this will contribute to projecting an image of your firm.

If you dress in blue jeans and athletic shoes, you may be projecting a casual image. If you are located in the fanciest shopping district, you are likely projecting an exclusive image. If you drive a Volvo, you are projecting a reliable image. If the people working for you have purple and orange hair, your image may be creative or wild—but it is certainly not conservative. *Ask yourself: What image do I personally project?*

There is also an expected image of your business. This is the perception of your firm that people carry in their heads even before they ever encounter your company—an idea of what they expect your business to be like. People expect an expensive jewellery store to be formal and elegant. They might expect the owner of a catering firm to look clean and perhaps wear a white lab coat. People don't expect a mural painter to be wearing a cocktail dress, or the director of a children's theatre troupe to be telling inappropriate jokes.

Now, we can often get people to sit up and take notice when we do things a little out of the ordinary. This is a keystone of successful advertising. But if we stray too far from the image that customers expect of us, it produces a kind of psychological discomfort in the customer. This discomfort is called **cognitive dissonance**. People tend to avoid it and, logically, to avoid businesses that make them experience it.

How would you feel about engaging a roof repair contractor who is wearing a $1200 suit and driving a Mercedes? How would you feel about a doctor whose washroom is always unclean? On the other hand, the messy washroom at a used tire dealer probably wouldn't bother you as much. It has to do with the images you expect.

There is nothing wrong with setting a tone for your business that is new or out of the ordinary. But this image must always be tempered by what your customers expect. *Ask yourself: What adjectives describe the image that customers will expect from my company?* Obviously, different customer groups will have different expectations. If you work as a travel consultant who specializes in seniors' bus trips, your image may have to be reliable, inexpensive, kindly, and caring. A travel consultant who works for professional sports teams must also have a reliable image, but in addition will need to be precise, tough, responsive, elitist, and expensive. It's what these clients would expect.

The image that your company projects should fulfill the general expectations of your customer groups, but it should also tell them that you are different from your competitors—sufficiently different that you will be seen as the *logical, exact, right, perfect,* and *only* choice for your customers to deal with. You are a specialist for those particular types of customers. If your customers are looking for cheap, you must project an image of being the cheapest. If they want reliability, you must be the most reliable. If they are looking for quality, you must represent the highest quality. And if they want hot, you will be the hottest.

Your image need not be totally clean, honest, and reliable—or even accurate. Think of the New York street hawker who rips open a packing case at a busy intersection and starts selling brand-name pantyhose on a *quick, cash, no-questions-asked* basis. Tourists, glancing over their shoulders, rush forward to make their purchases and quickly disappear back into the crowds. The street hawker's slightly crooked image may be far from the reality. Most likely, the vendor is fully licensed and has a credit account with the pantyhose wholesaler, pays all taxes, and is totally legal. But that's not the image that would work for these particular customers, excited by the adventure of a seedy deal. *Ask yourself: Have I ever seen a business that prospers by having a "seedy" image?*

✓ **Test Yourself 3.2**
True or False? The expected and projected images of your business must not be extremely far apart.

◇ **Get Help 3.1**
Ask friends or associates to come up with single words describing what your company should be like.

✓ **Test Yourself 3.3**
True or False? A company's image is the perception of the firm held in the mind of the company's owner.

Head Start Exercise

3.1   Make a list of adjectives that describe the image your company will project ($\frac{1}{8}$ page maximum).

Once you have decided on an image for your company, it's time to apply your image decisions.

NAMING THE BUSINESS   Most people would have worked out a name for their company long before this point in the business plan, probably because choosing a name is one of the more fun aspects of starting a business. But if you haven't done it yet, now is the time—and if you have done it, now is the time to do it properly. Doing it properly means considering *what* you're selling, *to whom* you're selling it, and the resultant image you wish to project.

Names chosen only for their personal meaning to you will not boost sales. If your last name is Goldstein and your partner's last name is Hornsby, you and your partner might think that "Goldhorn Bathtub Repair" is a great name for your company. It's not. It has meaning only for you and it doesn't sell.

Try and choose a name that will:
• Get attention.
• Be easy to remember.
• Project the image you want.

But choosing the name is a balancing act. *Naked Sex Clock Store* will surely get attention—and people aren't likely to forget it—but is it the image you want to project? Whatever name you choose, you should be able to explain, in your business plan, how the name works to project the appropriate image for your company.

✓ **Test Yourself 3.4**

True or False? Selecting a name should be the first step in planning a business.

Head Start Exercise

3.2   List at least five possible names for your business and note how they project different images. Identify the one that best satisfies your image needs. ($\frac{1}{3}$ page maximum.)

marketing mix The particular combination of marketing elements that a business uses to find and satisfy its customers; the marketing strategy, usually described in terms of its product/service, price, distribution, and promotion elements.

MARKETING STRATEGY   How you project your image—how you make yourself appear different from your competitors—is with your marketing strategy, or what professional marketers call the **marketing mix**. Over the years, a fairly standard method has evolved to explain a firm's marketing mix, and this is probably the best way to describe it in your business plan. The marketing mix is typically broken down into the following elements:

- product or service strategy
- pricing strategy
- distribution strategy and
- promotion strategy.

◇ **Get Help 3.2**

Call some prospective customers and do an informal survey. If consumers will be your customers, get some secondary information on trends. For example, read recent copies of the *Trend Letter*, a widely quoted newsletter from the Global Network in Washington. This publication covers current trends in marketing, demographics, and technology, and is available online at **www.thetrendletter.com**.

The better you get to know your market, the more accurately you will be able to tailor your business to give customers what they want—what they *really* want, not the superficial or the impossible.[1] Customers may seem to want the impossible: the lowest prices, highest quality, best service, best terms, fastest delivery, and the like, but it can't be done. So you must develop a marketing strategy that will give the customers not everything, but those things that are most important to them.

✓ **Test Yourself 3.5**

True or False? *Marketing mix* and *marketing strategy* mean the same thing.

Head Start Exercise

3.3   Make a prioritized list of the things that are most important to the kind of customers you will have. (For example, price, atmosphere, speed, accuracy.) If you cannot identify their priorities based on your experience, then do some research to find these out. ($\frac{1}{3}$ page maximum.)

✓ **Test Yourself 3.6**

True or False? Production is one of the elements of the marketing mix.

What Combinations of Things Will I Sell?

SERVICE/PRODUCT STRATEGY   The particular combination of things you sell is your *product* or *service strategy*. It describes the variety and quality of goods and/or services that you sell. The fewer different things you sell, the more specialized your business will be—and specialization is profitable. However, the choice of things you will sell is another balancing act that depends on your chosen market. You must try to ensure that you are offering everything your customers expect of you. (You don't want them to go to competitors for some of their needs, which could end up with you losing the customer.) On the other hand, you don't want to tie up your money or energy in a huge variety of products or services that won't make profit for you.

Imagine you are a computer-training consultant who sells courses and seminars to government departments and agencies all over your province. You specialize in web design courses, but have a very broad computer background. From your training experience, you know that the first time you teach something new you spend about four hours outside the classroom in preparation for every hour you spend inside the classroom. The second time you teach the same course, the ratio is about two hours outside for every one hour in class. The third, fourth, and subsequent times, the ratio can fall below one-quarter hour of preparation for every hour of teaching.

Now let's say you charge $700 per day for six hours of instruction. If you keep teaching the same old web design course over and over (even allowing time for customizing and improvement), you'll be making lots of money. On the other hand, if you teach web authoring software one week, networks the next, graphics the next, and office software after that, life will be less boring but you will have little profit to show: too much preparation time. Besides, if you present yourself as the "web training specialist," you will be a more obvious choice for this type of training compared to someone who is seen as a generalist.

This specialization of your product or service works only if it is appropriate for the kinds of customers you are chasing. Being a photographer who specializes in taking pictures of horses is fine provided that you are targeting horse owners or trainers in your area. And when you specialize your service or products, you have to keep the other elements of the marketing mix in mind. For example, if you open a bakery that sells only bagels, you will have a problem when customers can get similar bagels at a competitor's location where they can also pick up bread, doughnuts, and other items they might be looking for. In this case, being the "bagel specialist" will work only if your product is clearly different in terms of quality or price or some other feature.

Your product/service strategy includes not only the basic services and products you will offer, but also the variety of additional things you may do for your customers that will cost you money and time. *Ask yourself: What might I do for my customers that will add value to the product or service?*

Will you accept payment by Visa or MasterCard? Will you give your customers credit terms? Will you provide free installation? Will there be a warranty attached to your service or product? Will you supply free estimates? Free delivery? Free bags to carry home your product? Will you provide advice by telephone?

All these added services will provide value to the customer, and all will cost you money. The decision on which extra services you will provide must also be part of your overall strategy in catering to your chosen market groups and making yourself different from your competitors. The ability to give more personalized service is one of the competitive advantages of small firms over larger ones.[2] Nevertheless, the general rule for a new business is to offer relatively few products or services (compared to the competition), especially when you are just starting up. At the beginning, keep it simple. Then, later on, your business can grow by expansion of your offerings (*what* you are selling) or going after new markets (*to whom* you are selling). It is always easier to add something new than it is to stop providing something

✓ **Test Yourself 3.7**
True or False? Generally, it is more profitable for new businesses to specialize in fewer products or services than their competitors offer.

◇ **Get Help 3.3**
Interview the owner of an established business in your chosen field. Ask how the products or services the company offers now are different from those originally provided. Has the company changed the type of customers it was originally targeting?

that some of your customers have come to expect. A good exercise is to prepare a chart comparing the service/product mix of your proposed company to those of the competitors. See the example in Figure 3.1.

Figure 3.1

SERVICES COMPARISON FOR PET GROOMING COMPANIES

Product/service	Me	Competitor 1	Competitor 2	Competitor 3
dogs	X	X	X	X
cats		X		X
other pets				X
shampoo	X	X	X	X
styling	X	X	X	X
nail trim		X	X	X
store location		X	X	X
house calls	X			
show-prep	X		X	X
boarding			X	X
transportation			X	
obedience				X

Head Start Exercise

3.4   Create a chart showing the specific products or services you will offer compared to your direct competitors. The example in Figure 3.1 is for a pet-grooming service. (1 page maximum.)

What Prices Will I Set?

Your pricing strategy is measured in comparison to your competition. There are only three basic pricing strategies:

- You can price *lower than* the competition.
- You can price *higher than* the competition.
- You can price *the same as* the competition.

Ask yourself: How will I be priced compared to my competition? Why?

PRICING LOW   Pricing lower than your competitors is often appropriate for a new business, especially when potential customers have established relationships with your competition. The most obvious reason for customers to give you a try is that you are offering the same (or better) services/products for less than they pay now.

If this is your strategy, you have to be priced sufficiently lower than the competition so that it is worthwhile for customers to switch suppliers. But there are limits to how low you can go. *Ask yourself: How low can my prices go?*

Pricing lower than the competition is what professional marketers refer to as **penetration pricing**, since it can be used as a technique to "penetrate" new groups of customers. However, selling something at a loss just to get your foot in the door is only a good way to operate at a loss. Remember, you are in business to make a profit. The best way to ensure that you make an overall profit is to profit on every single transaction you have with a customer. This means that the price of everything you sell must include your costs plus an amount to cover all of your operating expenses (including the value of your own time) plus some level of profit.

penetration pricing Setting prices lower than those of the competition.

Even though you are setting your prices now, you will better understand your costs after you have completed the financial section of the business plan, and may well revise your pricing.

PRICING HIGH   It is a myth that "you always get what you pay for." But, like other myths, it is powerful because so many people believe it. Those who want the "best" often associate this with the "most expensive." Marketers often refer to a high pricing strategy as a **skimming** strategy, implying that it targets the upper-income brackets (or "skims the cream") of a market. If you are dealing with customer groups who want only the highest quality products, service, guarantees, and prestige, then likely they also expect the highest prices and you will have to provide them.

price skimming Setting prices higher than those of the competition.

Imagine you own a retail hat store in the high-rent shopping district. You cater to wealthy professional men who have offices in this area and your hat prices start at $100. One day, you find out about a wholesaler who is going out of business and is selling high-quality hats for $5 apiece. You calculate that if you were to buy the hats and sell them for $30 each, you would still be making several times your usual markup and could move the hats quickly. Bad idea!

The customers you are targeting don't come to you for $30 hats. They want $100+ hats. If you buy the $5 hats you will still have to sell them in the $100 range, in line with your customers' expectations. The danger here is that one of your customers may see the same hats on sale at a lower-priced competitor in the $15 range. Seeing this, a customer who believes he or she has bought a superior product will experience serious cognitive dissonance and the consequences will not be good for your business.

Ask yourself: How high can my prices go? For the most part, you will be priced higher than the competition only when you are dealing with an upscale market and offering a hard-to-get or superior product. But even then, there are limits to what you can charge—there is a limit to "what the market will bear." Rolls Royce and Rolex must do sophisticated analyses of the relationship between price and supply/demand to set their prices. They must also ensure that the price keeps their buyers in an exclusive category, without appearing to "price gouge." You will not have the same level of research as these companies and will have to rely on experience, observation, intuition, and asking a lot of questions. Make sure you can logically explain your specific prices in your business plan.

PRICING THE SAME   *Ask yourself: Why might I want to have prices pretty much the same as my competition?* Being priced *the same as* your competition is technically referred to as a **competitive pricing** strategy. Even though the public takes "competitive" to mean lower prices, this is not what it really means—be careful not to make this mistake in your business plan.

Generally, you will use a competitive pricing strategy whenever trying to "sell higher" will cost you customers, but at the same time you are not in a position to sell lower because of your costs or the ability of competitors to win a price war. Lots of consumer goods and services are widely found to be competitively priced—such as milk, gasoline, and movie tickets—as are many professional services such as dental fillings or some legal services.

In some cases, even though you may be an independent business, the rates you charge could be set, or strongly influenced, by a professional association (accountant, paralegal, chiropractor). So you are automatically stuck with a competitive pricing situation.

Your prices might even be determined by a collective agreement. This could be the case if you were a contract sound mixer for network television productions. In such an event, you would have to convince producers to use you based on your experience, or the fact that you use superior digital recording equipment, or some other advantage you have over your competitors.

It is perfectly fine to be priced the same as your competitors, provided you can explain why you are doing it and you can differentiate yourself from the competition by some other element(s) of your marketing mix: products/services, distribution, or promotion.

Head Start Exercise

3.5   Make a chart listing the products or services you will offer that are the same as or similar to those of your direct competitors. List the prices that each of your direct competitors charge. Now do the same for indirect competitors. (1 page maximum.)

NEGOTIATION   *Ask yourself: How will I handle it if I have established my list of prices and then a potential customer offers me less than my set price for one of my services or products?* Let's say you're a meeting planner who has been working for the local convention and tourist board on a three-month contract. You have done an outstanding job and are offered a two-month extension at the same daily rate. You feel that you should be paid at a higher rate, but don't want to risk losing the contract extension. It's time for **negotiation**, and that involves the following activities:

- *Doing your homework.* You must find out the going rates for your products/services, the market conditions, and, in some cases, your customer's circumstances. (For the meeting planner, that means how badly they might need you.)

- *Using a plan.* You must decide how much you will initially ask for, how much you really expect to get, and the least you will settle for. (In the case of the meeting planner, the *least* is what you're being paid now.)
- *Taking a co-operative approach.* You must sincerely try to get an agreement that will benefit both you and the other party. (In the case of the meeting planner, this could involve pointing out the cost savings to the convention and tourist board of not having to train a new planner, while you save the effort of not having to secure a new employer.)

In some businesses, a formal bidding process replaces negotiation. This is often the situation when large contractors are selling off smaller pieces of a project or when dealing with government. In such cases, doing your homework usually means checking the winning bids for previous similar contracts. The skill is in writing your bid/proposal.

In other kinds of business, active negotiation is constant. If you start a business selling used motorcycles, you will have a formal asking price based on your cost (which you have negotiated) as well as on market conditions. But realistically, you will expect to negotiate every sale.

Negotiation is a skill similar to salesmanship in that it involves an element of persuasion. There are lots of books with good negotiation advice that are worth reading, but you can't really learn a skill from a book. You have to practise it.

> **◇ Get Help 3.4**
> Check the library or a bookstore where you will find many negotiation titles. A couple of old standards are *You Can Negotiate Anything* by Herb Cohen and *Getting to Yes: Negotiating Agreement without Giving In* by Roger Fisher.

> **✓ Test Yourself 3.10**
> True or False? It is always best to take a co-operative approach when involved in a negotiation.

> **✓ Test Yourself 3.11**
> True or False? The best way to learn negotiation is by reading everything you can on the topic.

SMALL BUSINESS PROFILE 3.1
The Cereal House

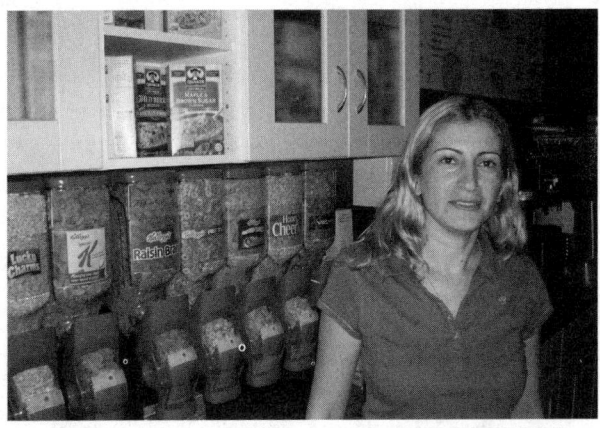

Nazli Erogu and her husband are both architects who immigrated to Canada from Turkey in 2004. Nazli's husband has stayed on in architecture working with a major construction company. Nazli, however, has opened a rather unusual restaurant where the main items on the menu are bowls of Cornflakes, Froot Loops, or other prepared breakfast cereals. Nazli came up with the inspiration shortly after arriving in Canada, seeing it as the perfect restaurant to target children, teenagers, and young adults. For a year she discussed the idea with friends and people in the business and everyone assured her that "it will never work." Why go to a restaurant for something you've got sitting at home? Finally, Nazli did an Internet search of her idea and found two companies in the United States that had opened establishments similar to her concept and both were experiencing significant success. Nazli was now committed to a plan.

A year later in the summer of 2006 The Cereal House cereal café was opened. During that time other so-called cereal bars had opened in different part of the country, but none close to The Cereal House. Nazli had found a site on a main street with high visibility that was close to a large elementary school, a high school, and a university campus—all within a short walk from the restaurant. Along with her husband, she designed the interior with bright colours, a clean layout, and a highly efficient work area. A major hiccup occurred during the renovation phase when the municipal regulations changed to require separate male and female washrooms, a staff washroom, and a barrier-free washroom for disabled customers. Nazli had installed only three washrooms to conform to the old regulations she had been informed about at City Hall, but approval to open was delayed until the alterations were made.

Regardless, the delays and frustration were worth it. Nazli's advice to those considering entrepreneurship is "to keep your courage up, even when you are the only one that believes in your idea."

How Will My Products or Services Get to the Customer?

distribution A company's strategy for getting services or products from the producer to the end-user. Distribution is sometimes referred to as place, so that the elements of the marketing mix can be described as the Four Ps: product, price, promotion, and place.

distribution channel The legal or contractual elements of how a service or product gets from the producer to the end-user.

physical distribution The chain of production storage and delivery that products move through, from producer to end-user.

The answer to this question is through your **distribution** strategy. Distribution is how goods and services actually get from a producer to the final user; in the business plan it is commonly broken down into **distribution channel** and **physical distribution**. *Ask yourself: What is the difference between distribution channel and physical distribution?*

DISTRIBUTION CHANNEL   *Channel* refers to the legal or contractual elements of how goods and services get from the producer to the final consumer.

Imagine that you are a trained hairstylist who would like to start a business that is somewhat different from the other salons. You decide to become a visiting hairdresser, specializing in hospitals and nursing homes. The fact that you go to the customers is what makes you different from your competition, but this is only a physical element of the distribution. Equally important is the issue of whether you are working on a contract with the nursing home, which might pay you a single fee for cutting the hair of its patients. Or do you approach the patients directly and get paid by each of them personally? In either case, the actual hair being cut still belongs to the patients, and you are still working at the nursing home locale, but the channel (the customers you are contracting with) is different.

For most new small businesses you will be using a "direct" form of distribution: you contract with and provide your services or products directly to the end-user. But let's say you start an interior decorating business, specializing in décor for elevators. The real beneficiaries of your service are those who ride the elevators, but they are not your customers. Who is the real user of your service? Maybe you will be working directly for the building owners. Maybe you will be working through an intermediary: a larger design firm that is decorating the entire building but subcontracts the elevators to you. Maybe you are acting as an intermediary yourself, going out and getting the design contracts then paying independent designers to do the work.

The owner of a business based on a new product must often choose among many channel options. What if you were to invent and patent a Teflon-type liquid protection for golf balls: just rub it on and the balls resist grass or mud stains and cracking and—most importantly—fly farther. But who would actually buy and apply your product: golfers themselves? Pro shops? Golf ball manufacturers?

And if the actual user is to be the golfers themselves, to whom do you sell? Will you have a store where the golfers can come to buy? Or will you sell directly to pro shops, which will in turn sell your product to the golfers? Perhaps you will sell to a sports wholesale company, which will then sell your product to sporting goods stores, hardware chains, and pro shops, and the golfers can buy from any of them. The choices are many, but the channel decision for getting the product to the end-user must be clarified in your plan.

In some cases you might even be an agent (real estate, theatrical, travel), in which case you are an intermediary who arranges a deal between a buyer and a seller, but you do not get directly involved with the product/service being sold. As an agent, your customers are often both the buyers and the sellers, and you must have strategies for selling to both.

In Section 1 of the business plan you clearly defined your business: *what* you are selling and *to whom* you are selling it. But after the process of clarifying your distribution channel, you may wish to reassess and redefine *who your customers really are*—not necessarily the end-user of the product, but those to whom you are selling. For example, you may be publishing an electronic pet-care newsletter on the Internet. You may have put a lot of research into understanding and measuring the potential readers of your product, but they are not your real customers. Those who pay you are the veterinarians and dog-food companies that advertise in your cyber-mag, so your channel of distribution is directly to these advertisers.

Head Start Exercise

3.6 Clearly state in one or two sentences to whom you are legally selling your product or service. Is this the ultimate user of your product or service? If not, explain. Are you an intermediary in providing your product or service? Make notes to explain. ($\frac{1}{2}$ page maximum.)

Test Yourself 3.12
True or False? Agents do not own the services or products that they are selling.

PHYSICAL ISSUES   *Physical distribution* commonly refers to the issues of moving tangible products, although some elements of this topic still apply to service businesses. For product-based firms, it can involve many complex issues. Some examples are:

- *Inventory.* Will your strategy be to carry lots of inventory or little (compared to your competitors)? Which is appropriate for your customers?
- *Ordering.* Will you need special methods for ordering replacement inventory because of the length of time it takes to get, or the fact that it spoils quickly?
- *Storage.* Will you need to rent warehouse space because you will be selling seasonal products? Will you be dealing with customs brokers as an importer? Will you need special provisions for sorting products?
- *Order process.* Will you require complicated order forms or an electronic database that will automatically order from your suppliers for your customers?
- *Transport.* Will you do your own deliveries? Will you need to ship overnight by courier or will your strategy be to always send orders by the cheapest method?

Depending on your choice of a business, there is a wide variation in which of these factors might be pertinent to your business plan. Increasingly, the term **supply chain** is being used to describe all of the processes and inputs for both the *channel* and *physical* elements of distribution. For large businesses, mapping and controlling complex supply chains has become an area of specialized study. For most new small firms, however, the method of physically getting the product or service to the user is simple and obvious. If you're starting an aromatherapy products store or an art gallery, the customers will come to you. If you're starting a tree-removal service or a bottled water delivery company, you will have a truck that goes to them. But your physical distribution strategy goes even further than that.

supply chain All of the contractual and physical aspects of bringing a product or service from its most basic components to the end-user.

Test Yourself 3.13
True or False? The fact that a product might be sold to a wholesaler, then a retailer, then a consumer refers to physical distribution.

DISTRIBUTION AND IMAGE   There is a close relationship between your company's image and physical distribution. The only impression future customers might have of your lawn maintenance business is the look of your truck when it pulls up to their neighbour's yard. The décor of your office or store is often the first means of projecting your image to new customers, so it has to fit with the rest of your marketing mix.

The owner of a second-hand bookstore may be enormously wealthy, but would be foolish to use his money for sprucing up the store to make it look new and fresh. Used book stores are better to look run-down because that's the kind of place where people expect to find cheap stuff—and that is the image that book bargain hunters will respond to. If the customers come to you, you should explain in the business plan how the décor, fixtures, lighting, furniture, displays, and so on will contribute to projecting your image. Some of these decisions may require going back to the feasibility section of your business plan and rewriting the costs of leasehold improvements.

Head Start Exercise

3.7   Make notes to explain any décor or physical set-up of your place of business that will have an impact on customers ($\frac{1}{3}$ page maximum.)

✓ **Test Yourself 3.14**
True or False? It is never appropriate for a business to have a run-down look.

How Will I Inform and Persuade Customers?

promotion strategy The approach a business uses to inform and persuade its customers, including techniques of advertising, publicity, personal selling, and sales promotion.

Promotion strategy means the methods you will use to let prospective customers know about your business and persuade them to buy from you. *Ask yourself: How am I likely to promote my business?*

"By relying on word of mouth" is the wrong answer to the above question! Many new business people, especially those in some form of self-employment or contract work, are not comfortable with notions of promoting themselves or their business. Perhaps they associate it with the ideas of peddling or bragging. Their solution to the problem of promotion is to take a passive approach, to rely on others to talk about their superior skills or products. These entrepreneurs often say they will rely on *word of mouth* to promote their services/products.

Business history is full of contests between entrepreneurs with superior products versus entrepreneurs with superior promotion. Superior promotion usually wins, and you are well advised to have a plan for actively promoting your business—one that projects your chosen image.

In a business plan, it is common to have the promotion strategy broken down into:
- advertising media
- advertising content
- publicity
- one-on-one selling
- sales promotion

advertising The attempt to persuade through mass communications media.

ADVERTISING MEDIA   **Advertising** for your new business must be entered into cautiously: a huge proportion of the money spent by small firms on advertising is totally wasted. Commonly, consultants, freelancers, and contract workers, who rely on personal selling, believe that they do not advertise at all. However, many of the tools that assist their personal selling efforts are indeed forms of advertising (business cards, résumés, cover letters, portfolios, brochures, phone book listings) and these should be prepared using the same care and principles used for preparing a major TV commercial.

Ask yourself: What advertising medium might I use? For advertising, most mass media charge according to the number of people that will see or hear the ad. So, most TV and radio stations or big city newspapers charge more for advertising space or time than new businesses can afford to pay. Even if you can afford it, in many cases it isn't sensible, especially if you are specializing in a narrow customer group. Why pay to advertise to a huge group of people, most of whom will never consider dealing with you?

Of the many advertising media available, the one most overlooked by small firms but potentially the most valuable for those who specialize is **direct mail**. Direct mail can mean a lot of different things. It can involve sending out letters (hard copy or e-mail), brochures, flyers, or catalogues to individuals or organizations—precisely of the kind you are targeting. Direct mail can be addressed personally to the customer, and even though some of it is classified as "junk mail" people do read it and respond.

In most cases, the mailing piece that you prepare is distributed using one of the following methods:

- *Postal tracts.* If you are going after customers that are all in the same geographic area, you will be able to draw your target area on a map as a **postal tract**. It is a simple matter to get a postal code directory and find the postal codes where your customers are located. The post office can deliver your *mailing piece* to every business or home within those codes at bulk mailing rates. Alternatively you can enlist an independent handbill delivery company or bulk mailer—or you can even do it yourself.

- *Customer lists.* Once you have actually started your business, your most important future customers will be your past customers. Think about it. People repeat the same behaviours over and over. Of all the people in the world, the ones most likely to buy from you are those who already have. Sure, there are a very few exceptions, but the vast majority of enterprises rely on repeat business. This being the case, it only makes sense that you maintain a list of the names, addresses, and phone numbers of your past customers. They are the ones you most want to send your future advertising to. Mailing list software is cheap (it is already a part of most word processors) and the associated hardware (printers and scanners) has tumbled in price over the past few years. It is also possible, in some cases, to buy or rent someone else's **customer list** when they have the same target customers as you but are not in competition.

- *Subscription lists.* Most publishers of trade journals, magazines, or newsletters are willing to rent out the names and addresses of their subscribers, either directly or through a mailing list company. If everyone in your target group is likely to read a particular periodical, that's the list for you. In many cases, the publisher is willing to send the list only to a third party (called a letter shop or mailing house) that will inexpensively label, print, sort, and deliver your mailing piece to the post office. The third-party involvement is so you don't make an actual copy of the **subscription list** and therefore will have to rent it again the next time you wish to use it. Similarly, you can rent lists of members in particular organizations, delegates to particular conventions, subscribers to cable TV, and so on.

? Get Help 3.5
For excellent examples of advertising campaigns, see the Canadian online magazine *Marketing* at **www.marketingmag.ca**.

✓ Test Yourself 3.15
True or False? Small businesses or freelancers are best to rely on word of mouth to promote their business.

direct mail A form of advertising that communicates individually with large numbers of potential buyers through postal or electronic mail.

? Get Help 3.6
For information on postal tracts, see the Canada Post website at **www.canadapost.ca**.

postal tract A geographic area that is made up of a series of adjacent postal code districts.

✓ Test Yourself 3.16
True or False? Direct mail tends to be a relatively good promotional investment for small firms.

customer list A database of the names, addresses, phone numbers, purchases, and so on of those who have purchased from a company.

subscription list The names and addresses of customers for particular publications or services. These can be rented (at relatively low cost) for the mailing of advertising pieces.

? Get Help 3.7
Check the Yellow Pages under "Mailing Lists and Services." Call a couple of suppliers and ask for a free catalogue of their lists. You may also want to search the Internet for "Canada Mailing Lists."

compiled list The names and addresses of prospective customers that have been gathered to meet the specifications of a business; compilation is usually an expensive process.

✓ **Test Yourself 3.17**

True or False? The most valuable mailing lists for most companies are their own customer lists.

✓ **Test Yourself 3.18**

True or False? Subscription lists tend to be more expensive than compiled lists.

Internet advertising A variety of evolving promotional options through the medium of the World Wide Web; still relatively lacking in data as to cost-effectiveness for small firms.

? **Get Help 3.8**

Check your local college to see if they offer a program in webpage design or Internet management. The program co-ordinator may advise you on set-up costs or refer you to a senior student who will assist you at a reasonable price.

ecommerce The selling, ordering, and at times distribution of goods and services via the Internet.

? **Get Help 3.9**

Your web hosting service or one of the various consulting services listed on the web is commonly used as the agent to apply for a domain name. Alternatively, you can visit the Canadian Internet Registration Authority (**www.cira.ca**) for a list of Canadian certified domain name registrars.

community newspaper A smaller-circulation newspaper targeting a specific geographic area, often published weekly.

specialty newspaper A smaller-circulation newspaper targeting customers who have a particular interest or are of a particular ethnic background.

- *Compiled lists.* **Compiled lists** are lists specifically put together for your purposes. You can do it yourself or hire a mailing list company to do it for you. There are so many databases around these days that mailing list companies can "merge and purge" to produce a list of just about any possible customer group. The narrower the list, however, the more expensive it will be to compile. In fact, compiled lists can run up to several dollars per name. But with time and patience it is also possible to produce your own mailing list.

Let's say you're a retired professor of accounting and wish to work as a financial adviser targeting college professors in your city. Knowing that the vast majority of professors use e-mail, you could check the websites of the various colleges in your city, access the internal phone books, and save the e-mail addresses of everyone with the title "professor." You now would have the perfect list to merge with your promotional letter.

The varieties of **Internet advertising** are still evolving to include online publications, browsers, commercial websites, and, most important of all, your own website. The biggest consideration for going on the web is how it might redefine the customer segment you are going after. Proportionately, large firms spend more than small ones on Internet advertising[3] simply because the Internet is geared to target the global market of many large firms. However, rather than having "everyone in the world" as a potential customer (a strategy that you know won't work), you can choose your target groups by the types of links that will bring customers to your site.

Even though the initial set-up can run from inexpensive (using common web page software) to many thousands of dollars for a complex, professionally designed site, a website can be a powerful advertising tool. But your site will need to be maintained and updated on a regular basis.

Ecommerce takes your use of the Internet beyond just advertising and into your broader marketing strategy involving sales, ordering, and distribution. Commercially available software allows you to have a "virtual store" where customers can place orders 24 hours a day and pay with their credit cards using secure transactions. The range of complexity in ecommerce is huge, from a fairly simple desktop operation that can get you going for a few hundred dollars to operations that require dedicated servers, databases, and expensive software.

For most small businesses, it's just too expensive to have even a small ad in one of the large mass-circulation daily newspapers. Even a listing in the classifieds can be prohibitive—and, in most cases, you would still be paying to advertise to a wider audience than your own target customers.

Unlike using the big dailies, by advertising in smaller **community newspapers** you could hit your entire market at a low cost. This happens when the customers you are targeting all live within the same geographic area that is serviced by the paper.

You may be targeting customers who live in different geographic areas but all have the same ethnic or language background. For example, you may be starting a language school that will teach English to recent immigrants from Hong Kong. It's a pretty good bet that all your potential customers will read the Chinese newspaper in your area, therefore that particular **specialty newspaper** is the place to run your ad.

There are other sorts of newspapers that specialize in people who attend the same college, who are involved in business finance, who are retired, who are of a particular religion, who are in the computer field, and so on. If your target market coincides with one of these publications you may be able to communicate with all your potential customers inexpensively. *Ask yourself: Which specialty newspapers do I read? Is the advertising in them aimed at people like me?*

The line between newspapers and magazines is becoming increasingly blurred. While newspapers can often publish your ad within a day or two, many magazines require the ad to be ready a full three months before readers will actually see it. With the advent of Internet publishing, however, online magazines can offer an almost instant response to advertisers.

The most important magazines for small, new specialty businesses are **trade journals** (not the mass-market consumer magazines). Trade publications are written for those involved in specific industries. There are literally thousands of such magazines and they are widely used by those within the industries they serve. For example, a freelance clothing designer looking for contract work might run an ad in *Canadian Apparel Manufacturer*, knowing that pretty much everyone in the industry reads this publication. A computer parts importer knows that his or her potential customers read *Computer Dealer News*, and a custom lamp designer knows to advertise in *Lighting Magazine*. Magazine advertising can be expensive, but cost is geared to circulation. *Ask yourself: Are there any publications that my potential customers will subscribe to?*

For some industries where most of the practitioners work freelance (professional photography, motion picture arts, theatre arts), professional **directories** are published on a periodic basis. In some industries it may be almost mandatory to have a listing in these directories. For most firms, however, the issue around directories is simply whether or not to list in the Yellow Pages.

Depending on the size of your community, Yellow Pages advertising can get incredibly expensive, ranging from hundreds of dollars for a simple listing to twenty or thirty thousand dollars for a full-page ad. So make sure you're spending the money wisely.

People usually turn to the Yellow Pages for *infrequently used* services—tow trucks, taxis, florists—services that are used so irregularly that most people don't have a normal supplier. So a restaurant in the downtown tourist district (where people from out of town don't know where they should eat) may find a Yellow Pages ad useful. A suburban restaurant where people go because they have seen it in the neighbourhood or it has been recommended may be wasting money on a Yellow Pages ad. *Ask yourself: Are customers likely to look for my service or product in the Yellow Pages?*

Advertising media such as transit cards and billboards tend to be too expensive for a micro-enterprise, but other forms of **outdoor advertising** may be appropriate: posters, handbills, vehicle lettering, sandwich boards.

If you are starting a retail business, of course, your most significant piece of advertising may well be your business sign. Illuminated store signs are expensive, so plan to have it for a long time. Make sure the sign clearly identifies the store and clearly projects the image you wish to send out. Don't forget, the sign will often be the first impression potential customers have of your business.

Head Start Exercise

3.8   Identify the primary advertising technique you will use in your first year. Make an estimate (call around) of what this will cost you. ($\frac{1}{4}$ page maximum.)

ADVERTISING CONTENT   Writing advertising copy (letters, newspaper ads, telemarketing pitches) is an area where many people seem to think they have some talent. It's one of those

---

? Get Help 3.10
Check the Yellow Pages under "Internet Products and Services" for Internet service providers and ecommerce consultants.

✓ Test Yourself 3.19
True or False? To be effective, a website must be maintained and updated regularly.

trade journals Magazines written for people involved in specific industries; for example, a commercial fishing publication or a professional teachers' magazine. See Chapter 2 for a discussion of trade journals as a marketing research tool.

✓ Test Yourself 3.20
True or False? It is almost always better to advertise in the big papers because so many more people read them than the smaller community papers.

directories Published lists of suppliers for particular goods and services; for example, a trades directory, an antique dealers directory, a directory of professional actors.

? Get Help 3.11
A number of commercial directories for both Canadian and international suppliers are available online; for example: the Canadian Trade Index (**ctidirectory.com**), Frasers' Industrial Suppliers Directory (**www.frasers.com**) or Thomas Global (**www.thomasglobal.com**).

outdoor advertising Visual promotion aimed at passing vehicle and pedestrian traffic.

? Get Help 3.12
Try to find a student majoring in journalism, advertising copy, or public relations to act as a low-cost editor for all your advertising writing. This can be done through quick email exchanges.

✓ Test Yourself 3.21
True or False? The Yellow Pages are excellent for advertising services that are used frequently.

things that you may believe is easier and cheaper to do without outside help—after all, you have been exposed to advertising your whole life. But thinking that this means you know how to prepare advertising is like thinking you know how to cook just because you have been eating your whole life. At the very least, you should have as many other people as possible read anything you've written (even letters). And don't get defensive when it's criticized! Instead, carefully weigh the comments of your proofreaders.

All of your advertising activities should try to achieve the following:

- *Grab attention.* This is most easily done by mentioning something specifically important to the viewer or reader.
- *Project the right image.* This applies not just to what you may have written, but even how it was sent, the type of paper, the colour, the overall look. Keep in mind the *cognitive dissonance* issue discussed above.
- *Get action.* This is most easily done by directly telling people what you want them to do: "Drop by today for a free estimate," "Please call as soon as you have seen my portfolio."

If you choose to advertise, you should be prepared to explain in your business plan your choice of media, why they are likely to be effective, and how you will know whether you are spending your money wisely. This means measuring and keeping records. Indicators of advertising effectiveness that you will want to keep track of include:

- *Activity.* How much did your advertising increase the number of calls you get, people coming into the store, website hits, or the number of order forms coming in?
- *Sales.* Did you bring in more dollars when advertising? If activity went up but sales didn't, you can see that the advertising had an effect but you need to adjust some other element of your marketing mix, such as your product/service offering.
- *Profit.* Never lose sight of profit as the purpose of all your business activity. If your advertising increased your sales but after the cost of the advertising there was no new profit, you may have to adjust your prices or other aspects of your marketing mix.

Head Start Exercise

3.9 Make a list of ways you will measure the effectiveness of any advertising you do ($\frac{1}{4}$ page maximum).

publicity Promotion by spreading information about a company, product, or service without directly paying for the use of media space or time.

PUBLICITY Publicity means free advertising—a misleading definition because, as you know, nothing is free and that includes publicity. In the case of publicity you pay, but only indirectly.

Let's say you start a service to help plan and organize weddings: Bride's Aid Wedding Planners. You might then mount a campaign (letters, clippings, brochures, free T-shirts) trying to convince the producer of a local radio call-in show that you would be an ideal guest for a show about wedding disasters. If the producer goes for it, you get to be on the show answering questions, giving comments, and generally demonstrating the value of having someone like you plan a wedding. You hope that the host of the show will work in, as often as possible, the fact that today's guest is "the owner of Bride's Aid Wedding Planners, located at. . . ." Now this is valuable exposure that you did not pay for, but it did cost you time and money to convince the producer and appear on the show.

Giving a free talk at the local public library (and later handing out your business cards), writing an unpaid article (which clearly identifies you and your business) for a local community newspaper, donating your product or service to a school or volunteer fire department (which ends up with you being interviewed on the local TV news)—these are all examples of valuable publicity.

Head Start Exercise

3.10 Make a list of at least three ways you could get publicity ($\frac{1}{4}$ page maximum).

ONE-ON-ONE SELLING Traditionally, **personal selling** has meant dealing physically, one on one, with a *salesperson*. But since the growth of telemarketing and online communications, the lines between advertising and personal selling are becoming less clear. Nevertheless, salesmanship—the skill of meeting potential customers and convincing them to buy your service or product—is the key to success for many entrepreneurs. At the same time, for many it is the most dreaded aspect of being in business. *Ask yourself: Can I see myself in the role of salesperson?*

personal selling Promotion of services/products through person-to-person interaction between the supplier and the potential customer.

Many new entrepreneurs are uncomfortable with the idea of themselves as salespeople, preferring to see themselves as professional service providers. As a result, when it comes to developing a promotional strategy for the business plan, they wrongly choose to rely on some form of advertising. In some cases, this is just a way of avoiding the discomfort of calling on prospective customers. Even when some alternative promotional tool is properly employed, however, for most new enterprises the entrepreneur must, to some extent, act as the salesperson in order to foster the relationship with the customer.[4]

If you feel that you have no selling abilities, keep in mind that selling is a skill, and as such you will improve with practice. Before you can get the practice, however, you must overcome any initial fear. As with public speaking for some, going to the dentist for others, or skydiving for most of us, the process of overcoming fear is pretty much the same:

- Analyze what you're really afraid of (rejection? failure? embarrassment? responsibility?).
- Imagine the worst-case scenario (your worst fears coming true).
- Decide to accept and live (or die) with the worst-case scenario (should it come about).
- Go ahead and do what you're afraid of (it won't be that bad!).
- Do it again! (already you can see improvement).

The steps in the personal selling process are quickly learned, and you'll do best by sticking to the basics. But knowing the steps is not a substitute for building your skill through practice. The selling steps are:

- *Prospecting.* This means finding prospective customers. Other types of promotion (when people respond to your advertising or when you talk to delegates after your publicity presentation) are ways of accomplishing this. Referrals (sometimes paid for) can come from existing customers or businesses that are complementary to yours. Sometimes, however, it comes down to manually building a list of prospects by checking through directories (such as the Yellow Pages) for your kind of potential customer.
- *Approach.* The first contact with your prospect can come with the prospect's response to your ad. It is also possible to have other people (such as telemarketers) generate leads and set up appointments for you. For new businesses, however, it is often a matter of *cold*

calling, where with no previous contact you either phone or visit the prospect, introduce yourself, and explain why you are contacting them.

- *Qualifying.* You don't want to waste a minute of your selling time talking to people who are never going to buy from you. Qualifying means finding out whether your prospect really is the kind of customer who could benefit from your product or service, whether they are in a position to buy, and whether you are in fact dealing with someone who has the authority to make the buying decision. You qualify the prospect by asking questions—lots of questions.
- *Presentation.* A good sales presentation should explain to the prospect the *benefits* of your service or product as quickly as possible—for the sake of your time as well as the prospect's. And it must be flexible. New salespeople face the danger of rigidly sticking to a sales presentation (especially if it's one they're proud of) when the customer is bored (already knows the information) or even when the customer is trying to interrupt in order to buy.
- *Closing.* Getting the customer to actually agree to buy is what we mean by closing. It seems so obvious an objective. Nevertheless, new salespeople are known for making an elaborate presentation, thanking the prospects for their time, and leaving without ever asking "So, will you buy?" "Do we have a deal?" "When would you like delivery?" "Can we set a date to start the work?" or "Will you sign the contract for that amount?" All of these are closing questions and you should never leave the prospect without asking one.
- *Managing objections.* If someone has a legitimate objection (a reason why they cannot buy from you) you want to find it out as quickly as possible so you won't be wasting time. But it's part of human nature to avoid making decisions (including the decision whether to buy your service or product), and prospects will typically come up with reasonable (but untrue) objections so they can avoid decision-making. Your job as the salesperson is to deal with the objection by requalifying the prospect (asking more questions) or by using the objection to close the deal. "So, the reason you don't want to buy is that you feel the price is too high? Well, if I could give you a lower price, would you sign the contract today?" After a few sales encounters, you'll have heard most of the objections you're likely to encounter and you will develop an appropriate closing response for each.

Head Start Exercise

3.11 List the steps in the selling process. Identify which will be the easiest and which will be the most difficult for you, personally. Explain why. ($\frac{1}{2}$ page maximum.)

Preparation should involve rehearsing your sales presentation (find a willing critic) and organizing tools to assist you. Sales aids can include everything from your business card to samples, an order book, a laptop computer (for demonstration or ordering), your portfolio, résumés, a cell phone, overhead transparencies, and so on.

If personal selling is the logical way of getting business from your type of customers, don't try to get around it by looking for promotional alternatives. If you can't learn to do it yourself (although you probably can without too much trouble), the options are hiring a salesperson, getting a partner who can sell, or changing your distribution strategy (provided there is an alternative).

If you decide to hire a salesperson, you are now into the role of sales manager. This may involve decisions about territory, compensation, training, and motivation for the salesperson.

✓ **Test Yourself 3.22**
True or False? Owners of new service businesses should try to avoid personal selling as a promotion technique.

Ironically, it is much easier to manage salespeople if you have some selling experience yourself. Still, an introductory marketing text will tell you the basics of getting others to sell.

SALES PROMOTION   **Sales promotion** is not some sort of discrete marketing activity. Instead, it's just a convenient way of lumping together any kind of promotional activity that is not clearly in the categories of advertising, publicity, or personal selling. Sales promotion is a big grab bag of creative promotional techniques, which are fraught with dangers for the new entrepreneur. *Proceed with extreme caution* when using any of the following techniques:

- *Giveaways.* These include items like pens, mouse pads, lighters, fridge magnets, and T-shirts printed with your company name and likely the phone number. The problem with giveaways is that much of it (that you will have paid for) ends up in the hands of people who are not part of your target market and will never buy from you. *Ask yourself: Do I own any pens showing the names of companies that I have never otherwise heard of or am extremely unlikely to ever deal with?*

- *Coupons.* The idea behind coupons is to get new customers to deal with you once, see how good you are, and then become regulars. Let's say you're a hairdresser, targeting elderly women in the neighbourhood of your salon. You distribute coupons for "$25 off the price of a perm" to the entire neighbourhood, trying to get new customers. But it could turn out that almost all of the coupons that come back to you are from existing customers, who are now paying $25 less for a perm that they would have bought anyway at full price.

- *Premiums.* Two-for-one deals, buy something and get something else free, the second entrée at half-price—these are all means of using premiums to promote your business. The danger, as in coupons, is giving away something that established customers would have paid for anyway. At the same time you are unsure if you are bringing new customers in. There is some evidence to show that retail price promotions are generally of more benefit to the manufacturer than to the retailer.[5]

- *Events.* Having skydivers land in your parking lot, a book signing by a celebrity, a face-painting contest—these are all promotional events. They often involve high cost and high risk: the weather may turn bad, the celebrity might be a no-show, a bigger event somewhere else may kill your turnout.

- *Trade shows.* If all of your potential customers annually attend a particular trade show or conference, you will be able to economically contact your entire market at one time,[6] provided you can afford the fee to rent a booth. Depending on the size of the show and the location, a two- to three-day booth rental can run from a few hundred dollars to many thousands—and this will not include the actual cost of setting up your display and providing handout material. The major risks are that the traffic won't appear (especially with shows that are not established), that your booth will be outclassed by the competition, or that your service really requires personal selling and you won't have time to talk to many customers.

- *Displays.* This usually means providing displays for someone else to sell your service. For example, you may be a pilot offering charter fishing flights to tourists visiting your town. You get customers by paying a commission to local hotels and travel agencies and you provide them with your company's brochures, maps, and price lists along with a display rack to put them in. But the display rack that you paid for could end up in the back room holding magazines or be used to display your competitor's brochures advertising a dinner-theatre.

- *Free samples.* Remember the "image" issue of something being worth what you pay for it? If you're selling a professional service, free samples will not help your image, where a money-back guarantee in your contract might. On the other hand, for some businesses

Get Help 3.13
Again, start with the library. An introductory marketing textbook (it doesn't have to be new or even particularly recent) will tell you the basics of salesmanship and sales management. Avoid slick popular works that promise miraculous sales results.

sales promotion A collection of techniques for getting potential customers to buy goods or services. These techniques do not fit into any of the more discrete categories of advertising, publicity, or personal selling.

you cannot promote your product without samples. For example, if you plan on selling frozen perogies to restaurants you have to let them taste the product first and try them out on their clientele.

Because of the high risk involved in most forms of sales promotion, if you decide to use one of these techniques, as in advertising, you should predetermine a method to measure the cost-effectiveness of your campaign.

Head Start Exercise

3.12 Identify any sales promotion techniques you might use and make notes to justify your choice ($\frac{1}{4}$ page maximum).

Keep in mind that your marketing strategy is a series of trade-offs or compromises that will give you the best mix of product, price, distribution, and promotion for the particular kind of customers you are specializing in. Learn from the most profitable businesses: Tim Hortons arguably does not have the best coffee. Canadian Tire does not consistently offer the best prices. Leon's does not have the greatest number of furniture outlets. But they all owe their success to having the right marketing mix for the customers they target.

SMALL BUSINESS PROFILE 3.2
The Bird House and Binocular Shop

The Bird House and Binocular Shop in St. John's, Newfoundland, was started by Wanda Crocker in 1996. At the time, she was a social worker with a hobby interest in birds but was having trouble finding the kinds of books and equipment she needed. Recognizing a need, Wanda opened a store where she could get the cheapest rent. Then, having proved the concept, she moved to a more central area with lots of tourist traffic. In 2001, by putting a greater emphasis on personal selling, she was able to increase sales by 62 percent. The next change to the marketing mix was a product expansion to include quality camera equipment suitable for bird photography. This was unsuccessful for several reasons. High-end cameras and their fast-changing digital components required high expertise and high sales volume to keep inventory from becoming obsolete. Wanda found that she was not able to compete with her indirect competition, the big box electronics retailers, in this area. So the line has been dropped.

Wanda is, however, expanding her "optics" lines, bringing in new magnifiers, binoculars, and monoculars. She is also preparing to offer cottage rentals on the edge of a local ecological preserve where she can conduct birding tours. Even with no direct competition in the St. John's area, Wanda still advertises. She uses local newspaper advertising, especially around Christmas time to capitalize on gift-giving. She also advertises in brochures aimed at tourists arriving on cruise ships, and she is listed in the local business directory sponsored by the St. John's Downtown Development Commission. As well, her website will finally be under construction in the near future.

The fact that Wanda is constantly re-assessing and modifying her marketing mix undoubtedly contributes to the success of this business.

✓Answers to Test Yourself Questions

3.1 Every business has an image of some sort. *True*

3.2 The expected and projected images of your business must not be extremely far apart. *True*

3.3 A company's image is the perception of the firm held in the mind of the company's owner. *False*

3.4 Selecting a name should be the first step in planning a business. *False*

3.5 *Marketing mix* and *marketing strategy* mean the same thing. *True*

3.6 Production is one of the elements of the marketing mix. *False*

3.7 Generally, it is more profitable for new businesses to specialize in fewer products or services than their competitors offer. *True*

3.8 A new firm should always try to price under the competition. *False*

3.9 Competitive pricing means trying to price lower than your competition. *False*

3.10 It is always best to take a co-operative approach when involved in a negotiation. *True*

3.11 The best way to learn negotiation is by reading everything you can on the topic. *False*

3.12 Agents do not own the services or products that they are selling. *True*

3.13 The fact that a product might be sold to a wholesaler, then a retailer, then a consumer refers to physical distribution. *False*

3.14 It is never appropriate for a business to have a run-down look. *False*

3.15 Small businesses or freelancers are best to rely on word of mouth to promote their business. *False*

3.16 Direct mail tends to be a relatively good promotional investment for small firms. *True*

3.17 The most valuable mailing lists for most companies are their own customer lists. *True*

3.18 Subscription lists tend to be more expensive than compiled lists. *False*

3.19 To be effective a website must be maintained and updated regularly. *True*

3.20 It is almost always better to advertise in the big papers because so many more people read them than the smaller community papers. *False*

3.21 The Yellow Pages are excellent for advertising services that are used frequently. *False*

3.22 Owners of new service businesses should try to avoid personal selling as a promotion technique. *False*

Questions for Discussion

1. Discuss how the average person misuses the term "marketing." Try to identify the reasons for this.

2. Pick several small businesses in your area and discuss the types of image that the names of those companies imply. Are these images appropriate for these firms? Suggest better ones.

3. Discuss the "product mix" of dollar stores. Why might this be appropriate for their target market?

4. Do you negotiate all or most of your retail purchases? Discuss reasons for people's reticence to negotiate lower prices on consumer purchases.

5. Try to identify the reasons that most new entrepreneurs are reluctant to engage in personal selling. How can an entrepreneur overcome this reluctance?

Recommended Reading

Booker, Dianna. *From Contact to Contract.* Chicago: Dearborn Trade Publishing, 2003.

Buskirk, Bruce, and Molly Lavik. *Entrepreneurial Marketing: Real Stories and Survival Strategies.* Mason Ohio: South-Western (Thompson), 2004.

Calvin, Robert J. *Sales Management.* New York: McGraw-Hill, 2001.

Epstein, Kevin A. *Marketing Made Easy.* Madison, WI: Entrepreneur Press, 2006.

Meisner, Chet. *The Complete Guide to Direct Marketing.* Chicago: Kaplan Publishing, 2006.

Schiffman, Steven. *Cold Calling Techniques (That Really Work).* Avon, MA: Adams Media Corporation, 2003.

Withers, Joan, and Carol Vipperman. *Marketing Your Service.* North Vancouver: Self-Counsel Press, 2006.

The Business Plan, Section 3: Marketing

IMAGE

1. Describe the image that your company will project and explain why this is appropriate for your services or products and the expectations of the customer groups you are targeting.

_____

_____

_____

_____

_____

_____

_____

BUSINESS NAME

2. Give the name that your business will be operating under and explain how this name projects the appropriate image for your products/services and customer groups.

_____

_____

_____

_____

_____

_____

_____

SERVICE/PRODUCT MIX

3. Provide a detailed explanation of the products or services you will offer, comparing your range to that of your major competitors. Explain why this strategy is appropriate for your type of customers.

_____

_____

_____

_____

_____

_____

_____

4. Explain any "added value" services that you will offer and why they are appropriate.

_____

_____

_____

_____

_____

_____

PRICING

5. Outline the pricing strategy that you will be using and explain how it fits in with the rest of your marketing mix.

_____

_____

_____

_____

_____

_____

6. Prepare a price list showing the specific products or services you will offer and the prices you will charge. Indicate any discounts you will offer for specific types of customers or volumes, or any ranges within which you will negotiate prices.

_____

_____

_____

_____

_____

_____

DISTRIBUTION

7. Explain clearly who the ultimate users of your products/services are and where your business fits into any chain of distribution. Identify your "legal" customers and the details of any contracting arrangements.

_____

_____

_____

_____

_____

8. Explain how your service or product will physically get to your customer. If the customer is coming to you, describe in detail the set-up, décor, and tone of your site. Explain how the site design is in keeping with the image you wish to project.

_____

_____

_____

_____

_____

_____

_____

_____

PROMOTION

9. Identify any advertising medium you will use, the nature of the advertising piece, and the frequency of advertising.

_____

_____

_____

_____

_____

_____

_____

_____

_____

10. Explain any publicity you will get and how you will arrange this exposure.

_____

_____

_____

_____

_____

_____

_____

_____

_____

_____

11. Describe any personal selling you will engage in, explaining how you will get your prospects, how you will approach them, and any sales aids you will use.

_____

_____

_____

_____

_____

_____

_____

_____

_____

_____

12. Explain any sales promotion techniques that you will use and any risks involved.

_____

_____

_____

_____

_____

_____

_____

_____

_____

PROMOTION EVALUATION

13. Explain how you will measure the effectiveness of the promotional means you have chosen and outline any backup plans for redirecting your promotional efforts.

_____

_____

_____

_____

_____

_____

_____

_____

Operations:
How Will I Organize the Work?

LEARNING OBJECTIVES

On completion of this chapter, you should be able to:

- *Identify the main considerations for the layout of office space.*
- *Identify the main considerations for the layout of retail space.*
- *Identify the main considerations for the layout of manufacturing and storage space.*
- *Discuss the objectives of purchasing systems.*
- *Explain various techniques for monitoring and controlling business processes.*
- *Discuss systems for managing information in a small business.*
- *List and define the major functions of management.*
- *Discuss techniques for effective leadership.*
- *Identify various issues of government regulation in business.*
- *Access sources of information and assistance for dealing with government.*
- *Prepare the operations portion of a business plan.*

So far, in your business plan you have explained what business you're getting into, you have presented evidence of why it will work, and you have explained the business strategy that you will use. Now, in Section 4 of the business plan, you will give the specifics of what you will do on a day-to-day basis.

How Will I Manage the Space and Equipment?

ACQUIRING NECESSITIES   Most of us enjoy shopping. On top of that, we like new "toys": the thrill of unpacking them, setting them up, and (for a few of us) reading the instruction manuals. So it's no wonder that one of the strongest urges for the new entrepreneur is to get out there and start buying fun things for the new business.

Slow down! A business is not a hobby (even though the idea may have started out that way). And business decisions are based on profit, not fun (even though entrepreneurs consider it fun to make profit). Any equipment acquisitions should be appropriate for *what* you are selling and appropriate for satisfying the needs of those *to whom* you are selling. If you're starting a recording studio that will make demo CDs for amateur bands, top-of-the-line equipment might be what you want. But for your market it is not necessary and you could go bankrupt trying to pay for it. Don't acquire anything more than you have to.

Ask yourself: What are the problems that arise when you treat your business as a hobby? When buying the things you really need, keep in mind that the equipment doesn't have to be new. Newspaper classifieds, sales by **tender**, and auctions (remember all those businesses that go bankrupt?) are good places to look for used equipment.

tender Sale of an item by requiring sealed bids from potential buyers, all of which will be opened at the same time, with the sale going to the best bid. Government contracts (as well as contracts for some businesses) are often given out this way.

Items you already own but will use in your business are considered part of your investment in the company. This is important for claiming depreciation expenses on your tax return and for demonstrating to lenders how much of an investment you have made personally.

Head Start Exercise

4.1   Make a list of all the personal belongings that you could invest into a new business (for example, a desk, car, computer, filing cabinet, tools, and so on) ($\frac{3}{4}$ page maximum).

In many cases when acquiring equipment you will have a choice between leasing and buying.

lease The long-term rental of property or equipment. Most leasing contracts for equipment (such as vehicles) include an agreement to ultimately buy the equipment.

Frequently, the **lease** deals available to small firms (for items like computers, vehicles, construction equipment, or machinery) are just another way of financing the purchase. Instead of you borrowing the money and going out and buying items in the name of your company, the leasing company buys it and title stays in its name while you use the equipment and make monthly payments.

In a great many of these leases, however, you are actually agreeing to buy the equipment by paying a final fee at the end of the lease. For these types of leases, careful comparison will often show that it is actually cheaper to finance the outright purchase of the equipment from the beginning. In fact, the requirements to borrow the money are likely no more stringent than the requirements for leasing.

So, shop carefully and keep in mind that lease prices, just like purchase prices, are negotiable.

Head Start Exercise

4.2   Make up a list of any equipment you will have to buy for your business along with ballpark prices. The prices are important for Section 5 of your plan ($\frac{1}{2}$ page maximum).

OFFICE SET-UP   Almost all enterprises have some sort of office, which is really just a place for processing and storing information. As such, an orderly arrangement of communication devices, work areas, and filing equipment is only to be expected. But most of the real processing of information (the planning and the decision making) takes place inside the head of the entrepreneur. Therefore, the office set-up must take into consideration your personal work habits, idiosyncrasies, and needs. Other office issues include:

- *Efficiency.* Self-employed people can spend a huge amount of their time on the phone, yet relatively few invest in an inexpensive headset (better than a speaker phone) that will keep both hands free for the computer or other work. Frequently used information (phone lists, current projects) should be close to hand, and work areas should reflect the process or flow of work.
- *Flexibility.* As office equipment becomes more portable (laptops, printers, hand-held communication devices) the actual office space itself can become more fluid and portable.[1]
- *Ergonomics.* If your business operations basically consist of you sitting at a computer, your productivity (and even your long-term health) could depend on a design that reduces eye, joint, and muscle strain, not necessarily the most comfortable. (An **ergonomic** study of laboratory seating showed a relationship between productivity and correct seat height.[2])
- *Visitors.* Visitor space is only important if customers, and to a lesser extent suppliers, come to your site. Considerations for the visitor might include issues of a comfortable reception or waiting area and on-site displays or advertising. In addition, you may need meeting space separate from your work areas to maintain confidentiality of your records and materials.

Head Start Exercise

4.3   Make a quick sketch of the office set-up you might need (1 page maximum).

RETAIL SET-UP   For a retail store, the business plan should outline the organization of storage and work areas. It should also show (using drawings) the layout for actual selling space, with the objectives of minimizing cost and maximizing sales in mind.[3] Considerations for use of the store space include:

- *Volume of shelf space allocation.* Since the business will have limited shelf space and some items take up more room than others, the question becomes how much space will be allocated for each item sold. These decisions can depend on the rate of sale (for restocking), shipping quantities, and the profitability of the item.

✓ Test Yourself 4.1
True or False? Leasing vehicles or equipment is usually more economical for a small firm than purchasing.

ergonomics The study of how work environments affect human health.

? Get Help 4.1
Numerous publications and websites cater to the needs of the small office/home office (SOHO) businessperson. In addition, small business and computer equipment publications frequently carry columns or special articles about the SOHO. Check out **www.entrepreneur.com** and click on *Home Based Biz* for useful articles.

✓ Test Yourself 4.2
True or False? A healthy investment for the small office is likely to be the most comfortable chair you can find.

- *Positioning of merchandise.* Putting items in the more visible and easier-to-reach spaces will, on average, increase the sales of those items. Logically, the more profitable items and impulse items (things the customer did not intend to buy, but may decide to after seeing the item) would receive the prime positions. In addition, similar items should be stocked together to make it easier for customers to find them.
- *Security.* For many retailers it is important to have the cash register positioned so the operator can see the entire store and at the same time monitor the entrance. It may also be important to keep the cash area well lit and visible to the street or mall traffic. *Ask yourself: Why might it be wise to place cash registers so they are visible to the street?*

Keep in mind that the overall tone of the store has been established in your marketing strategy (Section 3 of the business plan). Therefore, the actual layout, fixtures, and décor should be selected to project the image you have already decided on. Even security issues (like the placement of cash registers) should be in keeping with your image.

⟨?⟩ Get Help 4.2

If you are starting a retail operation, it is worth spending some time on the website of the Retail Council of Canada at **www.retailcouncil.org**.

Head Start Exercise

4.4   Make a preliminary sketch of any selling space or product demonstration or display areas (1 page maximum).

MANUFACTURING OR WHOLESALE SET-UP   Both manufacturers and wholesalers must carefully plan the shipping and receiving functions to allow for the orderly movement of raw materials or parts *in* and the rapid dispatch of products *out*.

The storage set-up is a balance between maximum use of the space and maximum ability to locate and access materials and finished products when they are needed. Let's say a wholesaler imports hang glider kits from Europe for distribution to the North American market. The kits would be fairly large, but there would be relatively few models and the boxes would be labelled. So, even though lots of space would be needed, the organization might consist of just piling the boxes on top of each other, label facing out. On the other hand, a business that builds and repairs custom guitar amplifiers would require very little storage space even though it might have hundreds of tiny electronic parts. Here, a complex labelling and ordering system would be needed.

Head Start Exercise

4.5   Make a sketch of any storage areas you will need for holding materials or finished products (1 page maximum).

process set-up A manufacturing layout that groups similar types of equipment or activities into separate areas.

product set-up A manufacturing layout that places machinery and equipment in the order that they are used for producing a particular product; an assembly line set-up.

Manufacturers of custom, made-to-order products generally use a **process set-up**, grouping together types of equipment that perform similar functions. However, businesses that mass-produce the same items over and over are likely to use a **product set-up**, where machinery and equipment are lined up in the order they are used for production. For example, in a small, custom furniture plant all the sanding machines will be together—a process set-up. On the other hand, a wood shop that mass-produces table legs may have one sanding machine near the beginning of the line (to smooth the wood after shaping on the lathe) and another one near the end (to sand between coats of lacquer)—a product set-up.

Let's say you want to custom-make model trucks as gifts for truck drivers. (You will provide a scale replica of the rig the trucker actually drives.) It sounds simple, but to make it pay you may need a fairly complex manufacturing process that has part of your shop devoted to a process set-up (which will make large numbers of popular brands of trucks which will be stored) and part of your shop devoted to a product set-up (that will take the correct model of truck from storage and modify and paint it for the individual client). Manufacturing firms, like this example, will need some kind of manufacturing plan. This will normally include a floor plan, an analysis of machinery use, and a detailed explanation of costing and scheduling methods.

For a small manufacturer, a flexible manufacturing space could be ideal, so that the set-up can be changed for different orders, seasons, and so on. So far, this is generally not economical, although there is some research looking for ways to make manufacturing space more dynamic.[4]

> **? Get Help 4.3**
> Industrial engineers (not to be confused with industrial designers) have expertise in designing maximum efficiency workplaces for manufacturing and storage. There are also several software programs to assist with layouts. See ***www.instantplanner.com***.

> **✓ Test Yourself 4.3**
> True or False? A product set-up is laid out like a traditional assembly line.

Head Start Exercise

4.6   Make a sketch of any production set-up you might need, labelling all equipment and showing (with arrows) the direction that products will follow as they go through your process (1 page maximum).

SERVICE SET-UP   This category could include everything from construction contractors to dry cleaners to music schools to psychotherapists. The category is defined as a service since most of the cost involved in what you're selling comes from labour and expertise as opposed to the cost of some physical product (even though a physical product may be an important part of what you're selling).

For many service firms, the only space and equipment considerations will be for an office. For others, such as restaurants and garages, your explanation of equipment and space use may include all the components of office, retail, and manufacturing set-ups.

For example, someone with a background involving theatrical makeup and hairdressing might decide to start a business making custom wigs for cancer patients. In this case, the business plan would have to include sketches of the set-up for the area where clients will be dealt with (identifying reception area, chairs, mirrors, storage areas, equipment, and lighting) as well as the workshop area where the wigs are made (showing moulds, work benches, tool areas, and so on).

> **✓ Test Yourself 4.4**
> True or False? A firm may be selling a physical product and still be classified as a service type of business.

Tropical North

Tropical North in Barrie, Ontario, is recognized locally as the cool place to buy a board. The store sells snowboards, skateboards, surfboards, and sailboards, but most of the revenue these days comes from selling clothing and accessories popular with the "boarder" crowd. This subculture, originally a small group of extreme sports enthusiasts, shares tastes in apparel, footwear, and even music. Brands are important to this group because of their traditional concern for equipment quality. The segment has expanded in numbers and age range over the past few years, to the point where it has become increasingly mainstream. But a larger market also means more competitors. Large malls have chain stores like West 49 with both their purchasing and advertising power competing for many of Tropical North's customers.

The location of the business—Barrie, Ontario—has proven to be excellent because of the city's explosive growth over the past few years as well as its proximity to several ski resorts. Young middle-class families have been moving into the city's new subdivisions, doubling the population over a ten-year period. Like many smaller cities, the downtown area has been rejuvenated with specialty stores and services that do not compete directly with the chains and big box stores. The site for Tropical North offers excellent visibility with high levels of pedestrian and auto traffic. The older buildings in this section, however, make the layout more of a challenge. The long, narrow store is set up with the cash register two-thirds of the way toward the back, pulling buyers in to see the entire inventory. There are lots of impulse items at eye level around the cash register and at other strategic spots in the store. The high ceilings are used to excellent advantage with maximum display of inventory.

Pulling this off, of course, takes experience. Owner Jeff Borgmeyer's advice to would-be store owners is to "get a minimum of three years' experience in retail, working for someone else, before going on your own."

How Will I Manage the Process?

logistics The study and management of the planning, procurement, transportation, and storage of products.

It's not enough that your business plan explains what goes where. It must also show that you have worked out the details of *how* you will do things.

just-in-time An inventory management system that plans to have products delivered shortly before they are required in order to reduce storage costs.

supply chain management Planning, implementing, and controlling all of the contractual and physical aspects of bringing a product or service from its most basic components to the end-user.

LOGISTICS   The term **logistics** originally applied to the planning and carrying out of military movements. Large manufacturing firms eventually adopted it, primarily to describe the transportation and storage of products. Large firms also came to believe that their profits were more and more linked to their ability to cut inventory costs, especially with **just-in-time** delivery systems. (Many small firms have also tried to follow this trend, but with less success.[5]). Over the years, the meaning of logistics has broadened to include issues of purchasing, production planning, and customer service. At the same time, a greater emphasis on logistics has taken place in the wholesale and retail sectors, and even service industries have adopted many logistics concepts. Often the term *logistics* will be used interchangeably with **supply chain management**. The *supply chain* was mentioned in Chapter 3 as involving both the channel and physical elements of distribution.

In Canada, the study of logistics has become more formalized, with many post-secondary courses available. The Logistics Institute confers a professional designation (P.Log.) for trained practitioners in the field. These logisticians are experts in developing systems that ensure the supply of products, when they are needed, as profitably as possible. You are applying many of the principles of this discipline as you figure out the most economical way to secure and manage materials.

If your business must manage high volumes, or a wide variety of materials, or if it has a complicated distribution process, it may be necessary to get the advice of a professional to prepare this part of your business plan, especially considering that smaller firms tend to be poor at more formal approaches to logistics.[6] *Ask yourself: Are there elements of my business that will need logistics planning?*

For most new ventures, however, it is sufficient to show some basic logic in your plan for keeping your business supplied in an economical fashion.

PURCHASING   The topic of purchasing is not about the one-time purchases of equipment at the start-up of a business. Rather, it is about the ongoing buying of materials, supplies, and services that your business will need on a regular basis. The idea is that every time you buy or contract something for the business, you don't want it to be a big decision-making exercise. Instead, you will have figured out a system for making purchases in advance.

The purposes of your purchasing system are:
- to prevent your business from running out of inventory or supplies (you can't make money if you don't have the supplies needed for your service), and
- to reduce your costs by keeping as little inventory as possible (you don't want to spend money financing and storing inventory that you don't need to).

Ask yourself: Which is the lesser of two evils, to have too much inventory or to have too little inventory? Obviously, you have to strike a reasonable balance between these two objectives. But the general rule is this: better to have too much (you can reduce prices to move the stock) than too little (and risk losing the customer as well as the sale).

How much work you put into this issue will depend on the nature of your business. If you plan on being a yoga instructor, your ongoing purchases will be only minor supplies—and going too heavily into business cards won't bankrupt you. But if you plan on opening a vegetable market, cases of unsold rotting avocados could be your undoing.

If your business depends on inventory, your business plan must show your method for knowing *when* to order stock and for knowing *how much* to order at one time. Small entrepreneurs often explain that knowing these things comes from experience. But a careful analysis of their "experience" really shows that most have worked out a purchasing system (often informally) that is based on things like:
- the rate of use of a particular product
- the amount of storage space available
- the order quantities offered by suppliers
- the delivery cost of an order
- the amount of time it takes to get replacement stock

Get Help 4.4

Look in the Yellow Pages under "Business Consultants" for specialists in the area of logistics. See also the website of the Logistics Institute at **www.loginstitute.ca**.

Get Help 4.5

Manufacturers and some retailers often depend on "economic order quantity" formulas for their purchasing decisions. Purchasing textbooks offer lots of these formal methods, but if you have problems using them try contacting someone who teaches purchasing or manufacturing operations at your local college. There are also excellent articles on inventory management at **www.inventoryops.com**.

✓ Test Yourself 4.5

True or False? One of the objectives of a purchasing system is to maximize the amount of inventory.

✓ Test Yourself 4.6

True or False? The terms *logistics* and *supply chain management* are commonly used interchangeably.

- the rate at which the stock spoils
- the peak-demand times of the year
- the production schedule

and various other factors particular to their own industries.

Head Start Exercises

4.7   If your business will depend on any specific supplies, make a list of the factors that will affect your ordering decisions ($\frac{1}{3}$ page maximum).

4.8   If your business will be carrying products for resale, estimate how much inventory you will need to carry, what this stock will cost you, and how often it will have to be replaced ($\frac{1}{2}$ page maximum).

---

barter The exchange of goods and services in lieu of cash payment. (This term is also synonymous with negotiation, but the former definition is the more common in a business context.)

Even if your business doesn't purchase products, it may well have to buy services from other professionals or businesses. Before starting up, new entrepreneurs may get a wide variety of outside help for the preparation of their business plan. Advisers may include teachers, bankers, engineers, accountants, marketing consultants, lawyers, appraisers, and so on. Many of these resources will provide free advice, but others will charge hefty professional fees. Don't hesitate to ask how much someone intends to charge for advice or assistance, and then compare those prices. Even though professional bodies publish suggested fee schedules, you may still find a huge variation in the price two different law firms will charge to register a simple corporation. Always try to negotiate (you may even be able to **barter** your own services in lieu of cash), and be prepared to challenge any bill that seems too high.

Head Start Exercise

4.9   Make a list of any paid advisers or consultants that you might need to hire in order to prepare your business plan. Estimate what this will cost you ($\frac{1}{3}$ page maximum).

---

accounting The recording, classifying, analyzing, and reporting of financial information.

accountant A person holding one of several professional designations who oversees, reports on, and makes recommendations on financial decisions.

bookkeeping The clerical or mechanical elements of accounting.

retainer An amount of money paid to a professional adviser (such as a lawyer) before any services have been given. This amount ensures that the services of the retained professional will be available when required, and charges for service are then deducted from the retainer.

Once their businesses are running, self-employed people typically use the **accounting** services of **accountants** or **bookkeeping** firms on a regular basis. Other consultants tend to be used as required, although some entrepreneurs (especially in fields where contract disputes are likely to arise) will pay **retainers** to particular law firms to keep their services available.

Your business may also purchase the services of other businesses on an ongoing basis. For example, you may have a landscape design firm where you create layouts for home gardens. Some of your customers will also want porches, gazebos, or other structures, and you could have a deal with an architectural engineer to prepare all of your drawings in order to get building permits. Or, if you work as a personal image consultant to senior executives, you could have subcontract arrangements with a tailor, a hairdresser, a public speaking consultant, and a fitness trainer, any of whom you will bring in as needed. With each of these service suppliers, you must have already worked out a price at which they will provide their services through your company.

Head Start Exercise

4.10 Make a list of any advisers or subcontractors you will have to use on a regular basis once the business is running. Estimate the total expense for their services on a monthly basis ($\frac{1}{3}$ page maximum).

PROCEDURES   For most of us, it doesn't take very long to perform the morning chores of washing, grooming, getting dressed, and getting ourselves to work or school. But these apparently simple tasks could fill hours and hours if we had to make new decisions on how to proceed at each step of the process:

- Brush the teeth before or after showering?
- Put the toothpaste on before or after wetting the brush?
- Start with the front teeth? With the outside surfaces of the teeth?
- Work in which direction?

We don't have to spend time making any of these decisions because we have worked out a system that we follow the same way each day. Similarly, the major tasks of your business should be worked out in advance to ensure that they are performed efficiently.

There are a variety of ways that you can demonstrate in your business plan that you have worked out orderly procedures. Typical techniques include sequential lists, bar graphs, flow charts, and continuity charts.

Lots of businesses will follow the same linear process for each job or customer. This is true for many retailers, consultants, and contractors who merely have to explain what they will do first for the customer, what they will do second, and so on.

For example, a company that paints parking lots for building owners might follow the procedures shown as a **sequential list** in Figure 4.1.

> ✓ **Test Yourself 4.7**
>
> True or False? It is possible to make business deals with customers or suppliers that do not involve the exchange of money.

> ✓ **Test Yourself 4.8**
>
> True or False? *Bookkeeping* and *accounting* are interchangeable terms.

> **sequential list** A simple, chronological ordering of procedures that will be followed by a business.

Figure 4.1   **LOT PAINTING COMPANY, PROCEDURES**

1. Schedule job with client and confirm new parking lot markings.
2. Divide lot into sections equal to one day's painting work.
3. Notify lot users of date on which their spaces will be unavailable.
4. Barricade section to be painted before lot opens.
5. Black out previous lines/markings.
6. Survey lot section for new lines/markings.
7. Place guides.
8. Paint new lines.
9. Stencil new markings.
10. Remove/transfer barricades.
11. Repeat steps 4–10 until job completion.

bar graph A chart that can be used to monitor and control project activities, showing time along the *x* axis and business activities along the *y* axis.

Businesses that involve overlapping activities or that have various jobs in progress at the same time may use a **bar graph** to plan and track those activities to completion. This type of graph when used to show both "scheduled" and "completed" activities is known as a Gantt chart. In the business plan, however, it only needs to show the planning process. For example, a conference planner can rely on this type of chart to ensure that all steps in the process have been completed on time. See the example in Figure 4.2.

Some businesses require the customer to make specific choices leading to different paths that a service will take. These optional routes are usually offered in a specific order and can be outlined in a **flow chart**. The example in Figure 4.3 is for a day spa that offers a series of different aesthetics packages to its customers. Note that the hair removal option is not available with some of the other services, either because of scheduling or possible irritation to the client's skin.

flow chart A map showing the various services offered by a business and the different routes that can be taken through these services.

Another method to graphically show a sequence of procedures over time is a PERT chart (program evaluation and review technique) or CPM (critical path method)—both of which show more details of time use. These **continuity charts** can be very useful in the business plan for "project" sorts of activities. For example, a theatrical costume designer may demonstrate a four-month costuming project as shown in Figure 4.4.

continuity chart A graph of the sequence of procedures and the time frame for each that must be followed for a project.

Figure 4.2 **CONFERENCE COUNTDOWN**

Weeks Until Conference

Figure 4.3

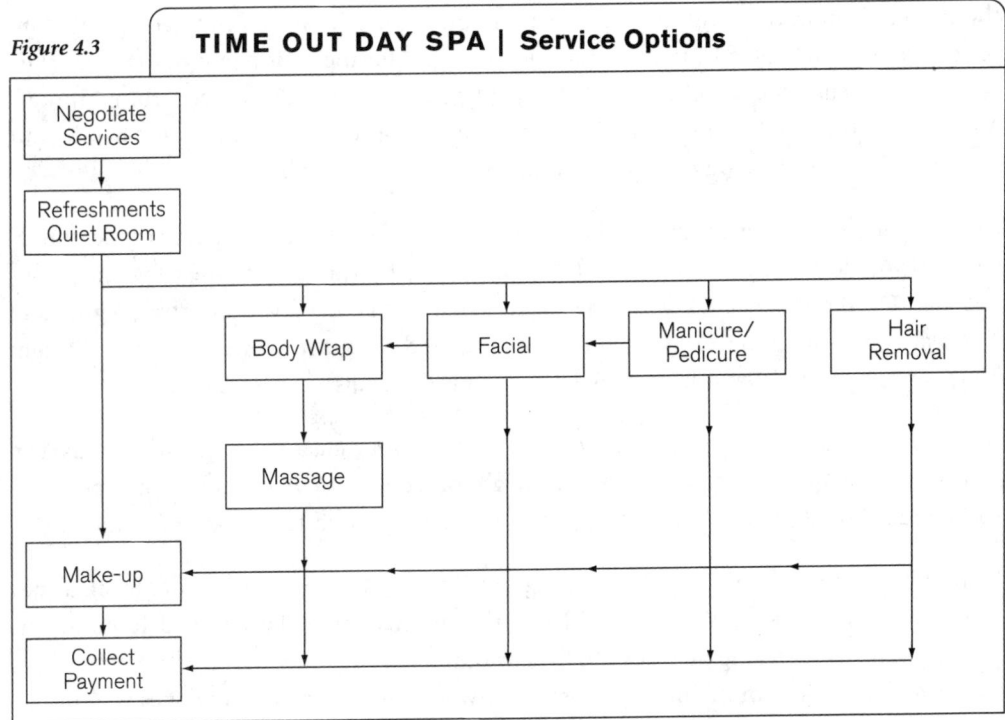

TIME OUT DAY SPA | Service Options

✓ **Test Yourself 4.9**
True or False? A Gantt chart is a type of bar graph.

✓ **Test Yourself 4.10**
True or False? A flow chart shows the single chronological series of procedures that a business uses.

◇ **Get Help 4.6**
If your business plan requires extensive technical detail (and writing is not your strength), you may have to hire a technical writer. Check the Yellow Pages under "Manuals Preparation" or get leads from writing programs at your local college.

Figure 4.4

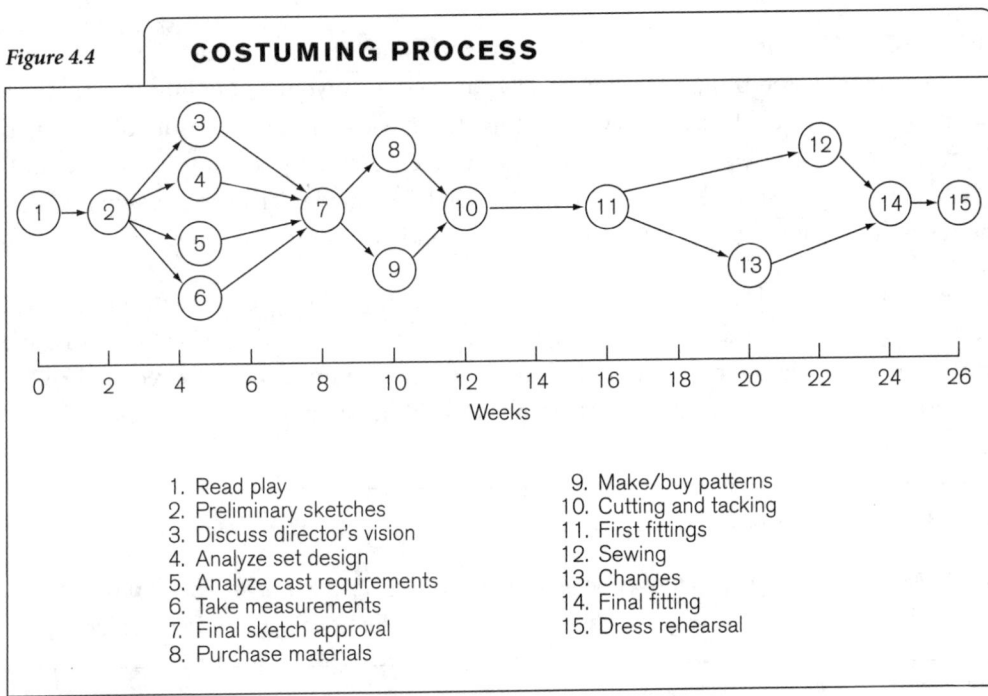

COSTUMING PROCESS

1. Read play
2. Preliminary sketches
3. Discuss director's vision
4. Analyze set design
5. Analyze cast requirements
6. Take measurements
7. Final sketch approval
8. Purchase materials
9. Make/buy patterns
10. Cutting and tacking
11. First fittings
12. Sewing
13. Changes
14. Final fitting
15. Dress rehearsal

For very simple endeavours, the business plan may require only a short paragraph or two to explain your procedures. Extremely complex processes may require a detailed operations manual attached as an appendix (see Chapter 10, "Systemization").

QUALITY AND CUSTOMER SERVICE *Ask yourself: Am I committed to giving my customers the highest possible quality?* Perhaps you shouldn't be. Lots of business people talk about their "commitment to quality," always implying the "best" or "highest" quality. But your commitment should be to the "right" quality: right for the customer groups you are targeting. Some customers will demand stringent quality standards and control methods.[7] Additionally, true quality control is about ensuring not only that you do not fall below your standards, but also that you do not exceed them at unnecessary cost.

Let's say you're in the business of making novelty candy for special events. It may be important that you do not ship any of your 100-gram chocolate animals that are below the promised size. On the other hand, you can't make money by giving away an extra 25 grams of chocolate on each animal. You have to have a method for setting lower *and* upper weight limits along with a system of checking that each product falls within those limits.

Ask yourself: What will my standards of quality be? For your custom chocolate animals, you may decide that quality means a particular weight range, a particular standard of appearance (no smudged bits, no extra bits), and a particular standard of taste (no bitter flavour).

Some entrepreneurs think they are ensuring quality with their personal guarantee that they will correct any complaints "to the satisfaction of the customer." This approach dumps the responsibility for checking quality onto the customer: the customer has to complain for it to work. But what about those unhappy customers who don't complain—the ones who just go somewhere else with their business and bad-mouth you for the rest of their lives? You can't rely on the customer to complain. You have to check quality yourself.

Ask yourself: How will I check quality? Quality control is all about checking. This applies not just to product-based businesses, but equally to services. Anyone going into business as a flight instructor would be acutely aware of this. The most significant measure of quality in aviation training is safety, and the control system to ensure safety (quality) is the checklist. Pilots live by checklists (literally). The checklist can be adapted to ensuring quality for businesses as diverse as moving companies, nightclubs, and pest control services.

Other means of checking quality can range from a simple visual inspection to formal, detailed customer surveys. In most cases, however, it's simply a matter of setting aside time to ask the customer: "How's your meal?" "Just calling to check that everything was delivered on time," or "We wanted to make sure there were no problems with the basement waterproofing job."

Head Start Exercise

4.11 Write single sentences to explain what "quality" will mean in the service or products you offer. Jot down some ways in which you could measure quality ($\frac{1}{3}$ page maximum).

How Will I Manage Information?

What appointments will you have to keep? To whom do you owe money, and who owes you? What remains to be done on each of your jobs/projects? Whose phone calls do you have to return? How much inventory do you have on hand? How much is your next tax payment? Which letters do you have to send? These are just a few examples of the things you have to know when you're in business for yourself, and since you can't remember them all, you need systems to keep this kind of information at your fingertips. *Ask yourself: How well organized am I? Am I good at writing down important things I have to remember?*

KEEPING RECORDS For some new entrepreneurs, the habit of good record keeping comes the hard way: only after losing a legal dispute, losing a customer, or paying more taxes than would otherwise be necessary. Get into the habit of good record keeping right from the very first day you even consider working for yourself. If you drive somewhere to buy a *Small Business* magazine, save and file the receipt and record the date and mileage of your trip. These are legitimate business expenses, but only if they are properly recorded and saved.

Ask yourself: For how long do I have to save my records? Popular lore maintains that a business has to keep important records for seven years before they can be destroyed. But in some cases, even this will not meet the legal obligations of the business owner. Especially for a new business, a better rule is *When in doubt, don't throw it out.* Better to set up some sort of *permanent* storage file for items such as business registrations, basic employee information and deduction records, tax returns, contracts, financial statements, and anything else with legal or tax implications.

Just as you organize your personal workspace, you must develop a system for recording and saving information, a system that you will come to use by habit. For some, a simple appointment calendar and shoebox for receipts will be enough. For others, it will take a filing cabinet with separate files for all the functional areas of the business, a large desk calendar that includes appointments, and a to-do list. And for many, the entire record-keeping system will be computerized using desktop, notebook, or handheld computer equipment or some combination of these.

Head Start Exercise

4.12 Write a short explanation of any manual, paperwork, or record-keeping systems you plan on using ($\frac{1}{4}$ page maximum).

SMALL-BUSINESS SOFTWARE Over the past few years, small-business computer programs have been evolving, becoming increasingly more comprehensive in the types of tasks they handle for the independent businessperson.

Today, the most commonly used programs are integrated office management packages incorporating word processing, email, fax, list management, graphics, database, web, video, and calendaring; some packages even include business plan and financial statement templates and numerous other capabilities. Examples are Microsoft Office and Lotus SmartSuite.

Many software packages that started out as programs to manage small-business accounting have evolved into comprehensive management information packages; these programs include QuickBooks and Microsoft Small Business Accounting.[8] Increasingly, these have the capability to integrate with office software packages that typically offer the following features. *Word processing* commonly includes templates for letters, invoices, reports, quotations, and so on for hard copy or email transmission or faxing from the computer screen. But even though today's inexpensive software has the capability for letterhead macros and embedded pictures, *you* may not have the capability because you haven't had time to learn it all. Few independent businesspeople can afford the time to develop high levels of software expertise unless this is specifically how they make their money. For most of us, the main consideration is whether it is easy to use. *Ask yourself: How computer literate am I?*

Email is now viewed as the most important business communication innovation. It's fast, it's cheap, it can be secure, and it documents your communication. At times, it may seem easier to just use the phone, but if you deduct the time you spend on hold and consider the advantages of being able to edit your words and attach pictures, graphs, and so on, email is an area where it might be worth building some skill.

web authoring The creation of documents and other media using the necessary language and protocol for transfer via the World Wide Web.

Office packages also provide **web-authoring** capability, but if your business has a sophisticated website or you use electronic-commerce transactions you will likely need advanced *web management* software and a higher level of expertise to use it.

These are features that help with both decision making and actually doing the work. *Doing-the-work* software can include everything from forms design (templates are available for a wide variety of forms) to purchase orders to job tracking and project management charts. Specific time-tracking and billing programs are available for many professions.

database software A program that stores many pieces of information in the form of tables, allowing the information to be sorted and reported in many different formats.

Many of the decision-making tools are database applications. **Database software** can record large amounts of information in particular files (for example, customer files) with many pieces of information in each file, stored in particular fields (for example, customer name, product order, or customer postal code). Information can be retrieved from the database by combining any number of files and it can be presented in many different formats (for example, sales reports, inventory reports, or customer rankings) as well as different styles of graphs and charts.

Setting up a database management system involves a fairly long learning curve—or, more likely, bringing in expert help. However, a number of database templates are commercially available for specific businesses such as restaurants, machine shops, and retail stores, and the list will continue growing.

In some cases, your web browser can be used as a tool to help you find prospective customers, and your own website can be a form of advertising. Mailing lists for fax, hard copy, or email are fairly easy to develop and these can be used for a variety of direct mail approaches. (See Chapter 3, "Advertising Media.")

presentation software Programs that help to create a series of "slides" or pages of information that can be viewed on a computer screen, computerized projector, over the web, or in hard copy. Typically used for training and promotion, the most widely adopted program is Microsoft PowerPoint.

Presentation software helps you create professional sales presentations with dramatic audio-visual effects. Some software includes job costing and estimating forms that are especially good for manufacturers, contractors, and various types of consultants. This information can be automatically transferred to quotations and ultimately invoices. For large contracts, it is also relatively easy to develop your own proposal outlines and contract templates.

For a business that relies heavily on one-to-one selling, quality software is available that will help you manage your sales time with calendars, customer contact files, and summaries of sales information.

How much of your own record keeping and accounting you choose to do will depend on:

- the financial complexity of your business activity
- your own abilities and training
- how much you can afford to pay an accountant to do the work, and
- your accounting software (if any).

Ask yourself: How much do I know about accounting? Some self-employed people do no more record keeping than putting all of their receipts in one location and writing down all their deposits, withdrawals, and payments in a chequebook. Then, typically, they will sit down with their accountant on a monthly basis and explain each of the transactions while the accountant enters the data. The accountant will provide monthly, quarterly, and/or annual reports and prepare the necessary tax returns. Sounds simple, but this is an expensive and time-consuming way to handle what is largely a matter of routine bookkeeping.

It is better to have your accountant help you set up a software (or paper) accounting system where you (or an employee who costs a lot less than the accountant) regularly record all of the transactions. This way, the accountant is just there to check reports and handle non-routine occurrences.

The first step in organizing your accounting system is to set up a **chart of accounts**. This is a list of specific categories in which your business will have transactions. For example, almost all businesses will have a cash account (money in the bank) and an **accounts payable** account (that shows bills owing). But a freelance writer is unlikely to have an **employee deductions** account, whereas a restaurant most likely will. A furniture dealer will have an inventory account, but a lawyer likely will not. Typical charts of accounts for many specific kinds of businesses are included in small-business accounting software.

A **general journal** is a tool that records each of your financial transactions in chronological order, noting which of your accounts the transaction affects. With some minimal training in bookkeeping you can probably record your own transactions (buying something, paying a bill, depositing a cheque), saving the money you would have had to pay your accountant for this job. The software takes care of updating the individual accounts that are affected by each transaction. You must decide your own capabilities in this area.

The status of a company's accounts is reflected in the **financial statements**. (See Chapter 5.) The financial statements show a company's profitability and its position as far as what it owns and what it owes. A major advantage of accounting software is that the entrepreneur (with a little expertise) can see up-to-date financial statements at any given time.

Accounting software also includes planning tools, which can be used for **cash flow** planning. This is one of the most valuable spreadsheet applications for entrepreneurs. The rows and columns of financial information on the spreadsheet can produce instant calculations allowing the entrepreneur to play *what-if* games for planning purposes; for example: "What if half my customers are two months late in paying their bills? How will this affect my bank balance?"

In selecting computer software, try to choose a package that has all the features you want. But use only those features you need. You don't have to adopt any package in its entirety (and

✓ **Test Yourself 4.13**
True or False? Database and presentation software are typically part of office management packages.

chart of accounts A list of the particular financial categories in which a business will have transactions. The chart assigns a name and number to each financial area, or "account."

accounts payable A list of the bills a business owes that will have to be paid in the near future.

employee deductions Money taken from the gross pay of employees to pay for such things as employee income tax, employee pension contributions, and employee benefit contributions.

◇ **Get Help 4.7**
For information about employee deductions look at the Canada Revenue Agency webpage ***www.cra-arc.gc.ca/tax/business/topics/*** and click on *payroll*.

general journal A book or computer document that forms part of a company's accounting system, in which all financial transactions of the firm are recorded in chronological order.

financial statements Accounting reports that summarize the position of a business and the financial changes that have taken place over a period of time. See Chapter 5.

cash flow The analysis of how money comes into and goes out of a business and the factors that affect the cash balance. See Chapter 5.

✓ **Test Yourself 4.14**
True or False? Your accounts payable represents money you expect to collect from your customers.

Get Help 4.8
How much you are going to rely on your accountant for choosing, setting up, and running your systems will depend on your own training and how fast you can learn new skills.

Get Help 4.9
Check computer magazines and search recent issues for reviews of the latest business software to help you purchase a package that has all of the tools you need.

management The setting and achieving of a company's goals and objectives, often through the work of others.

goals Things to be achieved in the long term, usually expressed as broad concepts.

objectives Things to be achieved in the short term, usually expressed as specific numbers with specific dates.

Test Yourself 4.15
True or False? A business owner with no employees can still be considered a manager.

Test Yourself 4.16
True or False? The terms *goals* and *objectives* are interchangeable.

end up having the software shape the operation of your business). For example, your accounting package may offer a slightly cumbersome on-screen personal organizer that would take you 15 minutes to update each day. But if working with a small pocket calendar is more efficient for you, there is no need to commit to its computerized counterpart. Pick and choose your tools.

How Will I Manage Myself and Others in the Firm?

Ask yourself: What is management? **Management** really means "getting people to do work." But what if there are no people other than yourself? This is the situation for lots of self-employed people.

Ask yourself: If I have no employees, am I still practising management? What about in the case of a partnership? Are the partners managing each other? The simple answer is that many of the techniques and principles of managing others can be applied equally well to managing yourself, partners, subcontractors, suppliers, and, at times, even customers. Management is about answering the questions:

- What are we trying to accomplish?
- Who will do what?
- Is the plan working?
- How can we accomplish more?

PLANNING: GOALS AND OBJECTIVES   The first question (*what are we trying to accomplish?*) involves the management function of planning: setting **goals** and **objectives** and communicating them to those being managed. In fact, that's exactly what you've been doing by creating a business plan. You have been explaining exactly what you wish to achieve and setting it down in a format that can be understood and referred to by partners, lenders, or outside investors—even yourself.

As an entrepreneur, clearly your goal is to make money. But you will ultimately achieve this by accomplishing a whole series of small objectives along the way: you will have a customer list completed by Tuesday; you will be making a particular number of sales calls per day next month; you will have so many dollars in sales by the end of six months; and so on.

There is no point in telling an employee that the goal is to help you make money and leaving it at that. Clearly, you must agree on a series of realistic objectives (involving numbers and a time line) that you expect the employee to achieve. This can be easily documented in a confirming memo: "Just to confirm our decision of this morning: we agreed that. . . ."

Planning is rarely a solitary activity and should more often involve those affected by the planning process: partners, employees, customers, and suppliers—getting the necessary agreement to make the plan work.

DIVIDING THE TASKS   In a new one- or two-person business, you can expect to do everything from unloading the truck to strategic planning to negotiating a contract to cleaning the washroom—whatever needs to be done. However, there is an unfortunate tendency for entrepreneurs to hire help on the same basis: "Working for me, you'll do a little of everything. Whatever needs to be done." *Ask yourself: What's wrong with that?*

Doing "whatever needs to be done" is not what employees want. They want a clearly defined job: salesperson, secretary, janitor, installer, proofreader, instructor. It is unreasonable to expect an employee to function as an entrepreneur; that's your role. Besides, there is some evidence that small firms with clear organizational structure perform better.[9]

The best way to handle this is to start thinking of your business as a collection of different specific jobs, right from the start. True, you may be the only employee, but think of yourself as alternating between jobs as the marketing director, the accountant, the repairperson, the writer, the computer programmer, and so on. Thinking of your business this way makes it easier to divide up the work among partners (partners can each take responsibility for several specific jobs), and as the business grows it becomes clear which specific jobs you will hire new people into. *Ask yourself: Which specific jobs could my business be made up of?*

A very complex business will have lots of jobs and these will have to be represented on an **organization chart**. It is perfectly reasonable to show an organization chart with more jobs than there are actual people working in the company. In this sense, the chart is a planning tool (for when you are finally in a position to hire people for all the jobs).

An organization chart, in fact, only names the jobs and shows any reporting relationships (that is, who will be whose boss). It does not actually explain the function of each job. For that you need job descriptions.

Like an organization chart, **a job description** can be an excellent planning tool and it can even form the contract between the employer and the employee.

A good job description can be written on a single page. It should state the general **responsibilities** of the job, or those things that the employee is obligated to look after. It should also outline the **authorities** of the job, specifying the areas where the employee has the right to make decisions. In addition, it should provide some indication of the job's **accountabilities**, or those things on which the employer will judge the performance of the employee. If you work with partners you can still use job descriptions, likely having more than one apiece. But the "who does what" question should also be addressed in your partnership agreement. Remember, the more detailed your agreement, the fewer partnership disputes you will have.

LEADERSHIP: ACCOMPLISHING MORE   *Ask yourself: If management is about getting people to work, then what is leadership?* **Leadership** is about getting people to work *harder*. It is about motivating to achieve. Leadership may be more skill than science, but there is a huge body of research on the effects of different management practices on things like

Get Help 4.10
If you need to make an organization chart, get a human resources management text from the library. You should easily find one with lots of chart examples. As well, the Service Canada website offers tips on hiring at **www.hrmanagement.gc.ca**.

organization chart A graphic representation of the structure of an organization, showing who is whose boss.

job description A statement of the duties, responsibilities, and other issues pertaining to a particular job within a company.

responsibility The tasks that an employee is obligated to complete.

authority The specific area within which an employee has the power to make decisions.

accountability Those particular activities on which the performance of an employee is measured.

leadership The motivational aspects of management that encourage greater productivity from employees.

SMALL BUSINESS PROFILE 4.2
Harvey Katz Cushion Company

There is no Harvey Katz associated with this company. In fact, the company is not really in the cushion business. The name is the creation of business owner Colin Meikle, who designs and manufactures upholstered furniture. Trained as a jazz musician (electric and double bass), Colin's hobby was sketching and building his own lamps and small furniture items, which he sometimes sold. Realizing the opportunities for making money as a musician were extremely limited, Colin wanted to go into a business where he could still exercise his creativity. At the time, Colin's mother had been in her own upholstery business for about ten years and Colin's wife had taken an upholstery course. Interestingly, Colin has never worked with either his mom or wife in the business, but somehow it just seemed an obvious route for him to take. Starting in 2002, for the first three years, Colin worked out of his home until the demands for space were just too great. In 2005, he rented a studio in an artist co-op building with room for a bright showroom as well as work and storage space.

Colin makes custom pieces of his own design and made-to-order pieces for a large manufacturer and a wholesale distributor in the U.S. as well as for Canadian retailers. The business has grown so much that Colin says, "I haven't had to make a sales call in the last three years." The industry is very much about specialization—for example, a furniture manufacturer may have a line of sofas that would benefit from having matching storage ottomans. Colin will get the contract for the ottomans and then contract out the framing to a wood manufacturing company.

The business is basically a one-person company, although Colin will hire the occasional temporary help. He does his own bookkeeping using QuickBooks and sends the files to his accountant at year-end. He has a simple but logical system for scheduling, ordering materials, and billing, and has his cell phone always close by. Colin recognizes that his tastes are not always what the customer is looking for. So his advice to new entrepreneurs is "listen, really listen to the customers and they will tell you what they want."

? Get Help 4.11

Read the history of management theory from an up-to-date text. Try subscribing to a management newsletter.

✓ Test Yourself 4.17

True or False? It is possible for a small business to have more jobs on its organization chart than there are people working for the company.

productivity, employee turnover, and absenteeism. From these works of applied psychology, we can get many practical ways to improve our own leadership style. Following are five practical leadership tips:

- *Measure behaviour.* You can't know if your management approach is improving things (getting your employees to make fewer errors, increasing your own sales rate, having your partner be more punctual) if you don't actually measure and record specific behaviours.

- *Reward improvement.* Look for employees, associates, and yourself doing something right (better), then reward that behaviour. It doesn't take much to be a powerful reward—a thank-you, some recognition, or a small treat usually works well. And when you reward improvement, the result is that you get more improvement—at an accelerating rate.

- *Take responsibility for employee well-being.* Paternalism from entrepreneurs toward employees is certainly out of fashion. Studies consistently show, however, that employees highly value (more so than wages) the security provided by group benefit packages. Even more important might be taking a personal interest in your employees ("Are your kids getting over the measles?"), as it encourages loyalty and productivity.

- *Provide opportunity.* Everyone, to varying extents, needs recognition, challenge, or some definition of success. As an entrepreneur you may recognize these needs in yourself, but fail to recognize them in others. Even though the opportunities for promotion, recognition, and prestige are documented as potent motivators, entrepreneurs are notoriously selfish about allowing employees to participate in even token ownership of the business. British tycoon Richard Branson, however, attributes his enormous wealth to giving others the opportunity to get rich.
- *Practise dynamic leadership.* The best leaders are those who can change their leadership style to meet the changing requirements of the circumstances, the employees, and the business. This means at times giving orders, at other times seeking group consensus, and sometimes letting others make decisions. It also means continuously growing and learning new skills as a leader.

GETTING PAID The issue of who gets paid how much and when can be an employer/employee issue, it can be an issue between partners, or, if you're on your own, it can be a personal budgeting issue.

Ask yourself: How much should I pay my employees and on what basis? When it comes to compensation, small business owners are often victim to two false beliefs:

- That money is the strongest motivator for employees.
- That small firms cannot afford to pay the same rates as large firms.

Studies have shown time and again that money rarely motivates employees to work above a minimal effort: money is not a motivator. But it can be a potential *demotivator.*[10]

Ask yourself: In your current job, would you be prepared to work 15 percent harder for an additional 15 percent in pay? If you answer honestly and you're like most of us, the answer is no: money is not a motivator. But let's say you have a job working for a uniform supplier, doing clothing alteration. One day, you encounter several other people doing basically the same job as you do and through them you learn that you are being paid about 5 percent less than any of them. The next day, your boss asks you to put in an extra effort for a particularly large order. If you stay late, you will be paid overtime rates. *Ask yourself: How motivated would you be to put in extra effort? Even to stay late for overtime pay? What if the boss promises you a promotion for handling this order well?* The fact that you now feel underpaid will hamper any other efforts to motivate you. In this sense, the issue of money has become a demotivator.

So the trick, as an employer, is not to overpay employees (you'd just be wasting your money), but rather to make sure that they feel they are paid fairly. At that point, you can then go on to motivate them to higher productivity by other means. (See above, "Leadership.")

Ask yourself: If I should pay employees fairly, it should be fair compared to what? Employees want to feel that they are paid fairly compared to others in the same firm (based on relative responsibility, job requirements, experience, and seniority) as well as compared to others doing the same job in different firms (that is, the *going rates*). You can get information about industry averages from trade sources and various salary surveys.

✓ **Test Yourself 4.18**
True or False? *Accountability* refers to those things on which a person's performance will be measured.

✓ **Test Yourself 4.19**
True or False? *Authority, accountability,* and *responsibility* all have the same meaning.

✓ **Test Yourself 4.20**
True or False? *Leadership* and *management* are interchangeable terms.

◇ **Get Help 4.12**
Up-to-date salary survey information showing the pay range for a wide selection of job categories in your area is often available from the local chamber of commerce. Major newspapers such as *The Globe and Mail* periodically publish national salary surveys. Also, look up specific jobs and check out the salary information on *www.jobfutures.ca.*

Equally dangerous to viewing money as a motivator is the myth of the small employer being unable to compete with big firms when it comes to compensation. Skilled labour is a commodity, like oil or lettuce. Is it reasonable for a small manufacturer to expect to pay less for electricity than General Motors does just because of size? If you try to rationalize underpaying employees "because you can't afford the going rates," expect serious motivation problems.

This same principle holds when it comes to **employee benefit** packages, including extended health care, dental care, drug plans, disability insurance and so on. True, the large employers can usually buy group benefits more cheaply because of their size, just like Wendy's gets a deal on their lettuce that an independent sandwich shop can't get. However, insurance companies are increasingly offering benefit packages for self-employed people and small-business owners at competitive rates. (See Chapter 2, "Small Business Insurance.")

Remember that benefit packages satisfy the employee's need for security, and therefore become powerful motivators.

Head Start Exercise

4.13 Calculate the monthly amount you will have to pay for any employees, including the expenses for any employee benefits or required employer contributions ($\frac{1}{2}$ page maximum).

If you are working as a sole proprietorship or in a partnership, the money the business operates on is considered the personal funds of you or of you and your partners, so money that you pay to yourself is really your own cash that you are drawing out of the business activity. This is referred to as **drawings.**

Sometimes your business will have more cash in the bank than at other times, and there is an unfortunate tendency to take out more money for your personal use at these times. But cash is not the same thing as profit, and you must carefully consider whether the money you decide to *pay yourself* should be earmarked for other purposes, such as paying bills that haven't come due yet.

A safer approach is to treat drawings like a regular salary. Predetermine how much you need to pay yourself and take a standard amount on a regular schedule, keeping your personal finances separated from the business finances.

In the case of a corporation, your personal finances are legally separate from the business finances and you would normally set up a regular salary payment for yourself or other working partners. But you also have the option of paying to yourself the business profits (or any part of the profits) in the form of dividends. When a business makes profit, there can be tax advantages in how you split your remuneration between salary and dividends.

Be cautious at start-up. Many ventures are extremely cash-hungry at the start and take a long time to show a profit. Early on, it's easy to be overly optimistic about how profitable working

employee benefits The non-monetary compensation of employees, through items such as pension plans, extended health care, and other insurance programs.

◇ **Get Help 4.13**
If there is a business association for your field, call and ask if they offer a group benefit plan for members and their employees.

drawings Cash withdrawals from a business by an owner of the company and intended for the personal use of the owner.

✓ **Test Yourself 4.21**
True or False? Salary is classified as an employee benefit.

◇ **Get Help 4.14**
Paying yourself is another area where you will likely rely on your accountant. If you are skilled in accounting, however, you can make decisions on the best way to pay yourself by using a variety of tax return software and running a series of different compensation scenarios.

for yourself can be at the beginning. A safer approach is to rely on little or no cash from the business until you have established a clear pattern of growth.

✓ **Test Yourself 4.22**
True or False? It is better for independent business owners to pay themselves regular salaries than it is to take money out of the business as it is needed for personal use.

Head Start Exercise

4.14 Estimate how many months you can survive without having to rely on the business for income. After that period, how much would you have to pay yourself each month? ($\frac{1}{8}$ page maximum)

How Will I Manage the Government?

The largest common source of irritation among those who work for themselves is "the government": the government as regulator, the government as taxer, the government as the place where you wait on hold trying to get information. It may come as a surprise when you become newly self-employed just how much of your life you will spend trying to find out what the government wants you to do and then how much time you will spend doing it. During all of that time you are doing things that don't make you any profit, but you must do them just to stay in business. On top of all that, you have three different levels of government to deal with: federal, provincial, and municipal, each for different issues.

Ask yourself: How will I handle the frustration of dealing with government? Step one is to remind yourself that your competition must deal with the same governments and the same frustrations. Step two is to start building some skill in efficient government dealings. This includes learning to be patient and assertive and to talk to the right person.

? **Get Help 4.15**
One of the most valuable resources for dealing with the federal and provincial governments is the *Scott's Government Index* published by Southam Inc. This is a listing of government administrators (by name or department) with full names, titles, phone numbers, and email addresses. This up-to-date loose-leaf service can be found in larger libraries or purchased online at **www.scottsinfo.com**.

LICENCES AND PERMITS   Depending on the nature of your business, licences and permits may be required from any of the three levels of government, although this is most commonly a municipal issue. Municipalities can require a variety of permits, from general vendor's permits to trade contractor licences to specific retail and service licences for businesses like bars, dry cleaners, taxis, street vendors, and restaurants. In addition, you will likely need building permits (for any remodelling you do to your place of business), sign permits (if you have any public signage), and parking permits (if your business is in a major urban area).

? **Get Help 4.16**
Check the blue pages of your phone book for the licensing or clerk's office in your municipality.

Provinces affect most businesses in the area of transportation, requiring driver's licences and motor vehicle permits. As well, provinces may require licensing for a host of other endeavours such as real estate sales, travel agencies, motor vehicle sales, nursing homes, daycare centres, and collection agencies.

? **Get Help 4.17**
Find the provincial ministry that issues licences, using your phone book's blue pages.

Federal licensing is most likely to affect the independent entrepreneur in the area of import and export licences or if you are involved in aviation or an industry using radio frequency communications.

? **Get Help 4.18**
For an overview of import permit requirements, call the automated customs information line at 1-800-461-9999. For information on export assistance see the Team Canada website at **exportsource.ca**.

TAXATION   Not only does a businessperson have to pay his or her own taxes, but in many cases the businessperson is also the designated tax collector working on behalf of the government to collect, record, and remit taxes from those they do business with. Examples would be provincial sales taxes or the federal goods and services tax (GST). (You must collect GST if your sales are more than $30,000 per year, so get a GST number from Canada Revenue Agency right away. This number is being used for an increasing number of other government registrations.) Another example is the federal excise tax on manufactured goods. You are also the collector for employee income taxes, Employment Insurance, and Canada Pension (and/or provincial pension) contributions. Don't try to get around this by having true employees bill you for services as though they were subcontractors. Check with your accountant. Manufacturers may also have to pay federal excise tax.

Federal income taxes are easiest to deal with when you are a sole proprietor or general partner since your business income calculation is part of your personal income tax return. The federal government collects for most provinces as well as itself, but the rules change a little every year. Even if you are competent with tax return software (your accounting package may include this), it is still a good investment to have an accountant make sure you are paying no more tax than necessary.

If you're incorporated, things become a little more complicated. You have to pay your corporate income tax to the province and the federal government separately, and this is also separate from your personal income taxes (which may include salary and dividends from the corporation). *Ask yourself: Now do I think I need an accountant?*

Depending on your deal with your landlord (if you have one), your business activities may also have to deal with property or service taxes levied by the municipality. (This also includes your business's share of property taxes on a home where you have your business.)

REGULATIONS   Sole proprietorships and partnerships must register in the province where they are operating. This is a fairly simple and inexpensive process involving the filling out of forms and a **name search** at the provincial business registration office. Your registered business certificate can now be used for obtaining licences and permits or opening business bank accounts.

If you're starting a corporation you have the choice of whether to incorporate provincially or federally. If you know that you are going to be operating in more than one province, then it may be easier in the long run to incorporate federally. Do-it-yourself software, books, and kits are available, although many people prefer to have a lawyer set up their corporations.

There is a large body of law that governs the function of businesses and the conduct of entrepreneurs. There are federal laws concerning contracts, competition, shareholders, and lenders, as well as laws that govern the relationships between employers and employees. These laws rarely affect the small businessperson. Even if you have employees, your business is likely to be covered under provincial employment law. (The exception here is if you are in a federally regulated business, such as aviation or radio broadcasting.)

Provincial employment laws in the areas of employment standards (hours of work, holidays, minimum wage, and so on), health and safety (including office environments), and human rights (including pay equity) are those most likely to affect the small employer.

Sidebar notes:

✓ **Test Yourself 4.23**
True or False? Building and sign permits generally come from the provincial level of government.

◇? **Get Help 4.19**
Canada Revenue Agency has a valuable small business information section on its website **www.cra-arc.gc.ca**.

name search An inexpensive check, by computer, to make sure that a business is not being registered under a name already in use.

✓ **Test Yourself 4.24**
True or False? For a sole proprietorship, business taxes are calculated as part of the personal tax return.

Pamphlets summarizing the provisions of the applicable laws are generally available from the provincial ministries.

Municipal regulation of businesses can cover zoning, land use, hours of operation, and even issues such as the appearance of retail storefronts. A local chamber of commerce can often help provide direction on these issues.

PROFESSIONAL AND INDUSTRY ASSOCIATIONS   Professional and industry associations are not owned or run by the government, although in some cases they form a type of government themselves to oversee the regulation and licensing for a profession. For example, there are self-governing bodies for the different types of accountants, for lawyers, for engineers, and for different classes of health care professionals.

Most associations, however, do not have control over the practices of their members. Rather, they exist to provide information and services to people in particular endeavours. There are organizations representing car dealers, funeral directors, hairdressers, artists, musicians, writers, grain farmers, commercial travellers, insurance agents, actors, marketing researchers, ice suppliers, and hundreds of other industries. (There's even an association for people who run associations.)

A significant, sometimes unofficial, function of both the regulating and non-regulating associations is to act as government lobby groups on behalf of the specific industry they represent. When legislation that would directly affect your business is pending, you are most likely to be kept informed about it and have the opportunity to influence such legislation through your industry association. There is also an organization that lobbies on behalf of independent entrepreneurs right across the country: the Canadian Federation of Independent Business.

Get Help 4.20
There is a Canada Business Service Centre in most major cities, with information on federal, provincial, and municipal regulations. Check the Canada Business website at *canadabusiness.gc.ca*.

Get Help 4.21
The Canadian Federation of Independent Business is a major source of information about issues affecting entrepreneurs: see *www.cfib.ca*.

✓Answers to Test Yourself Questions

4.1 Leasing vehicles or equipment is usually more economical for a small firm than purchasing. *False*

4.2 A healthy investment for the small office is likely to be the most comfortable chair you can find. *False*

4.3 A product set-up is laid out like a traditional assembly line. *True*

4.4 A firm may be selling a physical product and still be classified as a service type of business. *True*

4.5 One of the objectives of a purchasing system is to maximize the amount of inventory. *False*

4.6 The terms *logistics* and *supply chain management* are commonly used interchangeably. *True*

4.7 It is possible to make business deals with customers or suppliers that do not involve the exchange of money. *True*

4.8 *Bookkeeping* and *accounting* are interchangeable terms. *False*

4.9 A Gantt chart is a type of bar graph. *True*

4.10 A flow chart shows the single chronological series of procedures that a business uses. *False*

4.11 An entrepreneur should strive to always deliver the highest quality product or service possible. *False*

4.12 In Canada, all business records can be thrown out after seven years. *False*

4.13 Database and presentation software are typically part of office management packages. *True*

4.14 Your accounts payable represents money you expect to collect from your customers. *False*

4.15 A business owner with no employees can still be considered a manager. *True*

4.16 The terms *goals* and *objectives* are interchangeable. *False*

4.17 It is possible for a small business to have more jobs on its organization chart than there are people working for the company. *True*

4.18 *Accountability* refers to those things on which a person's performance will be measured. *True*

4.19 *Authority, accountability,* and *responsibility* all have the same meaning. *False*

4.20 *Leadership* and *management* are interchangeable terms. *False*

4.21 Salary is classified as an employee benefit. *False*

4.22 It is better for independent business owners to pay themselves regular salaries than it is to take money out of the business as it is needed for personal use. *True*

4.23 Building and sign permits generally come from the provincial level of government. *False*

4.24 For a sole proprietorship, business taxes are calculated as part of the personal tax return. *True*

Questions for Discussion

1. Try to explain the human tendency to buy things that we really don't need. Use personal examples and discuss how entrepreneurs can guard against this.

2. How is a classroom an efficient layout for the activities of teaching and learning? Find improvements for the room you are in now.

3. Speculate about why small entrepreneurs are slow to adapt new methods and systems for efficient ordering, delivery, and inventory control. What advantages do they have over larger competitors?

4. Discuss whether money can be a motivator for employees and under what circumstances. What are the most powerful employee motivators?

Recommended Reading

Drucker, Peter F. *The Essential Drucker: The Best Sixty Years of Peter Drucker's Writings on Management.* New York: HarperCollins Publishers, 2001.

Ellis, Carol W. *Management Skills for New Managers.* New York: American Management Association, 2005.

Kemp, Sid. *Quality Management Demystified.* New York: McGraw-Hill, 2006.

Ricci, Monica. *Organize Your Office in No Time.* Indianapolis: Que Publishing, 2006.

Various. *Ready-To-Use Business Forms.* North Vancouver: Self-Counsel Press, 2002.

The Business Plan, Section 4: Operations

SPACE AND EQUIPMENT

1. Briefly list all the equipment, furniture, and vehicles you will need to run your business. (Include both the items you already own and those you need to acquire.) Justify your needs.

_____

_____

_____

_____

_____

_____

_____

2. If yours is a retail or consumer service business, sketch a layout of the store identifying entrances, windows, displays, cash, and so on. If there is a wholesale or manufacturing component to the business, sketch a layout of the work and storage areas, identifying all equipment and explaining the use of each area.

_____

_____

_____

_____

_____

_____

_____

LOGISTICS

3. Explain your systems for buying, ordering, and storing any supplies that your business will depend on.

_____

_____

_____

_____

_____

_____

4. Identify any subcontractors or suppliers that you intend to use. Explain the services or products that they will provide and the details of contracting arrangements that you will have with them. Be sure to include any professional advisers you may use, such as accountants or lawyers.

_____

_____

_____

_____

_____

_____

_____

_____

METHODS AND PROCEDURES

5. Briefly explain and/or chart the process that you will use to complete a typical client or customer transaction.

_____

_____

_____

_____

_____

_____

_____

_____

6. Explain any methods or systems you will have for ensuring quality and handling customer complaints.

_____

_____

_____

_____

_____

_____

_____

_____

SYSTEMS

7. Explain the paperwork and/or software systems that you will use to control your business in terms of scheduling, inventory, billing, work progress, client records, and accounting.

_____

_____

_____

_____

_____

_____

_____

_____

ORGANIZATION

8. If more than one person will be working in the business, explain who will do what, who has what authorities, and who is whose boss. If you have one or more partners, refer to details in the partnership agreement. If you will have employees, attach an organization chart along with one-page job descriptions for each major job as appendices.

_____

_____

_____

_____

_____

_____

_____

_____

9. Explain how and when you, any partners, and employees will be compensated (hourly, salary, drawings), and any payroll deductions or contributions you will make for taxes, benefits, and so on.

_____

_____

_____

_____

_____

_____

_____

REGULATION

10. Identify any registrations, licences, or permits that you will be required to have for your business.

_____

_____

_____

_____

_____

_____

_____

_____

_____

11. Identify any professional groups or business associations that you will belong to and explain the reason for your membership. (Note any fees.)

_____

_____

_____

_____

_____

_____

_____

_____

_____

Finances:
How Will I Manage the Money?

LEARNING OBJECTIVES

On completion of this chapter, you should be able to:

- *Explain the purpose of financial statements.*
- *Outline the asset requirements for a new business.*
- *Define the accounting equation.*
- *Describe how profit is calculated.*
- *Apply the concept of "break-even" in calculating a break-even point.*
- *Identify various needs for cash-flow planning.*
- *Identify sources of help for financial management.*
- *Compare a variety of sources for start-up financing.*
- *Complete the finances portion of the business plan.*

The finances section of the business plan outlines:

- How much money you need to start into business.
- How much money you need to operate as a business.
- Where the start-up money will come from.
- How you will be able to keep paying your bills.
- How much profit you will make and when.

This may sound like a lot of information, but you already have the basis for most of it in the previous sections of your business plan. It's largely a matter of organizing the information and shopping around to see what things will cost you.

How Will I Explain the Business Finances?

You don't have to know a lot about accounting to run your own business. In fact, the more you get advice from your accountant, the better for the business.[1] But if you're going to talk to other businesspeople (banker, investor, consultant) about the finances for your venture, you have to acquire some basic accounting vocabulary. This is where it gets just a little confusing because accountants have several different terms for each accounting idea. But don't worry. You don't have to know all the financial jargon in order to understand the financial concepts.

Don't underestimate how much you already know about business finance. It's really no different from personal finance, and most people have some experience with handling problems in that area. The issues are simple: you own some things; you owe some money; you have money that comes in; you have money that goes out. What you want is more coming in than going out so that you can own more and owe less. It's the same with business.

FINANCIAL STATEMENTS   The standard way of explaining the finances of any business is with financial statements. These are documents that show what has happened to the business financially over a period of time and where the business stands at a particular moment in time. There are a variety of different documents that can be called financial statements, but a business plan is usually only concerned with the three main types:

- **Balance sheet:** Shows where the business stands in terms of what it owns, what it owes, and how much investment the owners have in the business.
- **Income statement:** Shows the sales of the business over a period of time (for example a year), what it cost to conduct business during that period, and how much profit (or loss) was made during that period.
- **Cash-flow statement:** Represents the same period as the income statement and gives details of cash coming into the business, cash going out of the business, and how these have affected the bank balance of the business. This is usually broken down on a monthly basis.

Ask yourself: If a business doesn't yet exist, how can it have financial statements? The business plan for a brand-new venture must use **projected financial statements** to explain the financial plan for the business. These represent your expectation of what's going to happen financially over the first three (or more) years of business activity.

- *Projected balance sheets.* You will have several of these. They will show where the business will stand financially on opening day, at the end of the first year, at the end of the second year, and at the end of the third year.
- *Projected income statements.* You'll have three of these, one for each of the first three years of business. They will show the year's expected sales, costs, expenses, and profit (or loss). In a sense, they will explain why the balance sheet (the company's financial position) will have changed each year.
- *Projected cash-flow statements.* There will be three of these covering the same periods as the income statements. By planning when cash comes in and goes out of your business, you will demonstrate that you will always be able to pay the bills that are due.

balance sheet A statement of the financial position of a business at a particular point in time.

income statement A statement of a business's profit or loss over a given period of time.

cash-flow statement A statement of cash going into and out of a business over a given period of time, and how this has affected the cash balance.

projected financial statements Statements predicting what the financial performance and position of a business will be in the future. Sometimes called *pro forma* financial statements.

Get Help 5.1
Many small accounting firms specialize in working with small businesses or self-employed people. Ask some entrepreneurs whom they use. In some cases you can get help from a senior student—ask a business teacher at your local college.

Even when you have an accountant prepare the statements for you, however, the actual planning decisions are yours. Furthermore, it is not economical to pay an accountant to ask you all the little details about the finances of your venture. Instead, you can organize all the information needed for the projected statements *before* you start paying for the accountant's time. All you have to know are a few basic terms; for example, *assets, liabilities,* and *equity.*

ASSETS   You or your accountant will need information about **assets** in order to complete the *opening-day balance sheet. Ask yourself: What are my assets?*

assets Things that are owned and have monetary value.

You may consider the fact that you're physically strong or particularly good-looking to be an asset. But when it comes to finance, an asset is something that is *owned*, rather than a personal attribute. It must also have some monetary value. You may have legal title to the 15-year-old Chevrolet with no engine sitting in your backyard. So you own it. But it's not an asset because it has no monetary value—it's going to cost more to tow it away than you could sell it for.

Doubtless, you will need some assets to operate in business. For a math tutoring business, the assets are little more than a telephone and some pencils and paper. For a building foundation contractor, assets may be vehicles, heavy equipment, and cash. Some of the assets you might already have. Others you will have to acquire.

Assets are traditionally divided into two categories. Those that tend to be more permanent in value (vehicles, equipment, machinery, land, buildings) are called **fixed assets**. Others are less permanent in value, or more *liquid*. They tend to be used up or change their form quickly (within a year) and are called **current assets**. Current assets include office supplies, inventory, prepaid expenses (like insurance or licences), any money that your customers owe you (this is called **accounts receivable**—but you shouldn't have any on opening day), and, of course, the cash you will need in your bank to run the business.

fixed assets Things that are owned and that tend to keep their value or form for long periods (in excess of a year). Examples are buildings, machinery, and equipment.

current assets Things that are owned and tend to be impermanent in value or form. Examples are cash, inventory, and prepaid expenses.

accounts receivable Assets in the form of money that is owed to a company by its customers.

Head Start Exercise

5.1   Complete Table 5.1 to indicate the materials, supplies, insurance, cash, inventory, and so on that you will need to come up with before your business can open. (Do not include equipment or machinery.) Estimate the monetary value of each item and enter it into the appropriate column to indicate whether you already own it or must buy it. (1 page maximum.)

At this point you will only be guessing how much cash you will need on hand to operate the business. Later, when you look at how cash will come into your business and when bills will be due, you can more accurately predict how much of a cash cushion you will need to stay operating.

Table 5.1

MATERIAL AND OPERATING CASH NEEDS (for start-up)		
Materials and Cash (Current Assets)	**$ Value**	
	Already Have	**Need**

Head Start Exercise

✓ **Test Yourself 5.2**
True or False? Cash is an example of a current asset.

5.2   Use Table 5.2 to list the fixed assets you will need in your business. Estimate the monetary value of each item and enter it into the appropriate column to indicate whether you already own it or must purchase it. Do not include items that will be leased or rented for the business. (1 page maximum.) (Refer to Section 4 of your plan.)

liabilities Legal debts; money owed by a business.

LIABILITIES   Now that you've listed the business assets (things owned), you must consider the liabilities (things owed). It's not a **liability** to owe a favour to your unemployed brother-in-law (whom you may consider to be a liability himself). We're talking here about *legal debts*, with monetary value.

Like assets, liabilities come in two varieties: current liabilities and long-term liabilities. It's not critical that you know the difference, but it will save time (and money) when explaining your anticipated debts to your accountant. **Current liabilities** are any debts that will be paid off within a year. This would include things like short-term loans, credit terms which suppliers might give you, and even the last 12 months worth of payments on a long-term loan.

current liabilities Short-term debts that will have to be paid off within a year or less.

Head Start Exercise

5.3   Write down any credit terms you expect to get from suppliers. Would you expect to owe anything to suppliers on the first day of business? How much? ($\frac{1}{3}$ page maximum).

Table 5.2

EQUIPMENT NEEDS (for start-up)

Equipment (Fixed Assets)	$ Value	
	Already Have	Need

Long-term liabilities are debts that will take more than a year to pay off and include things like long-term loans for buying vehicles or equipment and mortgages on land and buildings. By this point in your planning you will have an idea of whether you will have enough money to buy everything you need to get into business. You will also need some extra cash to run things at first, before you get regular income from customers. If you (and your partners or investors) won't have enough of your own money, you may have to borrow. Expect to revise your thinking on this several times while refining your plan.

long-term liabilities Debts that will have to be paid off within a period greater than one year.

Head Start Exercise

5.4 Make a note of any long-term loans you think you will need, indicating what the money will be used for ($\frac{1}{8}$ page maximum).

EQUITY   Equity is the amount of financial claim an owner has on an asset. It measures wealth. *Ask yourself: Who is the richest person I know? How rich are they?*

equity The amount of claim an individual has on an asset; or the measure of an individual's wealth.

Perhaps you are thinking of someone who lives in a $400,000 home and drives a new $60,000 Cadillac. That's $460,000 worth of assets right there. But think of someone else who lives in a $100,000 home and drives an older, used car that's worth only $10,000. *Ask yourself: Which of these two people is richer?* Well, you don't know. You can't judge how rich someone is by their assets alone. You must also consider their liabilities.

Let's say the Cadillac driver purchased his or her home with a 25-percent down payment and still owes $300,000 on a mortgage. If the house were sold for $400,000, $300,000 would go to pay off the bank and the owner would only get to keep the $100,000. So, this person only has $100,000 claim, or *equity* in the home. If the Cadillac was bought with a $5,000 down payment, $55,000 would still be owing on the car and the owner would only have the $5,000 as equity. This would give the Cadillac driver a total equity of $105,000.

But let's say our used-car owner owns the $100,000 home outright, with no mortgage owing. This person paid cash for the $10,000 car, and has no other debts. This used car driver's equity, or wealth, totals $110,000. This is the richer one. How rich someone is, or their equity, is not just a measure of the assets they own but also of the debts they owe—their liabilities. This can be expressed as an equation:

$$Equity = Assets - Liabilities$$

This equation can also be expressed in a slightly different way, with the assets on the left:

$$Assets = Liabilities + Equity$$

If you don't know enough mathematics to understand that these equations are the same, just accept it. It's true. And it is this second way of expressing the equation that is important to your accountant, because this is the **accounting equation.**

accounting equation The basis for the balance sheet, showing that the value of assets is equal to the sum of the values of liabilities and equity.

✓ **Test Yourself 5.3**
True or False? The balance sheet is an example of a financial statement.

It means that the value of all the "stuff" in the business (*assets*) is equal to the amount of money owed by the business (*liabilities*) plus however much the owners have invested of their own money (*equity*). For example, you may be a musician with a $5,000 sound system (*assets*), but you still owe $1,000 to a finance company (*liability*) from the purchase. You, therefore, have a $4,000 investment (*equity*) in your business.

$$\$5,000 = \$1,000 + \$4,000$$
(asset)   (liability) (equity)

Head Start Exercise

5.5 Estimate how much equity you will have in your new venture by adding up the value of any cash or assets that you already own that will be used in the business ($\frac{1}{4}$ page maximum).

BALANCE SHEET   The information that you have put together in Head Start Exercises 5.1–5.5 is all that's needed to assemble an opening-day balance sheet. When you give the information to your accountant you will be saving him or her lots of time (and yourself some money) since the information is already organized.

✓ **Test Yourself 5.4**
True or False? The accounting equation is "assets = liabilities − equity."

You may want to save even more by creating the balance sheet yourself and just having the accountant check it over. This won't be hard since you already know the basis for the format of the balance sheet—the accounting equation, or

$$Assets = Liabilities + Equity$$

Just as the left side of the equation must balance with the right side of the equation, the left side of the balance sheet must balance with the right side.

Figure 5.1 is the balance sheet from a new company that installs video surveillance equipment. The company has $21,179 worth of assets (on the left) and this same amount is the value of the liabilities and equity (on the right). They have to be the same because a balance sheet must balance.

| Figure 5.1 | **OPEN EYE EQUIPMENT \| Balance Sheet** |

(Date)

CURRENT ASSETS			CURRENT LIABILITIES		
Cash	$ 4,000		Accounts payable	$ 122	
Inventory	2,100		Total	122	$ 122
Accounts receivable	nil				
Prepaid expenses	1,106		LONG-TERM LIABILITIES		
Office supplies	73		Car loan	$ 8,400	
Total	7,279	$ 7,279	Bank loan	2,750	
			Total	$11,150	$11,150
FIXED ASSETS					
Automobile	$11,300		TOTAL LIABILITIES	$11,272	$11,272
Computer equipment	1,700				
Furniture/fixtures	900		OWNER'S EQUITY		$ 9,907
Total	13,900	$13,900			
Total Assets		**$21,179**	**Total Liabilities and Owner's Equity**		**$21,179**

Typically, balance sheets no longer divide the page into left and right; rather, the right side just follows along below the left side, as in the example for a formalwear rental business shown in Figure 5.2. Nevertheless, people still talk about the "left" and "right" sides of the balance sheet. The date on the balance sheet is critically important because it shows how the company stood at a particular moment in time: the following day supplies could be used up and customers might pay some bills, so the balance sheet would change.

COSTS AND EXPENSES   *Ask yourself: Is there a difference between "costs" and "expenses"? In regular usage, the terms *cost* and *expense* are used interchangeably. For the purposes of the business plan, however, we will need to distinguish between the two.

As much as possible, the term *cost* should refer to what we pay for something that we resell to our customers. This is referred to, more precisely, as **cost of goods sold.**

Cost of goods sold is a critical element of the income statement. The sales of our business minus the cost of goods sold equals our "gross profit." For example, a store selling western hats may have had $300,000 in sales last year, but the owner of the store paid $140,000 (cost of goods sold) for those same hats. So, this has produced a **gross profit** of $160,000. The

✓ **Test Yourself 5.5**
True or False? Referring to Figure 5.1, the owner of Open Eye Equipment has a personal investment of $9,907 in the business.

✓ **Test Yourself 5.6**
True or False? Referring to Figure 5.1, at the time of the balance sheet, no one owes money to Open Eye Equipment.

◇ **Get Help 5.2**
If you wish to better understand balance sheets, find someone with training in this area (a bookkeeper, accounting student) and discuss the example line by line.

cost of goods sold What a business paid for the goods that it purchased and resold over a given period of time.

gross profit The sales of our business minus the cost of goods sold over a given period of time.

Figure 5.2	**TRES HOT FORMALS	Balance Sheet**

Opening Day   **(Date)**

ASSETS

CURRENT ASSETS

Cash	$ 2,010	
Rental inventory	14,500	
Prepaid expenses	2,230	
Supplies	400	
Total current assets		$19,140

FIXED ASSETS

Store fixtures	$ 4,250	
Equipment	1,000	
Vehicles	9,950	
Total fixed assets		$15,200
Total Assets		**$34,340**

LIABILITIES

CURRENT LIABILITIES

Accounts payable	$ 1,080	
Short-term loans payable	3,500	
Other current liabilities	nil	
Total current liabilities		$ 4,580

LONG-TERM LIABILITIES

Long-term loans payable	$ 8,000	
Other long-term liabilities	nil	
Total long-term liabilities		$ 8,000

OWNER'S EQUITY

| Total investment | | $21,760 |
| **Total Liabilities and Owner's Equity** | | **$34,340** |

owner of the store cannot go out and buy a vacation condo with the $160,000, however, because much of that money must be used to pay for rent, insurance, advertising, and so on. These are the operating **expenses** of the business.

If the hat business has expenses totalling $110,000, the owner now has $50,000 net profit to do with as he or she sees fit (after paying taxes, of course). This is the essence of the income statement, as shown in Figure 5.3.

expenses All the money a company pays out (other than cost of goods sold) in order to stay in business. This includes things like rent, utilities, supplies, advertising, salaries, and so on.

Figure 5.3

HAT BUSINESS | Income Statement

For the one-year period ending (Date)

Sales	$300,000
Cost of Goods Sold	$140,000
Gross Profit	$160,000
Operating Expenses	$110,000
Net Profit	$ 50,000

For many straightforward, service-type operations, the only money to be shelled out will be in the form of expenses, since there are no goods to be resold. If your business is reselling goods, you already have a sales forecast and you should have a rough idea of what your products will cost you (as a percentage of your selling price). It won't be hard to estimate, from your sales forecast, your cost of goods sold for the first year of business.

Head Start Exercise

5.6   If you will be selling tangible products, estimate your cost of goods sold for your first year of business. Base this on your sales forecast from Section 2 of your business plan. ($\frac{1}{4}$ page maximum).

As you have been preparing all the elements of your business plan to date, you have been identifying your various operating expenses. Since you have identified the site for your business, you are now able to figure out how much you will have to pay each year for your rent, utilities, property taxes, and so on. Since you have identified your advertising techniques, you can add up what you will pay to advertise for a year. You also know what you will have to pay for insurance, salaries, and so on. Next, you will go through all of your plan thus far and estimate what your annual operating expenses will be in each area.

But there is one important expense that you have not yet considered: **depreciation**. Depreciation is the loss in value of an asset over time. Let's say you invest $1,000 in a lawn mower that you will use to start a lawn maintenance business. This is your equity. If you pay all your basic expenses and then spend the "profit," at the end of two years you will find that your lawn mower is totally worn out and must be replaced. You have essentially "spent" the equity in your business and will need another $1,000 to buy a new mower if you are to keep operating. Instead, you should treat the wearing out of the lawn mower as an operating expense. In this way, you can set aside money to replace depreciating assets.

Assets decline in value not just from getting worn out. They also become obsolete.[2] Let's say you buy high-quality video editing software for your business at a price of $1,000. Two years later, the software may be working exactly as it did on day one, but in the meantime

Get Help 5.3

You can look up the average percentage that cost of goods sold represents of sales for your industry (or a similar industry) in the small-business profiles published by Statistics Canada. These are available in many libraries. Or, check Performance Plus at **www.sme.ic.gc.ca**.

depreciation An asset's loss in value over a given period of time.

✓ Test Yourself 5.7

True or False? Gross profit is the difference between sales and cost of goods sold.

Get Help 5.4

There are often choices in how to depreciate an asset, and your accountant is your best adviser. Commonly, however, small businesses use the standard "capital cost allowance" rates allowed by Canada Revenue Agency. These rates are listed in the *Business and Professional Income Guide* available at any tax office, or go to the CRA website **www.cra-arc.gc.ca** and search *Business and Professional Income*.

better software has become available for only $300. What is your asset worth now? It has depreciated because it is obsolete. This depreciation is an expense of your business.

Head Start Exercise

5.7 Using Table 5.3, analyze all of your planning so far and estimate all of your operating expenses for the first year (1 page maximum).

Table 5.3	**ONGOING EXPENSES**	
Expense		**Annual $ Amount**
rent		
utilities		
equipment lease		
salaries (include yourself)		
insurance		
depreciation		
interest		
maintenance		
professional fees		
advertising		
supplies		
delivery		
travel		
other		
total		

INCOME STATEMENT In order to prepare a projected income statement it is necessary to figure out what your sales will be. You have already done this in Section 2 (Feasibility) of your business plan. You have now listed your costs of goods sold and your operating expenses, so there is sufficient information for you or your accountant to draft projected income statements. You will likely need one for each of your first three years of business. Figure 5.4 is a typical projected income statement for the first year of business. In this case, the operation is a small software retailer that expects to get some of its revenue from software sales and the rest from program set-ups and customizing work.

Figure 5.4   **SOFTWARE SOLVERS | Income Statement (projected)**

For the First Year of Business

SALES

Product sales	$110,000	
Programming services	35,000	
Total sales income	$145,000	$145,000

COSTS

Cost of goods sold		$ 61,000

GROSS PROFIT

Gross profit		$ 84,000

EXPENSES

Rent	$11,000	
Utilities	2,600	
Salaries/drawings	45,000	
Insurance	1,560	
Depreciation	8,400	
Interest	840	
Professional fees	1,800	
Advertising	6,500	
Supplies	300	
Travel	4,200	
Total operating expenses	$82,200	$ 82,200

NET PROFIT

Net before income tax		$ 1,800	$1,800
Income tax			600
Net Profit after Income Tax			**$1,200**

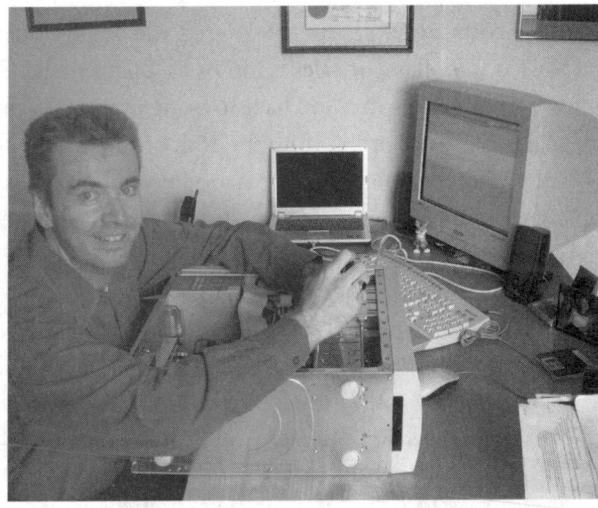

SMALL BUSINESS PROFILE 5.1

iJET Technology Services

Tim MacDonald is an information technology consultant specializing in networking and trouble-shooting for small- and medium-sized professional firms such as law offices and medical clinics. This is a second venture for Tim, the first being a marketing services company where a number of family members were involved in the business. That partnership failed but from it he learned the lessons of having precise, well-written agreements and clear decision-making authority. The path from the failed family business to Tim's current venture was not a direct one.

Tim had been working for a major airline using planning and scheduling systems for which the airline provided extensive software training. He was laid off in 2001, with the downturn in the airline business, so he set out to gain Microsoft certification in order to secure a job. During this period, through his personal contacts, Tim started to get small jobs for software installation and network trouble-shooting that became progressively larger. By the summer of 2002, Tim, working from home, found himself running a full-time business, all from repeat and referral clientele.

Even today, working from the office where he moved in 2005, Tim still does minimal promotion (ads in a legal newsletter and through his website—*www.ijet.ca*) but the business remains strong. For Tim, the office is almost unnecessary as he runs a practically paperless operation, scanning and transferring any paper he does get into electronic files. Tim feels that he should be able to access any document related to his business from anywhere that he happens to be.

The most significant financial lesson that Tim has learned along the way is to "trust your instincts when it comes to extending credit." The one time that Tim could not collect was from a new client that he felt uncomfortable about extending credit to, although he could find no logical reason for this. Regardless, his feelings proved right. Now, for large contracts, he always gets substantial deposits and with his established customers, the occasional late payment requires nothing more than a reminder call.

How Will I Track the Finances?

BREAK-EVEN *Ask yourself: Why would I be interested in just breaking even, when the goal of my business is to make a profit?* The purpose of financial statements is to help you plan and track what is going on in your business, ultimately to make sure you make a profit. But these are complex tools, and often difficult for the average self-employed businessperson to use. It's not unusual for small-business people to look at their financial statements only at the end of each quarter or, in some cases, only at the end of the year when they have their personal tax return completed.

But if you have to wait months to find out if you're making a profit, you may already be out of business by the time you get the news. What you need is a tool that will help you gauge on a monthly, weekly, or even daily basis whether you are making a profit. What you need is a break-even number.

break-even The point at which a company starts to make a profit. The point where sales are sufficient to cover all of the costs and expenses of a company.

Break-even is the point at which all of your costs and expenses are covered and where you are starting to make a profit. It can be expressed in dollars, or sales units, or as a percentage. For example, if you are a safety consultant you might know that you have to bring in $3,600 worth of billings each month before you are making any net profit. If it's the 15th of the month and you have only brought in $1,250, it's time to either get nervous or make a lot of phone calls to potential customers. As a bicycle shop owner, you may know that you must sell 12 bikes a week in order to break even. If you have 15 bikes sold by Thursday afternoon, you know it's going to be a good week. As a bed-and-breakfast owner, you may know that you must have a 30-percent occupancy rate to be profitable. If your place has been at least half full every day for the past month, you know you're making money. *Ask yourself: What measurement would be the most appropriate way for me to think of break-even: dollars? a number of units sold? a percentage of my capacity? What period is most important for me to consider break-even in: monthly? weekly? daily?*

Break-even is a *guideline:* it is not a very precise tool, but still can be extremely valuable in helping you track your performance. It can be expressed as a single number or shown on a chart where you can see your amount of profit at different sales levels. You can calculate an annual break-even amount using the information on your income statement. On most income statements, the operating expenses are broken down into two categories:

- **Fixed expenses:** These are the expenses that do not vary with sales. In other words, things you would have to pay whether or not you had any sales. These would include rent, insurance, utilities, and so on, and are normally shown first in the expenses area of the income statement.
- **Variable expenses:** These tend to vary with your sales (or go up as your sales go up). Examples are packaging, delivery, travel, casual labour, and often advertising.

To calculate an annual break-even value, you must first figure out the *contribution ratio*. This just means the portion of each sale that is left after paying its *cost of goods sold* and *variable expenses*. This is the amount that can be used to either pay off the *fixed expenses*, or, when they are paid off, can be kept as profit.

$$\text{Contribution ratio} = \frac{\text{Gross profit} - \text{Variable expenses}}{\text{Sales}}$$

You can now calculate break-even as a dollar value.

$$\text{Break-even} = \frac{\text{Fixed expenses}}{\text{Contribution ratio}}$$

This is only one formula to calculate break-even. There are lots of methods. You may wish to include this valuable tracking tool in your business plan.

CASH FLOW *Ask yourself: Is there a difference between "cash flow" and "profit"?* Lots of potentially profitable business ventures go **bankrupt**, not because they can't make a profit but because the entrepreneurs fail to plan for the way their money comes in and goes out. For most businesses, **revenue** comes in on one schedule but bills become due on a totally different schedule. Because of this, you could find yourself in a position where you are making a profit, but the cash has not yet come in from your customers. At the same time, your **creditors** are taking you to court for non-payment.

In a situation like this there is little use in running to the bank asking for money to tide you over, because few loan officers will feel comfortable lending money to someone who is being chased by creditors, even if they can demonstrate their profitability on paper. The trick is to plan for any future cash shortages before they happen. You must arrange for any financing needs well in advance, when it's not urgent, and when your reputation is intact. You do this with **projected cash-flow** statements. These are also called *cash budgets* and they represent the same periods as your projected income statements. Typically, they are broken down into 12 monthly columns, with rows of information showing:

- the expected sales
- the cash expected to come in
- the cash that will have to go out
- the changes in the bank balance.

Lots of rows of information make cash flow look a little complicated at first, but most of the rows just explain these four basic pieces of information.

fixed expenses Expenses of a business that tend to remain constant, regardless of the sales level of the business. Examples include rent, utilities, and permanent salaries.

variable expenses Expenses of a business that tend to fluctuate with sales. Examples include supplies, packaging, and delivery expenses.

Get Help 5.5
A competent business or accounting student should be able to help you quickly calculate a break-even point.

Test Yourself 5.9
True or False? A break-even number is a very precise financial tool.

bankruptcy When a business does not have sufficient assets or earning power to repay its debts and legal action is taken to dissolve the company and compensate the creditors as much as is possible.

revenue The income of a business from sales.

creditors Those to whom a business owes money.

projected cash flow A statement predicting how money will flow into and out of a business during a given period in the future. Also known as a cash budget.

Test Yourself 5.10
True or False? *Cash flow* and *profit* are interchangeable terms.

Figure 5.5

PROJECTED CASH FLOW | First Year of Operation, New Look Upholstery

MONTH	May	Jun	Jul	Aug	Sep	Oct	Nov	Dec	Jan	Feb	Mar	Apr
Sales	$1,000	$3,000	$5,000	$8,000	$12,000	$16,000	$20,000	$10,000	$15,000	$15,000	$20,000	$25,000
CASH IN-FLOW												
Cash sales	500	1,500	2,500	4,000	6,000	8,000	10,000	5,000	7,500	7,500	10,000	12,500
Account payments received	–	–	500	1,500	2,500	4,000	6,000	8,000	10,000	5,000	7,500	7,500
Cash borrowed from line of credit	–	–	1,600	2,700	1,600	–	–	–	–	–	–	–
Total Cash In-flow (a)	500	1,500	4,600	8,200	10,100	12,000	16,000	13,000	17,500	12,500	17,500	20,000
OPENING Cash Balance (b)	14,000	7,000	2,050	100	100	70	330	1,690	210	7,690	10,370	15,420
CASH OUT-FLOW												
Rent	800	800	800	800	800	800	800	800	800	800	800	800
Utilities	200	200	200	220	230	240	240	240	260	260	250	240
Vehicle expenses	200	250	250	280	300	300	300	240	260	260	300	300
Supplies	800	200	300	400	600	800	800	400	600	500	800	1,000
Loan payments	–	–	–	100	100	1,500	4,400	–	–	–	–	–
Payroll/drawings	4,500	4,500	4,500	4,500	7,500	7,500	7,500	10,000	7,500	7,500	9,500	9,500
Advertising	1,000	500	500	500	600	600	600	200	600	500	800	800
Taxes	–	–	–	1,400	–	–	–	2,600	–	–	–	8,200
Total Cash Out-flow (c)	7,500	6,450	6,550	8,200	10,130	11,740	14,640	14,480	10,020	9,820	12,450	20,840
CLOSING Cash Balance (a + b − c)	7,000	2,050	100	100	70	330	1,690	210	7,690	10,370	15,420	14,580

The example shown in Figure 5.5 is for an upholstery shop that gets about half of its business from consumers who pay with cash, and the other half from business customers who can take up to two months to settle their accounts. If you're looking at a cash-flow projection for the first time, don't panic. Just concentrate on one column, one item at a time, as you try to make sense of it. And remind yourself that it's only a tool to check that you won't run out of cash when your bills are due. It will become more clear as you assemble the information that will go into it.

The first task in preparing a cash-flow projection is to look at your annual sales forecasts and then break these down into monthly forecasts. This is part guesswork, part experience, and part logic. Virtually all businesses have some seasonal fluctuation. For example, December, July, and August are big vacation months, which means lots of business for tourist restaurants. However, there is also a decrease in new project starts or capital expenditures by larger organizations (which might make up your customers) during these months.

Many businesses have their own unique patterns. An ice sculptor may be extremely busy in the summer (wedding decorations) and February (winter carnivals) but really slow the rest of the year. A florist may sell more roses around Valentine's Day than during all the rest of the year put together.

For a new business, the problem of monthly fluctuations is compounded by the expected pattern of growth. This issue was examined when you prepared your sales forecast and now must be considered again when you look at sales by month.

Get Help 5.6
Check trade journals for your industry, looking for articles on seasonal fluctuations in business.

Head Start Exercises

5.8 Write down the main issues that will affect how your business will fluctuate monthly throughout the year. Also write down the issues that will affect the initial growth of your business. ($\frac{1}{4}$ page maximum)

5.9 Using Table 5.4, take the sales forecast from Section 2 of your business plan and break it down into monthly sales predictions for the first three years of business. Keep the issues of growth and seasonal fluctuation in mind. (1 page maximum.)

Go back and make sure that your totals are the same as your annual sales forecasts shown in Section 2 of your business plan, and that they also match any figures you have used for your projected income statements. If the totals don't match, it may be time to rewrite one or both components.

Test Yourself 5.11
True or False? Almost all businesses have some form of seasonal fluctuation in sales.

For many businesses the cash comes in as soon (or almost as soon) as the sale is made. These include businesses that accept payment by credit card, debit card, cheque, or automatic withdrawal, as well as actual cash money. In these cases, the cash flow will show exactly the same information in the *sales* row as in the *total cash in* row.

But let's say you give your customers 30 days to pay and you know from experience that only half of them will pay within the 30 days. The others will take between 30 and 60 days to actually get the money to you. If your sales are $10,000 in your first month, none of that money will flow into the business during that month. Half of it, $5000, will come in during the following month, and the other $5000 will arrive two months after the sale. This situation is shown in Table 5.5.

Table 5.4	SALES FORECAST BY MONTH		
Month	Year 1	Year 2	Year 3
1	$	$	$
2			
3			
4			
5			
6			
7			
8			
9			
10			
11			
12			
Total Sales Forecast	$	$	$

Table 5.5	CASH COMING IN			
	Month 1	Month 2	Month 3	Month 4
Sales	$10,000	12,000	14,000	16,000
Cash in		5,000	11,000	13,000

The cash in during Month 3 is made up of half the sales from Month 1 ($5000) and half the sales from Month 2 ($6000).

Ask yourself: How complicated can it get to predict the cash coming into my business? Imagine that some of your customers will pay cash at the time of sale, some will get 30 days to pay (with a third of those taking 60 days to pay) and some will get 60 days (with some of those actually taking 90). It would become a very complex chore to figure out how much money would be coming in each month. *Ask yourself: Do I want to reconsider my credit-granting policy?*

Head Start Exercise

5.10 Review your credit and collections decisions from Section 2 of your business plan. Write some notes that will explain any time gap between when your sales are made and when the cash will come in to your bank account. ($\frac{1}{3}$ page maximum)

The cash that you put out for costs and expenses is called **expenditures**. In planning for your projected income statements, you have already listed the ongoing costs and expenses you will have to pay for a full year. In order to plan your cash flow, however, you will have to provide some more detail about when you will actually pay these bills. And unfortunately, many of your bills won't come due in nice equal monthly amounts.

For example, you may have insurance to pay of $1,000 per year (as shown on your income statement), but the insurance company might require that you pay 6 months in advance. That means that you will have prepaid $500 before opening the business (this will show as a **prepaid expense** on your balance sheet), but you will have to pay another $500 every 6 months. So your cash-flow projection will show a $500 payment in your 6th month of operations and another $500 payment in your 12th month.

You may plan to run a weekly ad in your local Saturday newspaper, and the paper will bill you on a monthly basis. This means that you won't have any advertising expense to pay in your first month, because the first month's advertising bill won't arrive until the second month. Simple. Unfortunately, not all months have four Saturdays; some have five. So when it comes to planning your advertising expense you will have to sit down with a calendar and plan for a bigger bill in the months following the months with five Saturdays. Not so simple.

The people who are best at financial planning are imaginative thinkers—those with the ability to visualize the future *comings and goings* of money. Use your imagination for this process when you write down each of your conclusions about when bills will have to be paid.

expenditures The money a business pays out in a given period for costs and operating expenses.

prepaid expenses Expenses of a business that must be paid in advance, such as insurance and legal retainers. The value of the prepaid expense shows as an asset on the balance sheet and the value goes down as the value of the expense is used up.

Head Start Exercise

5.11 Use Table 5.6 as an aid to analyzing when you will be making various payments. You have already worked out the first two columns in preparing for your income statement. (1 page maximum.)

After you (and likely your financial adviser) have completed your first draft of the cash flow, you will probably want to go back and re-assess how much cash you will need on hand at start-up to ensure that you will be able to continue paying your bills through the growth period.

Ask yourself: Approximately how much cash do I think I'll need at the start of my business? Typically, new entrepreneurs will underestimate their need for operating cash and the cash-flow projection will demonstrate this by showing a negative bank balance. There are two ways to fix this, of course:

- Replan the expense portions of your business plan, coming up with ways to do things more cheaply, or
- Find a way to get more money (from lenders or investors) to be able to cover your planned expenses.

In fact, you may well do some of both, which leads to the final big question of planning to work for yourself: *Where will I get the money?*

Table 5.6

CASH GOING OUT | Ongoing Costs & Expenses (worksheet)

Cost or Expense	Annual Amount	Payment Period (monthly or other: specify)	Amount per Period

Where Will I Get the Money?

This is the last big question to answer in planning to work for yourself. It is only here at the end of the start-up planning process that the question can be answered. Until this point, there was nothing to get money for. But now there is a clear plan to be financed; the next step is to look at the different sources of funding. *Ask yourself: What are my options for getting start-up money?*

PERSONAL SOURCES   Sometimes a business starts with no financial input from the entrepreneur, but this is rare. More commonly, the new business owner contributes materials and equipment or personal cash, or puts up other personal assets as **collateral** for borrowing money. Many new entrepreneurs risk pretty much everything they have. At first, this sounds pretty daunting—especially when you consider the high rates of new-business failure. But it's not nearly as bad as it sounds. A *business failure* is not necessarily a bankruptcy. Lots of entrepreneurs find that they aren't making any money with their venture and close the operation down before losing very much of their personal assets.

collateral Assets of a borrower that are pledged to a lender in the event of non-payment of a loan.

Risking your own money in a business is critically important if you plan on asking others to risk theirs. Potential lenders and investors want to know how much you're risking; not just as a percentage of the total investment, but also as a percentage of everything you've got in the world. For example, you may ask someone to invest $25,000 in a business that you are putting $5,000 into. If they find out that you are worth $100,000 (you might have this much equity in your home), how would they feel? On the other hand, if they find out that $5,000 is everything you've got in the world (you had to sell your TV to get some of the money), they are going to feel a very different sense of commitment on your part. In both cases, however, you're still only investing $5,000.

✓ **Test Yourself 5.12**
True or False? Collateral refers to assets that a lender may seize if you fail to pay back a loan.

Your own cash is not the only *personal* source of funding. A significant portion of the start-up (or "seed") money for new businesses is borrowed from family and friends. In Canada, this is one of the major sources of start-up capital. This may be due in part to our immigration policies, which give priority to family reunification, the likelihood of immigrants living in an extended family unit, and the fact that immigrants are more likely to start new businesses than are native-born Canadians.

Ask yourself: Who in my family would be able and likely to lend me money for business purposes? This source of seed capital is referred to as **love money** because it is largely loaned on the basis of the relationship as opposed to the strength of the business plan or the amount of collateral. Interestingly, the ease of access to love money seems to be culturally related, with some ethnic groups setting a higher priority on family entrepreneurship.[3]

love money Money that is borrowed from relatives and/or friends for a business venture.

Just because love money might be available to you doesn't mean you'll take it. You may choose other sources, such as banks or partners, since there can be potential problems with love money. Family members with little business background often cannot distinguish between debt and equity. They might lend you money thinking that this makes them your partner. Not only might they wish to interfere in the operation of the business—but also, in some cases, the debt will be never-ending, even after it has been long paid back: "See where she is today? She owes everything to me. I'm the one who got her started. Without me she'd be no place." *Ask yourself: Does this sound like any of my relatives?*

The fact that your uncle will not require a business plan before lending you money is not all good news. The very process of creating the plan increases your chance of a successful start-up and in the long run could save your relationships with family members. In addition, any loans from family should still be formalized with a written agreement explaining all the terms and conditions.

Head Start Exercise

5.12 If you plan on borrowing money from family members or close friends, make a note of the contract terms that you will try to negotiate and how these will avoid potential "love money" problems ($\frac{1}{2}$ page maximum).

GOVERNMENT PROGRAMS   Many millions of dollars are earmarked each year by the federal and provincial governments to assist small entrepreneurs in one way or another. But politicians and bureaucrats are much like managers in other large institutions: they need to prove their accomplishments with statistics. The best kind of stats for entrepreneurial funding programs show lots of activity generated at low administrative cost to the taxpayer. And the administrative cost for making a small loan is just about the same as it is for making a large loan. So if it comes to a choice between making lots of small loans or fewer but larger loans, the big loans win.

This explains the frustration sometimes felt by new entrepreneurs looking for small loans. At times it looks easier for an existing business to borrow $500,000 than it is for a new venture to get $30,000. This has always been a problem when dealing with banks (a problem for which many politicians have criticized the banks), but the same problem is true of government funding.

The other major problem with government programs is that they are always changing. Some programs expire, others run out of money, and for some the rules change. Sometimes a change of government means the end of a program that is brought back to life under a new name. It's hard to keep track. But all that aside, there has been a steadily growing commitment at all levels of government to encourage entrepreneurship, and it is worthwhile for anyone planning self-employment to see what assistance is available.

The **Business Development Bank of Canada (BDC)** is a financial institution owned by the federal government. The BDC offers excellent assistance to entrepreneurs through lending, investing, and reasonable-cost consulting programs. For new small ventures and young entrepreneurs they offer micro-loans (usually up to $25,000), and for early-stage and established businesses they have loan programs going all the way up to $5 million. In addition, they offer numerous specific programs (for example, loans to help companies create a web or ecommerce component of a business or loans for Aboriginal or exporting ventures). They even have a growing *Venture Capital* initiative where they can hold equity in certain businesses. The mandate of the BDC allows it to make loans with less emphasis on collateral than would be typical of banks.

If you want to borrow money for the purchase of fixed assets, you may consider a loan under the **Canada Small Business Financing Program (CSBF).** These loans are negotiated through a regular bank but are like a student loan in the sense that repayment is mostly guaranteed by the federal government. You can borrow up to 90 percent of the value of the assets at reasonable repayment rates, although there are usually some administration fees.

In addition to loans, there are some government grants available for specific purposes. These usually come in the form of tax credits or payments to third parties for specified services. (It's rare to get cash from the government that you could use to purchase tangible assets.) More typically, the money is available for staff training, technical research, tourism development, or export market development. If you have to do some of these things anyway, be sure and check if any of this "free money" is available to you.

If your business is based on some technical innovation or adaptation, there may be financial or expert assistance available from one of the programs of the National Research Council or Industry Canada.

?> Get Help 5.7

There are a number of publications (available in many libraries) that list government funding programs for business. One of the best is the *CCH Government Assistance Manual*, since it is a loose-leaf service that is updated frequently. For additional information try *www.cch.ca*.

BDC The Business Development Bank of Canada—a federal government agency charged with lending money to small and medium enterprises, under reasonable terms.

?> Get Help 5.8

Check the blue pages of the phone book to find your closest BDC office. It is worth a visit even just to collect the wide variety of free pamphlets that are available. Or, check the website at *www.bdc.ca*.

CSBF The Canada Small Business Financing Program, which provides federal government guarantees to banks that lend money to small and medium enterprises for the purchase of fixed assets.

?> Get Help 5.9

You can get information on CSBF loans from branches of most banks. Or, use the search feature of the Strategis website at *www.strategis.ic.gc.ca*.

Human Resources and Social Development Canada (HRSDC) has for some time offered the Self-Employment Benefit Program through various private-sector partners. This is one of the most extensive grant programs for new entrepreneurs and can include personal income support for up to a year as well as training and other support. They finance numerous other programs, especially in the areas of employee training and counselling services.

For Aboriginal entrepreneurs there are several federal initiatives offering training and financial support. In addition, some Canadian Aboriginal bands offer financial assistance to their own members who become entrepreneurs.

The federal government supports a number of regional programs (The Atlantic Canada Opportunities Agency, The Federal Office of Regional Development—Quebec, The Federal Economic Development Initiative for Northern Ontario, Western Economic Diversification Canada) that offer specific regional support to entrepreneurs. As well, there are numerous provincial programs, municipal programs, and co-operative programs involving more than one level of government. Provincial governments produce many free guides on business start-up and often have toll-free information numbers that can direct you to provincial funding programs.

Government should represent more than an information source or source of funding for the new entrepreneur. You may consider government as a group of potential customers—big customers who can always pay their bills. Governments buy a huge range of goods and services and a firm government contract can be an import advantage when seeking other forms of funding.

CHARTERED BANKS   Banks basically lend money to small entrepreneurs in two ways:

1. *Term loans.* These are loans given with a fixed repayment period, usually for fixed assets at a fixed interest rate. They are typically used for things like store fixtures, vehicles, or equipment.
2. *Lines of credit.* These allow a borrower to "overdraft" a chequing account up to a pre-set amount. Typically, the borrower pays back a portion of the outstanding balance each month at a variable interest rate. The amount the borrower has access to is often a percentage of inventory or accounts receivable.

Banks make their lending decisions based on the viability of the business plan, the strength of any collateral you offer, and your personal credit history. The lending decision is made within the bank's policies, but usually it is the person you are dealing with at the branch level who has the final say. The loans officer or branch manager may find it more convenient to imply that some decisions (like loan refusals) are made anonymously at head office, but in most cases you are negotiating with a person holding the necessary authority. And as you know: *everything is negotiable*, from interest rates to the amount of collateral needed.

It is normally difficult for new ventures to get bank financing. But just because a bank turns you down, it doesn't mean you can't get the money. There are lots of competing banks. Try them all. But be sure to always clarify the reasons for a refusal. It may be a matter of restructuring your

---

HRSDC Human Resources and Social Development Canada, the department of the federal government concerned with training and employment. It has various programs that support entrepreneurship and provide training assistance to small business.

? Get Help 5.10
Export Development Canada offers various forms of financial assistance to firms that will be exporting products and services from Canada. Check its website at **www.edc.ca.**

? Get Help 5.11
See the National Research Council website at **www.nrc.ca** or find out about the Government of Canada Innovation Strategy at **www.innovationstrategy.gc.ca.**

? Get Help 5.12
Check out the Human Resources and Social Development Canada website at **www.hrsdc.gc.ca.**

✓ Test Yourself 5.13
True or False? Government grants are rarely available for the purchase of tangible assets.

? Get Help 5.13
Look at the Aboriginal Business Canada website. Start with **www.strategis.ic.gc.ca** and click on the *Site Map* and then *Aboriginal Business Canada.*

? Get Help 5.14
Carefully check the blue pages of your phone book to identify provincial offices that offer information about small business funding. Look for a "Canada Business Service Centre" or check their website at **canadabusiness.ca.**

credit bureau An organization that gathers and reports information on the financial status and borrowing and repayment histories of consumers and businesses.

? Get Help 5.15
You can register to be a supplier to the federal government by calling your regional office of Public Works and Government Services Canada (check the blue pages) and asking for an application for registration or by logging on to **contractscanada.gc.ca**.

✓ Test Yourself 5.14
True or False? Banks typically give lines of credit for the purchase of fixed assets.

? Get Help 5.16
To get a copy of your credit report, call Equifax Canada at 1-800-465-7166 or TransUnion Canada at 1-800-663-9980. The websites are **www.equifax.ca** and **www.tuc.ca**.

✓ Test Yourself 5.15
True or False? Credit bureaus must allow a consumer to see any credit information that they have on that consumer.

business plan or it may be an issue related to your *credit history*—the bank gets this information from a **credit bureau.**

Credit bureaus are provincially regulated and in most provinces may not show your file to anyone without your permission. In addition, you must have access to your own file should you want to check the accuracy of information. And if you plan on borrowing money you should check your file *before* applying for a loan. Then you can attempt to have any inaccuracies corrected. Because of the millions of credit transactions taking place daily, mistakes happen—lots of them. Credit bureau files are full of inaccurate entries and you don't want an error to prevent you from being able to secure financing. Check first.

INVESTORS   When someone invests in your business operation, it means that they will have an *equity position*, that they will own part of the business. They may or may not be active partners in the business. If you have a general partnership, however, don't forget that any partner you may bring in will have the right to be involved in managing the business. In this case, the decision to bring in a partner is far more than an issue of securing funds. *Ask yourself: Other than for investment money, do I really need a partner?*

If you're set up as a corporation, however, it will be easier to maintain control of the business after you bring in investors (as long as you keep at least 51 percent of the shares). Don't forget that there are strict limits on selling the shares of a privately held corporation to avoid the highly regulated and expensive area of publicly traded shares.

You can bring in formal investors in the form of venture capital companies, although it is extremely rare (it does happen) for them to invest in start-up ventures. These firms are large pools of money (from their own investors) intended for investing in other firms. Generally they are looking to invest substantial amounts (millions) in companies that are "high-tech" and that offer high rates of return (30% or more). However, if you are starting a business based on the proprietary rights for a product or technology (that is, you have a patent or the Canadian distribution rights), then you may wish to investigate this source.

More likely, any corporate investors you get will be of the informal variety: **angels.** These are relatively wealthy individuals (often senior or retired professionals) who enjoy taking some risk with a portion of their capital by investing in small business, especially those where they can see themselves providing advice.[4] Most angels seek an opportunity to personally contribute to the venture, at least in an advisory capacity. This implies that *asking for advice* may be a significant tool of persuasion when it comes to recruiting an angel.

angels Wealthy individuals who invest in independent small businesses and who are not related to the business owners.

? Get Help 5.17
You are most likely to find an angel investor through personal contact or an introduction by some other professional such as an accountant, lawyer, or investment dealer. Ask around.

? Get Help 5.18
Check out the website of the Canadian Youth Business Foundation, which is full of valuable links and business-plan examples: **www.cybf.ca**.

OTHER SOURCES   One of Canada's best resources for writing a business plan comes from the Canadian Youth Business Foundation. The website of this not-for-profit organization offers great advice and many valuable links including a wide variety of business plan examples. The organization also has an outstanding loan program for new entrepreneurs between the ages of 18 and 34. Unsecured loans of up to $15,000 are available in conjunction with a free mentoring program.

There are many small local programs available involving prizes for great business plans and entrepreneurship awards. Also, some ethnic communities offer financial help to their own entrepreneurial members, and various service clubs and educational institutions have entre-preneurial awards. It can take a lot of digging to turn up these sources, so keep asking and spend time in the library.

Indirect financing can also be a resource. This would include such things as negotiating gen-erous terms from suppliers (difficult at start-up), helping to get you inventory that hasn't yet been paid for. In rare cases (for example, an art gallery) it could even mean getting inventory on **consignment** (where your supplier lets you display the item and, when you sell it, you share the proceeds with your supplier). It can also mean leasing equipment rather than buy-ing, to reduce any down payment or deposit.

Once you have examined all the possible sources of finance and identified which are avail-able to you, you must start approaching them with your business plan. Don't expect this to be a one-shot deal. You may have to change your plan to meet the requirements of potential investors or lenders. You may have to change the scope of your ideas to fit within the financ-ing available. You may have to do both. Often, it is a tedious, back-and-forth process of nego-tiation that will involve considerable rewriting of the business plan.

✓ **Test Yourself 5.16**
True or False? Angels are wealthy people who lend money to their family members.

indirect financing Methods whereby a business has the use of assets for which it has not paid.

consignment When an item is taken into inventory and held for sale by a business, but still remains the property of the supplier to the business. The proceeds of any sale are split between the supplier and the selling business.

SMALL BUSINESS PROFILE 5.2
Dave Johnson, Dairy Farmer

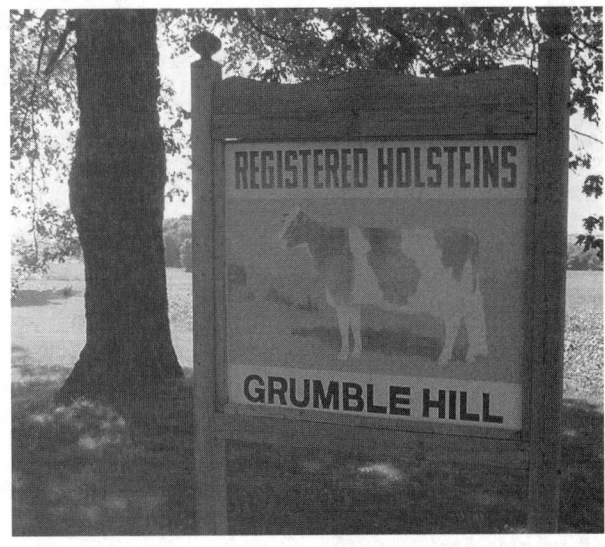

After Dave Johnson graduated from Ryerson, he was working in road construction and had absolutely no experience running a farm. But he knew that farming was what he wanted to do. With his own savings, the investment of two partners, and a big mortgage, he was able to buy a small dairy farm. Then Dave's partners set up a limited partnership to invest in high-quality purebred Holsteins, and Dave's farm was paid to board the cows. The limited partnership received certain tax advantages and the deal gave half of the off-spring of these cows to the farm. In this way, Dave was able to build a very high-quality herd that he could not have financed otherwise.

According to Dave, "Canadian cattle have always had a high repu-tation internationally for quality and health." This, combined with the lineage and high milk production of Dave's cows, meant that he could profitably export breeding cattle all over the world. Then in 2003, mad cow disease was found in Canada, and the U.S. immediately closed the border to all Canadian cattle. By the time of writing, the border has re-opened for Canadian beef, but only for cattle being sent to the U.S. for slaughter; no breeding stock. This ban has effec-tively killed Dave's exports, not only to the U.S., but also to Mexico and Latin America (Canadian cattle may not travel through the U.S. to these destinations), as well as to many other countries that follow the U.S. lead on import restrictions.

Despite all this, Dave still sees advantages in being a Canadian dairy farmer, partly because of Canada's marketing board system. Marketing boards (they may have different names in different provinces) have the authority to control and regulate the production distri-bution and pricing of specific commodities such as milk. They buy all of the production of milk, paying the farmers a fair return, and sell to the processors. The production is generally controlled to about equal the consumption so there are no wild fluctuations in supply and price. Because of this, Dave can count on a predictable, reliable cash in-flow for his business. Nevertheless, Dave's advice to would-be farmers is: "Marry a teacher. You get a steady income and good benefits."

The process of rewriting (and rewriting and rewriting) may be more necessary for the financial section of the business plan than any other. Every other planning decision you make will have some financial implications. Fortunately, the integration of word processors and spreadsheets has greatly reduced the time and effort required for this rewriting. So get started!

✓ Answers to Test Yourself Questions

5.1   The principles are the same for both personal finances and business finances. *True*

5.2   Cash is an example of a current asset. *True*

5.3   The balance sheet is an example of a financial statement. *True*

5.4   The accounting equation is "assets = liabilities − equity." *False*

5.5   Referring to Figure 5.1, the owner of Open Eye Equipment has a personal investment of $9907 in the business. *True*

5.6   Referring to Figure 5.1, at the time of the balance sheet, no one owes money to Open Eye Equipment. *True*

5.7   Gross profit is the difference between sales and cost of goods sold. *True*

5.8   Assets can depreciate, even if they are not being used in a business. *True*

5.9   A break-even number is a very precise financial tool. *False*

5.10 *Cash flow* and *profit* are interchangeable terms. *False*

5.11 Almost all businesses have some form of seasonal fluctuation in sales. *True*

5.12 Collateral refers to assets that a lender may seize if you fail to pay back a loan. *True*

5.13 Government grants are rarely available for the purchase of tangible assets. *True*

5.14 Banks typically give lines of credit for the purchase of fixed assets. *False*

5.15 Credit bureaus must allow a consumer to see any credit information that they have on that consumer. *True*

5.16 Angels are wealthy people who lend money to their family members. *False*

Questions for Discussion

1.   Take a poll of how many in the group suffer from "accountingphobia." Discuss the reasons for this and methods of overcoming it.

2.   How fast do cars depreciate? What are some myths and rules of thumb in this area? What are the factors affecting automobile depreciation?

3.   Why are the cash-flow projections in a business plan so important to lenders and investors? What typical mistakes might new entrepreneurs make in their cash-flow planning?

4.   Why are there so many government programs to support entrepreneurship? What sort of checks and safeguards might be built into these programs?

5.   Discuss methods for building a strong credit history. Why might this be important, even if you have no intention of ever borrowing money?

Recommended Reading

Hill, Brian E. *Attracting Capital From Angels: How Their Money—and Their Experience—Can Help You Build a Successful Company.* New York: John Wiley & Sons, 2002.

Mohr, Angie. *Bookkeepers' Boot Camp: Get a Grip on Accounting Basics.* North Vancouver: Self-Counsel Press, 2003.

Mohr, Angie. *Financing Your Business: Getting a Grip on Finding the Money.* North Vancouver: Self-Counsel Press, 2004.

Nobes, Christopher. *Penguin Dictionary of Accounting.* London: Penguin Books, 2005.

The Business Plan, Section 5: Finances

Entrepreneurs buying or buying into an existing business should complete Sections 1 to 5 of the business plan as well as this portion.

START-UP REQUIREMENTS

1. Complete Table 5.7, indicating all the current assets you will need to come up with before your business can open. This list will include things like office supplies, inventory, prepaid expenses (like insurance or licences), and the cash you will need in your bank account in order to run the business. (Attach this chart as an appendix to your plan.)

Table 5.7

MATERIAL AND OPERATING CASH NEEDS (for start-up)

Materials and Cash (Current Assets)	$ Value	
	Already Have	Need

2. Complete the equipment needs worksheet in Table 5.8 by reviewing the list you have made and establishing prices for what you need or the value of things you already have. (Attach this chart as an appendix to your plan.)

Table 5.8	**EQUIPMENT NEEDS (for start-up)**		
Equipment (Fixed Assets)		**$ Value**	
		Already Have	**Need**

OWNER(S)'S INVESTMENT

3.   Briefly explain how much you, your partner(s), and any other investors (angels, venture capitalists) will be contributing in order to start the business. (Do not include any borrowed money.) Be sure to include the value of those things you already own (cash, equipment, or materials) that will be used exclusively for the business. Also include any expenses you have already paid.

_____
_____
_____
_____
_____
_____
_____
_____
_____
_____

BORROWED MONEY

4.   Indicate any money your business will have to borrow. Identify the lender(s), the interest rate, and the repayment terms. (This amount may have to be estimated for a first draft, then recalculated after completing the balance sheet, and again after completing the cash flow.) Indicate any collateral that may be required.

_____
_____
_____
_____
_____
_____
_____
_____

BALANCE SHEET

5. Prepare a balance sheet for the opening day of your new business (Figure 5.6). After you have completed the rest of the financial section, prepare projected balance sheets for the end of the first, second, and third years (Figures 5.7a, 5.7b, and 5.7c, respectively) of business to indicate how the financial position of the firm will change.

Figure 5.6 | **Balance Sheet**

Opening Day   **(Date)**

ASSETS

CURRENT ASSETS

Cash   _____

Accounts receivable   _____

Inventory   _____

Prepaid expenses   _____

Other current assets   _____

Total current assets   _____

FIXED ASSETS

Land and buildings   _____

Fixtures   _____

Equipment   _____

Vehicles   _____

Other fixed assets   _____

Total fixed assets   _____

Total Assets   ════════

LIABILITIES

CURRENT LIABILITIES

Accounts payable   _____

Short-term loans payable   _____

Taxes payable   _____

Other current liabilities   _____

Total current liabilities   _____

LONG-TERM LIABILITIES

Mortgage payable   _____

Long-term loans payable   _____

Other long-term liabilities   _____

Total long-term liabilities   _____

OWNER'S EQUITY

Total investment   _____

Total Liabilities and Owner's Equity   ════════

Figure 5.7a

Balance Sheet (Year End, Year 1)

(Date)

ASSETS

CURRENT ASSETS

Cash _____

Accounts receivable _____

Inventory _____

Prepaid expenses _____

Other current assets _____

Total current assets _____

FIXED ASSETS

Land and buildings _____

Fixtures _____

Equipment _____

Vehicles _____

Other fixed assets _____

Minus accumulated depreciation (_____)

Total fixed assets _____

Total Assets ════════

LIABILITIES

CURRENT LIABILITIES

Accounts payable _____

Short-term loans payable _____

Taxes payable _____

Other current liabilities _____

Total current liabilities _____

LONG-TERM LIABILITIES

Mortgage payable _____

Long-term loans payable _____

Other long-term liabilities _____

Total long-term liabilities _____

OWNER'S EQUITY

Capital investment _____

Retained earnings _____

Total owner's equity _____

Total Liabilities and Owner's Equity ════════

Figure 5.7b | **Balance Sheet (Year End, Year 2)**

(Date)

ASSETS

CURRENT ASSETS

Cash _____

Accounts receivable _____

Inventory _____

Prepaid expenses _____

Other current assets _____

Total current assets _____

FIXED ASSETS

Land and buildings _____

Fixtures _____

Equipment _____

Vehicles _____

Other fixed assets _____

Minus accumulated depreciation (_____)

Total fixed assets _____

Total Assets _____

LIABILITIES

CURRENT LIABILITIES

Accounts payable _____

Short-term loans payable _____

Taxes payable _____

Other current liabilities _____

Total current liabilities _____

LONG-TERM LIABILITIES

Mortgage payable _____

Long-term loans payable _____

Other long-term liabilities _____

Total long-term liabilities _____

OWNER'S EQUITY

Capital investment _____

Retained earnings _____

Total owner's equity _____

Total Liabilities and Owner's Equity _____

Figure 5.7c **Balance Sheet (Year End, Year 3)**

(Date)

ASSETS
CURRENT ASSETS
Cash _____
Accounts receivable _____
Inventory _____
Prepaid expenses _____
Other current assets _____

Total current assets ════════

FIXED ASSETS
Land and buildings _____
Fixtures _____
Equipment _____
Vehicles _____
Other fixed assets _____
Minus accumulated depreciation (_____)

Total fixed assets _____

Total Assets ════════

LIABILITIES
CURRENT LIABILITIES
Accounts payable _____
Short-term loans payable _____
Taxes payable _____
Other current liabilities _____

Total current liabilities _____

LONG-TERM LIABILITIES
Mortgage payable _____
Long-term loans payable _____
Other long-term liabilities _____

Total long-term liabilities _____

OWNER'S EQUITY
Capital investment _____
Retained earnings _____

Total owner's equity _____

Total Liabilities and Owner's Equity ════════

COSTS AND EXPENSES

6. Complete the ongoing costs and expenses worksheet (Table 5.9) by carefully reviewing all the earlier parts of the business plan and estimating how much you will need to pay annually, as well as on a regular monthly basis, to operate the business. For costs or expenses that are paid on an irregular basis over periods longer than monthly, provide notes to indicate approximately how much and when these items would be paid for—examples might include semi-annual licence fees or large inventory purchases. Be sure to fill in both the annual and monthly (or other period) columns. (Attach this chart as an appendix to your plan.)

Table 5.9 **Ongoing Costs & Expenses (worksheet)**

Cost or Expense	Annual Amount	Payment Period (monthly or other: specify)	Amount per Period

INCOME STATEMENT

7. Using the above information and your sales forecast from Section 2, prepare projected income statements for the first, second, and third years of business (Figures 5.8a, 5.8b, and 5.8c, respectively).

Figure 5.8a | **Income Statement (projected) First Year**

For the One-Year Period Ended: (Date)

SALES

Sales from source #1 _____

Sales from source #2 _____

Total sales income _____

COSTS

Cost of goods sold _____

GROSS PROFIT

Gross profit _____

EXPENSES

Rent _____

Utilities _____

Equipment/lease _____

Salaries/drawings _____

Insurance _____

Depreciation _____

Interest _____

Maintenance _____

Professional fees _____

Advertising _____

Supplies _____

Delivery _____

Travel _____

Total operating expenses _____

NET PROFIT

Net before income tax _____

Income tax _____

Net Profit after Income Tax ========

Figure 5.8b | **Income Statement (projected) Second Year**

For the One-Year Period Ended: (Date)

SALES

Sales from source #1   _____

Sales from source #2   _____

Total sales income   _____

COSTS

Cost of goods sold   _____

GROSS PROFIT

Gross profit   _____

EXPENSES

Rent   _____

Utilities   _____

Equipment/lease   _____

Salaries/drawings   _____

Insurance   _____

Depreciation   _____

Interest   _____

Maintenance   _____

Professional fees   _____

Advertising   _____

Supplies   _____

Delivery   _____

Travel   _____

Total operating expenses   _____

NET PROFIT

Net before income tax   _____

Income tax   _____

Net Profit after Income Tax   _____

Figure 5.8c	**Income Statement (projected) Third Year**

For the One-Year Period Ended: (Date)

SALES

Sales from source #1 _____

Sales from source #2 _____

Total sales income _____

COSTS

Cost of goods sold _____

GROSS PROFIT

Gross profit _____

EXPENSES

Rent _____

Utilities _____

Equipment/lease _____

Salaries/drawings _____

Insurance _____

Depreciation _____

Interest _____

Maintenance _____

Professional fees _____

Advertising _____

Supplies _____

Delivery _____

Travel _____

Total operating expenses _____

NET PROFIT

Net before income tax _____

Income tax _____

Net Profit after Income Tax _____

SALES INCOME BY MONTH

8. Take the sales forecast from Section 2 (feasibility) of your business plan and break it down into monthly predictions (Table 5.10). (Attach this chart as an appendix to your plan.)

Table 5.10

PROJECTED SALES INCOME BY MONTH			
Month	Year 1	Year 2	Year 3
1	$	$	$
2			
3			
4			
5			
6			
7			
8			
9			
10			
11			
12			
Total Sales Forecast	$	$	$

9. Give logical reasons for this monthly breakdown, considering items like seasonality and growth of the business.

_____
_____
_____
_____
_____
_____
_____

10. Specify any credit or payment terms you will provide to your customers and when you expect them to actually pay. Explain the pattern of *when* cash will actually be received for your sales.

_____
_____
_____
_____
_____
_____
_____
_____
_____
_____

11. Describe any credit or payment terms you will expect from your suppliers or subcontractors and note how this will affect your cash disbursements.

_____
_____
_____
_____
_____
_____
_____
_____
_____
_____
_____
_____
_____

12. Prepare projected cash-flow statements for each of the first three years of business, broken down by month (Figures 5.9a, 5.9b, and 5.9c, respectively).

_____
_____
_____
_____
_____
_____
_____
_____
_____
_____

Figure 5.9a   **CASH FLOW**

PROJECTED CASH FLOW

FIRST YEAR OF OPERATION: (date)

MONTH	1	2	3	4	5	6	7	8	9	10	11	12
Sales												
CASH IN-FLOW												
Cash sales												
Payments received												
Other cash received												
Total Cash In-flow (a)												
OPENING Cash Balance (b)												
CASH OUT-FLOW												
Equipment purchased												
Inventory purchased												
Rent paid												
Utilities paid												
Loan payments												
Salaries/drawings												
Supplies purchased												
OTHER expenses paid												
Total Cash Out-flow (c)												
CLOSING Cash Balance (a + b − c)												

Figure 5.9b

CASH FLOW

PROJECTED CASH FLOW

SECOND YEAR OF OPERATION: (date)

MONTH	1	2	3	4	5	6	7	8	9	10	11	12
Sales												
CASH IN-FLOW												
Cash sales												
Payments received												
Other cash received												
Total Cash In-flow (a)												
OPENING Cash Balance (b)												
CASH OUT-FLOW												
Equipment purchased												
Inventory purchased												
Rent paid												
Utilities paid												
Loan payments												
Salaries/drawings												
Supplies purchased												
OTHER expenses paid												
Total Cash Out-flow (c)												
CLOSING Cash Balance (a + b − c)												

Figure 5.9c **CASH FLOW**

PROJECTED CASH FLOW

THIRD YEAR OF OPERATION: (date)

MONTH	1	2	3	4	5	6	7	8	9	10	11	12
Sales												
CASH IN-FLOW												
Cash sales												
Payments received												
Other cash received												
Total Cash In-flow (a)												
OPENING Cash Balance (b)												
CASH OUT-FLOW												
Equipment purchased												
Inventory purchased												
Rent paid												
Utilities paid												
Loan payments												
Salaries/drawings												
Supplies purchased												
OTHER expenses paid												
Total Cash Out-flow (c)												
CLOSING Cash Balance (a + b – c)												

Pippa's Patty 'N Pie

About the Sample Business Plan

Pippa's Patty 'n Pie is the start-up business plan for the first venture of Ethel and Elliot Wilson. The partners are a brother and sister of Caribbean and German descent from Weyburn, Saskatchewan, now living in Southern Ontario—in other words, typical Canadians. Ethel is 35 years old, married to a chartered accountant, and has two children. Ethel's youngest child has just started going to school full-days and her part-time work teaching at a local college is not what she really wants to do. Ethel holds a Bachelor of Business Administration and worked as a business analyst for a credit-reporting firm before teaching. She and her husband have been paying down the mortgage on their small home and have about $90,000 of equity plus an additional $30,000 worth of securities in their investment portfolio. They have no other debts. Ethel and her husband have agreed to cash in the portfolio and use the money to start the business, lending $10,000 of it to Elliot for part of his investment.

Elliot is 26 and has been in and out of school and various jobs (mostly part-time) for the last seven years. He has no significant assets and owes about $16,000 in student loans. This year, he graduated from a two-year Culinary Management program and intended to use his credential to work on cruise ships and in hotels around the world. Then, Ethel and Elliot's 85-year-old Jamaican-born grandmother came up with the idea for the business. The patty recipe they intend to use is a modified version of Gramma's own. As well, Gramma has promised to give Elliot $10,000 toward the business (repayable if it is a success). She is also willing to provide some small additional security for loans.

Pippa's Patty 'n Pie Business Plan—September 20XX
Confidential: Please store in a secure location
Ethel B. Wilson 905–555–5555
Elliot Wilson 519–555–5555

Section 1: The Summary and Concept

SUMMARY

Pippa's Patty 'n Pie will sell inexpensive fast food to a middle-class youth market in Westdale, an upscale residential neighbourhood in Hamilton, Ontario. The fast food market is growing and Pippa's represents an opportunity to outprice the competition and satisfy the tastes of the youth market. Pippa's will be a family business owned by a brother and sister, who together have business finance, culinary, and fast food experience.

Westdale has a thriving commercial core with many restaurants, but only four direct fast food competitors. There are a huge number of students (elementary, secondary, college, and university) that frequent and traverse the area. Sales forecasts for the first three years are $206,000, $275,000, and $300,000, with costs remaining relatively stable.

Pippa's will project an image of *value*, *speed*, and *cleanliness*. It will be at the lowest end of the fast-food price range, producing its own beef and chicken patties and re-selling some baked goods from other suppliers.

Both owners will work in the business (one in the kitchen, one dealing with the customers and administration). Initially, there will be one part-time and one full-time employee.

The business will require just over $60,000 in start-up capital with over $40,000 of that coming from the entrepreneurs, who will take a bank loan for the remaining $20,000. Most of the investment will be for the purchase of quality, used restaurant equipment ($37,000), which can serve as primary collateral for the loan. Paying a reasonable salary to the owners, the business will pass the break-even point within the first four months and make a small profit ($800) in the first year and a significant one-year profit ($24,000) by the third year.

INTRODUCTION

Pippa's Patty 'n Pie, although technically classified as a "bake shop," will be a non-seating fast food outlet (limited-service restaurant). The business will primarily sell baked meat patties along with complementary food products and beverages to a local student market as well as a broader, mealtime market from the local consumer traffic. Pippa's will depend on high volume and a fast customer turnover. The menu will be limited and prices will be at the lowest end of the fast food range. Pippa's will be located in the Westdale section of Hamilton, Ontario, a middle-class area with a high concentration of educational facilities. Some of the food products will be made at the shop and others will be bought from local suppliers.

PRODUCTS AND SERVICES

The products offered by Pippa's are intended to satisfy hungry young appetites inexpensively. This means a generally high-starch, high-fat product, although all products can be produced as "trans-fat free," since this is a growing health concern.

Most of the products sold by Pippa's will be consumable using only one hand and no utensils—ideal for on-the-go snacks or a stand-up meal (with a patty in one hand and a drink in the other). Although Pippa's will not have seating, there will be several narrow countertop areas where customers can remain inside and stand to consume their food.

THE CUSTOMERS

The primary customer groups for Pippa's will be students of the elementary school, secondary school, and business college, all of which are within a three-minute walk of this business. A secondary target will be the many university students from the McMaster campus and medical centre about a six-minute walk away. Many of these students frequent the Westdale retail neighbourhood where Pippa's is located. The general traffic of consumers who live and work in this area forms another segment. A specific Caribbean immigrant segment will not be targeted although Pippa's will likely get some customers from this and other immigrant groups since the business concept is similar to one widely used in Africa, Europe, and the Caribbean. Nevertheless, the immediate location has a relatively low immigrant population.

THE OPPORTUNITY

The fast-food industry has clear leaders in the categories of hamburgers, pizza, submarine and pita sandwiches as well as in the coffee and donut areas. Pastry or pie shops, common in Africa, the Caribbean, and Western Europe (all having immigrant populations in Canada), represent an unexploited approach to fast-food customers. As well, the market for fast food is still growing. According to the Canadian Restaurant and Foodservices Association, there was an 8.5% sales increase in the first quarter of this year for "limited service restaurants."[1] Also, as lifestyles become busier, we are eating on the go more. By 2005, 6 out of every 10 restaurant meals were eaten "off-premise."[2] These factors indicate that the timing is excellent for a new product mix entry into the fast food market.

THE OWNER(S)

The business is owned by Ethel and Elliot Wilson, a brother and sister. Ethel Wilson is a graduate of Kwantlen University College, where she graduated with a BBA in entrepreneurship. She has several years' experience working for a large credit-reporting firm in the role of analyzing small- and medium-sized companies and preparing credit reports on them. She is currently teaching part-time, but her youngest child is now old enough to attend school full days and Ethel is ready to return to a full-time endeavour. Ethel's husband, a chartered accountant, is committed to supporting Ethel in this venture. He will not be working for Pippa's in any paid capacity, as he works full-time and wishes to devote more time to childcare, especially when Ethel is busy. Elliot graduated from Niagara College's Culinary Management Co-op program. His training has provided him with baking and kitchen management skills. As well, he has worked full-time and part-time in a range of restaurants from fast food to fine dining.

Neither of the partners has experience as an entrepreneur, although other family members own businesses. The partners are both goal-oriented as shown by their completion of their post-secondary programs. Because of gender and age differences (nine years) between Ethel and Elliot, sibling rivalry is not a significant issue. The partners come from a close-knit family, work well together, and share a similar sense of humour. They have complementary skills (Ethel is more strategic and Elliot is more hands-on) and have the high levels of trust that are found in family relationships. The timing is good for them to open a business together since Ethel is looking to re-enter the workforce on a full-time basis and Elliot is looking to establish a career with more focus and long-term prospects.

The partners will each draw a salary of up to $2,500.00 per month from the time the business seems to be in positive cash flow. Ethel, with the support of her husband, could survive indefinitely without turning to the business for money, and Elliot has the support of his parents, with whom he will be living. The parents have agreed to cover all of Elliot's basic living expenses for up to two years, or until the business becomes profitable, whichever comes first. Both partners are prepared to waive their monthly salary any time the business is facing a cash shortage. (See Resumes as Appendix 1.)

THE LEGAL ORGANIZATION

The business is a corporation, under the Canada Business Corporations Act. One hundred voting shares of the corporation have been issued: 49 shares to Elliot Wilson and 51 shares to Ethel Wilson.

The company has been organized as a corporation in order to protect the personal assets of Ethel Wilson and her husband (including the home they own) against any catastrophic liability of the company. Federal incorporation was chosen, simply because of the ease of the online incorporation feature available at the time. Elliot and Ethel Wilson will be the only directors of the company, although there is already a volunteer Advisory Board consisting of:

- the outside accountant that Pippa's will use

- a former food services professor of Elliot's

- a retired vice-president of marketing of a large company (family friend)

- the branch manager of a bank (personal friend of Ethel).

This board will meet one month before start-up and every six months after that, at Pippa's. Members will receive a $100 honorarium for each meeting and a free meal.

There is a partnership agreement between the two shareholders, attached as Appendix 2. The agreement allows Ethel to lend Elliot $10,000, half of his share of the owners' investment in the company. Elliot agrees that his share of any dividends that the company pays out will automatically be turned over to Ethel, until all the loan (plus interest at an annual rate of 5 percent) has been paid back. As well, there is a dispute settlement mechanism in the partnership agreement. Even though Ethel has voting control and can overrule Elliot on any day-to-day decisions, for important strategic decisions on which the partners disagree, they will use one of the members of their advisory board as an arbitrator.

(See Partnership Agreement as Appendix 2)

Section 2: Feasibility

LOCATION

Pippa's Patty 'n Pie will be located in the Westdale section of Hamilton, Ontario, right in the thriving commercial section referred to as Westdale Village. Hamilton is a city of half a million people, in the centre of the London to Oshawa industrial corridor. The Westdale area is a solid middle-class section of the city with owner-occupied homes and small rental apartments. Many of the residents are families with children. The entire city of Hamilton has a median family income[3] that is well above the national average and Westdale would be well above the city average. Assuming that pedestrians will use a fast-food outlet within a seven-minute walk of where they work, live, or go to school, Planning Department information indicates a residential population of about 10,000[4] within the 1.75-km radius around the site. As well, the two closest schools in the neighbourhood have a combined student population of 2,500.[5] In addition, a personal estimate of the number of people who work in the shops, offices, and small service businesses within the 1.75-km[2] drawing area would add about another 600 potential customers.[6] This would total about 13,100 potential customers, not counting the drive-by traffic. Hundreds of McMaster University students would pass the site on a daily basis en route to school or the Westdale Village, but most would be in cars so they have not been included. Also, numbers for the elementary students have not been included because of the lower likelihood of their making their own lunch purchases.

This location is also important because it is very close to a medium-sized commercial bakery that will be the supplier of important items on Pippa's menu. There is also easy access from the 403 highway for bringing in supplies from food wholesale operations and fresh items from the Ontario Food Terminal. If for no other reason, Hamilton is a good location because it gave birth to the greatest Canadian fast food success story: Tim Hortons. This may be because it is in the very centre of Canada's densest population and could allow for easy contiguous expansion of a business.

SITE

The site is a 1,000-square-foot store in a three-unit strip plaza on Paradise Road. There is a large retail window and on-street parking as well as parking for three cars in the front. The unit on one side of the site is a denture clinic and on the other side is a tax service office. The road is the main access into West Hamilton and the large grocery store (The Barn) directly across the street also generates a great deal of automobile traffic. A study of automobile traffic has not been performed. Drivers are not a primary target since no drive-through capacity is possible at this site. (*Note*: None of the competing fast-food services have drive-throughs either. A three-day sample of pedestrian traffic (Thursday, Friday, Saturday) showed an average of 502 people[7] walking in front of the site between the hours of 8:00 am and 6:00 pm and many hundreds more walking on Main Street, from which the site is clearly visible.

The front door is wide enough to be considered wheel-chair accessible, and there is no bump or elevation change on entry. But there is no automatic door opening mechanism.

The site is appropriate in that it is naturally divided into two large areas that will become the serving area and the kitchen, with a small office in between them. The site is also accessible to the targeted younger market physically (it is easy to see into and the window is close to the sidewalk). It is also accessible in a psychological sense in that it is an average-looking store, not intimidating or exclusive as are some of the high-end retailers in the village.

SITE EXPENSES

A conditional offer to lease has been accepted by the landlord at the site. In return for one month's rent as security deposit, the partners have six weeks to arrange financing for the business. (If the lease is not finalized, the deposit becomes non-refundable.) When the condition is removed and the lease finalized, the security deposit will be considered paid and the partners will pre-pay the first month's rent at that point.

The lease is for five years at a flat monthly rent of $1,400 plus a one-third share of the maintenance costs (garbage removal and snowplowing etc.), which will run as high as $185 per month. Central heating and air conditioning for the building are included with the rent. The lease allows for the rent to increase each year in proportion to the annual Consumer Price Index as reported by Statistics Canada. There is no provision for the rent to go down if the CPI were to drop. The lease is renewable for an additional five years, but at that point rent can increase above the base rent if sales of the business are in excess of $400,000. The annual increase will be equal to 1 percent of sales in excess of $400,000.

MARKET POTENTIAL

The market potential for Pippa's would be the total fast-food expenditure of the 13,100 potential customers in the drawing area. Higher income brackets (which would apply to Westdale) spend about $3,070 per person annually on food.[8] Of this, about 7 percent is spent on fast food. Therefore the total market potential would be (7% × $3,070 × 13,100) $2.8 million.

COMPETITION

There are 18 restaurants in the Westdale Village area, but only four of them are direct fast-food competition: Basilique Gourmet Pizza, Pita Pit, Subway Subs, and Tim Hortons. All are within 400 metres of Pippa's. Three out of the four are successful national franchises. The average fast-food sales of the four is about $700,000 (1/4 of the market potential) and may be considerably higher because some percentage of the automobile traffic coming through Westdale (not included in the market potential) would stop to use well-known national franchises. Pippa's sales will come from taking local pedestrian customer sales from these establishments and by competing on price and speed of service.

Indirect competition will include the small food counter in The Barn grocery store across the street, as well as school cafeterias and vending machines. Pippa's will be superior to The Barn in price and food quality and superior to the school cafeterias in terms of food appeal and environment.

SALES FORECAST

The food and beverage industry has total annual sales in Ontario of about $32 billion[9] and employs approximately 170,000 people,[10] for average sales of about $188,000 per employee. Considering that Pippa's will have three full-time employees in total, one estimate of sales could be $188,000 × 3 = $564,000. The average sales per fast food business in Ontario is $480,000. On average for Canadian limited service eating places, the ratio of revenue to equity is 34.2:1.[11] Despite the balance sheet, Ethel and Elliot will have about $30,000 of true equity in the business (Elliot must repay $10,000 to Ethel), so using this ratio the sales would on average be 34 × $30,000 = $1,020,000. Elliot's experience includes several months of working in a submarine sandwich shop in a location similar to Pippa's. Based on memory, he estimates that the sub business was bringing in about $1,000 per day. Using only 300 days per year, this would give an estimate of $300,000 in sales. Based on limited knowledge, Elliot's former food services professor gave a best-guess estimate of "somewhere around a quarter million" as his sales forecast. In rank order, these estimates are:

> The equity to revenue ratio: $1,020,000
>
> Ratio of sales to employees: $564,000
>
> Average per fast-food business: $480,000
>
> Elliot's similar-business estimate: $300,000
>
> Expert opinion (guess): $250,000

Since Pippa's will have none of the brand recognition of its competitors, it is reasonable to use the most conservative estimates. Averaging the bottom two gives a sales rate that could be achievable by the end of the first year ($275,000). It will take time (estimate of six months) to build up to this rate, starting from a sales rate of 0 on the first day. So the first year forecast for Pippa's will be ($275,000 × 0.75). A small increase will be forecast for the third year.

> Year 1 $206,000
>
> Year 2 $275,000
>
> Year 3 $300,000

PROTECTING THE BUSINESS

A comprehensive small business package covering liability, fire, theft and retail window insurance has been quoted at $1,900 annually, payable in quarterly pre-paid instalments of $475. The business will not carry life insurance on the partners at this time since both are currently covered by family policies and the business capital is not yet enough to be concerned about.

A coded security alarm system is already in the unit and Pippa's will only have to pay the $30 per month monitoring fee. Only one person at a time will have access to the cash register and a new cash float will be started anytime there is a switch in cashiers.

A trademark will be applied for on the name Pippa's Patty 'n Pie and the $350 fee will cover the cost, provided that the trademark is accepted without objection. Pippa's will not extend credit to customers or accept third-party credit cards. However, it will accept debit payment since teenagers find this a prestigious way to make a purchase. If it becomes too costly with too many debit transactions for small amounts, a minimum order size will be applied to these transactions.

Section 3: Marketing

IMAGE

The main elements of Pippa's image will be:

Value. This is important to younger people who have relatively little disposable cash and are not prepared to pay for the frills of fine dining.

Speed. Fast food should be that. When you're hungry, you shouldn't have to wait for the kitchen to prepare something and Pippa's will be the fastest.

Cleanliness. This is important to the middle-class customers being targeted who (although they won't admit it) carry most of the values of their middle-class parents.

BUSINESS NAME

The name "Pippa's Patty 'n Pie" projects the three mainstays of the image. Traditionally, meat pies have been heavy, filling, and high *value*. The name has a *speedy* staccato sound to it, making it natural to say it quickly. (Try saying it slowly and feel how odd it is.) The name Pippa is not Caribbean, but rather Scandinavian, with the appropriate reputation for *cleanliness*. Finally, the company has a human name, like Harvey's or Wendy's or Tim Horton's, as opposed to Burger King or Red Barn. Just looking at the most successful franchises indicates that this might have some value.

SERVICE/PRODUCT MIX

The initial menu will consist of

Breakfast:
Ham 'n Egg Pie	$1.35
Cheese 'n Egg Pie	1.35
Sausage Roll	1.75

Regular
Beef Patty	$1.35
Chicken Patty	1.35
Veggie Patty	1.75
Spicy Beans	.95
Spicy Rice	.95
Veggie Sticks	1.75

Beverages
Canned Soft Drinks	$1.10
Coffee	1.10 / 1.35
Tea	1.10 / 1.35
Juice	1.10

Desserts
Apple Pie	.95
Cherry Pie	.95

All pies, patties, and sausage rolls will be served in an open-ended waxed paper envelope imprinted with Pippa's logo. Veggie sticks will consist of a small serving of carrot, celery, and zucchini sticks in a poly bag, which is sealable for freshness.

Spicy beans or rice will be served in a ten-ounce styrofoam cup with a plastic lid. Plastic spoons will be provided but enterprising youth will probably take to eating (drinking?) the beans or rice directly from the cup. Drinks will be served in the original container only. The only value-added service will be that customers will have the option of eating at the two stand-up counters in the serving area.

PRICING

According to the Canadian Restaurant and Foodservices Association, the average per-person expenditure at chain restaurants is just over $5.00.[12] The pricing strategy to appeal to the younger market will be to keep the price of a snack (patty and drink) under $ 3.00 and to keep the price of a meal under $4.00. So, for example, a customer could get a beef patty, drink, and apple pie; or a patty, spicy beans, and a drink; or two patties and a drink—all for under $4.00.

No individual pricing discounts will be offered but a family value meal may be introduced (if it seems that customers are buying take-home-for-dinner quantities). The meal would contain 6–8 patties, a large order of beans, rice, and veggie sticks. (Price to be determined.)

DISTRIBUTION

Distribution is direct from Pippa's to the end-user, but Pippa's is acting as an intermediary for several products that come from the manufacturer (sausage rolls, fruit pies, etc.). As well, some of the products (carrots, zucchini, celery) will come from a wholesale distributor.

The site is designed for speed, with customers coming in, reading the menu, ordering and paying at the cash (close to the entrance), moving to their left to pick up orders, and moving again to their left to make room for new customers. The serving area is a narrow workspace for efficient service. The colours will be predominantly white (sterile) with purple, orange, and green highlights. All surfaces will be of easy-clean materials, and lighting and fixtures will be of simple, plain designs.

PROMOTION

Because Pippa's is targeting a small geographic segment, no mass media will be used. The sign will be the major form of advertising. Small ads in yearbooks will be taken, more as a community gesture than good advertising. A press release will be sent to community media one week before the official opening and press will be invited to a small opening ceremony where free samples will be distributed. The only personal selling will be asking early customers if they have tried this or that (things on the menu that they did not order).

Around start-up, high levels of product wastage are expected because of slow sales. For this reason, patties, etc. that have been in the warming ovens near their maximum time will be removed, cut in half and placed on a tray. Ethel or Elliot will take the tray into the street (weather and time of day permitting) and offer free samples to passersby.

PROMOTION EVALUATION

Promotion will frequently be evaluated by engaging customers in conversation during slow periods, always asking, "What made you come in the first time?" A record of responses will be kept in a notebook by the cash register for analysis.

Section 4: Operations

SPACE AND EQUIPMENT

Pippa's will need the following standard commercial kitchen equipment, which can all be purchased used and in excellent condition: 35-ft. commercial refrigerator; under-counter 14-litre refrigerator; 35 cu. ft. freezer; portable blast freezer; 3 commercial microwave ovens; commercial gas grill (installed); and commercial gas oven (installed). The following equipment will be needed new: (more difficult to find used, in good shape) commercial pastry roller, kitchenware, and utensils. Unfortunately, the building currently has commercial carpet throughout. The kitchen and customer areas will need this replaced with commercial vinyl and seven different counter areas will need to be installed. A second two-piece washroom must be installed. Labour for paint and other décor will be provided by the partners. The partners also have a computer and office furniture that they will contribute to the business.

An outside illuminated sign of stretched canvas (to conform to existing signs and as required by the lease) will be ordered at a price of $2,300. An illuminated sign with menu item pictures will be ordered for behind the counter. Part of the sign will be a reader panel where individual menu items, along with prices, can be listed and easily changed. This will cost $1,850.

LOGISTICS

The ordering system will be refined based on proven usage rates. But the plan at start-up is to have a minimum of three weeks' supply of all patties and pies and sausage rolls on hand, even though the lead time required at the bakery is only one week. Nevertheless, this will ensure a safety margin in case of supply interruption. All poly bags will be labelled with a date of receipt, and a first-in-first-out policy will be used for all foods, to maximize freshness. When the inventory reaches the minimum level plus a one-week supply, another week's supply will be ordered. At present, there is little cost advantage to ordering and storing really large quantities. Supplies to make the patties are easily available.

The Lindsay Commercial Bakery, located in Ancaster, just south of Hamilton, has been identified as a supplier of individual sized quiche (cheese or ham) that will be renamed as Ham 'n Egg Pie, etc. Lindsay will also supply sausage rolls. (Only beef fat and unsaturated vegetable oils will be used to minimize trans fats, as per Pippa's specifications.) These items will be flash-frozen at Pippa's in vacuum poly bags to prevent freezer damage. As well, Lindsay will supply small individual fruit pies that will be refrigerated. Due to the high sugar content, spoilage is less of an issue. Lindsay is not yet prepared to extend credit terms, but will accept Pippa's company cheque on delivery.

A lawyer has been hired for the partnership agreement at a cost of $620. The company accountant has not yet provided any direct services but will be used for tax and financial statements and planning at an annual cost of about $1,200.

METHODS AND PROCEDURES

All patties, egg pies, and sausage rolls will be frozen (patties will be frozen immediately after baking and cooling, and egg pies and sausage rolls immediately after delivery from the commercial bakery). Items will be sealed in polyvinyl bags with most of the air removed and the bags labelled for baking date. Patties and pies will be microwaved to an edible temperature (about 3 minutes for 8 pies from frozen) and transferred to the warming ovens where they can safely remain from 3 to 12 hours, depending on the product.

Beans will be prepared from commercial canned beans with the addition of desiccated onions and spices. Rice will be cooked from parboiled on a boiler on the grill and spiced with commercial salsa. Both beans and rice can remain covered in the Crock-Pots for an entire day with minimal loss of quality.

For wastage, Pippa's can be expected to discard on average one-half tray of ham 'n egg and cheese 'n egg pies after breakfast each day (16 to a tray); one-half tray of beef and chicken pies and veggie pies, after lunch rush hour and at the end of the day; one-half tray of sausage rolls, one-half cooker of beans, one-half cooker of rice, for total wastage of about $18.00 per day at cost. Some of this may be recouped through storing and freezing waste and selling it to local pig farmers. Over the next couple of years, however, legislation might ban all animal product contents in feed because of concerns about mad cow disease. Therefore no income is shown as coming from this source.

Quality control will depend on checking temperatures coming from the microwaved products until cooking times for all products are precise enough to maintain food at about 55 degrees Celsius. Pippa's policy will be to replace any item that a customer finds unsatisfactory with the same or an alternative of the customer's choice.

SYSTEMS

All financial and inventory records will be kept using QuickBooks, with which Ethel is already familiar. A separate journal will be kept of all batch numbers of products that are baked or received for freezing. In case a problem occurs with a particular batch, it can be traced back to the time of baking or receipt.

ORGANIZATION

Ethel will handle all administrative duties and Elliot will perform all kitchen duties. The full-time employee will work the counter serving customers, assisted and replaced by either Elliot or Ethel depending on the time of day. Generally Ethel will open in the morning, preparing the first batches of food and the full-time employee will arrive at about 7:30 am, working through the breakfast and lunch rushes until 3:30 pm. Elliot will arrive in the mid-afternoon and both he and Ethel will work the counter for the after-school rush. Then at 4:00 pm, a part-time employee will work with Elliot, and Ethel will leave. In the evening, with the part-timer on the counter, Elliot will do the day's baking and lock up at around 10:00 pm as a closing time. (The area appears quiet around then, even in the summer, but the schedule can change to meet demand.) For the Saturday schedule, the part-timer will cover the 7:30 am to 3:30 pm shift and Sundays, the shop will close.

The employees will initially be paid just above minimum wage, which, including employer CPP contributions, will work out to about a total cost of $9.50 per hour for the part-timer and $11.00 for the full-timer. CPP contributions will be made for both Elliot and Ethel based on their salary.

REGULATION

Since Pippa's is technically a bakeshop, as opposed to a restaurant, it does not have to meet local requirements for separate male and female and disabled washroom facilities. Nevertheless, a single wheelchair accessible washroom is being added to the facility for customer use. Because it is a food preparation business, the employee washroom cannot directly access the food preparation area so an additional door must be built in the kitchen area.

Pippa's will require a Bakeshop Licence from the City of Hamilton at a cost of $185 annually. There are no plans to join any business associations during the start-up phase.

Section 5: Finances

START-UP REQUIREMENTS

See chart: MATERIAL AND OPERATING CASH NEEDS (For Start-up), attached as Appendix 4.

See chart: EQUIPMENT NEEDS (For Start-up), attached as Appendix 5.

OWNER(S)' INVESTMENT

Ethel and Elliot will be contributing $42,100 in equity. ($20,000 each in cash and $2,100 in equipment.)

BORROWED MONEY

Pippa's will need to secure a loan of about $20,000 for operating expenses as the business gets off the ground. This should be at an annual interest rate of about 9.5% and paid off over the first three years of the business at monthly payments of $640. The $36,000 of kitchen and restaurant equipment and fixtures could be used as collateral.

SALES INCOME BY MONTH

See chart: Projected Sales Income By Month attached, as Appendix 6

Most of the variation in sales for the cash flow is the result of growth in the business. Sandwich and pizza sellers in Westdale estimated that loss of student business in the summer was offset about equally by the increase in holiday traffic. Increasingly, colleges and universities are running courses right through the summer, and the good weather makes it more likely that people will be out for lunch.

The business will operate almost entirely on a cash basis until credit can be established with Pippa's own suppliers. There are no foreseeable circumstances of Pippa's extending credit.

Endnotes for Sample Business Plan

1. Canadian Restaurant and Foodservices Association Report, "Foodservice Sales Jump," *www.crfa.ca/research.*

2. Canadian Restaurant and Foodservices Association, "Six in 10 Restaurant Meals Eaten Off-Premise," *www.crfa.ca/research/2005.*

3. Statistics Canada, "Composition of Family Income for Census Families for Both Spouses or Partners," 2001 Census.

4. Hamilton Planning and Economic Development Department, Tax Roll information and maps.

5. Calls to Westdale Secondary and Columbia Business College.

6. Personal observation and estimate.

7. Site observation by partners during May when high schools and elementary schools were in session but college was between winter and spring terms (although some students were still about).

8. Statistics Canada, Catalogue no. 62-554, 2001 data.

9. City of Hamilton, Economic Development Department, "Hamilton Food and Beverage Industry Profile."

10. Ontario Job Futures, "Overview of Ontario Employment Patters," 2004.

11. Industry Canada, Performance Plus, small business ratios for Limited Service Eating Places, NAICS Number 7222, 2002 data.

12. Canadian Restaurant and Foodservices Association, "Menu Trends: Chains vs. Independents," *www.crfa.ca/research/2005/menu* (adjusted for inflation).

PIPPA'S PATTY 'N PIE INC. | Balance Sheet

Balance Sheet (Opening Day)

ASSETS

CURRENT ASSETS

Cash	$20,000	
Accounts receivable	0	
Inventory/supplies	1,750	
Prepaid expenses	3,460	
Other current assets	100	
Total current assets		$25,310

FIXED ASSETS

Land and buildings	0	
Fixtures	17,950	
Equipment	18,670	
Vehicles	750	
Other fixed assets	0	
Total fixed assets		$37,370
Total Assets		**$62,680**

LIABILITIES

CURRENT LIABILITIES

Accounts payable	0	
Short-term loans payable	0	
Taxes payable	0	
Other current liabilities	0	
Total current liabilities		

LONG-TERM LIABILITIES

Mortgage payable	0	
Long-term loans payable	$20,000	
Other long-term liabilities	0	
Total long-term liabilities		$20,000

SHAREHOLDERS' EQUITY

Capital investment	$42,680	$42,680
Total Liabilities and Equity		**$62,680**

PIPPA'S PATTY 'N PIE INC. | Balance Sheet

Balance Sheet Year End (Year 1)

ASSETS

CURRENT ASSETS

Cash	$21,158	
Accounts receivable	0	
Inventory/supplies	1,750	
Prepaid expenses	3,460	
Other current assets	100	
Total current assets		$26,468

FIXED ASSETS

Land and buildings	0	
Fixtures	16,150	
Equipment	14,270	
Vehicles	750	
Other fixed assets	0	
Total fixed assets		$31,170
Total Assets		**$57,638**

LIABILITIES

CURRENT LIABILITIES

Accounts payable	0	
Short-term loans payable	0	
Taxes payable	0	
Other current liabilities	0	
Total current liabilities	0	

LONG-TERM LIABILITIES

	0	
Mortgage payable	0	
Long-term loans payable	$14,169	
Other long-term liabilities	0	
Total long-term liabilities		$14,169

SHAREHOLDERS' EQUITY

Capital investment	$42,680	
Retained earnings	789	
Total equity		$43,469
Total Liabilities and Equity		**$57,638**

PIPPA'S PATTY 'N PIE INC. | Balance Sheet

Balance Sheet Year End (Year 2)

ASSETS

CURRENT ASSETS

Cash	$21,026	
Accounts receivable	0	
Inventory/supplies	1,750	
Prepaid expenses	3,460	
Other current assets	100	
Total current assets		$26,336

FIXED ASSETS

Land and buildings	0	
Fixtures	14,650	
Equipment ($15,000 new equip.)	21,570	
Vehicles	750	
Other fixed assets	0	
Total fixed assets		$36,970
Total Assets		**$63,306**

LIABILITIES

CURRENT LIABILITIES

Accounts payable	0	
Short-term loans payable	0	
Taxes payable	0	
Other purrent liabilities	0	
Total current liabilities	0	

LONG-TERM LIABILITIES	0	
Mortgage payable	0	
Long-term loans payable	7,835	
Other long-term liabilities	0	
Total long-term liabilities		$ 7,835

SHAREHOLDERS' EQUITY

Capital investment	$42,680	
Retained earnings	12,791	
Total equity		$55,471
Total Liabilities and Equity		**$63,306**

PIPPA'S PATTY 'N PIE INC. | Balance Sheet

Balance Sheet Year End (Year 3)

ASSETS

CURRENT ASSETS

Cash	$25,954	
Accounts receivable	0	
Inventory/supplies	1,750	
Prepaid expenses	3,460	
Other current assets	100	
Total current assets		$31,264

FIXED ASSETS

Land and buildings	0	
Fixtures	13,150	
Equipment ($18,000 new equip.)	34,870	
Vehicles	750	
Other fixed assets		
Total fixed assets		$48,770

Total Assets | | | **$80,034**

LIABILITIES

CURRENT LIABILITIES

Accounts payable	0	
Short-term loans payable	740	
Taxes payable	0	
Other current liabilities	0	
Total current liabilities		740

LONG-TERM LIABILITIES

Mortgage payable	0	
Long-term loans payable	0	
Other long-term liabilities	0	
Total long-term lliabilities		0

SHAREHOLDERS' EQUITY

Capital investment	$42,680	
Retained earnings	36,614	
Total equity		$79,294

Total Liabilities and Equity | | | **$80,034**

COSTS AND EXPENSES

See chart: Ongoing Costs & Expenses (Worksheet) attached as Appendix

---

PIPPA'S PATTY 'N PIE INC. | Income Statement

Income Statement (Projected) for the One-Year Period Ended: (Year 1 End)

SALES

Sales	$206,000

COSTS

Cost of goods sold	$ 78,280

GROSS PROFIT

Gross profit	$ 127,720

EXPENSES

Rent	$ 16,800
Utilities	0
Equipment lease	0
Salaries/deductions	89,000
Insurance	1,900
Depreciation expense	6,200
Interest	1,849
Maintenance	2,220
Professional fees	2,800
Advertising	1,200
Supplies	4,300
Delivery	0
Travel	500

Total operating expenses	$126,769

NET PROFIT

Net before income tax	$951
Income tax	$162
Net Profit after Income Tax	**$789**

PIPPA'S PATTY 'N PIE INC.	Income Statement

Income Statement (Projected) for the One-Year Period Ended: (Year 2 End)

SALES

Sales	$275,000		

COSTS

Cost of goods sold	104,500		

GROSS PROFIT

Gross profit		$170,500	

EXPENSES

Rent	$ 16,800		
Utilities	0		
Equipment lease	0		
Salaries/deductions	115,070		
Insurance	1,900		
Depreciation expense	9,200		
Interest	1,346		
Maintenance	2,220		
Professional fees	3,000		
Advertising	1,200		
Supplies	4,300		
Delivery	0		
Travel	500		
Total operating expenses		$155,536	

NET PROFIT

Net before income tax			$ 14,964
Income tax			2,968
Net Profit after Income Tax			**$ 11,996**

PIPPA'S PATTY 'N PIE INC. | Income Statement

Income Statement (Projected) for the One-Year Period Ended: (Year 3 End)

SALES

Sales	$300,000	

COSTS

Cost of goods sold	$110,400	

GROSS PROFIT

Gross profit		$189,600

EXPENSES

Rent	$ 16,800	
Utilities	0	
Equipment lease	0	
Salaries/deductions	120,048	
Insurance	4,400	
Depreciation expense	6,200	
Interest	585	
Maintenance	2,220	
Professional fees	2,600	
Advertising	1,800	
Supplies	5,328	
Delivery	0	
Travel	996	
Total operating expenses		$ 160,977

NET PROFIT

Net before income tax		$28,623
Income tax		$ 4,800
Net Profit after Income Tax		**$23,823**

PIPPA'S PATTY 'N PIE INC.

Projected Cash Flow

Year 1 of Operation

MONTH	1	2	3	4	5	6	7	8	9	10	11	12
Sales	5,000	7,000	8,500	12,000	14,800	21,900	22,000	22,800	23,000	23,000	23,000	23,000
CASH IN-FLOW												
Cash sales	5,000	7,000	8,500	12,000	14,800	21,900	22,000	22,800	23,000	23,000	23,000	23,000
Payments received	0	0	0	0	0	0	0	0	0	0	0	0
Total Cash In-flow (a)	**5,000**	**7,000**	**8,500**	**12,000**	**14,800**	**21,900**	**22,000**	**22,800**	**23,000**	**23,000**	**23,000**	**23,000**
Opening Cash Balance (b)	**20,000**	**11,996**	**7,437**	**3,609**	**1,426**	**38**	**3,152**	**5,403**	**8,975**	**12,471**	**15,962**	**19,356**
CASH OUT-FLOW												
Advertising	200	0	200	0	200	0	200	0	200	0	0	200
Inventory	1,900	2,660	3,230	4,560	5,624	8,322	8,360	8,664	8,740	8,740	8,740	8,740
Rent/maintenance	1,585	1,585	1,585	1,585	1,585	1,585	1,585	1,585	1,585	1,585	1,585	1,585
Insurance/prof. fees	1,275	0	0	725	0	0	725	0	0	475	0	1,500
Loan payments	640	640	640	640	640	640	640	640	640	640	640	640
Salaries/deductions	6,334	6,334	6,334	6,334	7,800	7,900	7,900	8,000	8,000	8,000	8,032	8,032
Supplies/equipment	1,000	300	300	300	300	300	300	300	300	300	300	300
Taxes	0	0	0	0	0	0	0	0	0	0	0	162
Other expenses	70	40	39	39	39	39	39	39	39	39	39	39
Total Cash Out-flow (c)	**13,004**	**11,559**	**12,328**	**14,183**	**16,188**	**18,786**	**19,749**	**19,228**	**19,504**	**19,779**	**19,336**	**21,198**
Closing Cash Balance (a + b − c)	**11,996**	**7,437**	**3,609**	**1,426**	**38**	**3,152**	**5,403**	**8,975**	**12,471**	**15,692**	**19,356**	**21,158**

PIPPA'S PATTY 'N PIE INC.

Projected Cash Flow

Year 2 of Operation

MONTH	1	2	3	4	5	6	7	8	9	10	11	12
Sales	23,000	24,000	24,000	24,000	24,000	24,000	20,000	20,000	23,000	23,000	23,000	23,000
CASH IN-FLOW												
Cash sales	23,000	24,000	24,000	24,000	24,000	24,000	20,000	20,000	23,000	23,000	23,000	23,000
Payments received												
Total Cash In-flow (a)	**23,000**	**24,000**	**24,000**	**24,000**	**24,000**	**24,000**	**20,000**	**20,000**	**23,000**	**23,000**	**23,000**	**23,000**
Opening Cash Balance (b)	**21,158**	**7,201**	**9,869**	**11,638**	**13,532**	**16,001**	**17,970**	**17,184**	**17,373**	**18,522**	**19,796**	**21,645**
CASH OUT-FLOW												
Advertising	200	0	200	0	200	0	200	0	200	0	200	0
Inventory	8,740	9,120	9,120	9,120	9,120	9,120	7,600	7,600	8,740	8,740	8,740	8,740
Rent/maintenance	1,585	1,585	1,585	1,585	1,585	1,585	1,585	1,585	1,585	1,585	1,585	1,585
Insurance/prof. fees	775	0	0	775	0	0	775	0	0	775	0	1,800
Loan payments	640	640	640	640	640	640	640	640	640	640	640	640
Salaries/deductions	9,589	9,589	9,589	9,589	9,589	9,589	9,589	9,589	9,589	9,589	9,589	9,589
Supplies/equipment	15,358	358	358	358	358	358	358	358	358	358	358	358
Taxes	0	0	700	0	0	700	0	0	700	0	0	868
Other expenses paid	70	40	39	39	39	39	39	39	39	39	39	39
Total Cash Out-flow (c)	**36,957**	**21,332**	**22,231**	**22,106**	**21,531**	**22,031**	**20,786**	**19,811**	**21,851**	**21,726**	**21,151**	**23,619**
Closing Cash Balance (a + b − c)	**7,201**	**9,869**	**11,638**	**13,532**	**16,001**	**17,970**	**17,184**	**17,373**	**18,522**	**19,796**	**21,645**	**21,026**

PIPPA'S PATTY 'N PIE INC.

Projected Cash Flow

Year 3 of Operation

MONTH	1	2	3	4	5	6	7	8	9	10	11	12
Sales	25,000	25,000	25,000	25,000	25,000	25,000	25,000	25,000	25,000	25,000	25,000	25,000
CASH IN-FLOW												
Cash sales	25,000	25,000	25,000	25,000	25,000	25,000	25,000	25,000	25,000	25,000	25,000	25,000
Payments received	0	0	0	0	0	0	0	0	0	0	0	0
Other cash received	0	0	0	0	0	0	0	0	0	0	0	0
Total Cash In-flow (a)	**25,000**	**25,000**	**25,000**	**25,000**	**25,000**	**25,000**	**25,000**	**25,000**	**25,000**	**25,000**	**25,000**	**25,000**
Opening Cash Balance (b)	**21,026**	**4,520**	**7,564**	**9,108**	**10,902**	**13,646**	**15,490**	**16,984**	**20,028**	**21,572**	**23,366**	**26,110**
CASH OUT-FLOW												
Advertising	300	0	300	0	300	0	300	0	300	0	300	0
Inventory purchased	9,200	9,200	9,200	9,200	9,200	9,200	9,200	9,200	9,200	9,200	9,200	9,200
Rent/maintenance	1,585	1,585	1,585	1,585	1,585	1,585	1,585	1,585	1,585	1,585	1,585	1,585
Insurance/prof. fees	1,250	0	0	1,250	0	0	1,250	0	0	1,250	0	2,000
Loan payments	640	640	640	640	640	640	640	640	640	640	640	640
Salaries/deductions	10,004	10,004	10,004	10,004	10,004	10,004	10,004	10,004	10,004	10,004	10,004	10,004
Supplies/equipment	18,444	444	444	444	444	444	444	444	444	444	444	444
Taxes	0	0	1,200	0	0	1,200	0	0	1,200	0	0	1,200
Other expenses paid	83	83	83	83	83	83	83	83	83	83	83	83
Total Cash Out-flow (c)	**41,506**	**21,956**	**23,456**	**23,206**	**22,256**	**23,156**	**23,506**	**21,956**	**23,456**	**23,206**	**22,256**	**25,156**
Closing Cash Balance (a + b − c)	**4,520**	**7,564**	**9,108**	**10,902**	**13,646**	**15,490**	**16,984**	**20,028**	**21,572**	**23,366**	**26,110**	**25,954**

chapter 6

The Purchase Alternative:

How Do I Buy (or Buy Into)
an Existing Business?

LEARNING OBJECTIVES

On completion of this module, you should be able to:

- *Compare the advantages of starting a new venture versus buying an existing business.*
- *Identify and describe the major risks in buying a business.*
- *Describe various approaches to buying or buying into a business.*
- *Explain the difference between purchasing shares or assets of a business.*
- *List the major provisions included in a purchase agreement for a business.*
- *Define ratio analysis as it relates to assessing a business for sale.*
- *Apply the return on investment concept to pricing a business.*
- *Distinguish between asset methods and earnings methods of pricing a business.*
- *Identify several specific techniques for business valuation.*
- *Outline a method for negotiating the price of a business.*
- *Prepare alternative components of the business plan related to buying a business.*

Chapters 1 through 5 have been concerned with starting a brand-new venture. An alternative
is to become the owner, or part owner, of a business that is already up and running. Either
method of getting into business will require a business plan—one that includes most of the
topics covered in Chapters 1 through 5. The plan for buying or buying into a business, however, will also require some additional elements, mostly related to calculating a value for the
existing company and the terms of sale.

Is Buying a Business Right for Me?

PERSONAL CIRCUMSTANCES   On average, buying a business is a less risky option than starting a brand-new business (buying a franchise is even lower risk). So, the selection of a start-up method will likely have something to do with your tolerance for risk. This is partly a reflection of your own personality, but it can be influenced by factors like the risk tolerance of your spouse or any business partners. Other commitments, such as supporting family members, children entering college, or assets you wish to protect, can also influence the amount of risk you are willing to take. *Ask yourself: How much risk am I willing to take?*

Your financial circumstances may also be a factor in how you go about becoming an entrepreneur. Buying an existing business is usually more expensive than starting a brand-new company. That's because when you start a new business, you can shrink the idea down to any size necessary to fit your available financing. For example, if you wish to start a new specialty dessert restaurant, but can't arrange financing, you may be able to finance a gourmet ice cream stand and build from there. But if you want to buy an existing specialty restaurant, you will have to buy the whole business as it exists. So, generally, those buying existing businesses have access to more personal financing than those starting new firms.

Sometimes, you just find yourself in circumstances where there is an opportunity to buy a business. And you have to make the decision whether to pursue that opportunity. Some examples are:

- Retirement or death of a business owner. This could be a business you are working for or have some other association with (customer, supplier) and you may be approached directly or hear of the opportunity informally.
- You may be part of an employee stock ownership plan (**ESOP**) where you have been accumulating shares of the company as part of your retirement plan. An opportunity may arise to significantly increase your holdings by buying additional shares from the principals or other employees.
- You are approached by other managers of the company where you work and asked to participate in a **management buyout** of the company. This usually involves each of the management team giving personal guarantees on a loan used to purchase a controlling interest in the company. There are lenders that specialize in financing management buyouts.[1]

Most of these circumstantial opportunities imply that a quick decision is needed on your part on whether to pursue the opportunity. But after you have declared your intentions, you do not have to rush the research and negotiations leading to a final agreement.

MERITS OF BUYING   *Ask yourself: What's the big advantage of buying an existing business?* When you buy an existing business you are usually buying one that has proven it can make money. In addition, the time-consuming, often frustrating, start-up work has been done for you, resulting in:

- *Efficient methods and procedures.* Presumably, company systems have been refined over time for some measure of efficiency that you would not have when starting a new business. In a new business there are many decisions (and many mistakes) to make—the best place to

---

✓ **Test Yourself 6.1**
True or False? Starting a brand-new company is, on average, higher risk than buying an existing business.

ESOP (employee stock ownership plan; also employee share ownership program) Allows employees to purchase shares in the company where they work as part of their retirement packages. Shares may be held within pension plans or Registered Retirement Savings Plans (RRSPs), with the associated tax benefits. In some cases provincial tax credits are also available.

management buyout This is where a group of employees, led by a management team, arranges to purchase a controlling interest in a company. Some merchant bankers and venture capital funds specialize in funding this type of purchase.

✓ **Test Yourself 6.2**
True or False? Starting a brand-new business is, on average, more expensive than buying an existing business.

put the cash register; how often to buy inventory; how to set up the bookkeeping . . . . The owners of the existing business should have already made (and corrected) most of the mistakes.

- *Defined markets.* Through trial and error, there should have come about a clear understanding of which particular customer groups are most likely to buy from this business.
- *Established customers.* The base of existing customers and the likelihood of their remaining as customers is primarily what we mean by the **goodwill** of a business. The past purchases of these customers form the basis of predictions for the future performance of the business.
- *Established suppliers.* Established suppliers are important, not just because of their proven reliability but also because of any credit terms that are in place with them. When you start a new business, suppliers are reluctant to extend credit terms, but when you take over an existing company it is often possible to continue any favourable payment terms that were established by the previous owner.
- *Trained employees.* Having employees in place not only keeps the business going and generating cash, but these employees can also serve as a resource to help train you as the new owner.

All these components contribute to a documented financial history of the company that can be used for making decisions about the future of the company—including the decision of whether or not to buy it.

Head Start Exercises

6.1 Briefly explain why buying a business is the most appropriate start-up method for you and your circumstances ($\frac{1}{2}$ page maximum).

6.2 Briefly describe the history of the company you are buying. *Note*: Students who are using the Head Start exercises as class assignments will each have to interview an entrepreneur whose business they will use as an example for the exercise assignments in this chapter ($\frac{1}{3}$ page maximum).

RISKS OF BUYING It is easy to underestimate the amount of work involved in buying a business; that is, in doing it properly. The amount of research required and the complexity of the business plan will likely exceed that required for a new start-up because:

- You are likely dealing with a larger entity than a start-up business, since the business you are buying will have gone through some growth since its own start-up.
- There is extensive investigation required in figuring out how much to pay for the business.

There are many potential problems associated with buying a business.[2]

- *Overvalued assets.* The problem of overvalued assets may be the single biggest danger for the naïve business buyer. You may, for example, be buying a shirt store with an inventory of $25,000 worth of shirts. Your accountant will confirm that the store did, in fact, pay $25,000 for the shirts, but that's not necessarily what they are worth. Many of them may be obsolete styles or inferior quality, worth far less than the value showing on the balance sheet. Or, you may be buying a business with equipment that has been depreciated to 30 percent of its original value. But the equipment may be totally worn out, worth nothing. *Ask yourself: How could I deal with this problem?* Every asset of a business must be carefully inspected,

✓ **Test Yourself 6.3**
True or False? Buying an existing independent business is lower risk than buying a franchise.

goodwill The amount paid for a business in excess of the value of its assets. The value given to a business's ability to make profit because of its established customer base. Sometimes considered an intangible asset of the business.

✓ **Test Yourself 6.4**
True or False? Goodwill refers to the intentions of business sellers to treat prospective buyers fairly.

 Get Help 6.1
Appraisers are listed in the Yellow Pages. Most specialize in one or two areas, so you may have to use more than one appraisal firm. Rates are usually reasonable and a worthwhile investment.

and where you cannot accurately assess value yourself you should bring in professional appraisers.

- *Redundant assets.* **Redundant assets** are things that a company owns that are not necessary for it to function at its current or expected income levels. For example, you may be considering buying a garden centre that has three pickup trucks for delivery, but two trucks are more than sufficient to deliver all the sales that the store can handle. In buying the business, why should you buy a truck you don't need? *Ask yourself: How could I deal with this problem?* In setting a price for the business, you should deduct the value of any redundant assets and perhaps give the vendor a chance to liquidate them before the sale.

- *Lease problems.* Escalator clauses and inability to renew are major problems. You may be looking at a business whose success depends on the site, but the lease for the property runs out in three years. *Ask yourself: How could I deal with this problem?* You will not be able to secure loans that must run longer than the existing lease. So you must deal with the landlord *before* buying the business and attempt to negotiate a lease that is conditional on your making a deal on the business. Alternatively, you can first make an offer on the business that is conditional on your being able to negotiate an acceptable lease with the landlord.

- *Impending loss of key employees.* Sometimes the success of a business depends on the knowledge and skill of one or two employees. You might be considering the purchase of a trail mix packaging company. The old-but-working machinery for mixing and packaging is maintained and operated by two brothers who each have 30 years of experience in the job. Your fear is that with a change in ownership, the brothers might retire. *Ask yourself: How could I deal with this problem?* If retirement is imminent, you may be able to contract with these employees to train replacements before they leave.

- *Impending location/site changes.* Retail and consumer service businesses depend heavily on location for their success, and changes in the geographic area (zoning changes, roadway changes, deteriorating neighbourhood) could be disastrous. *Ask yourself: How could I deal with this problem?* Research is the first step, usually conducted by visiting the planning department of your City Hall and asking a lot of questions. If planned changes will dramatically alter the traffic patterns around the business site, you may rethink your decision to buy.

- *Negative image.* Some businesses have a bad reputation among their potential customers. Even minimal research will turn up a company's bad image. But you may decide to buy anyway if you can get a bargain price. *Ask yourself: How could I deal with this problem?* Trying to reverse a negative image is among the most difficult of marketing problems. You can change the company name, but if you're buying a neighbourhood retail store, the old name will persist. You can put up "under new management" signs, but they can't stay up forever. You can redecorate, hire new staff, and send out letters. It *is* possible to change a negative image, given enough time and effort, but it is difficult to assess how much this will ultimately cost.

- *Non-transferability of contracts.* Some of the revenue for a business may come from particular contracts that are not transferable to the new owner(s). For example, you may want to buy a television repair service that makes much of its profit from servicing patient TVs in local hospitals. After buying the business, you find out that the hospital contracts are **personal services contracts** with the previous owner and give you no rights to the hospital business. *Ask yourself: How could I deal with this problem?* This is another issue that has to be dealt with in advance of buying the business, first by

redundant assets Assets owned by a business that are not necessary for it to produce profit at current or projected levels.

✓ **Test Yourself 6.5**
True or False? The most common danger in buying an existing business is the problem of overvalued assets.

✓ **Test Yourself 6.6**
True or False? The term "redundant assets" refers to assets that are not necessary for the business to carry on making a profit.

? Get Help 6.2
A lawyer is your first source of help in interpreting a lease. As well, some accounting firms have lease audit specialists on staff who can check whether a company is being properly billed for the many complex charges that can be part of a lease.

✓ **Test Yourself 6.7**
True or False? It is relatively easy to change an existing negative image of a small business.

personal services contract An agreement contracting with an individual rather than a company to perform particular services that is generally not transferable to another individual or business.

carefully checking all contracts with your lawyer. In a case like this, options include setting a price for the business that excludes revenue from personal service contracts, or making an offer to buy the business that is conditional on your being able to secure the contracts.

Head Start Exercise

6.3 Briefly identify any potential problems or areas of concern you have relating to the business for sale. Note how you will address these concerns. ($\frac{1}{3}$ page maximum.)

What's Involved in Buying a Business?

ASSESSING THE BUSINESS   Many of the risks in buying a business can be minimized by properly assessing the business. The assessment should logically cover most of the factors in the business plan, looking at whether the business is satisfactory in each area as well as identifying things you could improve if you owned the business. The business assessment checklist in Table 6.1 is a thorough list of the topics you would want to investigate in assessing a business.

Ask yourself: What is the most important question to ask about a business for sale? The key question to ask any business owner who wants to sell is "why are you selling?" Surprisingly, the answer to this question is very often a lie. The answer will likely be plausible and have an element of truth to it:

- "I'm 74 and been in this business for 40 years; it's about time I retired."
- "I need the money from the business to invest in a great opportunity I have."
- "I'm moving to Florida."

It could be that all of these statements are true, but they are not necessarily the underlying reasons for selling. After all, *ask yourself:*

- If the business was good enough for 40 years, why not 41?
- Why is your new opportunity better than your current business?
- Why move to Florida now?

Perhaps business sellers fear that their real reasons for selling are reasons that would prevent you from buying. Regardless, you must try to investigate the reasons for sale. Suppliers, employees, bankers, and neighbouring businesses are all potential sources of information.

Admittedly, you may never identify the real reason for sale. But if you do, you can have a strong negotiating advantage because you will understand how badly the seller wants to sell. And the real reason for selling may not be a reason that would prevent you from buying. For example, you may want to buy a barbershop that is situated across the street from a retirement community, close to a new college campus. The owner has told you

> ✓ **Test Yourself 6.8**
> True or False? Small problems in a business for sale that you know have inexpensive solutions should still be noted in your assessment of a business for sale.

Table 6.1

BUSINESS ASSESSMENT CHECKLIST/NOTES

✔	Factor	Description	Potential for Improvement
	BUSINESS DEFINITION		
	Existing business plan		
	Clearly defined products/services		
	Clearly defined market segments		
	BUSINESS FEASIBILITY		
	Advantageous location		
	Advantageous site		
	Acceptable terms of lease		
	Appropriately estimated market potential		
	History of accurate sales forecasting		
	Clearly identified competitors		
	Accurately estimated market share		
	Appropriate levels of insurance		
	Intellectual property protection		
	Full transferability of customer contracts		
	MARKETING		
	Appropriate image for target market		
	Appropriate product/service mix		
	Appropriate pricing strategy		
	Appropriate distribution channel		
	Effective physical distribution		
	Appropriate promotion methods		
	Effective advertising techniques		
	Effective sales techniques		
	OPERATIONS		
	Acceptable condition of fixed assets		
	Efficient space utilization/layout		
	Efficient purchasing system		
	Effective quality control systems		
	Appropriate record keeping systems/software		
	Up-to-date records		
	Clear lines of authority (organization chart)		

Table 6.1

BUSINESS ASSESSMENT CHECKLIST/NOTES (continued)

✔	Factor	Description	Potential for Improvement
	Clear job descriptions		
	Effective management policies		
	Appropriate salary levels for staff		
	Appropriate salary levels for owner(s)		
	Appropriate employee benefits		
	Up-to-date licences and permits		
	Full legal compliance		
	Beneficial association memberships		
	FINANCES		
	Up-to-date financial statements		
	Acceptable financial statement audits		
	Healthy key ratios		
	Healthy credit report		
	Healthy relationship with creditors		
	SALE/PURCHASE ISSUES		
	Appropriate asking price		
	High level of personal accord with seller(s)		
	High level of seller negotiating flexibility		
	Acceptable involvement of intermediaries		
	Acceptable involvement of advisers		
	Reason for selling		

only that he is moving from the area, but you find out from neighbouring businesses that in reality he is worried about losing his many senior citizen customers, who have several competing shops to choose from. The seniors have been complaining about the loud and unruly behaviour of college students who hang around in front of the barbershop. For you, this could be great news because your intention for the shop is to target the college students—none of the other shops in the area has pursued this market. Here, the seller's reason for selling is not a reason that would prevent you from buying, and now you have the negotiating advantage.

✓ **Test Yourself 6.9**
True or False? The critical question to ask the owner of a business for sale is "What is the price?"

Head Start Exercise

6.4 Note the reasons for sale given by the owner(s) and briefly speculate about alternative reasons ($\frac{1}{4}$ page maximum).

BUYING IN   Sometimes, when a business is in trouble the owners will look for new capital to keep the business afloat *until things turn around*. This scenario most often indicates a failing business and any new capital will just keep the business alive a little longer until it eventually fails, taking the new partner's money with it. If you are buying part ownership in a business, it should be because:

- The business is growing and needs capital for well-planned expansion, and/or
- You have some particular expertise that would be an advantage to the business and the current owners are willing to give up some equity in order to get you.

buying into a company Purchasing less than 50 percent ownership of a company.

taking over a company Purchasing more than 50 percent ownership of a company.

If you are buying just a portion of a company, the most common way to do this would be with the company set up as a corporation and with you buying a certain percentage of the shares. The expression **buying into a company** usually implies buying a minority share ownership (less than 50 percent), while buying a majority share ownership is usually referred to as **taking over a company**. If you are taking over a company, you essentially have full control to run the company as you see fit (as long as you look after the interests of the other shareholders). When you buy into a company, you may be doing so as an outside investor, with no active participation in the company, other than voting as a shareholder. More typically, with small businesses, you will be buying in with some particular active management role in the company.

Whether you are buying into a company as a general partner or as a working shareholder, you will need a partnership agreement. The agreement should cover issues such as:

- the amount of capital you are contributing and the percentage of equity (or shares), liability, profits, and losses that will be apportioned to you and each of the other partners;
- specific areas of management responsibility and restrictions on authority for each of the partners;
- rules for transferring ownership (or shares) in the business;
- specific salaries and benefits for the partners as well as rules for agreeing on paying out profit (as drawings or dividends) or equity to the partners;
- rules for dissolution or sale of the business;
- dispute settlement mechanisms to be used by the partners.

The partnership agreement is critical when you are buying into an existing partnership, because you are already at a disadvantage as the *new person* in the relationship. Your ultimate guarantee of fairness and equality within the partnership is the strength of your written agreement. Also, if you are buying all of an existing business in conjunction with a new partner, you must be careful not to focus on the purchase agreement to the exclusion of your partnership agreement. This partnership agreement will be at least as important to your long-term success as an entrepreneur.

core business The particular products and services and market segments that produce the majority of a company's profit.

outsource Find suppliers outside of a company to provide certain products or services that the company formerly produced internally.

BREAKING OFF A PIECE OF A LARGER FIRM   Large companies tend to go through cycles of expansion (adding to their products and services and widening their target markets) and contraction (where they become more specialized in their products/services, markets, and the kinds of activities they actually perform). During these contraction phases organizations sometimes *sell off* divisions or departments of the organization in order to concentrate more on the **core business**. At the same time they will try to **outsource** various supplies and services if it is more economical to do so. In times of reorganization like this, companies may entertain proposals—by employees, suppliers, or others—to take over some of the activities of the companies as separate firms.

Let's say you work for a large fast-food chain that uses plastic buckets for delivering liquid muffin batter to its franchisees. At a site separate from the main plant, the company has a department that brings back the empty buckets to clean and sterilize for re-use. A history of mechanical breakdowns and labour friction has made this department a problem area for the company. The company may consider selling off this division to you as your own business. This is most likely if the company is in a contraction phase and if the company can be convinced that by doing so they will have:

- a secure source of supply under a long-term contract
- a reliable quality of service
- a cost saving by outsourcing to you.

Ideally, you might be able to get the original company to accept payment for the assets you are purchasing over an extended period of time. This is most likely if you can demonstrate that the company will not be putting out any additional cash to do so, and if you can present a business plan showing your ability to pay off the assets within a reasonable time.

The starting point in taking over such a company is to write the mission statement for the new firm (*what* the company sells and *to whom* it sells) as an independent company, not as a former department. For example, you would describe your market as *fast-food chains* as opposed to specifying your former owner and only customer. Thus, right from the beginning you are seeing your business as an independent venture having growth potential.

INTERMEDIARIES   Real estate agents working on a commission basis sell many small businesses. There are also specialized business brokers who tend to arrange purchases of slightly larger businesses (rarely the smaller "mom and pop" operations), sometimes as part of corporate buyouts. Brokers may provide other professional services such as evaluation on a fee-for-service basis.

If you're looking for a business for sale, you can go to a real estate agent who will search the Multiple Listing Service to find a prospective business of the sort you are looking for. Then your agent will represent you in the negotiations by dealing with the seller's agent. If a deal can be reached, your agent will receive half of the commission paid by the seller. But the reality is that once negotiations start, your agent has little incentive to represent your best interests (ethical considerations aside) by perhaps advising you to walk away from the deal. The most economical use of the agent's effort is to try to persuade you to accept the deal on the seller's terms. And the higher the price, the higher the commissions.

An alternative strategy is to search the papers or Internet on your own to find a prospective business for sale. (This is not a difficult task.) Then, deal only with the listing (seller's) agent. In this case, when it comes down to final negotiations, the agent's financial interest will be in working to convince the seller to accept your offer. That's because this agent will get to keep all of the commission if the seller sells to you, whereas the listing agent will only get half if selling to buyers who are represented by agents of their own. In fact, when negotiations get tough, a listing agent may even be willing to forgo a portion of the commission to put a one-agent deal together.

✓ Test Yourself 6.10
True or False? Buying into a business typically means taking a majority ownership in the firm.

✓ Test Yourself 6.11
True or False? The *core business* refers to a company's primary products/services and primary market segments.

Get Help 6.3
The Canadian Real Estate Association's commercial real estate website is easy to use for finding businesses for sale by geographic area. Go to their website at **www.icx.ca**.

✓ **Test Yourself 6.12**
True or False? As a purchaser, it is a negotiating advantage to deal only with a listing broker or agent.

Head Start Exercise

6.5   Briefly describe the role of any intermediaries that will be involved in your purchase transaction ($\frac{1}{4}$ page maximum).

What Should the Purchase Agreement Include?

SHARES VS. ASSETS   When a business is a sole proprietorship or partnership, the assets and debts of the business are, technically, the personal assets and debts of the owner(s). So, in buying such a business, you are really purchasing the assets of the company, which you will be using (in a legal sense) in a brand-new business. The store, factory, or office will look the same and the company may have the same name and the same employees, but it will be a different legal entity consisting of you and any partners you may have.

When you are *buying* a company that is incorporated, you have a choice:
• You can buy the *assets* of the company, or
• You can buy the *shares* of the company.

When you buy only the assets, the original corporation still exists as a business entity and any debts or legal liability related to the past actions of the company remain with that corporation. When you buy the shares of the company, the corporate entity, even though it has a new owner, is still responsible for any liability resulting from past actions. For example, you might have bought a business whose taxes from two years ago were re-assessed and the tax bill was increased by $4,000. If you had purchased the shares of the company, you would now be responsible to pay this bill. If you had purchased the assets of the company, you would not.

lien The right of a creditor to take over a particular asset if a particular debt has not been paid as agreed.

warranty The legal promise that an asset will be delivered in the condition described in a contract.

When buying assets, you would ideally wish to purchase assets on a *free and clear* basis. This means having the seller agree to discharge all **liens** before the finalization of the sale. It will be your lawyer's responsibility to make sure this has been done. In some cases, you will be agreeing to take over certain liabilities from the seller as part of the purchase arrangements. In either event, you will have to negotiate any **warranties** provided by the seller. Assets may be sold on an *as-is* basis, where you must accept them in whatever their condition on closing the deal. Or you may have them fully warranted, where the seller has promised that they will be in good working condition.

✓ **Test Yourself 6.13**
True or False? It is possible to buy the shares of a sole proprietorship.

PAYMENT OPTIONS   In many cases, the seller will wish to have full payment due on the finalization of the sale. But if the seller is having trouble finding a buyer who can arrange this, or if there is a tax advantage to the seller, it may be possible to arrange payment—at least for part of the business—over an extended period; in essence, to have the seller help finance your purchase. This would mean having the seller extend you a loan for a portion of the purchase price of the business, and the loan would be secured against the assets of the business.

Rather than holding a loan against the business, some sellers may be persuaded to retain a *minority share position* in the company. This is more likely if the prospects for profits are high for the next few years. Such an arrangement may include a specific time frame for ultimately selling the minority shares to the new owner.

When a business for sale owns the property where it is situated, it may be possible to negotiate an arrangement with the owner to buy the other assets of the business but have the owner retain the property and lease it to you. At the end of the lease, depending on the profitability of the business, you may choose to negotiate to buy the property or to move the business. Such arrangements are often decided by the situation of the seller and where tax advantages lie. This kind of arrangement can also apply to other fixed assets such as heavy equipment.

Another option is to have an agreed-on price that is payable on closing, but with the possibility of additional payments that can be made if the business achieves certain levels of profit over the next few years. This approach can help make the deal when the buyer and seller cannot agree on the profit potential of the firm. It can also be used when someone is buying into a business as an active partner, as long as the additional payment levels are not so high as to take away the new partner's incentive to maximize the company profit.

The past relationship between the buyer and the seller, the financial/tax position of the seller, and the ease with which the business can be sold are all factors that can affect the kind of financing arrangements you can make with a seller.

NON-COMPETITION ISSUES   Purchase agreements will often include restrictions that prevent the old owner of a business from entering into any form of competition with the business. These usually specify a geographic range (five kilometres, for example) or a time limit (five years, for example). The need for such a restriction is obvious if the business has involved the personal services of the owner. For example, you could buy an automobile repair shop from a mechanic who has a long-standing relationship with most of the customers. Shortly after you buy the shop, the seller could open a competing shop close by, taking all of the customers that you paid for as the goodwill value of the business. Non-competition clauses have to be carefully drafted, because certain laws make any unreasonable restriction on a person's right to earn a living unenforceable.[3]

DISCLOSURE ISSUES   You will want to have a disclosure clause in your purchase agreement. This basically says that the seller agrees to tell you about anything that might adversely affect your decision to buy the business. This covers all of the items listed above in "Risks of Buying," such as the impending loss of key employees or problems with specific assets. The idea here is that if the business turns out to be less profitable than expected because of such a problem, the door is open for you to sue the seller. To be successful in your lawsuit you will have to provide evidence that the seller knew about the problem before the finalization of the purchase deal. You certainly do not plan on spending your time and money to take the seller to court. But it is important to have this clause, because it makes it in the seller's best interest to tell you everything the seller knows that might even possibly be a problem.

The negotiations to buy a business can also involve issues of non-disclosure. For example, if you have expressed interest in buying someone's business, you expect to be able to see

✓ **Test Yourself 6.14**
True or False? Compared to buying shares, buying the assets of a company provides greater protection against being sued for past actions of the company.

✓ **Test Yourself 6.15**
True or False? The right of a creditor to take over a particular asset because of an unpaid debt is referred to as a *lien*.

❓ **Get Help 6.4**
You will certainly need a considerable amount of your lawyer's time as you discuss specific provisions that you or the seller want in the purchase agreement. You can cut down on this time (and the associated expense) by studying a purchase agreement template, which you can buy for a few dollars at your office supply store. An example is the *Buy–Sell Agreement Kit* from Self-Counsel Press. See **www.self-counsel.com**.

✓ **Test Yourself 6.16**
True or False? A non-competition clause restricts a seller from disclosing company secrets to a competing firm.

financial statements, customer lists, operating methods, and anything else that will help you assess the business. The seller does not want to have you learn all the intimate details of the business, change your mind about buying it, and then go tell everything you know to the competition. Therefore, you will likely be required to sign a non-disclosure agreement before having access to confidential information about the company. Non-disclosure can also be required of the seller. If you buy the business, you will not want the seller to reveal confidential information to competitors—including the selling price or financing arrangements for the business.

CONTINUING ASSISTANCE   It is a fairly common practice to have the old owner of a business remain with the business as an employee or adviser, often for an extended period after the business is sold. This can be arranged as a condition of the purchase agreement, usually with some form of salary payment involved. The old owner is able to help the ownership transition by:

- training the new owner
- keeping the business running and creating cash flow during the transition
- introducing the owner to customers, suppliers, and employees to help transfer these critical relationships.

Ask yourself: What problems could arise from these types of arrangements? It sometimes happens that deals keeping the old owner in the business must be renegotiated to a shorter time period. This is usually the result of personal conflicts that develop between the new and old owners of the business relating to:

Test Yourself 6.17
True or False? A disclosure clause in a purchase agreement requires the seller to tell anything they know about the company that might prevent the buyer from completing the sale.

- *Supervision of employees.* The new owner is trying to establish authority while the old owner continues in the long habit of being the boss.
- *Changes in methods.* The new owner has bought the business with a view to improving things, while the old owner acts defensively to changes, interpreting them as a criticism.

When negotiating for the continuing help of the previous owner, it is wise to leave some flexibility in the planned duration of the arrangement.

Head Start Exercise

6.6   Briefly note any provisions you would require in the purchase agreement ($\frac{1}{4}$ page maximum).

How Much Should I Pay?

VALUATION CONCEPTS   A business is constantly changing and adapting to the *marketplace,* the environment in which it lives. It grows, it shrinks, it gets sick or healthy. And people can be very subjective, even emotional, about a business. It is impossible to set a definitive monetary value on any business since no two people will view it exactly the same way. But people do agree on certain general concepts and approaches toward estimating the value of a business.[4]

SMALL BUSINESS PROFILE 6.1

A McAfee & Associates Insurance Brokers Ltd.

Adelle McAfee owns A McAfee & Associates Insurance Brokers Ltd. Over a 17-year period, Adelle went from being part-time employee of the firm, to full-time employee, to half owner, and finally to full owner. This was all part of an orderly planned succession for the business leading up to the retirement of the previous owner. And there is a succession plan in place for when Adelle retires. Today, the firm has eight full-time employees and one part-timer. At the time of buying the business, putting a value on the company was relatively easy. There is a pricing formula that is widely used for the insurance industry, based on the commissions generated by a brokerage, so negotiations tend to be minimal.

The insurance industry, by its very nature, tends to be conservative and slow to change, but during her time in the business, Adelle has seen significant changes in the market—less so in technology. Her firm is still using the primary software that it purchased in 1991, although the provider updates the program regularly for an annual maintenance fee. Changes in legislation and more competition among financial service providers over the last few years have allowed for a greater range of products and insurers that Adelle can offer to her clients. It has also required greater knowledge on the part of the broker. This means constant training for Adelle and her employees. Part of this requirement comes from the provincial Insurance Brokers licensing and regulating body that requires annual training in legislation as well as ethical issues in order to maintain a broker's licence. Then there is the huge amount of product and market information that has to be absorbed. "Education never stops, once you get into a profession," says Adelle.

Ratio Analysis: You would never consider buying a business without having an accountant examine the financial statements for that company. The financial statements can reveal a lot about a company—is the firm profitable, is it able to pay its bills, does it have a good inventory turnover, and so on. The accountant doesn't draw these kinds of conclusions just by glancing at the numbers and relying on experience. Instead, the accountant will perform a *ratio analysis*. This means using the numbers on the financial statements to calculate certain **key ratios**, which will help to build a picture of the company's financial health.

> **key ratio** A financial indicator for a company, obtained by dividing one specific value from the company's financial statements by another specific value from those statements.

These ratios help to describe the company in terms of:
- *Profitability.* The most common measure of profitability is *return on equity*.

$$\text{Return on Equity} = \frac{\text{Net Profit}}{\text{Owners' Equity}}$$

- *Liquidity.* This **liquidity** ratio indicates whether a firm is in a position to keep paying the bills that are due.

> **liquidity** The ability of a company to pay its short-term financial obligations.

$$\text{Current Ratio} = \frac{\text{Current Assets}}{\text{Current Liabilities}}$$

Another ratio that tests liquidity is called the *quick ratio,* or sometimes the *acid test ratio.* In this case, inventory is not counted as a current asset because it may take some time to turn inventory into cash.

◇ **Get Help 6.5**

Financial ratios are available, classified by industry, on Industry Canada's Performance Plus site: *sme.ic.gc.ca*. You can access the site free of charge. Statistics Canada also sells ratio information in its document *Financial Performance Indicators for Canadian Business*, which you may be able to access through your library or accountant. Key ratios are often difficult to read because they are sometimes expressed as percentages and sometimes as fractions. You may well need the help of an accountant for this.

solvency The ability of a firm to pay all of its financial obligations (short- and long-term).

$$\text{Quick Ratio} = \frac{\text{Current Assets} - \text{Inventory}}{\text{Current Liabilities}}$$

- *Management efficiency.* These profitability ratios also indicate how efficiently the company is able to use its assets, as well as its purchasing and sales efficiency.

$$\text{Return on Assets} = \frac{\text{Net Profit}}{\text{Total Assets}}$$

$$\text{Gross Margin} = \frac{\text{Gross Profit}}{\text{Sales}}$$

- *Debt management.* These ratios indicate the **solvency** of a company. The *debt to equity ratio* indicates how much a firm relies on borrowed capital compared to capital invested by the owners.

$$\text{Debt to Equity} = \frac{\text{Total Liabilities}}{\text{Owners' Equity}}$$

How much debt a company carries can affect profits because of the related interest expense. Most industries have their own standard for what is considered a healthy debt ratio.

$$\text{Debt Ratio} = \frac{\text{Total Liabilities}}{\text{Total Assets}}$$

- *Cash management.* How long it takes a company to collect money that is owed to it can affect its ability to pay its own bills.

$$\text{Average Collection Period} = \frac{\text{Accounts Receivable}}{\text{Average Sales per Day}}$$

Key ratios by themselves still tell you relatively little about the financial health of a company. It is only when these numbers are compared to the averages for your industry that you can see a company's *relative* liquidity, profitability, or efficiency.

Rate of Return: In estimating the *rate of return* to expect from a company that is for sale, ratio analysis will show you the past rate using the return on equity ratio. But other ratios are also important here, because things like the relative efficiency or debt management of a company give hints about the likelihood of that particular level of profitability continuing.

Imagine that you have inherited some money that you would like to invest. You know that the higher the risk associated with any investment, the higher the return on investment (ROI) you should expect. You also know that the more liquid the investment (the easier it is to get your money back in cash) the lower the return. For example, if you put your money into a daily interest savings account, your money is insured and guaranteed (up to a maximum of $100,000 at the time of writing). The money is also totally liquid, in that you can take it out of the account at any time. But with such low risk and high liquidity, the return (the annual interest rate) will only be a percentage point or two.

Putting your money into Canada Savings Bonds is also low risk. But these are a less liquid investment, in that you have to wait for the bonds to mature in order to get your interest. So, they should give a higher return. For the sake of the example, let's say that the bonds will be paying around 5 percent this year. If you would like to assume more risk you could look to the securities markets, where you might be able to find a mutual fund that has a

✓ **Test Yourself 6.18**
True or False? The return on equity ratio is an indicator of a company's profitability.

✓ **Test Yourself 6.19**
True or False? The quick ratio is an indicator of a company's management efficiency.

✓ **Test Yourself 6.20**
True or False? The collection period indicates how long, on average, it takes a company to get money owed to it by customers.

pretty consistent return of, let's say, 9 percent. Ultimately, there are no guarantees with such an investment, but based on past performance you might still consider the risk to be moderate.

Ask yourself: What if I were to invest in a small business? What rate of return would I want from such a risk? The high failure rate of small firms means that this tends to be high risk. Also, your investment has very low liquidity in that you can get your money back only by selling the business, which could take some time. So you certainly wouldn't be willing to accept a return of 1 percent or 5 percent or even 9 percent. Perhaps you will decide that if you are going to take the risk of buying a business, you will want a return of 15 percent. But this is only a general decision on your part.

The specific rate of return that you will want from any particular business will depend on the risks associated with that business. The higher the risk, the higher the return you must expect. Risk factors include:

- How long the business has been established.
- The stability of the particular market.
- Dependence on individuals in the firm who may leave.
- Growth in the competition.
- Rate of change in technology.

And many other factors that you will investigate while assessing the business.

Head Start Exercise

6.7   Choose a rate of return that would be acceptable for your investment in a business. Explain your choice ($\frac{1}{4}$ page maximum).

Present Value: The concept of *present value* starts with the idea of future value. If you were to invest $100 today at an annual interest rate of 5 percent, at the end of one year you would have $105. And at the end of two years, because the interest is compounded, you would have $110.25. At the end of five years you would have $127.63. So if you entered into a deal with someone who was going to pay you $127.63 at the end of five years, you know that's not the same as getting paid $127.63 today. The *present value* of that $127.63 (considering 5-percent annual growth) is only $100. There is a formula to calculate the present value of any future amount of money you are expecting:

$$PV = \frac{FV_n}{(1 + i)^n}$$

where:

PV = Present value

FV_n = The amount of money to be received in year "n".

n = The number of years in the future that the money is to be received.

i = The annual interest rate that the money will grow at.

Try the formula using FV_n = $127.63, i = 0.05, and n = 5, just to test your math skills. The application of present value is, of course, when you can reasonably predict the future profit

✓ **Test Yourself 6.21**
True or False? The lower the liquidity of an investment, the lower the expected rate of return should be.

✓ **Test Yourself 6.22**
True or False? The higher the risk of an investment, the higher the expected rate of return should be.

Get Help 6.6
Present value can be calculated by formula or by using a present value table. These tables are often found in business math and accounting textbooks, or can be downloaded from the Internet. For example, the business and legal publisher CCH has a Business Owner's Toolkit site at **www.toolkit.cch.com/tools/ tools.asp** where you can click on *Present Value Tables*.

Test Yourself 6.23
True or False? Present value calculations are based on the idea that money is more valuable if received now rather than later.

going concern An operating business that is expected to continue operating into the foreseeable future.

Test Yourself 6.24
True or False? Liquidation value is typically a lower amount than book value.

of a business and then calculate the present value of that profit at some reasonable growth rate. This gives you an indicator of what that future profit is worth today, or how much you might be willing to pay for a business that would make that future profit.

VALUATION METHODS   There are two main considerations in putting a monetary value on a business:

- The value of the assets that you are buying.
- The projected value of the future profits of the business.

Each of these considerations has its own set of methods for determining business value: asset methods or income methods. Within these two groups of methods, there are lots of specific techniques for setting a value on a business. A broad sample, but certainly not all of these techniques, is presented here.

ASSET METHODS for setting a value on a business are also known as *balance sheet methods*, since it is the balance sheet that provides the information for their calculation. Imagine that you are considering buying Best Bronze Tanning Bed Distributors, whose recent balance sheet is shown in Figure 6.1. This supplier of commercial tanning beds sells several brands of beds to spas and tanning studios throughout your province. In addition, Best Bronze has just secured the exclusive Canadian distribution rights for a new, safer type of bed that produces no increased risk of skin cancer.

Liquidation value is the lowest possible value for a business and is more valid for a failing business than it is for a **going concern**. The liquidation value estimates what the value of the assets would be if they were sold at auction (or otherwise quickly disposed of) and deducts from this amount the liabilities of the business. The remainder represents the liquidation value of the company. Using the Best Bronze example, Figure 6.2 shows the value of the company's assets as appraisers and an auctioneering firm have estimated their quick-sale value.

From the liquidation value of the assets ($288,987) the value of the company liabilities ($236,230) is deducted. This leaves $52,757 as the liquidation value of the business. Obviously, this is far from any fair market value for the business. However, it is important to calculate this value to show the range of possible values for a business—especially for the buyer, who may use this information in negotiations.

The *book value* of a business is the value of its assets, as shown on the balance sheet, minus the value of its liabilities—in other words, the owners' equity. So, in the case of Best Bronze, the book value would be $159,100. The main problem with book value is that the value of assets stated on the balance sheet may be quite far from any market value of the assets. For example, companies have choices in how they can depreciate assets for maximum tax advantage, but this could result in assets being undervalued on the balance sheet.

Adjusted book value attempts to correct for problems with book value by trying to represent all assets and liabilities at fair market value. For example, in Figure 6.3 you can see that for Best Bronze the following figures have been adjusted:

- *Accounts receivable.* Further investigation showed that two of the accounts still carried on the books had been outstanding for some time and were from companies known to be in

Figure 6.1

BEST BRONZE TANNING BED DISTRIBUTORS | Balance Sheet

December 31, 20XX

ASSETS

CURRENT ASSETS

Cash	$ 4,752	
Accounts receivable	16,228	
Inventory	72,225	
Prepaid expenses	1,005	
Total current assets		$ 94,210

FIXED ASSETS

Land and building	$262,000	
Warehouse equipment	12,210	
Office equipment	4,160	
Truck	22,750	
Total fixed assets		301,120
Total Assets		**$395,330**

LIABILITIES

CURRENT LIABILITIES

Accounts payable	$ 29,994	
Short-term loans payable	3,946	
Taxes payable	10,620	
Total current liabilities		$ 44,560

LONG-TERM LIABILITIES

Mortgage payable	$ 177,252	
Long-term loan payable	14,418	
Total long-term liabilities		191,670
Total Liabilities	**$236,230**	
Owners' Equity	159,100	
Total Liabilities and Owners' Equity		**$395,330**

deep financial trouble. Since there was little chance of ever collecting on these, they were deducted from the receivables.

• *Inventory.* A careful inspection of the inventory revealed some old stock, including a couple of models of a tanning bed that was considered obsolete. Because of safety considerations, there was no hope of ever selling these beds and they could not be returned for refund since the manufacturer was out of business. Their value was therefore deducted from the book value of the inventory.

Figure 6.2	**LIQUIDATION VALUE OF ASSETS FOR BEST BRONZE TANNING BED DISTRIBUTORS**	

	Balance Sheet (Book) Value	Liquidation Value
CURRENT ASSETS		
Cash	$ 4,752	$ 4,752
Accounts receivable	16,228	3,245
Inventory	72,225	28,890
Prepaid expenses	1,005	0
Total current assets	$ 94,210	$ 36,887
FIXED ASSETS		
Land and building	$262,000	$225,000
Warehouse equipment	12,210	8,700
Office equipment	4,160	1,900
Truck	22,750	16,500
Total fixed assets	$301,120	$252,100
Total Assets	**$395,330**	**$288,987**

- *Land and building.* This asset was revalued upward to reflect steady increases in real estate prices and because of a building inspection that revealed the structure and facilities to be in excellent shape.
- *Warehouse equipment/office equipment.* These also were revalued upward. The accounting system used by Best Bronze had depreciated both assets at the standard *capital cost allowance rates* indicated by the Canada Revenue Agency on tax returns. The equipment, however, had been well maintained and was worth much more than the book value. Because of an active market in both used warehouse and office equipment, it was easy to establish fair market values.
- *Truck.* Recent increases in new-vehicle prices also resulted in increased market value for used vehicles. In addition, this particular truck had logged very few kilometres and was in excellent condition, resulting in the new higher value.

The adjusted value of the assets ($409,957) minus the value of the liabilities ($236,230) gives an adjusted book value of $173,727.

Replacement value is a useful technique for comparing the cost of buying a business with the cost of starting a similar business from scratch. Assets are revalued at what it would cost to replace them—not necessarily with brand-new assets. But even available used assets will almost always cost more than the depreciated book value of existing assets. Figure 6.4 shows the assets of Best Bronze at their replacement cost.

Obviously, the value of assets like cash and accounts receivable will remain unchanged. Assets like inventory and prepaid expenses are valued higher because prices will likely have gone up between the time these things were purchased and the present. The replacement

Figure 6.3

ADJUSTED VALUE OF ASSETS FOR
BEST BRONZE TANNING BED DISTRIBUTORS

	Balance Sheet (Book) Value	Adjusted Value
CURRENT ASSETS		
Cash	$ 4,752	$ 4,752
Accounts receivable	16,228	7,000
Inventory	72,225	63,000
Prepaid expenses	1,005	1,005
Total current assets	$ 94,210	$ 75,757
FIXED ASSETS		
Land and building	$262,000	$287,000
Warehouse equipment	12,210	16,500
Office equipment	4,160	5,500
Truck	22,750	25,200
Total fixed assets	$301,120	$334,200
Total Assets	**$395,330**	**$409,957**

value of assets like buildings and equipment is generally higher than the adjusted value because replacing assets can include fees like real estate transfer taxes, legal fees, or delivery and installation costs. The $445,240 replacement value of the assets minus the $236,230 in liabilities produces a business replacement value of $209,010.

✓ **Test Yourself 6.25**
True or False? Replacement value is an asset method of business valuation.

INCOME METHODS put a value on a business based on the ability of that business to earn money. Many of the income techniques require you to predict the future earnings of the business, which is arguably a more fair way to assess value. But it can also be a less accurate way, since the value is no more accurate than your ability to predict the future.

The capitalization of earnings technique for pricing a business starts with establishing your desired rate of return. For example, you might want at least a 15-percent return on any business that you would buy. But you must decide on the relative risks of this particular business. You know that the business has been established for many years and has shown a steady growth in sales and profit. Your ratio analysis shows that the business is financially healthy and well managed. The only outstanding risk you can identify is the potential for health problems related to tanning beds. You know that despite widespread warnings by dermatologists over many years, the tanning business has continued to grow. For ethical reasons, you would not be entering this industry, except for the recent innovation in bed safety for which Best Bronze has exclusive distribution rights. The German manufacturer of the new beds has indicated that supply will not be a problem.

✓ **Test Yourself 6.26**
True or False? Adjusted book value is an income method of business valuation.

After careful discussions with your advisers, you may settle on 15 percent as an acceptable return on any investment you would make in Best Bronze. You can then compare this figure to the profits of the business (the return) to calculate a price for the business

Figure 6.4

**REPLACEMENT VALUE OF ASSETS FOR
BEST BRONZE TANNING BED DISTRIBUTORS**

	Balance Sheet (Book) Value	Replacement Value
CURRENT ASSETS		
Cash	$ 4,752	$ 4,752
Accounts receivable	16,228	16,228
Inventory	72,225	74,500
Prepaid expenses	1,005	1,060
Total current assets	$ 94,210	$ 96,540
FIXED ASSETS		
Land and building	$262,000	$297,900
Warehouse equipment	12,210	16,800
Office equipment	4,160	5,700
Truck	22,750	28,300
Total fixed assets	$301,120	$348,700
Total Assets	**$395,330**	**$445,240**

(the investment). For example, look at the income statement of Best Bronze Tanning Bed Distributors shown in Figure 6.5.

Last year's net profit before tax was $30,210, and let's say that the average profit over the last few years has been around $30,000. You are looking for an ROI of 15 percent. Another way of writing this is:

$$\frac{R}{I} = \frac{15}{100}$$

Since you already know that the return (profit) will be $30,000, you can substitute that into the equation:

$$\frac{\$30,000}{I} = \frac{15}{100}$$

Now all you have to do is solve the equation for *I*, the investment: *I* = *$200,000.* This tells you that if you want a return on investment (ROI) of 15 percent and the return is $30,000, then you should be willing to pay $200,000 for the business.

Capitalized cash flow is another income method. In this context, it refers to net profit that has been adjusted by adding back in:
* *Depreciation.* This expense does not use up actual cash of the business.
* *Extraordinary salary, benefits, or "perks" received by the owner.* This solves the problem of properly accounting for these forms of earnings as discussed under valuation concepts.
* *Extraordinary one-time transactions.* This would include settlement of a lawsuit, a one-time licence fee, or some kind of windfall that would not be normal for the business but could dramatically affect the profit in the year it occurred.

Figure 6.5

BEST BRONZE TANNING BED DISTRIBUTORS |
Income Statement

For the One-Year Period Ending December 31, 20XX

SALES

Equipment sales	$602,015	
Installations and repairs	104,725	
Total sales		$ 706,740

COSTS

Cost of goods sold		$331,110

GROSS PROFIT

Gross profit		$375,630

EXPENSES

Salaries/benefits	$287,865	
Depreciation	12,135	
Building maintenance	11,055	
Utilities	8,190	
Professional fees	6,100	
Advertising	6,328	
Supplies	5,922	
Insurance	7,445	
Miscellaneous expense	380	
Total expenses		$345,420

Net Profit Before Tax **$30,210**

In the income statement shown for Best Bronze, the only adjustment would be for the $12,135 of depreciation. So, let's say that this business had an average cash flow over the last three years of $30,000 + $12,000 = $42,000. Dividing this cash flow by your expected return of 15 percent would give you a price of $42,000/15% = $280,000 for the business. This is the same math as in the previous example, just expressed in a shorter form.

Discounted cash flow is yet another income method. This way of pricing a business depends on your ability to predict future cash flow of the business by using the same projection techniques used throughout your business plan to project sales costs and expenses. If cash flow for Best Bronze has been growing at roughly 10 percent a year for the last few years, you may decide to project this same growth rate for the next five years (this is the outside length of time considered feasible for small-business projections). In the last year, cash flow was $42,000, so next year it will be 110% × $42,000 = $46,200, and so on. And if we look up the 15 percent ROI that we want (also called a **discount rate**) on a present value table, we will find the present value factors for each of the years shown in Figure 6.6.

This figure shows us that the present value of the cash flow that the business is expected to produce (at a 15-percent ROI) is $184,145. Assuming that your projections are correct, this is the amount you should be willing to pay for the business based on this method.

Earnings multipliers represent another method of pricing a business. If you knew the selling price of several recently sold firms in your industry, as well as the profits of those companies,

discount rate The yearly rate of return that is used to calculate the present value of future cash inflows.

Figure 6.6

BEST BRONZE TANNING BED DISTRIBUTORS | Discounted Cash Flow at Discount Factor of 15%						
	Year 1	**Year 2**	**Year 3**	**Year 4**	**Year 5**	**Total**
Projected cash flow	$46,200	$50,820	$55,902	$61,492	$67,641	
Present value factor	0.869565	0.756144	0.657516	0.571753	0.497177	
Present value	$40,174	$38,427	$36,756	$35,158	$33,630	$184,145

you would be able to calculate a ratio between the selling price and the earnings. For example, on average, the companies may have sold for five times their earnings (before-tax net profit). It would then be a simple matter to multiply the recent average earnings of the company you are pricing by five (the multiplier) to get an estimate of the current market value of the firm. *Ask yourself: Where could I get the information to calculate an earnings multiplier?*

In all likelihood, sale price information will be based on your own experience and observation, insider information, or industry gossip. Corporate directories and credit reports will also give earnings information, and it is possible to deduce selling prices from them by comparing before and after sale reports. You can also get an indication of the multiplier for your industry by using the average **price–earnings ratio** of publicly traded companies in your field. This information is easily available but will apply to companies that are many times larger than the small firm you are pricing. Keep in mind that this number will change with volatility in stock prices and so the price–earnings ratio should be averaged over some period of time.

price–earnings ratio (P/E) The ratio comparing the current market price of an ordinary share of a company with the profit per share for that company over the last year.

Earnings multipliers are considered to be a **rule-of-thumb pricing** method. Many industries have their own traditional rule-of-thumb methods for setting values on companies. Primarily based on profit, rule-of-thumb pricing can also use factors such as sales income, units sold, or assets to produce the ratio with price. For example, gas stations might be priced, on average, at $0.30 multiplied by the number of litres of gas sold each month. Some industry associations and periodicals track and publish current information about multipliers for calculating business prices.

rule-of-thumb pricing Using a ratio showing a relationship between the average price of a business in a particular field and some other factor such as profit to calculate the price for a specific company.

Other valuation techniques include:
- adjusted tangible net worth
- discounted future earnings
- capitalization of after-tax earnings
- discounted after-tax discretionary cash flow.

Get Help 6.7

Various financial services and other companies offer websites that give stock information, including P/E information for the shares of specific companies traded on Canadian exchanges. For example, see **www.liveinvestor.com**.

And there are many many variations on all of the techniques listed.

Head Start Exercise

6.8 Outline the business valuation techniques you plan to use to put a price on the business. Identify any professional advisers you will use. ($\frac{1}{3}$ page maximum.)

NEGOTIATING PRICE   In determining a price to pay for a business it is necessary to use a variety of different techniques for estimating the value of the firm. These will produce a variety of values, which you can use to help establish:

- a fair market price for the business
- the lowest reasonable price you think the business could be purchased for
- the maximum amount you are personally willing to pay for the business.

These are the numbers you need to prepare for your price negotiations.

One method for establishing a fair market price is to use a weighted average of your different business values. You may have used several techniques to estimate the value of the business, but some of those techniques are more valid than others. So you may have a discussion involving your accountant, perhaps a business valuation specialist, and some other advisers, where you come to a consensus about the relative weight that each of your valuation methods should be given; maybe on a scale of 1 to 10. For example, you may decide, as a group, that the liquidation value has little validity here since the business is financially sound. You may weigh book value at 5 since it does not take the established goodwill of the company into account. You may decide that discounted cash flow deserves a 10 weighting because of the steady historical growth in cash flow that the company has shown, and so on. As shown in Figure 6.7, the weighted values are averaged to estimate a fair market value for the business.

Get Help 6.8

Accountants who specialize in establishing the value of businesses often carry the CBV designation, showing that they have been certified by the Canadian Institute of Chartered Business Valuators. The institute's website, at **www.cicbv.ca**, can help you find a business valuation specialist in your area.

Test Yourself 6.27

True or False? Many industries have their own rule-of-thumb pricing methods using multipliers.

SMALL BUSINESS PROFILE 6.2
Kutters Hairstyling

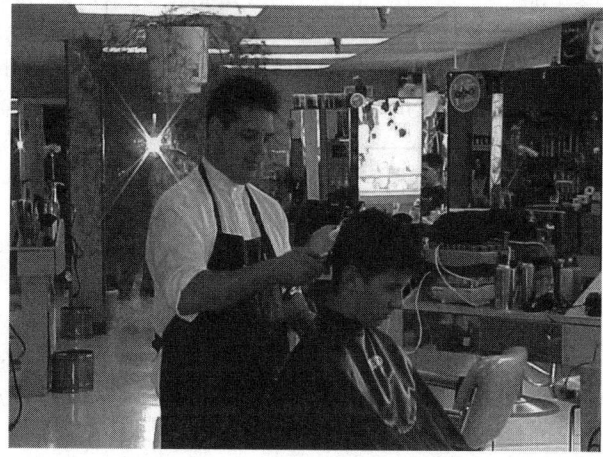

Melanie Graham bought Kutters Hairstyling, Whitehorse, Yukon, an upscale hair salon, ten years ago after working there as an employee for seven years. Melanie had started working for Kutters part-time when she was 13 years old. To buy the business, she was able to secure a bank loan and since that time the salon has expanded from the original 3 employees to 12. It has also expanded in the range of services that it offers, now including aesthetics, tanning, and massage. The change in ownership went smoothly with all of the former employees still remaining in the business.

At the time of the buyout, the agreement included a provision for the original owner to work in the salon on a "chair rental" basis, keeping her own fees and clientele but paying Melanie for the space and services. The other stylists (and all of the new hires since then) have worked as employees on a commission basis. This arrangement makes it more conducive for Melanie to invest in the training of "her team." In fact, Melanie's reputation for the training and development of her staff helped win her the Business Development Bank of Canada's *Young Entrepreneur Award* for 2001. Melanie emphasizes training not only to keep her staff on the "cutting" edge of hair fashion, but also as a team building activity. At the time of writing, she had completed arrangements to take her employees on a "training cruise" combining a holiday perk with serious development.

Recently, Kutters moved to new premises right in the heart of downtown. Melanie formed a partnership with her brother to buy the building, which is then leased back to the salon. The site is ideal for maximum pedestrian traffic and visibility and will allow for future expansion of the business. Melanie Graham's advice to new entrepreneurs is to "really try to learn the finance. Even if it's a simple business and even if you have a bookkeeper or accountant, you should still try to know as much as you can about finance and accounting."

Figure 6.7

BEST BRONZE TANNING BED DISTRIBUTORS | Weighted Average Business Value

Valuation Technique		Business Value ×	Weighting	= Weighted Value
Asset Methods	Liquidation Value	$ 52,757	1	$ 52,757
	Book Value	159,100	5	795,500
	Adjusted Book Value	173,727	7	1,216,089
	Replacement Value	209,010	4	836,040
Earnings Method	Capitalized Earning	200,000	5	1,000,000
	Capitalized Cash Flow	280,000	6	1,680,000
	Discounted Cash Flow	184,145	10	1,841,450
	Earnings Multiplier	198,000	8	1,584,000
Totals			46	$9,005,836

$$\text{Weighted Average Business Value} = \frac{\$9,005,836}{46} = \$195,779$$

This process can now help you plan for negotiations by first determining *the lowest reasonable value that you think the business could be sold for*. This should be your *opening offer*. Using the Best Bronze example, you may decide to set the opening offer close to the book value of the business, with only a token amount ($6,000) included for the goodwill of the business—let's say, $165,000. This leaves you more than $20,000 of negotiating room to get to your fair market value of $195,779, but you are still within the range in which the business could conceivably sell.

The next step is to set the *maximum amount you are willing to pay for the business*. You would certainly not want to pay above your assessment of a fair market value. But if you have come this far in the buying process, you have already invested a considerable amount of your time, effort, and no doubt money for professional fees in buying the business. Let's say you estimate the cost at $2,500. If you don't make the deal, not only are you out by this amount, but you also will have to spend it all over again on the next business you consider buying. So, in an effort to avoid going through the process again, you can add this amount to your fair market value and get your maximum price of $198,279. You now have the settlement range that you will negotiate within ($165,000 to $198,000), working hard to keep the price as low as possible by moving, when necessary, in very small increments.

The starting point for price negotiations is usually the asking price for the business.[5] Be careful not to let the asking price influence your opening offer.[6] The asking price itself tells you nothing about the value of the business. It does, however, give you some small indications about the negotiating style of the seller and about the nature of the final agreement. For example, if the asking price is ludicrously high, it could indicate that the seller has a totally unrealistic sense of the value of the business—in which case the negotiating challenge for you is to educate the seller. Or, it could indicate a seller who is looking to mislead a naïve buyer into paying too much—in which case you should be suspicious of everything the seller tells you and wary of all the seller's tactics. Careful questioning of the seller and checking their references and reputation are your best bets for distinguishing between the two reasons for such high pricing.

An unreasonably low asking price could be a warning sign that the seller is trying to hurry you into *snapping up a bargain* before you do a thorough investigation of the business. But it could also mean a seller who is in distress and needs to sell quickly. If this is the case, the seller will probably be looking for a short closing (a short time to the finalization date of the deal). The low asking price could also indicate a seller who truly underestimates the value of the business. This is more likely to be the situation when the seller does not have competent professional help to assist with the sale. Either of these last two situations presents an opportunity for a real bargain. *Ask yourself: Would I have a moral problem in taking advantage of a distressed or incompetent seller?* There is certainly an ethical line between negotiating a great deal and deceiving someone who is vulnerable because of a personal crisis or bad advice. Most ethical businesspeople would want to make sure that the distressed seller had full knowledge that a higher price could be secured by waiting. And it would be unethical to actively mislead a naïve seller, even by confirming misinformation the seller may have received from advisers. Besides, an incredible bargain of a deal, even after it is long closed, could still end up in court if there is evidence of deception.

An important principle of price negotiations is to bargain based on the documented verifiable facts only, not on something the seller may tell you *off the record*. For example, you may be negotiating to buy a golf course and the seller privately confesses to **skimming cash** for rounds of golf that require no receipts to the tune of $20,000 a year. The implication here is that you too can benefit by this illegal activity and that the business is really worth more than the value that the financial statements indicate. In such a case, you must remember that you do not know that the business has an additional $20,000 in revenue. All you know for sure is that the seller is a thief. *Ask yourself: What are the chances of a thief also being a liar?*

skimming cash The illegal removal of unreported cash from a business in order to avoid paying tax on that income.

A second negotiating principle that you should adhere to, as the buyer, is to negotiate for the business as it is—not as how you could make it. Beware when the seller is constantly pointing out that the business has this potential or that possibility of improvement. These are potentials that the seller did not take advantage of, improvements that the seller did not make. As a result, the seller is *not* entitled to compensation for them. Improvements to a business are worth money only if they have been implemented.

In buying a business or a share of a business, price is only one issue to be negotiated. But it cannot be separated from the other issues. For example, you will likely have to pay more if you can get the seller to agree to payment terms that favour you. On the other hand, if the seller wishes to retain the right to open a competing business within the next few years, this should reduce the price of the business. There will be many non-monetary issues that have to be negotiated, and the best way to deal with them is to set a monetary value on each of them in your negotiation planning. This may be more of a subjective process than actual calculation, but each issue can be priced. For example, if you would prefer to close the deal on May 30, but the seller would prefer April 30, you must estimate what it will cost you in cash and inconvenience to have to run around and hurry your preparations to advance the date— say, $1,000. This means that you will reduce your opening offer (or any offers currently on the table) as well as your maximum price by $1,000.

To simplify the negotiating process, it is often a good tactic to seek agreement, in principle, on as many non-monetary issues as possible before discussing price. This reduces the number of times that you will have to recalculate your price position during the talks.

✓ **Test Yourself 6.28**

True or False? Cash skimming by the previous owner should be factored into the price of a business.

Head Start Exercise

6.9   Briefly list the negotiating tactics you will use in arranging the purchase agreement ($\frac{1}{4}$ page maximum).

✓Answers to Test Yourself Questions

6.1   Starting a brand-new company is, on average, higher risk than buying an existing business. *True*

6.2   Starting a brand-new business is, on average, more expensive than buying an existing business. *False*

6.3   Buying an existing independent business is lower risk than buying a franchise. *False*

6.4   Goodwill refers to the intentions of business sellers to treat prospective buyers fairly. *False*

6.5   The most common danger in buying an existing business is the problem of over-valued assets. *True*

6.6   The term "redundant assets" refers to assets that are not necessary for the business to carry on making a profit. *True*

6.7   It is relatively easy to change an existing negative image of a small business. *False*

6.8   Small problems in a business for sale that you know have inexpensive solutions should still be noted in your assessment of a business for sale. *True*

6.9   The critical question to ask the owner of a business for sale is "What is the price?" *False*

6.10   Buying into a business typically means taking a majority ownership in the firm. *False*

6.11   The *core business* refers to a company's primary products/services and primary market segments. *True*

6.12   As a purchaser, it is a negotiating advantage to deal only with a listing broker or agent. *True*

6.13   It is possible to buy the shares of a sole proprietorship. *False*

6.14   Compared to buying shares, buying the assets of a company provides greater protection against being sued for past actions of the company. *True*

6.15   The right of a creditor to take over a particular asset because of an unpaid debt is referred to as a *lien*. *True*

6.16   A non-competition clause restricts a seller from disclosing company secrets to a competing firm. *False*

6.17   A disclosure clause in a purchase agreement requires the seller to tell anything they know about the company that might prevent the buyer from completing the sale. *True*

6.18   The return on equity ratio is an indicator of a company's profitability. *True*

6.19   The quick ratio is an indicator of a company's management efficiency. *False*

6.20   The collection period indicates how long, on average, it takes a company to get money owed to it by customers. *True*

6.21   The lower the liquidity of an investment, the lower the expected rate of return should be. *False*

6.22   The higher the risk of an investment, the higher the expected rate of return should be. *True*

6.23 Present value calculations are based on the idea that money is more valuable if received now rather than later. *True*

6.24 Liquidation value is typically a lower amount than book value. *True*

6.25 Replacement value is an asset method of business valuation. *True*

6.26 Adjusted book value is an income method of business valuation. *False*

6.27 Many industries have their own rule-of-thumb pricing methods using multipliers. *True*

6.28 Cash skimming by the previous owner should be factored into the price of a business. *False*

Questions for Discussion

1. What are the personality differences between entrepreneurs suited to buying a business versus those suited to starting their own new business?

2. What is the cheapest way to get into business for yourself? The most expensive? Outline some scenarios where buying a business could be the cheapest.

3. Identify some instances where you have bought something and ended up feeling cheated. How could these situations be similar to buying a business?

4. Is it possible to buy a business with little or no cash? Outline any stories you may have heard of this happening. What could you negotiate instead of cash for taking over a business?

5. What is the single most important thing to find out before buying a business? Argue your position.

6. Discuss the issue of *skimming cash*. How prevalent is this among small businesses? Which businesses would be ideal for this practice? How can it be discouraged?

Recommended Reading

Balanko-Dickson, Greg. *Tips and Traps When Buying a Business.* New York: McGraw-Hill, 2006.

Feldman, Stanley, Timothy Sullivan, and Roger Winsby. *What Every Business Owner Should Know about Valuing Their Business.* New York: McGraw-Hill, 2003.

Lambing, Peggy A., and Charles R Kuehl. *Entrepreneurship*, 4th ed. New Jersey: Pearson Education Inc., 2007.

Tuller, Lawrence W. *The Small Business Valuation Book.* Avon, MA: Adams Media, 1994.

The Business Plan, Alternative Module:
Business Purchase

Entrepreneurs buying or buying into an existing business should complete Sections 1 to 5 of the business plan as well as this portion.

1. Briefly describe why buying or buying into a business is an appropriate start-up method for you and your personal circumstances.

_____

_____

_____

_____

_____

_____

_____

2. Describe the history of the company you are buying (or buying into) and any specific advantages of buying now.

_____

_____

_____

_____

_____

_____

3. Describe the investigation methods you used to assess the business and to get the information for completing Sections 1 to 5 of the business plan.

_____

_____

_____

_____

_____

_____

4. Briefly describe the reason for sale by the owner(s) as determined by your investigations.

---

5. Generally describe your purchase transaction in terms of what you are buying (a piece of a business, a partnership role, a whole business) and from whom you are buying it. Attach, as an appendix, a draft of any partnership or shareholder agreement that will apply.

---

6. Briefly identify and describe the roles of any intermediaries in arranging the sale.

---

7. Briefly outline the main provisions of your purchase agreement and attach a draft of the agreement as an appendix.

_____

_____

_____

_____

_____

_____

_____

_____

_____

8. Describe the financial health of the company being purchased, referring to the analysis of the key business ratios.

_____

_____

_____

_____

_____

_____

_____

_____

9. Identify what you consider an acceptable rate of return for investing in a business. Give your rationale.

_____

_____

_____

_____

_____

_____

_____

_____

_____

10. Identify a fair market value for the business. Briefly explain your valuation methodology and sources of assistance. Attach, as an appendix, a detailed valuation of the business using several techniques from both asset and income methods.

_____

_____

_____

_____

_____

_____

_____

_____

_____

_____

11. List your opening offer and the maximum price you are willing to pay for the business. Explain your rationale.

_____

_____

_____

_____

_____

_____

_____

_____

_____

12. Describe your plan for conducting negotiations.

_____

_____

_____

_____

_____

_____

_____

_____

_____

The Franchise Alternative:
How Do I Buy a Franchise?

LEARNING OBJECTIVES

On completion of this chapter, you should be able to:

- *Name and describe the various franchising formats.*
- *Discuss the growing trend for franchise disclosure legislation.*
- *Assess your own suitability as a franchisee.*
- *Identify a variety of information sources on franchises for sale.*
- *Outline a typical process of arranging to buy a franchise.*
- *Explain the major issues in assessing a franchisor.*
- *Name and describe the methods of financial assistance commonly used by franchisors to assist franchisees.*
- *Describe and discuss the major provisions commonly found in franchise agreements.*
- *Prepare alternative components of the business plan related to buying a franchise.*

Every year some portion of Canadian franchises fail. But buying a franchise is, on average, a lower risk start-up method than either starting a brand-new business or buying an existing business. Because of this, franchising has grown at a very high rate over the last two decades, to include more than 90,000 franchise units in Canada. And during this time, what we mean by a franchise has grown to cover an assortment of legal arrangements and product/service distribution systems. Just a tiny sample of the kinds of franchises for sale includes home inspection services, schools, funeral homes, water delivery services, employment agencies, driver training centres, management consulting firms, computer retailers, logistics companies, accounting firms, car repair shops, and, of course, fast-food outlets. There are even franchises that help people to buy franchises. If you decide to buy a franchise, you will need a business plan that includes all of the topics covered in Chapters 1 to 5. As well, your business plan will need to include the additional topics covered in this chapter.

How Does Franchising Work?

FRANCHISE TYPES The word **franchise** refers to a set of rights (the right to use a company's name, products, trademarks, copyrights, design, and style of business) that are sold by a **franchisor** to a **franchisee**. But within that definition, there are still lots of different things that we call *franchising*. The field of franchising is changing so rapidly that there has not been time for a standard classification system to evolve. Nevertheless, by using the following five broad categories you will be able to communicate sensibly with other businesspeople about franchising issues.

Licensing: A traditional franchising format—**licensing**—is where the franchisor sells the right to produce and sell the franchisor's products or services, using the franchisor's name and trademarks. Soft drinks and frozen treats are often franchised this way. The franchisee is often not bound to producing the franchisor's products exclusively and may have licences from more than one franchisor (usually not in direct competition). At the same time, the franchisee may even produce products under the franchisee's own brands.

Dealerships: Dealerships are generally retailers operating under the trade name of the franchisor, which is the manufacturer and/or wholesaler of products carried by the franchisee. Car dealers, hardware stores, snowmobile dealers, and gas stations can all be examples of **dealership franchising**. Some franchises in this category are not limited to carrying only the brands of the franchisor, or necessarily only products supplied by the franchisor. For example, hardware franchisors generally offer relatively few products under their own house brands, while they may distribute many competing national brands. Car dealers may be obliged to carry new models manufactured by their own franchisor only, but a DaimlerChrysler dealer will certainly have used Fords on the lot for sale.

Conversion: A long-standing trend in dealership franchising has been **conversion franchising**. This is where an independent business converts to becoming a franchise. So, an independent gas station/garage called Jim's Garage could become a Petro-Canada station, a franchise still owned by Jim. This would involve putting up the Petro-Canada sign and carrying the Petro-Canada products. At the end of the franchise agreement, Jim would have the opportunity to renew the franchise, return to independent status, or convert to another franchisor's brand.[1]

Traditionally, dealerships afforded generous management freedom to franchisees, which resulted in considerable variation among individual franchises. For example, at one time you could find substantial individuality among Canadian Tire dealerships or Shell stations. Over the past few years, however, as franchisors have refined their retailing systems, they have insisted on greater conformity in décor, layout, and merchandising systems. As this trend continues, it blurs the line between dealerships and *business format* franchises (see below).

MLM: Multi-level marketing differs from other forms of franchising in that there are usually minimal selection criteria for the franchisees and rarely a true franchise agreement or fee. However, there are usually start-up costs relating to sales kits and initial inventory. MLM is a method of selling the franchisor's products through independent salespeople (usually working from their homes) who sell directly to consumers, often in the customers' homes or via telephone. Typically MLM is used to sell household cleaning products, cosmetics, giftware, kitchen products, vitamin/herbal supplements, books, jewellery, and even

franchise The particular set of rights that are sold by a company, allowing others to use its products, intellectual property, and style of doing business.

franchisor A company that sells the rights to duplicate its system and style of doing business or to distribute its products and services. (*Note* U.S. spelling: franchiser.)

franchisee An individual or company that purchases the rights to distribute the products of or use the intellectual property and business style of another company.

licensing The selling of the right to produce and distribute a particular brand of product or service.

✓ **Test Yourself 7.1**
True or False? The word *franchise* refers to a fast-food outlet, typically found in a high-traffic suburban area.

✓ **Test Yourself 7.2**
True or False? A franchisor is a buyer of a complete method of doing business.

dealership franchising When a retailer has the rights to carry the products of and operate under the trade name of its supplier.

conversion franchising The adapting of an independent small business to become a franchise outlet.

✓ **Test Yourself 7.3**
True or False? The manufacture and sale of Popsicles uses a form of franchising called licensing.

long-distance telephone service. As an MLM franchisee, you make some profit by selling the franchisor's products or services. However, you can also make commissions on the sales of new salespeople that you recruit. And, ultimately, you can make a commission on the sales of new sellers recruited by your recruits and so on for several levels of commission.

This is the draw of MLM—it is often touted by the franchisor as a road to wealth by having multiple levels of salespeople making money for you. And there is no doubt that a small minority of people involved with MLM do get wealthy. But these people are the exception. They are often people involved early in a new market or at the start of an industry's growth cycle. However, these are the examples held up by the franchisors to recruit new sellers. A good tip-off to the approach of an MLM franchisor is to check the company's website and see if it emphasizes the quality and benefits of its products. Or does it tell you to *stop being a loser and join a team of rich happy winners?*[2]

Most franchisors who use other formats are reluctant to recognize MLM as a type of franchising, largely because of its history involving now-outlawed **pyramid selling** schemes. Some of the pyramid selling elements still prevail in MLM. For example, training is often heavily motivational, as opposed to informational, with franchisees sometimes paying to attend expensive conferences and seminars put on by the franchisor. There certainly are cases of MLM franchisors with quality products, reasonable prices, and long-time franchisees who make a reasonable living and enjoy the work. But many people who enter into MLM put in long hours in saturated markets and end up working for less than minimum wage before leaving in frustration. Because it is so easy to get into, there is a tendency to avoid any research in favour of *just seeing how it works out*. Even minimal research, though, could save you a great deal of time and effort if the MLM venture you are considering is less than it promises.

SMALL BUSINESS PROFILE 7.1
Guardian Security

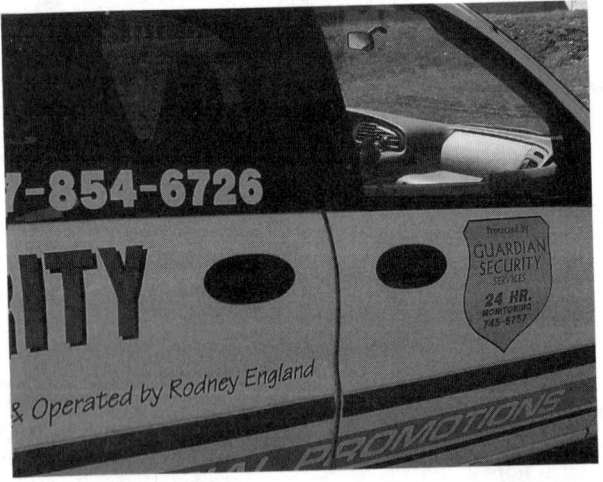

Guardian Security is centred in Mount Pearl, Newfoundland. Owner Rodney England started the company in 1998, working by himself selling alarm systems and monitoring services to homes and businesses as an ADT dealer. Within 4 years he had built the firm to more than 80 employees, and since then he has been carefully following his own plan for expansion.

Authorized dealerships or distributorships tend to be at the lower end of the franchise spectrum in terms of franchisor control. Typically, the dealer will contract with a manufacturer for training and the rights to sell and service a product. The authorized dealer sells and installs the product to the standards prescribed by the manufacturer, but otherwise dealers run their company as they see fit. In the case of Guardian, they sell ADT security equipment and ADT monitoring services, but in addition they offer security guards, surveillance, secret shoppers, closed-circuit TV, patrols, anti-bugging, bodyguard services, and many other types of security products and services.

This industry has grown dramatically over the last few years, partly because of technical innovation reducing security system costs. As well, there has been increased legislation for things like smoke and natural gas detectors and we also have an aging, more vulnerable but wealthier population who can afford these services. These conditions plus Rodney England's own strategic approach to growth have produced Guardian's rapid expansion. According to Rodney, the first expansion priority now is to "grow geographically because we can just reproduce a system we've got down pat." Following this approach, he has opened branches in Grand Falls and Corner Brook, Newfoundland, and Dartmouth, Nova Scotia. See the company website at **www.guardian-security.com**.

Business Format: Sometimes called *full-business format*, or *entire business format*, this is the most common form of franchising. Usually targeting consumer markets, this type of contract has the franchisor prescribing, in great detail, the marketing and operational procedures of all franchisees to the point where, to the customer, each outlet seems virtually identical. Even within **business format franchising**, however, there are many possible variations of the franchise agreement. Some examples are:

business format franchising
Buying a complete method of doing business under the trade name of, and with the products and systems of, the franchisor.

- *Single-unit franchise.* This is the simplest franchise arrangement, where the franchisee operates a single outlet or provides service to a defined geographic area. For example, you could have a lawn maintenance franchise, where your several trucks operate from a single garage within one particular suburban territory.

- *Multi-unit franchise.* This is where a single franchisee purchases more than one franchise site or territory from the same franchisor. This situation may arise when a successful franchisee is given the opportunity to buy additional sites or territories as they become available. In some cases, additional franchises could be planned for in the original franchise contract. For example, you could buy a photo shop franchise in a fast-growing suburban area. You know that a new mall is planned for several years in the future, a few kilometres from your shop. So, your franchise contract gives you the *right of first refusal* on buying any franchise that the franchisor grants in this mall, or even any area adjacent to your territory. Some franchisors encourage multi-unit deals because they give expansion opportunities to franchisees, producing greater commitment to the franchisor.[3] As well, it can reduce training costs and minimize conflict among adjoining franchisees.

? Get Help 7.1
For information about MLM and other business practices, look at Canada's Competition Bureau website at **www.competitionbureau.gc.ca**.

✓ **Test Yourself 7.6**
True or False? Pyramid selling is an outlawed activity.

✓ **Test Yourself 7.7**
True or False? Wendy's uses business format franchising.

- *Multi-brand franchise.* As franchisors have become bigger and bigger corporate entities, there has been a tendency toward takeovers of complementary franchise companies. For example, at the time of writing, Yum Brands! Inc. owns the Pizza Hut, KFC, and Taco Bell brands. So if you were looking to buy a fast food franchise for a tourist gas-stop, Yum may be willing to sell more than one franchise brand to you, a single franchisee.

- *Territory franchise.* For this type of contract, the franchisee buys the rights to service a geographic area with the franchisor's products or services. The franchisee has the responsibility to open as many outlets, or hire as many service people, as the territory requires.

- *Master franchise.* In this arrangement, the master franchisee buys the right to sell franchises to others within a given territory. Commonly, the master franchisee provides the training, support, and administration for the individual franchisees. This set-up works well for American franchisors, which can sell a master franchise for all of Canada or for specific regions. The Canadian master franchise can then modify the marketing and operational approaches of the American franchisor to fit the Canadian market or regional markets.

Head Start Exercise

7.1 Identify the franchisor and briefly describe the format of the franchising system you will be buying into ($\frac{1}{3}$ page maximum). *Note:* Students who are using the Head Start Exercises as class assignments will each have to interview an individual franchisee whose business will be used as an example for the exercise assignments in this chapter.

LEGAL ISSUES Compared to the United States (which has strict federal legislation as well as some state laws), franchising in Canada has been very poorly regulated. At the time of writing, only Alberta and Ontario have laws that specifically regulate the sale of franchises, and legislation is imminent in PEI and New Brunswick. The Canadian Franchise Association, an

0₃

✓ **Test Yourself 7.8**
True or False? A master franchise provides the right to sell franchises to others within a given area.

default Failing to fulfill the terms of an agreement.

litigation Being involved in a lawsuit as either suing or being sued.

❓ **Get Help 7.2**
The full Code of Ethics of the Canadian Franchise Association is available on its website, at **www.cfa.ca**. You can also use this site to check whether a particular franchisor is a member in good standing of the association.

disclosure The revealing of confidential information.

✓ **Test Yourself 7.9**
True or False? When the same franchisee owns both a Harvey's and a Swiss Chalet at the same site, this is an example of multi-unit franchising.

❓ **Get Help 7.3**
You can see the disclosure document requirements for the Alberta Franchises Act on the website for the Alberta Queen's Printer at **www.qp.gov.ab.ca/display_regs. cfm**. Search for *Franchises Regulation*.

✓ **Test Yourself 7.10**
True or False? Canada tends to have stricter franchising regulations than most of the United States.

organization of franchisors, does have a code of ethics that its members agree to follow. The major provisions of the code are:

- Freedom for franchisees to form and join associations that promote their own interests.
- Reasonable training and management support of franchisees.
- Reasonable notice of, and opportunity to correct, any franchisee **defaults** on franchise agreements.
- Reasonable effort to solve complaints from or disputes with franchisees.
- Encouraging prospective franchisees to contact existing franchisees for research purposes.
- Full disclosure to the franchisee of all relevant information about the franchisor (including past and present **litigation**), and about the franchise agreement, a reasonable length of time before the franchisee has to make a binding commitment.

It is this last item, **disclosure**, that forms the key provision of the existing franchise laws. Without this, you could find yourself signing a franchise agreement with someone who has past convictions for defrauding franchisees. Or you could find out too late that most of the franchises sold by the company have failed. If you are in an area where there is no franchise legislation, you can still request that the franchisor supply you with all of the disclosure information that would otherwise be required. A refusal, naturally, should give you second thoughts about the franchisor. Be careful about relying on franchisor disclosure as a means of protecting yourself as a franchisee. Just because a franchisor is willing to disclose something about the company or the agreement does not render it harmless. In fact, disclosure can work in favour of an unscrupulous franchisor. That's because the franchisor, once having disclosed something in writing, cannot be accused of having misled the franchisee in that area. In this sense, disclosure requirements put the responsibility for protecting yourself as a franchisee squarely on your shoulders.

Buying a franchise in Quebec is subject to provincial language legislation: the Charter of the French Language. This means that the franchisor must be willing to prepare the franchise agreement in French. It may also require the translation of operations manuals and training and promotional materials. Signage must be either French or bilingual, with French clearly predominating. The province's Civil Code, based on the French system of law, may also require some revision of the franchise agreement's content to meet the Code's standards for clarity. For franchisors that operate on a nationwide basis, an even greater flexibility of language options may be required for New Brunswick and parts of Ontario, where there are large bilingual areas. If your franchisor is new to these areas, your negotiations with the franchisor may have to involve educating the franchisor on the cultural issues of the country.

The federal Competition Act can affect franchise operations across the whole country, especially in the area of price setting.[4] For example, if you own a motorcycle dealership, the franchisor can advertise a manufacturer's suggested retail price for each model of new bike you carry. But the franchisor cannot dictate to you a minimum selling price for any product, as this would inhibit competition. Franchises do, however, have many exemptions from the Competition Act because of the relationship between the franchisor and the franchisee. For example, Tim Hortons may run a national campaign advertising strawberry doughnuts at a particular price with every franchisee expected to use that price. This would not be a violation of the act because there is no significant impairment of competition—there are still lots of competing franchises where you can get your doughnuts.

The contract, or Franchise Agreement, governs the relationship between the franchisor and the franchisee. Thus, the relationship is subject to the great body of contract law that has evolved, including various **precedents** resulting from past cases between franchisors and franchisees. But this murky area of the law is complex and expensive to pursue, especially when litigating against the deeper pockets of an established franchisor. To avoid going to court, get the help of an experienced franchise lawyer *before* you sign an agreement.

precedent A decision by a court that will set the pattern for subsequent decisions on similar matters.

Head Start Exercise

7.2   Describe the level of disclosure your franchisor is committed to, either by legislation or code ($\frac{1}{4}$ page maximum).

Is Franchising Right for Me?

MERITS OF FRANCHISING   Buying a franchise from an established, growing, and ethical franchisor can have a great many benefits that add up to reduced risk and potentially higher returns for your new business. These advantages come from:

- *Marketing research.* Well-run franchisor operations spend a significant amount of their revenue on marketing research, both at the national level (for developing corporate strategy) and at the individual site level. As a potential franchisee, the research relating to your future location/site can be critical to your success. This is especially true for retail and consumer service businesses.

- *Brand strategy.* Established franchisors have developed in the minds of potential customers clear images of their company **brands**.[5] For example, most urban Canadians would easily be able to rank, in order of expense, the cost of a chicken dinner at KFC, Swiss Chalet, or the Keg. *Ask yourself: How do they rank?* Part of this strategy is the careful selection and targeting of market segments and a diligent monitoring of competitors' strategies.

- *Existing customers.* If you buy a franchise from an established national or regional franchisor, the day your franchise opens, you have existing customers. They have never actually bought anything from you, but they already see themselves as your customers and you didn't have to win them. This won't be the case, for example, if you open a brand-new independent coffee shop. Prospective customers will have lots of reasons to hesitate before buying from you: "Will the coffee taste okay?" "Is it clean inside?" "Is it expensive?" But if you open a Tim Hortons franchise, there is no such hesitation. And these existing customers mean that you are creating cash flow as soon as you open.

- *Training.* Some of the more sophisticated franchisors have their own training institutions, with various certificate and diploma programs for franchisees and their staff. Some manufacturing franchisors have long-term in-factory training programs for the franchisee's technicians. But generally, franchisors offer short, intensive training programs, for the franchisee only, running from one to six weeks, with the average at around three weeks. Additionally, there may be some on-site assistance to train new staff for start-up of the franchise.

- *Complete package.* Many franchisors advertise that they are selling **turn-key** packages, because a new franchise can be up and fully running in mere weeks. This also implies that the franchisor has determined the best way of doing things for the industry and worked out the bugs in the system. The efficient systems of the franchisor, especially in a business format franchise, provide much of the franchise's value. And a top-quality franchisor is constantly working to further refine these systems.

Get Help 7.4

Some of the provincial/territorial law societies have lawyer referral services that you can access by telephone to get the names of lawyers in your area identified by specialty. Try the white pages of the phone book under "Law Society." As well, you may try the website for Canadian lawyer referrals: ***www.canlaw.com***.

brand The name of a company or a trademark-protected word that identifies the company and that creates a specific image in the minds of consumers.

✓ **Test Yourself 7.11**

True or False? Members of the Canadian Franchise Association are franchisors.

✓ **Test Yourself 7.12**

True or False? Canadian federal regulations require franchisors to disclose all past litigation.

turn-key (*also* turnkey *or* turn key) Operations that are ready to go, with all set-up and preparation completed. You just "turn the key" and it goes.

✓ **Test Yourself 7.13**
True or False? A legal precedent is a court decision that sets the pattern for similar cases in the future.

✓ **Test Yourself 7.14**
True or False? A franchisor of tractor equipment may not dictate minimum selling prices to franchisees.

- *Advertising power.* Advertising may be the single biggest advantage of buying a franchise over owning an independent business. If you open your own independent sandwich shop, you may decide to set aside, say, 3 percent of your sales for advertising. For this amount you could perhaps run a weekly ad (one you wrote yourself) in your community newspaper. But if you had a Mr. Sub franchise, your 3-percent advertising fee would be combined with the 3 percent from each of the other Mr. Sub franchises. This would produce an advertising campaign that was not only quantitatively superior (a national multimedia campaign) but also qualitatively superior (written by professionals from a top agency). It is knowing the importance of this advertising power that has caused many franchisors to divide the royalties they charge into two distinct components: a general royalty and a separate advertising fee intended strictly for this purpose.[6]

DRAWBACKS   For some, the drawbacks of being a franchisee outweigh the potential benefits. Because the franchisor holds the power in the franchise relationship, the benefits depend to a great extent on the ethical practices of the particular franchisor. Even with an excellent franchisor, however, there are some general drawbacks to buying a franchise. They include:

- *Franchise fee.* This is a major start-up cost for which you do not get any tangible assets. One way of thinking of this fee is as a prepaid expense (prepaid for the entire duration of the contract) for renting the intellectual property of the franchisor.
- *Franchisor control.* Depending on the franchise agreement, the franchisee can have less decision-making authority than a mid-level manager in a large organization. In some cases, the franchisor can even limit the profit potential for a franchisee through things like changing supply prices, opening adjacent franchise territories, and raising lease prices for property and equipment. Thus, two of the great advantages of entrepreneurship are removed: the independence of being your own boss and the potential for unlimited profit.
- *Royalties.* These must continuously be paid regardless of whether the franchisor re-invests any portion of this money in the development and promotion of the organization.
- *Advertising.* A separate advertising fee can sometimes give a franchisee a false sense of security in the belief that this money is being spent on effective advertising. For example, most of the money could be spent advertising for new franchisees as opposed to advertising for customers that will bring revenue to you.
- *Lack of goodwill equity.* When an independent entrepreneur works to build a business, there is the satisfaction of knowing that the business is increasing in value beyond the mere book value. That extra value, the value of the business's goodwill, will be realized in cash when the business is sold. At the end of many franchise contracts, however, the goodwill that the franchisee has worked to build accrues entirely to the franchisor, unless there is a specific buy-back condition stating otherwise.

PERSONAL REQUIREMENTS   *Ask yourself: What are the skills needed by a franchisee?* Each of the different start-up methods has its own average risk, going from highest risk in starting a brand-new business to lowest in buying a franchise. So, too, each method has its own requirements in terms of business skills. Starting a whole new business requires mostly entrepreneurial skills like innovation, motivation, and negotiation. Being a franchisee, on the other hand, requires mostly management skills like organization, planning, and supervision. Logically, the requirements of buying an existing independent business would be somewhere in between these two, as shown in Figure 7.1.

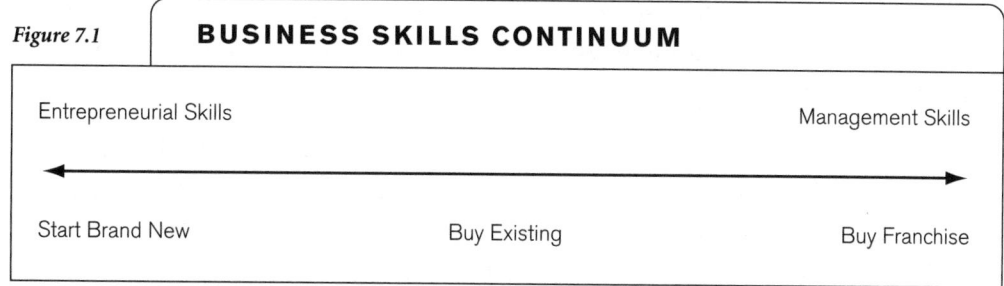

Figure 7.1

BUSINESS SKILLS CONTINUUM

Entrepreneurial Skills   Management Skills

Start Brand New   Buy Existing   Buy Franchise

Remember that you are not the only one to decide whether you and franchising are suitable for each other. Some franchisors have specific requirements in terms of skills, experience, and personality requirements. Occasionally, a franchisor may ask you to take some kind of formal test, but most often your suitability will be evaluated based on your résumé and the formal and informal interviews you have with managers from the franchisor. A stable financial history, good communication skills, and a mature, patient, conformist personality can all score points with franchisors.[7] Management experience, ambition, and dedication are also important characteristics that franchisors look for in potential franchisees. But still, the most important issue is: *Do you have the money?*

✓ **Test Yourself 7.15**
True or False? The ability to be innovative is an important characteristic for a franchisee.

Head Start Exercise

7.3   Explain why buying this franchise is a good route to business ownership for you personally ($\frac{1}{3}$ page maximum).

✓ **Test Yourself 7.16**
True or False? It requires more entrepreneurial skill to take over an existing business than to operate a franchise.

How Do I Choose a Franchise?

THE PROCESS   Checking out franchise magazines, franchise shows, and Internet sites, or talking with an existing franchisee are all common preliminary sources of information for anyone thinking of buying a franchise. But finding a franchise that is suitable for you is a much more difficult task than you would expect. It's not like buying a car, where if you want one with low fuel consumption you can within minutes find data to compare the gas mileage of every model of car for sale in Canada. In another few minutes, you can compare every car available for its warranty terms, and so on. Not so with franchises. There is lots of information about franchises that are for sale, but it is confusing and difficult to compare, partly because of the way franchises are promoted. Publishers gather information from franchisors using surveys where the franchisors report their own information. Different franchisors use different definitions of the reporting terms, so it becomes difficult to compare franchises based on published information. Here, for instance, are some commonly used terms that can be misleading:

- *Minimum investment.* Sometimes this term refers to the entire start-up cost of the cheapest franchise sold by that franchisor. Sometimes it refers to the amount of cash that the franchisee has to put up before being able to finance the rest of the costs. Occasionally, this includes the cost of real estate; usually the franchisee is expected to lease.
- *Initial franchise fee.* In some cases this refers to the entire franchise fee for the entire term of the franchise. In others it is an initial payment with the rest due on closing the franchise agreement, or at some other time.

unencumbered Being part of a person's net worth, consisting of free and clear assets that are not pledged as security against any debt. Money that, if you lose it, will not cause you to lose any of your other assets.

◇ **Get Help 7.5**
For links to and lists of franchises for sale in Canada, try *Canadian Business Franchise* magazine at **www.franchiseinfo.ca** Canada Franchise Opportunities at **canada.franchiseopportunities. com.**

✓ **Test Yourself 7.17**
True or false? The loss of unencumbered cash will not cause you to go bankrupt.

✓ **Test Yourself 7.18**
True or False? It is relatively easy for the average student to find out the terms of a franchise agreement.

- *Required capital.* Normally this refers to the minimum amount of **unencumbered** cash that a franchisee must have to invest in the franchise. Occasionally, it refers to the net worth of the franchisee.

The difficulty in getting clear information from franchise publications or even from a visit to a booth at a franchise show may well discourage some potential franchisees, since these are common first steps on the road to buying a franchise. If you are not discouraged, you may take the next step and request more information from franchisors, which will generally send you information kits and sometimes follow up with personal contact from sales representatives. This begins a series of contacts, each of which is designed to reveal a little more information about the franchisor while at the same time qualifying you as a potential franchisee as quickly as possible.

The information kit will likely tell you about the minimum financial and other requirements of the franchisor. It may also contain an application form, similar to a job application, but one that asks for your personal financial information—like a credit application. This approach can save the franchisor from wasting time on you if you are not qualified. But it also elicits some commitment from you on the basis of very little information from the franchisor. Your application could trigger several meetings with one or more representatives of the franchisor, serving as combination selection interviews and sales presentations, but without ever giving you the details of the franchise agreement.

During these meetings you may be asked to sign a non-disclosure agreement relating to any information you get from the franchisor or any franchisees you may interview. But before the franchisor actually gives you detailed financial information, any legally required disclosure information, or a copy of the franchise agreement, you may have to sign a conditional offer to purchase a franchise and pay a deposit. This offer is made conditional on the details of the franchise agreement being acceptable to you. Only then are you and your lawyer permitted to analyze (usually under time constraint) the details of the franchise agreement. If the agreement is acceptable, or if it can be negotiated to the point where it is acceptable, you will pay the rest of the franchise fee and set a closing date for the agreement. Then you must set up the franchisee company in a way that is compliant with the agreement.

In choosing a legal form for your franchisee company, all of the same considerations apply as for an independent new business. Because the business is a franchise, however, there may be some additional arguments for incorporation. This would be the case if you wished to protect personal assets that may be put at risk through franchisor policies. For example, you might own a fitness club franchise where one of your clients has been injured using a piece of exercise equipment and is suing for damages. It could be that the equipment was specified and supplied by the franchisor and that you maintained and supervised the equipment exactly as the franchisor trained you and specified in operations manuals. Nevertheless, you (and probably the franchisor as well) are being sued and, without incorporation, your personal assets could be at risk.

ASSESSING THE FRANCHISOR   Franchise magazines, which you can get in most bookstores, are a source of some basic information for contacting franchisors. But remember that these are essentially advertising vehicles for the franchisors. They are mainly published by franchise associations, which are trying to promote franchising in general as well as their individual members. So you will find mostly *good news* franchising stories—not exposés of franchisee abuse or editorials about high-handed franchisors. When it comes to assessing a franchisor, however, the best source is existing franchisees.[8] The checklist in Table 7.1 identifies the major areas you need to look at.

Table 7.1

FRANCHISOR ASSESSMENT CHECKLIST/NOTES

✔	Factor	Description	Potential for Improvement
	BUSINESS BACKGROUND		
	Clearly defined products/services		
	Clearly defined market segments		
	Growing market potential		
	Accurately estimated market share		
	History of consistent growth		
	History of franchisee success		
	History of litigation		
	History of accurate sales forecasting		
	Clearly identified competitors		
	Intellectual property protection		
	MARKETING		
	Appropriate image for target market		
	Brand recognition		
	Appropriate product/service mix		
	Appropriate pricing strategy		
	Effective distribution/delivery		
	Appropriate promotion methods		
	Effective advertising techniques		
	Effective sales approaches		
	OPERATIONS		
	Efficient space use in franchises		
	Efficient ordering system		
	Effective quality control systems		
	Appropriate record keeping systems/software		
	Effective management policies		
	Beneficial association memberships		
	FINANCES		
	Up-to-date financial statements		
	Healthy key ratios		
	Healthy relationship with creditors		
	Financial assistance program for franchisees		

Table 7.1

FRANCHISOR ASSESSMENT CHECKLIST/NOTES (continued)

✔	Factor	Description	Potential for Improvement
	FRANCHISE ISSUES		
	Appropriate franchise fee		
	Appropriate royalty fees		
	Appropriate advertising fees/controls		
	Acceptable sales/information approach		
	Acceptable involvement of advisers		
	Positive feedback from franchisees		

Get Help 7.6

So You Want to Buy a Franchise, by Douglas Gray and Norman Friend, is an excellent book with detailed lists of questions for evaluating a franchise. It is published by McGraw-Hill Ryerson and is out of print but available in libraries.

Head Start Exercise

7.4 Briefly describe the history of the franchisor you will be dealing with ($\frac{1}{3}$ page maximum).

ASSESSING THE OPPORTUNITY In addition to the general merit of the franchisor, the particular opportunity available to buy a franchise outlet or territory must also be assessed. This basically means conducting the feasibility analysis that makes up Section 2 of the business plan. This will include any marketing research information supplied by the franchisor on location and site. As the franchisee, you will be responsible to review and verify the franchisor's information and, if necessary, conduct your own research. Generally, you will look at:

- *The location.* This includes population size, trends, and wealth, as well as issues of transportation and competition.
- *The site.* Access, visibility, parking, surrounding businesses, and building condition are all elements of the site analysis.
- *The market potential.* If the franchisor does not have an estimate of market potential for the specific territory or **drawing area** of the franchise, it may be estimated from other data supplied by the franchisor.
- *The sales forecast.* Your main objective is to produce a reliable sales forecast and accurate projection of expenses. This will enable you to calculate the expected earnings for the franchise. The franchisor will likely offer you information on average sales and profits for franchises, but this information cannot be relied on to predict sales for your new franchise. For example, the average may be skewed by a very few outlets with exceptional sites. Or, the average may include franchisor-owned outlets whose management expenses are charged to the overall franchisor overhead, thus inflating the profitability of the outlet. Instead, you must try to get copies of actual financial statements for a sample of existing franchises that are as similar to yours as possible. Then you can make your predictions by performing correlations of sales, expenses, and net profit. For example, you could calculate the square footage of your proposed site and multiply it by the average sales per square foot of your sample. This will give you an estimate of sales. You could also estimate the total value of assets in your new site and multiply that value by the ratio of profit to assets calculated for the sample.

drawing area The physical location in which most of the customers of a business live or work.

Get Help 7.7

The case for getting professional accounting help is very strong here, not just because of the importance of the calculations but also because of the time restrictions for making a final decision that the franchisor will likely impose.

Only with these types of calculations will you be able to make an accurate estimate of the future earnings for the franchise. Then you can use that estimate to calculate the ROI (return on investment) that the business will provide. Here, the likely ROI calculation will be:

$$\text{ROI} = \frac{\text{Projected Annual Net Profit}}{\text{Total Equity Investment}}$$

Remember that the higher the risk and the lower the liquidity of an investment, the higher the return you should expect. Compared to other start-up methods, franchising tends to be lower risk, but your investment is far from liquid. You can get your money out only by selling the franchise, and this process is likely to be highly restricted by the contract. Remember also that if you are comparing different possible franchises there is more than a single type of ROI (return on investment) calculation that you can use for comparison.

Head Start Exercises

7.5   Briefly summarize the kind of data that you expect to get from the franchisor, which will help you to calculate your sales forecast ($\frac{1}{3}$ page maximum).

7.6   Briefly identify what you would consider to be an acceptable rate of return (return on equity) for investing in this franchise. Give reasons ($\frac{1}{3}$ page maximum).

BUYING AN EXISTING FRANCHISE   This special case is a combination of *buying an existing business* and *buying a franchise*. Because of this, you should use both Table 6.1 from Chapter 6, the checklist for assessing an independent business, and Table 7.1, the checklist for assessing the franchisor.

The legal complexity in a case like this can be very high since you may be dealing with an agreement to purchase from the current owner, as well as the franchise agreement. As in buying any existing business, of course, the key question is this: *Why is the business for sale?*

✓ **Test Yourself 7.19**
True or False? Buying a franchise is an investment with low liquidity.

There are lots of potentially valid reasons for selling a franchise, but each one of them should give you at least a second thought:

- The franchisor is forcing the sale because of poor management on the part of the current franchisee. If you are an experienced manager this could be an opportunity for you to buy the franchise cheaply and turn it around. But, *Ask yourself: Is this a case of an overly demanding franchisor that strictly enforces a tough contract?*
- The current franchisee is a partnership and one of the partners wants to get out, while the other will stay with you as the new partner. If the business is profitable, having a partner who knows the ropes could be to your advantage. But, *Ask yourself: Is this a case of a partner who is difficult to get along with?*
- The franchise was started as a franchisor-owned outlet but the franchisor is in an expansion phase and selling off company-owned units. This could be an advantage since the unit is already up and running with a financial history. But, *Ask yourself: Does this mean that there is more money in selling franchises than in running them profitably? What does this say about future franchise support?*
- The franchise agreement is up for renewal but the owner is retiring. This could be an opportunity to get the franchise for the remainder of the contract period at a lower price than you

SMALL BUSINESS PROFILE 7.2
Subway Franchisees

When Tao Jiang and his wife Xin Yu Wang came to Canada from China, Tao spent his first year here as a full-time college student in an information technology program. He abandoned school to work full-time, and eventually he and Xin Yu ended up working in Subway franchises, which both enjoyed. The challenge soon became to get one of their own. The couple worked in Subways for five years and along the way looked at other franchise options but settled on Subway partly because of the expertise they already had. The other reason was their belief that compared to the competition, the firm offered a superior product in terms of freshness and choice.

In 2004, Tao and Xin Yu approached the Subway head office and were offered a chance to take over an existing franchise that had been in operation for 14 years. The location was between a college campus and a high school in an area of lower-middle-class medium-density population. The site was in a small strip plaza on a busy street with both on-street parking and a lot in front. Tao and Xin Yu were impressed and signed a 20-year franchise contract. Financing was a combination of the couple's own savings, a loan from Tao's sister, and a bank loan.

Typical of fast food franchises, the franchisor leases the unit and sub-leases it to the franchisees, technically the numbered corporation owned by Tao and Xin Yu. As expected, the majority of customers are students (big sub eaters), creating a slow summer season for the business. But there has proven to be enough midday traffic (lunch is the busiest time for the chain) even when the schools are closed. The couple are pleased with the performance of the franchisor over their first two years of ownership. Even though there are constraints of the franchise contract (a handy ATM cannot be added to the store), Tao strongly feels that advertising power gives a huge advantage to franchises over independent sub shops. Tao's advice to those thinking of entrepreneurship is to "do something you enjoy because you spend so many hours in it."

✓ **Test Yourself 7.20**
True or False? Buying an existing franchise has greater legal complexity than buying a new franchise.

would have to pay for a new franchise. But, *Ask yourself: Why is the franchisor not buying back the remainder of the contract and selling a full-term franchise? Are the facilities old and worn?*

There are plenty of legitimate reasons for selling and buying an existing franchise, but there are also reasons that spell trouble. Thorough research is your best hope for ensuring a good deal.

How Can I Finance a Franchise?

FINANCIAL REQUIREMENTS   For a rough idea of the kind of franchise you might be able to afford, take a look at Figure 7.2. The "minimum cash equity" column shows how much debt-free cash you must personally have available in order to buy a franchise in each category. Of course, any lenders financing the rest of the franchise cost will have their own creditworthiness and security criteria. In addition, some franchisors require a certain minimum net worth that is in excess of the unencumbered cash investment you can make. This is the franchisor's own measure of financial stability. It can indicate how well you will be able to survive a temporary downturn in the industry or whether you might be able to afford future expansion of the franchise.

Figure 7.2	**TYPICAL RANGES OF CANADIAN FRANCHISE COSTS**		
Category	**Minimum Cash Equity[1]**	**Total Start-Up Costs[2]**	**Franchise Fee**
Home cleaning services	$13,000–30,000	$18,000–85,000	$12,000–20,000
Lawn maintenance services (including fertilizer and weed spray)	$18,000–40,000	$35,000–100,000	$15,000–30,000
Hair and beauty services	$20,000–50,000	$35,000–140,000	$7,500–25,000
Small fast-food restaurants (under 35 seating capacity)	$45,000–100,000	$125,000–250,000	$15,000–50,000
Automotive specialty services (e.g. muffler, transmission, lube)	$50,000–125,000	$150,000–275,000	$25,000–50,000
Large fast-food restaurants (over 75 seating capacity)	$150,000–350,000	$150,000–1,000,000	$45,000–55,000
Full-service restaurants (licensed dining rooms)	$200,000–500,000	$600,000–2,000,000	$40,000–75,000

1. The minimum amount of unencumbered cash that the franchisee must have available to invest in the franchise.

2. Not including real estate unless franchisee ownership of the building is required by the franchisor.

SOURCES OF FINANCE   For many franchisors, new franchisees are strictly a source of cash (franchise fees plus the sale of equipment and inventory) and the franchisees are left to arrange their own financing. However, it is becoming more common that business format franchisors pre-arrange a financing package with a major lending institution.[9] The lender has already completed a risk analysis on the typical franchise and has a predetermined lending formula that can be quickly applied to individual franchisees. The Royal Bank has developed a specific program for this, realizing that the bank can also reap the benefit of providing other banking services to franchisees. The bank has designated a team of *franchise specialists*, with training and experience in this area, who also make referrals to lawyers and accountants specializing in franchised businesses.

Another area where franchisors may help with financing is in the area of inventory. For example, if you have a gasoline dealership, the franchisor will provide you with the gasoline, which is paid for only as it is used. Because of the volatility in retail prices of gas, this is generally necessary for franchisees since a major price drop could have serious financial consequences. (On the other hand, any windfall profit from a price increase will go to the franchisor.)

Somewhat similar arrangements, called **floor plan financing**, are often available for larger manufactured products. For example, if you are a franchised dealer of recreational products, such as snowmobiles or personal watercraft, chances are that your franchisor has set up a private finance company that lends you the money to buy this expensive inventory. You will pay interest on each vehicle in your inventory from the day you receive delivery until the day you sell it. **Title** to each vehicle, however, will remain in the name of the franchisor until the day you sell it to your customer. Title is transferred to you and then your customer on the same day. The advantage of this arrangement to the franchisor is that if your franchise goes bankrupt, the franchisor is not at risk of losing the inventory.

For franchisees arranging their own financing, all the sources that might be pursued for starting a brand-new business can also be accessed to finance the purchase of a franchise. The franchisor, however, may have some restrictions on, or have to be involved with, some of these sources.

- *Personal sources.* Money borrowed from family and friends, *love money,* is sometimes easy to access on an informal basis. The franchisor, however, may have some restrictions

 Get Help 7.8

Check the Royal Bank website at ***www.rbcroyalbank.com***, click on *business* and then click on *franchise* to locate an RBC franchise specialist or links to other franchise information.

✓ **Test Yourself 7.21**

True or False? It requires about $40,000 personal net worth to purchase a McDonald's franchise.

floor plan financing A technique of lending money to a retailer for purposes of buying inventory, where title to the inventory remains with the supplier.

title Registered or legal ownership.

on how much money you can borrow to buy the franchise, stipulating a maximum debt-to-equity ratio.

- *Government programs.* Government programs typically do not differentiate between franchised or independent small businesses. There are a few exceptions, such as some franchise restrictions on student business loans from the Business Development Bank of Canada.

- *Banks.* Before lending you money to buy a franchise, banks may require information about average franchise performance that you have agreed to keep confidential, so the franchisor will have to agree to the release of this information. As well, a bank loan may have requirements that in the case of your franchise's failure the bank has first priority on the assets of the franchise. This may contradict your franchise agreement and so will also require the permission of the franchisor.

- *Investors.* Bringing in partners or investors will require a partnership or shareholder agreement that will likely need the approval of the franchisor for a variety of reasons. For example, your franchise agreement might require the appointment of a single individual from the franchisee company as the responsible party for the franchise. At the same time, your shareholder agreement might have a buy/sell clause, which allows another partner to take over in case of the death of the first. This means that the franchisor would have to pre-approve all partners as potential replacements for the designated responsible party. Similarly, the franchisor would likely wish to restrict the bringing in of future partners without the franchisor's approval.

✓ **Test Yourself 7.22**
True or False? Government lending programs generally treat franchises differently from independent small businesses.

Head Start Exercise

7.7   Briefly outline your sources of finance to buy the franchise ($\frac{1}{4}$ page maximum).

What Are the Contract Issues?

Lawyers working on behalf of the franchisor prepare the franchise agreement to ensure that every sentence of every paragraph benefits and protects the franchisor. As a result, the contract emphasizes the responsibilities of the franchisee but gives all the authority to the franchisor; even to the extent that the franchisor can often unilaterally change the contract merely by amending its operations manual. For an established successful franchisor, there will be little willingness to negotiate the terms of the franchise. So, as a potential franchisee, your interest in the contract is to:

1. Make sure that you understand the implications for each of its provisions, and
2. Decide whether or not you are willing to accept those conditions.

TERRITORY AND SITE ISSUES   If the contract provides a protected territory, the contract should also include a map, or detailed description, clearly showing the geographic boundaries where you will have exclusive rights. Ideally, you would also like to have adjoining territories indicated and, if they are undeveloped, the right of first refusal for opening new franchises in them. Also, when the adjoining territories are undeveloped, some identification of the point at which they could be opened (for example, when the population reaches a certain number, or when your sales surpass a certain level) would help to protect your franchise.

Some franchisors like to be, and some insist on being, the landlords for their franchisees. This means that the franchisor either owns the property where the franchise is to be situated or leases it and then sub-leases to the franchisee. The logic behind this approach is that it allows the franchisor to ensure that the site will remain available throughout the life expectancy of the franchise and that a third-party landlord will not be able to endanger the viability of the franchise through operating restrictions or unsupportable rent increases. If your landlord is your franchisor, however, you will have to ensure that the terms and conditions of your lease match those of the franchise agreement. If they don't match, it could give the franchisor the right to take an increased share of your profit. For example, if you have a 10-year franchise term and a 5-year lease, when it comes time to renew your lease the franchisor could raise your rent by an amount equal to the majority of your profits.

If your landlord is a company or individual other than your franchisor, the lease terms will probably require the approval of the franchisor. This is partly to ensure that your lease does not give your landlord the right to dictate your operating hours or other aspects of your business that may put you in violation of your franchisor's policies. But the franchisor will be primarily reviewing the lease with regard to specific rights (for example, entry onto the premises) for the franchisor. You will have to check the lease to protect yourself and your franchise. For example, you must be careful of how the terms for renewal of your lease are written. Let's say you have a 10-year lease with a 5-year renewal option, in order to match the 15-year term of your franchise. You could notify the landlord that you are exercising the option to renew, expecting a modest increase in rent. The landlord, however, may advise you that there will be a 100-percent increase in your rent. If you cannot negotiate an agreement on the new rent, depending on how the renewal conditions are written you may have to go to arbitration. If the landlord can present a case for increased costs, you may end up with a rent far more than you can afford. It would be better to have a renewal option that is geared to the increased sales of the franchise.

SUPPLY AND INVENTORY ISSUES   Items in the franchise agreement may require you to buy certain supplies or products from the franchisor exclusively. This should be fine with you as long as there is assurance that you will get the supplies at some reasonable market value or better. A provision allowing you to use other sources of supply (as long as the quality is acceptable to the franchisor) should be included.

The contract may also give the franchisor the right to set minimum inventory levels for certain products and supplies. You must ensure that this cannot be done arbitrarily or merely to improve the franchisor's cash flow. Rather, the contract provision must specify that all inventory levels must be set for reasonable turnover rates for the industry. Let's say, for example, that you own a chicken wing franchise where the franchisor requires you to maintain an inventory of 100 kilograms of frozen wings at all times. If neither you nor any of the other franchisees have ever run out of wings, but the franchisor nevertheless increases the inventory requirements to 200 kilograms, this would be considered unreasonable.

Note that the real test for the reasonableness of a contract provision is how important you think it is for being used against other franchisees (ones who are less competent and ethical than you). If you think a provision could stop some other franchisee from endangering the image of the franchise, then it is probably reasonable.

✓ Test Yourself 7.23
True or False? Franchise contracts are written in favour of the franchisor.

✓ Test Yourself 7.24
True or False? Major franchisors tend to be very willing to negotiate the terms of their franchise contracts.

✓ Test Yourself 7.25
True or False? A franchisor will want the right of approval for a franchisee's lease agreement with an independent landlord.

Get Help 7.9
An excellent book on franchising, which contains a good sample franchise contract, is *Franchising in Canada: Pros and Cons* by Michael M. Coltman. Older editions published by the Self-Counsel Press may be available at the library. A current edition is published (but not widely distributed) by the Parkland Community Futures Development Corporation in Manitoba. Their website is **www.pcfdc.mb.ca**.

RENEWAL AND TERMINATION ISSUES   The *carrot and stick* combination that the franchisor uses to control the franchisees is the hope for renewal of the contract (by being in good standing) and the fear of termination from being in default of the provisions of the contract. The conditions of renewal should be spelled out in the initial contract, although it may not be under the same conditions as the original contract. For example, the renewal period may be shorter than the original contract, or you may be required to sign any new standard agreement that the franchisor has adopted since the original contract.

The franchisor will likely have the right to terminate the franchise if you are in default of the contract or for other good cause. The agreement will give the franchisor the right to inspect your franchise to ensure compliance with the contract, which will include all of the regulations in the operations manual. The contract should allow you a reasonable amount of time to correct any deficiencies that the franchisor has found and given you notification of. However, the franchisor would have the right to terminate the contract without notice for some gross act of negligence, fraud, bankruptcy, or anything else that would fall under the heading of *good cause.*

Ideally, you would like to have a provision that when the agreement is terminated—or runs out and is not renewed—you will be compensated not just for the value of the business assets but for the increased value of the business due to its growth. So if the franchisor sells the business, or takes it over as a company-owned outlet, you will still be compensated for your work in developing the business.

TRAINING AND ASSISTANCE ISSUES   The nature and duration of training should be specified in the contract. Otherwise, you may find out that the training consists of letting you work, without pay, at another franchise or company-owned outlet for several weeks. True training should be active in nature with a specific training plan. The contract should specify if there are any additional training costs or if all costs are included in the franchise fee. The contract should also indicate whether the cost of training materials and manuals is included.

The manner of any ongoing assistance should also be specified so that it isn't just a case of *call us if you have any problems.* Help lines, regular meetings, seminars, conferences, publications, and websites to assist franchisees and their staff should all be listed along with any associated costs. Start-up training for a new franchisee and ongoing franchisor support are two of the main advantages of buying a franchise. As a result, they should be specified in detail in the contract.

✓ Answers to Test Yourself Questions

7.1   The word *franchise* refers to a fast-food outlet, typically found in a high-traffic suburban area. *False*

7.2   A franchisor is a buyer of a complete method of doing business. *False*

7.3   The manufacture and sale of Popsicles uses a form of franchising called licensing. *True*

7.4   A significant majority of multi-level marketing direct sellers eventually become wealthy. *False*

7.5   Petro-Canada uses dealership franchising to distribute its products. *True*

7.6   Pyramid selling is an outlawed activity. *True*

7.7   Wendy's uses business format franchising. *True*

7.8   A master franchise provides the right to sell franchises to others within a given area. *True*

7.9   When the same franchisee owns both a Harvey's and a Swiss Chalet at the same site, this is an example of multi-unit franchising. *False*

7.10   Canada tends to have stricter franchising regulations than most of the United States. *False*

7.11   Members of the Canadian Franchise Association are franchisors. *True*

7.12   Canadian federal regulations require franchisors to disclose all past litigations. *False*

7.13   A legal precedent is a court decision that sets the pattern for similar cases in the future. *True*

7.14   A franchisor of tractor equipment may not dictate minimum selling prices to franchisees. *True*

7.15   The ability to be innovative is an important characteristic for a franchisee. *False*

7.16   It requires more entrepreneurial skill to take over an existing business than to operate a franchise. *True*

7.17   The loss of unencumbered cash will not cause you to go bankrupt. *True*

7.18   It is relatively easy for the average student to find out the terms of a franchise agreement. *False*

7.19   Buying a franchise is an investment with low liquidity. *True*

7.20   Buying an existing franchise has greater legal complexity than buying a new franchise. *True*

7.21   It requires about $40,000 personal net worth to purchase a McDonald's franchise. *False*

7.22   Government lending programs generally treat franchises differently from independent small businesses. *False*

7.23   Franchise contracts are written in favour of the franchisor. *True*

7.24   Major franchisors tend to be very willing to negotiate the terms of their franchise contracts. *False*

7.25   A franchisor will want the right of approval for a franchisee's lease agreement with an independent landlord. *True*

Questions for Discussion

1.   Which types (in terms of products or services) of franchises do you feel have reached the point of market saturation? Give reasons. Which types of franchises do you feel have plenty of opportunity to continue growing? Give reasons.

2.   Would you rather buy a franchise with a lower franchise fee and higher royalty, or one with a higher franchise fee but a lower royalty? Discuss.

3.   What issues of complaint would a franchisor be likely to have about a franchisee? How could these be resolved?

4.   What issues of complaint would a franchisee be likely to have about a franchisor? How could these be resolved?

Recommended Reading

Gray, Douglas, and Norman Friend. *So You Want to Buy a Franchise.* Toronto: McGraw-Hill Ryerson, 1998. (May be out of print, but available in libraries.)

Mathews, Joe, Don DeBolt, and Deb Percival. *Street Smart Franchising.* Madison, WI: Entrepreneur Press, 2005.

Norman, Jan. *What No One Ever Tells You about Franchising.* Chicago: Kaplan Publishing, 2006.

Wilson, Tony. *Buying a Franchise in Canada: Understanding and Negotiating Your Franchise Agreement.* North Vancouver: Self-Counsel Press, 2005.

The Business Plan, Alternative Module:
Franchise Purchase

Entrepreneurs who are buying a franchise should complete Sections 1 to 5 of the business plan, as well as this portion.

1. Identify the franchisor and briefly describe the format and nature of the franchising system that you will be buying into.

    _____

    _____

    _____

    _____

    _____

    _____

    _____

2. Briefly describe any legislation, codes, or franchisor practices that will govern the franchisor's dealings with you.

    _____

    _____

    _____

    _____

    _____

    _____

    _____

3. Explain why buying a franchise is an appropriate business start-up method for you and your personal circumstances.

    _____

    _____

    _____

    _____

    _____

    _____

    _____

4. Describe in detail the history of the franchisor, outlining the franchise rates of success/ closings as well as any history of litigation. (*Note:* Franchisor permission may be required before disclosing this portion of your business plan.)

_____

_____

_____

_____

_____

_____

_____

5. Describe the strength of the franchisor's brand recognition and the overall marketing strategy of the company.

_____

_____

_____

_____

_____

_____

_____

6. In general terms, describe the nature and efficiency of the systems provided by the franchisor.

_____

_____

_____

_____

_____

_____

_____

7. Prepare a short analysis of the financial health of the franchisor and describe any financial assistance that is provided to franchisees. (*Note:* Franchisor permission may be required before disclosing this portion of your business plan.)

_____

_____

_____

_____

_____

_____

8. Outline the entire cost of setting up the franchise, your amount of equity investment, the franchise fee, and the rate at which you will have to pay royalties and any other franchisor charges. (*Note:* Franchisor permission may be required before disclosing this portion of your business plan.)

_____

_____

_____

_____

_____

_____

9. Using information from Section 5 of your business plan, calculate the return on equity that you expect to get, and explain why this is appropriate considering the risk and liquidity of your investment. (*Note:* Franchisor permission may be required before disclosing this portion of your business plan.)

_____

_____

_____

_____

_____

_____

10. Briefly outline the major provisions of your franchise agreement including provisions for territory assignment, sources of supply, inventory requirements, contract renewal, termination, assignment, and franchisor assistance. (*Note:* Franchisor permission may be required before disclosing this portion of your business plan.)

_____

_____

_____

_____

_____

_____

The Family Firm Alternative:
How Do I Take Over My Family's Business?

LEARNING OBJECTIVES

On completion of this chapter, you should be able to:
- *Discuss the nature of entrepreneurship in the family business.*
- *Identify major advantages of family firms.*
- *Discuss the problems in managing family firms.*
- *Explain techniques for reducing conflict between family members.*
- *Discuss the development of a successor to a family business.*
- *Outline the process of planning for retirement.*
- *Define basic estate planning terms.*
- *Describe the options for transferring a business to the next generation.*
- *Identify the major problems facing second-generation business owners.*
- *Prepare alternative components of the business plan related to taking over a family business.*

Ask yourself: Is a second-generation owner of a family business a true entrepreneur? If you think back to the definition of entrepreneurship found at the beginning of Chapter 1, you will remember that it involved *risking money to make a profit.* So let's say you inherit a family business worth $100,000. You are now faced with a choice:

- You can sell the business and spend the $100,000, or maybe just put it in the bank for safe-keeping. In this case you will definitely not be an entrepreneur.

Or,

- You can keep the business running—in which case, every day that you remain in business, your $100,000 is at risk. That makes you 100-percent entrepreneur. After all, someone who buys an existing business from a stranger is still an entrepreneur. It doesn't matter that you didn't start the business. It doesn't mean that you can't innovate and change the business as much as you want.

If there is any difference in the nature of the entrepreneurship between starting a new business and taking over the family firm, it is probably that it requires more personal courage to take over the family firm. That's because the long-term success rates for family businesses when they have been taken over by the second generation are not much different than the success rates for brand-new start-ups. However, in the family business the *cost* of failure is higher—not just because of the greater value of assets usually at risk, but because of the personal cost. Comparisons to a more successful founding parent (at least one who is seen that way[1]) or getting the blame for diminishing the family reputation or financial status can be painful. So, the second-generation entrepreneur is, at the very least, worthy of the respect accorded to a start-up entrepreneur.

When you take over a business that has been owned by members of your family, you will need a business plan that includes all of the topics covered in Chapters 1 to 5. As well, your business plan will need to include the additional topics covered in this chapter.

✓ **Test Yourself 8.1**
True or False? Someone who takes over ownership of a family business is not a true entrepreneur.

What Are Family Businesses?

DEFINITIONS   *Ask yourself: What is the definition of a family business?* It may be easier to recognize a family business than it is to define the term.[2] Which of the following could be considered family businesses?

1. A woman is the sole owner of a dental supply company in which her four adult sons are the senior managers.
2. Three brothers are equal partners in a house-building firm, which does not employ any other members of any of their families.
3. A childless couple jointly owns a catering business, which has no other employees.
4. A woman from a big family, but with no spouse or children of her own, owns a printing business. Every year she gives summer jobs to three or four of her nieces and nephews who work loading and unloading trucks.
5. A man has inherited full ownership of a bakery that was handed down from his grandfather and father. The owner's own children express no interest in the bakery and no other family members are involved with the company.
6. A man owns 49 percent of the shares in a furniture business where his son works as a cabinetmaker. The man's partner owns 51 percent and has no family members involved with the company.

family business A company where controlling interest is held within a single family and at least two members of the family work for the business.

The definition for a **family business** is usually along the lines of "a business where controlling interest is held by one or more (collectively) members of a family and where at least two members of that family are involved with the company." By this definition, scenarios 5 and 6 above do not qualify as family businesses. But it wouldn't take much for either of them to qualify: scenario 5 would qualify if one of the kids were to get involved, and scenario 6 would qualify with the transfer of 2-percent ownership. By some definitions, all of these scenarios would easily qualify as family businesses.

A less formal but widely held understanding of family business is that *ownership or management of the business will, to some extent, be by family relationship rather than merit.* In principle, this idea does not offend most people's sense of justice because one of the main reasons for starting a business is to be able to provide income and employment for family members.

Head Start Exercise

8.1   Briefly describe the history of your family business and explain which family members are currently involved with the firm ($\frac{1}{2}$ page maximum). *Note:* Students who are using the Head Start Exercises as class assignments will each have to interview an owner of a family business whose company will be used as an example for the exercise assignments in this chapter.

There are many benefits to family firms, including:

- The opportunity for family members to spend much more time together than would be allowed by most other types of employment.
- A common purpose and sharing among family members.
- A level of trust in family managers that is difficult to achieve with those outside the family.
- The opportunity to provide secure employment for family members.
- The chance to be involved with an organization that holds other values above the need for profit.
- The ability to leave a legacy for future generations of the family.

✓ **Test Yourself 8.2**
True or False? Any business that employs more than two people from the same family is a family business.

For immigrant families, there is the special benefit of being able to use the business as a way of sponsoring family members into the country. This is generally available in cases where you can demonstrate that you need a relative for a position of trust in the business and that the relative is qualified to do the job.

◇ **Get Help 8.1**
To find out more about sponsoring relatives to work in the family business as immigrants, check the Citizenship and Immigration Canada website at *www.cic.gc.ca* and click on *Sponsor Your Family*.

Head Start Exercise

8.2   Briefly describe how your family members would benefit from being in business together.

FAMILY VS. BUSINESS RELATIONSHIPS   Family relationships tend to be highly emotionally charged. Business relationships also have a strong emotional component. When the same relationship has both business and family elements, the emotions become magnified. The tendency to support one another is much stronger, but so is the tendency to fight with each other. *Ask yourself: Is it better to live a life with more emotional volatility or less of it?* Your answer will depend on your personality as well as family and cultural values.

Many family businesses consist of spouses or life partners working together as business partners. When you are in business with your spouse, this has practical advantages, such as saving on transportation costs to work. Or, depending on the nature of the business, you may take shifts alternating between work and home so that one of you is always available at the business. For some pairs, the extra closeness of living and working together is the ideal shared experience.

On the negative side, at start-up or other times when income from the business is slight, there is no steady source of cash from an employed spouse to rely on—and failure of the business means you are both unemployed. Also, when you are both entrepreneurs, you may have none of the **family benefits** (dental, extended health care, insurance) that are provided by many employers, adding to your financial stress. The stress of the extended time together can also put pressure on your relationship—and a breakdown in the relationship almost certainly means that one of you must give up the business, or possibly that the business will fail. The dynamics of spouses working together are magnified when other family members are involved in the same business.

Ask yourself: Why is it so difficult for parents to give driving lessons to their children? The most difficult individual to delegate to is your own child, because in **delegating** you have to give up authority. This means abandoning the role of parent. And even when parents are able to delegate, the tendency is to hover over the child, endangering the very self-confidence that they are hoping to encourage.

In North America there is only about a 30-percent chance of being able to successfully transfer a business from the older generation to the children.[3,4] This may be partly due to the freedom young people have to choose paths in life that they think will be more interesting than the family business, with which they are already familiar. But, more likely, the younger generation is trying to avoid spending their lives in what they see as the permanent dynamics of the parent–child relationship. This fear is influenced by the "sitcom view" that many young people have about their parents' personalities: that they are predictable and unchanging, like the characters in a long-running TV show. As a second-generation entrepreneur, however, you must get beyond this prejudice and realize that the current generation of family business owners is still in the process of maturing and learning new behaviours, and that they are capable of being influenced by you.

The natural rivalry between brothers and sisters (*I'm telling Mom and Dad and you'll be in trouble*) tends to disappear with age and become more of a mutually supportive relationship—but not in all cases. In some instances the vying for parental attention and approval continues well into adulthood. This is more likely to happen between children of the same gender who are close in age. When two such competitive family members both work in the family business, the real problem comes when one of them is put in charge and the other is unable to accept this authority.

Studies of birth order indicate that, on average, firstborns are greater achievers while later-born children tend to have more social skills and be better liked. *Ask yourself: Which would make the better candidate to take over the family business?* The answer will depend on a host of factors other than birth order, but it's not necessarily the eldest. The eldest male, however, is more likely to be selected as successor to the business, especially in families that have immigrated from other cultures. Today, this basis for selection is likely to produce resentment rather than acceptance in better-qualified siblings.

There are two categories of in-laws associated with family businesses: those who work in the business and those who don't but are married to family members who do. Those who work in the business can find themselves in an awkward position when non-family employees see these in-laws as part of the privileged group of family owners. Family members, however,

---

family benefits Fringe benefits paid for (at least in part) by many employers and which are extended to the spouse and dependent children of the employee. Such benefits typically include extended health care, dental care, and various types of life and disability insurance.

delegating Giving subordinates responsibility and full authority for completing specific tasks.

✓ **Test Yourself 8.3**
True or False? A family business can be used as a means of sponsoring the immigration of a foreign relative into Canada.

✓ **Test Yourself 8.4**
True or False? Fewer than one-third of family businesses are successfully transferred to the second generation.

may be unwilling to extend the same trust and authority to the in-laws that they would to blood relatives. So there is some potential for isolation and resentment in this role.

In-laws in the second category do not work in the business but are married to family members who do. The danger here is that these in-laws may take a hand in trying to manage the careers of their spouses in the firm. The *don't let them push you around* style of coaching can have a negative impact on otherwise stable family/business relationships. Understandably, those married to business family members may depend on the business for their livelihood, but have no real knowledge of or influence on the operation. Pressuring the spouse who works in the business is an attempt to achieve some sense of control.

MANAGING CONFLICT   There are proven techniques for dealing with most of the problems associated with the complex politics of family firms. History has shown that family businesses are more successful when there is a family culture, or a set of values that include the following ideas:

- The business is a long-term trust of the family rather than a source of cash and jobs for family members.
- What's best for the business is best for the family in the long run.
- The business is there ultimately for the benefit of the family, not the other way around. So it is not disloyal to the family to decide not to work in the business.
- Any decision relating to the business is *only business* and *not personal.*

These values can be aided by a set of clear policies to be followed in the operation of the business, including:

- A single family member will have administrative control of the business.
- Formal lines of authority will be followed and clear job descriptions will be available for all positions in the business.
- Family members seeking jobs in the business must formally apply and clearly demonstrate that they have the requirements to perform those jobs.
- Salaries for all positions in the business will be at competitive industry rates.
- The business will not lend money or act as guarantor for loans.

Another tool that has proven effective in reducing family conflict is the creation of a **family council** to involve those family members who are not directly working in the business: in-laws, family members who are employed elsewhere, retired family members, and even younger members who are still in school. All of these groups may have an interest in the business—financial or personal—but have to rely on second-hand information or gossip to know what is going on in the business. Through regular meetings, the council can provide a source of information and a forum for airing concerns about the business.

Head Start Exercise

8.3   List any informal techniques or formal company policies that are intended to reduce conflict among family members ($\frac{1}{4}$ page maximum).

Test Yourself 8.5
True or False? Siblings of the same gender who are close in age are more likely to continue rivalries into adulthood.

Test Yourself 8.6
True or False? Birth order studies indicate that younger siblings tend to be higher achievers.

family council A group of family members who meet regularly to receive information about and discuss concerns relating to the family business. Council members do not generally have any active involvement in the business and have no authority over the business.

Test Yourself 8.7
True or False? Conflict is reduced when an individual family member has administrative control of the business.

Test Yourself 8.8
True or False? The family business should be the place family members rely on for borrowing money.

How Do I Prepare for Running the Business?

✓ **Test Yourself 8.9**

True or False? A family council carries the same authority as a board of directors.

Preparation for taking over a family business cannot start too soon. Some important steps in preparing are declaring your intentions, apprenticing, studying business, getting outside experience, and building networks.

DECLARATION OF INTENTIONS   As soon as you see any serious possibility of a career in the family business, start to talk about this goal. Keeping your aspirations secret is a self-defeating habit. Unless you tell your goals to others they cannot help you achieve them. And, when you do express your goals, help, advice, and moral support can come from many directions. It is especially important that you tell your intentions to other stakeholders in the business, for a variety of reasons:

- *Founder/parents.* Business owners will often have secret hopes that someday one of their children will be interested in taking over the family business, without ever actually having a serious two-way conversation about this possibility. Your declaration of interest can start the conversation that will eventually lead to a plan for takeover. On the other hand, you may have an unspoken expectation of inheriting the business that is not part of the senior generation's plan. If taking over the business is not a serious possibility, it's better that you find out early and make alternative career plans.

- *Siblings.* Stating your hope of running the business can open negotiations with siblings who may have similar aspirations. If there is going to be competition for the role, making accommodations and getting it settled early will help prevent family feuds. In some cases, your announcement of wanting to run the business may bring a sense of relief to a brother or sister who feared getting stuck with the job.

- *Employees.* The sooner employees know about a long-term plan for a family member to take over the business the sooner they can adjust their own career plans. It is totally demoralizing for a long-term employee who harboured hopes of promotion or buying the business to find a family member "parachuted" in when the owner retires.

✓ **Test Yourself 8.10**

True or False? Any intentions you have of taking over the family business should be kept confidential for as long as possible.

Head Start Exercise

8.4   Explain why you are a suitable successor for leadership of the family business in terms of your personality, interests, and family position ($\frac{1}{4}$ page maximum). *Note:* Students who are using this exercise as a class assignment should identify likely successors to the example business and explain their suitability.

apprenticeship A skill training program where the trainee performs increasingly more complex and responsible jobs over a long period of time.

APPRENTICESHIP   Starting at the bottom and working your way up is a great way to learn a business. Serving an informal **apprenticeship** in the business means actually doing as many jobs as possible in the company to the point where you have developed some level of proficiency with each of them. The second generation of a family business will often start this process by taking summer and part-time jobs, and filling in for employees on vacation.

But if you intend to take over the business, this should not be a haphazard series of activities. Rather, there should be a clear plan of progress, perhaps working through all of the processing procedures of the company and then moving, step by step, to higher levels of responsibility.

Ask yourself: How will employees feel about my moving from job to job in the company? If employees do not have a clear understanding of the intention for you to eventually run the business, you will be perceived as the boss's kid dabbling in jobs that others must toil at for long periods—in some cases, whole careers. This opens the door for resentment and a lack of co-operation. But when people know that switching jobs is part of your training program, they are more likely to take a hand in helping you learn the job and understand its importance to the company.

Your own attitude during this process will make all the difference: *arrogance will get you nowhere.* Many business families instill in the younger generation a belief that, because of their privileged position, family members in the business must always work harder than employees doing the same jobs. Your struggles with learning new tasks will be a humbling experience, but one that will form a bond with employees rather than make you an object of derision.

STUDY Keep in mind that there are no formal educational requirements for taking over the family firm. But a business diploma or degree will give you a broad understanding of all the functional areas of business. In addition, some form of specialization in marketing, accounting, production, human resources, or information technology can be of great benefit, even though as a business owner you will not be working in just one narrow area. Having an in-depth understanding of one area of business gives you a greater appreciation for the complexity and depth of all of the areas.

Ask yourself: Why study business if I can learn it on the job? The big advantage of formally studying business is that it teaches you the system for classifying business information. Thus, when a problem arises in your business, you immediately recognize it as a marketing problem, or a production or accounting problem, and you are one step closer to a permanent solution through modifying your methods. The untrained business manager would tend to recognize the same problem as a problem with an individual employee or with a particular customer order and be more likely to seek a temporary fix. Understanding this system for classifying business information also allows you to analyze the good things about your business. It's amazing how many successful small business owners do not know *why* their businesses are successful. If you are trained to analyze your competitive advantages, you can capitalize on them to become even more successful. And when there is a threat to your business from changes in the market or the competition, you will be more likely to recognize it and take appropriate action.

OUTSIDE EXPERIENCE Working in someone else's business is an experience that is sometimes missed out on by those who have grown up with a family business. It can be humbling to be just another employee, not related to the boss. This can help you build **empathy** with your own future employees. Outside experience is another way to increase

> **Get Help 8.2**
> There are a huge variety of full- and part-time post-secondary business programs available right across Canada. Contact a business program coordinator at your local college or university or use *www.schoolfinder.com* to find programs.

> **Get Help 8.3**
> Northeastern University links more than 100 universities that have family business centres. Access their online magazine at *www.fambiz.com*. This site has a good search engine for family business articles.

> **Get Help 8.4**
> Management of the family business is becoming an area of specialization at more business schools. For example, the BBA program at Schulich School of Business (*www.schulich.yorku.ca*) offers a specialization in entrepreneurial and family business studies.

empathy The ability to experience the feelings and motives of others.

✓ **Test Yourself 8.11**

True or False? Formal education helps business owners to understand why their businesses are successful.

your credibility as the boss in your own business. And seeing the methods, problems, and management styles of another company can give you a new objectivity about your own family firm. Your outside employment doesn't even have to be in the same industry as your family business to teach you valuable lessons that you can bring home. And if you're not really sure about a career in the family business, working outside is one of the best ways to help you make up your mind.

✓ **Test Yourself 8.12**

True or False? Family business is a field of study available at various business schools.

Head Start Exercise

8.5   Briefly list relevant education and work experiences that make you a suitable successor for leading this business. *Note*: Students who are using this exercise as a class assignment should list the education and experience of likely successors to the example business. ($\frac{1}{3}$ page maximum)

⬦? **Get Help 8.5**

If you don't have time to read the newspapers daily, current events magazines such as *Maclean's* (***www.macleans.ca***) and *Time* (***www.time.com***) give good summaries of what's going on in the world at large.

networking The process of making contact and building relationships with people for purposes of mutual support.

NETWORKS   Networking is the process of making contacts and building relationships with people for mutual support. In preparing to take over a family business, part of your networking task is to make contacts with the various associates of your family's retiring generation. These include customers, suppliers, bankers, and professional advisers. Accompanying the current family owners to meetings can be used for initial contact, but often the real links are made in social situations. Intergenerational socializing can be difficult, but made easier if you are up to date on current events in politics, sports, movies, and music. Developing some level of skill in activities like golf, skiing, dancing (yes, dancing), and public speaking are all ways of increasing your ability to network.

You must also build your own network of contacts. Membership in associations is an excellent way to do this. Chambers of commerce, industrial associations, service clubs, and family business associations are all networking vehicles. The Canadian Association of Family Enterprise brings together people associated with family businesses to identify common problems and to lobby the federal government on behalf of family enterprise. The association also performs informational and educational activities. A similar Quebec-based organization is the Family Business Network *(Réseau des Entreprises Familiales)*. Although many of their documents have not been translated into English, this is still a valuable resource, as Quebec has long been a leader in entrepreneurship research and support. The Family Business Network also has a special interest in the role of women in family firms.

⬦? **Get Help 8.6**

The Canadian Association of Family Enterprise has a website at ***www.cafemembers.org***.

⬦? **Get Help 8.7**

The website for the Family Business Network is at ***www.fbn-i.org***.

✓ **Test Yourself 8.13**

True or False? The Canadian Association of Family Enterprise lobbies the federal government on family business issues.

How Do I Help Prepare Retiring Family Members?

When you own your own business, there is no official retirement age. But, as part of the baby boom generation, the majority of family business leaders in Canada expect to retire within the next few years. The majority of these, however, do not have any formal plans for what they will do when they retire, nor for passing on the business to family members.[5] This older generation of business owners may need a great deal of assistance, encouragement, and advice to prepare for handing over the reins of the business. A good starting point is to help them get lots of information and to find independent advisers.

INFORMATION AND ADVISERS   If you are the successor to the family business, you should *not* be in the role of chief adviser to the retiring generation. First, you are too close to the situation and have too much personal financial interest to give objective advice. Second, your retiring relatives deserve the benefit of good professional advice for such major decisions. And third, bringing in outside advisers prevents other interested family members from complaining of undue influence or favouritism in the estate planning process, and helps avoid future family conflict.

The key advisers needed are:

- *Accountant.* The accountant's main role is to advise on the tax implications of anything the retiring business owner may decide to do with the business or other assets, and to recommend ways of accomplishing the desired goals that will reduce or defer taxes.
- *Financial planner.* A qualified financial planner can help identify the kind of financial instruments that will produce the balance of income and security needed for a particular planned retirement lifestyle.
- *Lawyer.* The lawyer's role is to advise on wills, powers of attorney, trusts, shareholder agreements, and any other documents involved in transferring authority. In addition, lawyers are often knowledgeable about options in insurance coverage.
- *Personal adviser.* A wise and experienced friend or mentor who is not part of the immediate family can be an excellent source of advice in planning retirement and the **succession** of business ownership.

Head Start Exercise

8.6   Name the specific formal advisers who could help the current business owner(s) in planning for retirement and succession of the business ($\frac{1}{4}$ page maximum).

NEED/WANT IDENTIFICATION   Retirement from the business should not be seen as giving up a major source of satisfaction in one's life. Rather, it should be seen as the chance to intensely pursue those activities that will provide the greatest life satisfaction. For the average middle-aged business owner, when asked "What do you want to do when you retire," the honest answer is "I don't know." One way of getting to an answer is to start with a *wildest dreams* type of question: "If you could do or be anything in the world, limited only by your own fantasies, what would it be?" Extreme answers such as write a great novel, win the Canadian Open, become a famous movie star, travel around the world, discover a cure for heart disease, or coach in the NHL should be encouraged, regardless of how unrealistic they may seem. That's because this kind of exercise points in the direction of interest and satisfaction for the future retiree. Later, when the constraints of reality (such as health, skills, finances, agreement of spouses) are applied, achievable but fulfilling ambitions can be

---

? Get Help 8.8

The Canadian Association of Retired Persons offers many benefits to those over 50, both retired and planning retirement. This non-profit group lobbies governments on behalf of seniors' interests and publishes its own magazine covering a huge variety of retirement issues. Check out the website at ***www.carp.ca***.

✓ Test Yourself 8.14

True or False? The majority of family business leaders in Canada expect to retire within the next few years.

succession The taking over of control by the next in line to do so.

✓ Test Yourself 8.15

True or False? As successor to the family business, you should be the primary adviser to the senior generation on retirement and estate planning.

? Get Help 8.9

The Yellow Pages offers a category of Retirement Planning Consultants, which tends to be a combination of investment dealers, insurance brokers, and firms that make arrangements for chronic medical care. Nevertheless, careful checking of firms listed here could produce contacts of reliable specialists in the retirement field.

identified. So, writing a novel can become completing a college journalism diploma, movie stardom can become active membership in an amateur theatre group, world travel can become overseas work on foreign-aid projects. None of these more realistic ambitions means settling for less than one's dream. Instead, they are achievable steps in the direction that will provide individual fulfillment.

A retiring owner—especially a founder—may have a strong need for continuing involvement in the business in some capacity, and this should be incorporated into the succession plan. For example, the owner may go from being president of the company to chair of the board of directors, or chair of the advisory board.

Head Start Exercise

8.7   Briefly list the retirement goals of the current owner(s) ($\frac{1}{4}$ page maximum).

Future retirees must know what they want to do before they can figure out what it's going to cost. But aside from money to be spent on "want" satisfaction, retirees must plan for regular living expenses including food, shelter, gifts, transportation, and all the other items in the normal household budget. In addition, contingency planning for medical emergencies and possible disability becomes more important as one gets older.

Open and frank discussion should be held with all interested parties including spouses, children, other family members, and non-family managers in the business. One study indicates that the majority of family businesses have no clear plan in case of the death or disability of the controlling owner.[6] But for many business owners, "succession" is a difficult subject. The deep emotional attachment entrepreneurs can have to their businesses must be recognized and discussed, along with how they will cope with giving up authority.[7] A worst-case scenario is when the older-generation owner agrees that you will take over the business, but then has a change of mind during the transition phase before you have assumed any legal ownership.

estate All the assets owned by a person.

living will A statement of how a person wishes to be cared for in case of incapacitating or terminal illness.

trust An arrangement where a person transfers ownership of assets to a responsible party (the trustee), who may use the assets only for the benefit of certain parties (the beneficiaries) as instructed.

PREPARING A PLAN   The owner of a family business who is planning to retire should really make three separate but interrelated plans:

- *A retirement plan.* This covers retirement goals (education, travel, sports, arts, business, volunteer work, hobbies), living arrangements, health management issues, and a budget for retirement.
- *An estate plan.* The **estate** plan covers sources of retirement income, a will, powers of attorney (including a **living will**), and any **trusts** that are set up to manage assets.
- *A succession plan.* Decisions about who will eventually run the family business and how it will be owned are included here. It should also explain the transition role of the retiring generation.

For the steps in creating these plans, take a look at Figure 8.1, the retiring business owner checklist.

The succession is most likely to be successful if control is left in the hands of an individual family member. Remember, this does not necessarily mean majority ownership, just owning a majority of the voting shares. There are many Canadian examples of family businesses being damaged or destroyed when second-generation owners have spent their efforts in battles for control of the company rather than in managing it.

The succession plan should be written with clear timelines for transferring control of the business. Without this, as heir to the business you are left in the demoralizing position of waiting in the wings indefinitely. Clear dates for a transition period made up of steps of increasing responsibility are necessary for you to prepare yourself as an entrepreneur. A date for final transfer of power should be decided on. Interestingly, there is some research to indicate that family business owners are most likely to commit to a succession plan when they are in their fifties.[8] Prior to this, they are generally not ready to consider retirement—and after this decade, there seems to be an increasing reluctance to give up power. If the current owners of the family business are not able to commit to a timetable, this is the strongest of signs that they are not psychologically prepared to give up the business.

Head Start Exercise

8.8 Identify the projected date for the current owner(s) to retire from running the business and briefly explain the rationale for this time frame ($\frac{1}{4}$ page maximum).

✓ **Test Yourself 8.16**

True or False? The majority of family business owners in Canada have fully discussed issues of inheritance with their children.

◇ **Get Help 8.11**

There are several excellent books on estate planning. Two of the best are *Winning the Estate Planning Game* by Tim Cestnick, published by Prentice Hall Canada and *The Canadian Guide to Will and Estate Planning* by Douglas Gray and John Budd, published by McGraw-Hill Ryerson.

✓ **Test Yourself 8.17**

True or False? Setting a retirement budget is part of the succession plan.

◇ **Get Help 8.12**

The non-profit Centre for Family Business (**www.familybizcentre.com**) offers workshops, seminars, and

SMALL BUSINESS PROFILE 8.1
R. Vaillancourt Portes & Fenêtres

Carl Vaillancourt and his older brother Pierre own R. Vaillancourt Portes & Fenêtres, a manufacturer of doors and windows in Drummondville, Quebec. The business was started more than 55 years ago by Carl and Pierre's grandfather, Raymond, and their father, Réal. The original entrepreneurs started out in a small garage in their backyard. Today, the company has a modern facility of 60,000 square feet and more than 30 employees. Through the years, family involvement in the business has changed a number of times, with a third brother joining and leaving the firm and Carl becoming involved several years later.

The industry has changed greatly over the years with the growing consumer demand for attractive low-heat-loss windows and doors. The advent of moulded PVC casings and thermal glass in the 1980s started both the improvements in the products and a growth in retrofitting of windows and doors. R. Vaillancourt's main products are steel windows and doors including horizontal and vertical sliding windows, casement windows, single and double doorways, patio doors, and garage doors. Today, the company targets residential and commercial customers throughout the province of Quebec. It provides warranties on all of its products, some up to 20 years. Their promotional approach is to emphasize the advantage of dealing directly with the manufacturer rather than a "middle-man." See the company website at **www.rvaillancourt.com**.

The many changes experienced by R. Vaillancourt have all gone fairly smoothly. Carl attributes this to the continuity provided by his father, Réal—who, after he stopped being active in the day-to-day business, still maintained an office with the company, acting in an advisory capacity.

Figure 8.1

RETIRING BUSINESS OWNER CHECKLIST

Retirement

- ❏   Hold discussion with spouse
- ❏   Attend retirement workshops
- ❏   Read current literature on retirement
- ❏   Join retirement networking group
- ❏   Set retirement goals
- ❏   Decide on living arrangements
- ❏   Analyze income requirements
- ❏   Set retirement budget
- ❏   Create retirement schedule

Estate

- ❏   Read current estate planning books
- ❏   Identify and meet with advisers
- ❏   Evaluate estate (including business)
- ❏   Hold discussions with family
- ❏   Decide inheritance issues
- ❏   Create/revise will
- ❏   Decide incapacity/medical issues
- ❏   Create power of attorney

Business Succession

- ❏   Hold discussions with legal and financial advisers
- ❏   Project outlook for business
- ❏   Hold discussions with family
- ❏   Hold discussions with senior employees
- ❏   Identify successor(s)
- ❏   Decide on control of the business
- ❏   Negotiate roles of successors and other family members
- ❏   Identify transfer mechanism
- ❏   Create timetable for steps in transferring responsibility
- ❏   Set date for final take-over

What Are the Legal Issues?

Taking over the family business is really about two separate issues:

1. taking over management authority for the business, and
2. taking over legal ownership of the business.

As a second-generation leader of a family firm, you may find yourself in the chief executive role long before you have legal control of the company. And in some ways, you're never really the boss until you have legal ownership. There are various ways you can receive legal control of the family company, including:

- inheriting ownership through a will, on the death of the business owner
- receiving ownership in the business as a family gift or a series of gifts over time
- buying the business from the retiring generation, usually with payments spread over an extended period.

Some combination of these methods can be used. Depending on the method of transfer, the number of family members involved, and the time frame, the legal complications can be endless and certainly require professional help.[9] But the more you understand about the legal implications of transfer decisions, the more you can influence the process.

TAXATION ISSUES   When you buy an asset and keep it for a while, then sell it or give it away, the increase in value of the asset while you owned it is a **capital gain**. Capital gains are taxable. So if your parent started a business 20 years ago for a $10,000 investment and today the business is worth $900,000, the capital gain is $890,000. If your parent gives you the business as a gift, or sells it to you, then the *capital gains tax* on the business becomes payable.

And even though capital gains taxes fluctuate from time to time, you would still be looking at a tax bill in the hundreds of thousands of dollars. Even worse would be if your parent died and left you the business: you would likely have to pay **probate** fees on the estate on top of the capital gains tax.

There are exemptions to and methods of deferring capital gains taxes that should be employed wherever possible. These techniques include:

- Employing the *lifetime capital gains exemption,* which can allow up to $500,000 of capital gains to be exempt from tax on the sale or giving away of shares in a small-business corporation.
- Transferring or **bequeathing** shares of the family business to a spouse. This can be done without triggering the capital gains tax, and could be employed as a way of delaying the tax when the spouse is expected to outlive the business owner.
- Giving shares in the business to children early in the life of the business, before the shares have appreciated to the value they would have at the time of the owner's retirement.
- Employing an **estate freeze**. This fairly complicated manoeuvre allows the business owner to create two types of shares in the business. One type, retained by the owner, stays frozen at the current assessed value of the business. The other type, given to heirs, receives all the growth in value of the business from that point on. The capital gains tax becomes payable on the frozen shares only when they are passed on to the heirs. As long as the heirs retain the new shares, they do not have to pay tax on this increased value.[10]

✓ **Test Yourself 8.18**
True or False? Transferring a business to the next generation works best when control of the business is spread among as many family members as possible.

✓ **Test Yourself 8.19**
True or False? Business owners are most likely to commit to a succession plan when they are in their fifties.

❓ **Get Help 8.13**
Tax rules and rates are always changing. To find the latest information on any particular tax, check the Canada Revenue Agency website at **www.cra-arc.gc.ca**. They offer many helpful pages specifically for small-business tax issues.

capital gain The increase in value of an asset over a period of time.

probate The legal procedure of getting a court to declare a will valid. Probate fees are charged as a percentage of the estate and vary from province to province.

bequeath Leave assets to someone in a will.

estate freeze A legal manoeuvre designed to freeze the value of the shares of a business owned by the retiring owners. All the new value from the growth of the business can then be owned by the next generation of the family.

Get Help 8.14
The accountant who acts as an adviser on business succession taxes will typically have a CA (*www.cica.ca*) or CGA (*www.cga-online.org*) designation and should have specific experience in the transfer of family business ownership.

Get Help 8.15
The website for Canada Revenue Agency has a search feature that can produce regulations and a vast number of articles on specific tax issues. Start with the main menu at *www.cra-arc.gc.ca*.

- Using farm asset exceptions. If the family business is a farm, assets used in the business can be transferred to succeeding generations of family members free of capital gains.
- Using the capital gains reserve exception. When the shares of a small business corporation are transferred to succeeding generations of a family, payment of the capital gains tax may be spread out over a period as long as 10 years.

Identifying which of these and other transfer options have the greatest advantage for your own situation will certainly require the help of a tax professional. The process usually involves projecting various financial scenarios and assessing the relative risks and benefits. The earlier a knowledgeable accountant is involved in the planning process, the better.

LEGAL FORM ISSUES   If the business is not incorporated prior to succession of control, the retiring owners have the option of removing assets from the business (for example, land and buildings) so that they can keep personal title to these assets and then lease them back to the business. The assets can then become a source of income for the retired family members. At the same time, the possibility of having the succeeding generation put these assets at risk (by borrowing money against them) is minimized. At some future time, the assets could be sold to the company or willed to the successors of the business.

In order to take advantage of the $500,000 lifetime capital gains exemption, or to use the estate freeze as a way of avoiding taxes, the family business must be set up as a corporation. When more than one family member will be taking over the business, it can also be an advantage to have a corporation because it becomes easier to distribute varying percentages of ownership among the heirs. Also, by using two classes of shares (voting and non-voting), it is possible to distribute equal amounts of ownership among various children but to leave control of the company with a single member of the family or group of family members that will be directly involved with the business. With a corporation, the retiring generation can retain shares in the company for a source of income but give up control by keeping only non-voting shares.

Considering the various tax options in transferring corporate shares, this is often a more advantageous legal form for passing a business to the next generation. And, presumably, a family with a well-established business would have enough other assets that it would want to protect them by incorporating. Any corporation with more than one owner should have a *shareholder agreement.*

This may be even more critical to a family business because it can reduce the potential for conflict among family members. The shareholder agreement may include company rules on:
- paying dividends versus keeping earnings in the company
- salary limits for company officers
- protection for minority shareholders, requiring unanimous shareholder consent for certain decisions
- details of a **buy/sell agreement.**

buy/sell agreement A contract between owners of a company stating that in the event one of them dies, the remaining owners have the right and obligation to buy the deceased's share of the business.

The buy/sell agreement allows remaining shareholders to buy the shares of a shareholder who dies or becomes disabled. Usually, the money for this purchase will come from insurance policies carried on each of the shareholders.

The lawyer advising on succession planning should have experience in both family business matters and estate planning, or should belong to a firm with experts in each area who can be called on. Be sure to ask specific questions about experience.

Head Start Exercise

8.9   Briefly outline plans for how the business will be passed on to the successor(s) and how control will be distributed ($\frac{1}{3}$ page maximum).

INSURANCE ISSUES   Aside from the regular kinds of insurance required by a business, special coverage may be needed for a family business—especially a firm being passed from one generation to another. Insurance can help protect the business while ownership is in the hands of the older generation, during a transition phase, and when you take over the business. For example, if the business is highly dependent on the skills, abilities, and relationships of an older-generation entrepreneur, it may be wise to have this business owner covered by *key person insurance* while you and/or other family members are in training for this role.

During the transition phase you may be sharing ownership of the business with older-generation family members. Or you may be taking over the business in partnership with other family members. In these situations you will need life insurance on each other as partners or shareholders, so that in the event of death, you or other remaining partners/shareholders can purchase the shares of the deceased partner (from their heirs) as per your buy/sell agreement. Naturally, if you are the beneficiary of your family partners—thus inheriting their share of the business anyway—such insurance may not be necessary.

If you and other members of the family sit as directors on the board of the family corporation, you may require **directors' and officers' insurance**. This is because directors and officers of a company can be sued for decisions they make (or fail to make) that result in some harm to another party.

ALTERNATIVE COMPENSATION ISSUES   A general theme among succession planners is that when it comes to estate planning, business owners should treat their children *fairly,* not *equally.* For example, let's say you are one of four siblings with a parent who owns a business that has a net value of about $1 million, representing most of the parent's wealth. Of the family children, you are the only one who has shown interest in the business, and you have worked there for seven years while your brother and sisters have pursued alternative careers. There are unlimited numbers of ways the estate could be disposed of on the death of your parent, but consider these three:

• The entire business, representing most of the estate, could be left to you as a reward for your interest and work in the business. This would likely be perceived as unfair by your siblings, who may have been equally devoted to the parent but just not interested in the business. In this case they could have grounds for contesting the will, which would result in expensive litigation, as well as hard feelings among the family members.

• Shares of the business could be divided equally, four ways, among the siblings, giving you and each of the others about $250,000 of stock in the company. Even if the shares are

✓ **Test Yourself 8.20**
True or False? To use most of the tax deferral options available to family businesses, the company must be a corporation.

directors' and officers' insurance
Insurance policies that protect members of the board of directors or the senior managers of a company if they are personally sued for decisions or actions they take on behalf of the company.

classified to give you voting control of the company, you may well believe this to be unfair because the value of the company could be due, at least in part, to your hard work. And while you were working to make the company worth more, your siblings were making themselves wealthier through their own chosen fields.

- A more complex formula could be worked out to calculate the increase in value of the business during the time you worked there and award you that amount (or some portion of that amount), with the rest of the value of the estate being divided equally among you and the other heirs. This is the solution that, although not equal division, would most likely be perceived as fair by all of the parties.

✓ **Test Yourself 8.21**

True or False? In passing on the family business to the next generation, it is best to treat all children in the family equally.

If a business founder has lots of assets outside of the business, heirs not involved with the business could be fairly compensated with non-business assets. But for most Canadian business owners, the majority of their wealth is tied up in the business. In these cases, other techniques to achieve fairness in the distribution of an estate could include:

- Removing assets such as land or buildings from the business and giving these (possibly through a trust) to heirs not involved with the business. This would be done on condition that the assets are rented back to the business, with the heirs who now own them receiving rent on the assets as compensation.
- Arranging for heirs not involved with the business to hold notes payable by the business over an extended period of time.

SMALL BUSINESS PROFILE 8.2
West End Offset Plate Service

West End Offset Plate Service still provides complete pre-press services to commercial printers. But that end of their business, in just the last few years, has become almost obsolete, with the advent of automatic "computer-to-plate" systems. The business is more than 45 years old. Brothers Paul and John Moran started working there part-time as kids, for their father, the owner. As adults, Paul and John pursued their own interests in theatre and film and never expected to work in the family printing business. But when their father became seriously ill and died shortly after, the brothers stepped into the business as partners and started planning the long-term future of their firm.

With the rapidly changing technologies and markets in the printing industry, the Morans realized that they would need to find a more specialized niche. Capitalizing on their own arts backgrounds, they started offering unique printed products for visual media. For example, a TV commercial may be set in a kitchen containing boxes and jars of household products, which are realistic looking, but not actual consumer products. These "fake" products are one of the services that West End now provides. Books, posters, or any other printed product that a director or set designer might look for are also within their capability. The business now has three full-time employees and one part-timer, with good growth prospects.

After five years of working together, the brothers have specialized in their contributions to the company with John handling sales and customer service and Paul taking care of production inside the shop. Paul's advice to others who can never picture themselves in a career with the family business is "never say never."

What Takeover Problems Will I Face?

SECOND-GENERATION PITFALLS   There are a great many factors that contribute to the poor success rates for second-generation entrepreneurs. Typical mistakes of second-generation owners can be grouped into the general categories of hasty expansion, alienation of key employees, succumbing to family politics, and lack of strategy.

Hasty expansion: As a new successor to the business, you may feel a great urgency to assert your own identity, to start implementing your many ideas, and, unfortunately, you may feel in a rush to make the business grow. This will take money. You may be tempted to borrow money for expansion capital. In an established business, especially one with lots of assets, borrowing money for expansion can be almost too easy. But when you increase the debt load of the business, you have the extra expense of servicing that debt. This means you are operating closer to your break-even point. You will have reduced the safety margin of your company—a safety margin you will need in case there is an unexpected downturn in business.

This is where many recent business successors get caught. Any investment in expansion takes a while before it starts to produce cash flow. If there is a significant drop in the market while you're waiting for the expansion to produce cash, you may find yourself losing money. When your business is operating at a loss it's hard to borrow more money. And if the losses go on for long, creditors will start to go after the business assets. So begins the downward spiral of a failing business.

This does not mean that you should forget about expansion. The lesson here is that borrowing money to expand should not be entered into hastily. Expansion should be part of a well-planned strategy, building on the factors that have led to the success of the business so far. Expansion may be exactly what your business is ready for. But as a new leader, it is better to err on the side of caution.

✓ **Test Yourself 8.22**
True or False? Increasing the debts of the business by borrowing to expand is a common error of second-generation owners.

Losing key employees: When the older generation of owners retires from the business, this could be a trigger for senior employees to start thinking along the lines of retirement for themselves. And if you are taking over the business quickly (not a slow transition) it may be difficult to transfer the loyalty employees have felt for the previous generation to yourself. There may also be cases of long-term employees who held out hope of equity in the business who will see your appointment as an end to this hope. Combine all these factors with possible overzealousness on your part to get rid of a few problem employees. This will give everyone some concern about their job security—and the result could be employees looking for new jobs.

Being the new boss requires a careful balance between exercising firm authority and avoiding the alienation of key employees. When you first assume leadership of the company, it may be important to remind employees about the advantages of working for a family business: that the organization has values other than just the pursuit of profit. Assurances that you will uphold whatever values (tradition, quality, honesty, reputation) are associated with your firm can make long-time employees more comfortable. To ensure that you keep important non-family managers, you may also consider forms of profit sharing and even equity sharing while still retaining control of the company.

Succumbing to family politics: History has shown that family business leaders can be sidetracked from the job of running the company by the energy-draining feuds, power struggles, and favour-seeking of families. As leader of the family business, you may find yourself faced with a choice between doing something that is in the best interest of the business or in the best interest of an individual family member. Or you may face choices between the interests of one family member over another. Your best way of coping with these problems is to stick to business and stay out of family politics. You must make decisions based on the long-range interests of the business, explain your reasoning, and be clear that it is only business, not personal.

Failing to develop a strategy: The changes you eventually make in the business should be part of a long-term strategy. But some second-generation owners fail to become strategically focused after taking over the business. Reasons include:

- Long-held habits of dealing with operational problems as a junior manager.
- Over-conservatism, especially if the fortunes of many family members are dependent on the business.
- Indoctrination by the previous generation: *this is what has always worked for our business; this is what always will work for our business.*

Business training and outside experience will make you more aware that you need a strategy for responding to changing market conditions. This includes having a written business plan. Otherwise, changes you make in the business will be haphazard and maybe even unnecessary.

✓ **Test Yourself 8.23**
True or False? Leading the family business requires being deeply involved with the family politics.

An active board of directors (or in some cases a board of advisers) can be an excellent source of support and advice for broad strategic issues. As the day-to-day boss of the company you can easily lose sight of a long-term strategy for the firm, but board meetings should be primarily for this purpose. The board will likely be made up of family shareholders, and may include the previous generation of owners and senior, non-family managers of the business.

Many family-business consultants recommend keeping the board small and including directors from outside the family and the business. These outside directors are chosen for their broad business knowledge and their objectivity about the business. For a small business, directors generally get paid around $3,000 a year (depending on the size of the company) and attend about one meeting a month.

Head Start Exercise

8.10 Briefly describe your long-term plans for the business ($\frac{1}{4}$ page maximum).

MANAGING THE TRANSITION   When you take over the family business, in all probability your intention is not to continue running things the way the previous generation did. You will want to make changes. And even though those changes may be part of a well-thought-out strategy, and even though you will be the boss, you will run into resistance.

Ask yourself: Do most people resist change? Look at people's hairstyles. Many people sport the hairstyle that they had when they left high school, keeping it the same for 30 or 40 years—or longer! Yet many of those same people update their clothing styles on a fairly regular basis. This is mostly because of style changes in the clothing available for sale. Nevertheless, this tells us that most people will not initiate change (the hair) although they are perfectly capable of accepting it (the clothes). To actively resist change, however, people need a reason. The most common reasons that people resist changes in a business are:

- *Resistance to force.* People don't like to be bossed around, even when it's their employer doing the bossing. *Ask yourself: How do I feel when my boss at work suddenly tells me to do something a different way?*
- *Fear of losing an advantage.* Asking people to change an old work habit, one that took a long time to perfect, means extra work. It may be easier to find reasons why the change won't work.
- *Personal antipathy.* Not everyone is going to like having you as a boss. You may even find some with an active dislike of you to the point where they are obstructive when you try to make changes. It's not business; it's personal.

The ways you can overcome resistance to change include:

- *Providing ongoing communication.* This process should start with sharing your vision for the future of the company; the reasoning behind changes should always be explained.
- *Empowering employees.* Employees who have an active hand in the planning process are quicker to implement changes than those who are just receiving orders.
- *Rewarding support.* When employees can see a personal benefit to themselves for participating in the change process they are more likely to support it. And employees learn quickly from seeing others rewarded.
- *Exercising authority.* Sometimes, especially during a crisis, change must come about quickly. At such times your leadership may have to become less consultative and more decisive. And if there is an employee whose personal antipathy toward you affects job performance or the performance of the organization, you may have to exercise the full extent of your authority and dismiss the employee.

The transition phase should follow the steps outlined in the succession plan. Taking over management of the business is a process that's best done patiently and in stages. A transition of steadily increasing responsibility gives you the opportunity to:

- *Make mistakes.* Your right to make mistakes is an important issue to discuss with the retiring owner(s), especially if they are your parents. Getting agreement that the mistakes you make are less important than how you go about fixing them will help build confidence in your judgment.
- *Take advantage of the retiring founder's experience.* A true desire to learn from the retiring generation will build mutual respect. By asking more questions and expressing fewer opinions you are demonstrating how you value experience.
- *Build leadership skills.* Employees will need some time to adjust and accept a new boss. Asking them for advice in their areas of expertise is an important factor in achieving mutual respect.
- *Transfer customer loyalty.* In an abrupt transition of power, customers are likely to scrutinize the takeover, wondering if there will be problems with supply or service. A gradual transition will help maintain confidence in your company.
- *Leave your options open, just in case.* As you get closer to assuming full leadership of the company you may decide it's really not for you. Or, the retiring owners may decide that they just can't give up control. While the transition of power is not complete, there is always the option of changing plans.

✓ Answers to Test Yourself Questions

8.1 Someone who takes over ownership of a family business is not a true entrepreneur. *False*

8.2 Any business that employs more than two people from the same family is a family business. *False*

8.3 A family business can be used as a means of sponsoring the immigration of a foreign relative into Canada. *True*

8.4 Fewer than one-third of family businesses are successfully transferred to the second generation. *True*

8.5 Siblings of the same gender who are close in age are more likely to continue rivalries into adulthood. *True*

8.6 Birth order studies indicate that younger siblings tend to be higher achievers. *False*

8.7 Conflict is reduced when an individual family member has administrative control of the business. *True*

8.8 The family business should be the place family members rely on for borrowing money. *False*

8.9 A family council carries the same authority as a board of directors. *False*

8.10 Any intentions you have of taking over the family business should be kept confidential for as long as possible. *False*

8.11 Formal education helps business owners to understand why their businesses are successful. *True*

8.12 Family business is a field of study available at various business schools. *True*

8.13 The Canadian Association of Family Enterprise lobbies the federal government on family business issues. *True*

8.14 The majority of family business leaders in Canada expect to retire within the next few years. *True*

8.15 As successor to the family business, you should be the primary adviser to the senior generation on retirement and estate planning. *False*

8.16 The majority of family business owners in Canada have fully discussed issues of inheritance with their children. *False*

8.17 Setting a retirement budget is part of the succession plan. *False*

8.18 Transferring a business to the next generation works best when control of the business is spread among as many family members as possible. *False*

8.19 Business owners are most likely to commit to a succession plan when they are in their fifties. *True*

8.20 To use most of the tax deferral options available to family businesses, the company must be a corporation. *True*

8.21 In passing on the family business to the next generation, it is best to treat all children in the family equally. *False*

8.22 Increasing the debts of the business by borrowing to expand is a common error of second-generation owners. *True*

8.23 Leading the family business requires being deeply involved with the family politics. *False*

8.24 It is usually an advantage to include outside directors on the board of directors for the family firm. *True*

8.25 The majority of people do not like to initiate change. *True*

Questions for Discussion

1. Are there differences in the problems faced by male and female entrepreneurs when taking over a family business?

2. Discuss the advantages and disadvantages of working full-time with your spouse in a business where only the two of you are the owners and in a business where other family members also have ownership.

3. What are the major causes of intergenerational conflict? How do these manifest themselves in a family business?

4. What are the concerns and problems of non-family members who work for a family business? How can these be dealt with?

5. Why is it important for everyone to have a will? Why are people reluctant to prepare their wills?

Recommended Reading

Carter, Tom. *Write Your Legal Will in Three Easy Steps.* North Vancouver: Self-Counsel Press, 2005.

Cestnick, Tim. *Winning the Estate Planning Game.* Toronto: Prentice Hall Canada, 2001.

Gray, Douglas, and John Budd. *The Canadian Guide to Will and Estate Planning,* 2nd ed. Toronto: McGraw-Hill Ryerson, 2002.

Lancaster, Lynne. *When Generations Collide: Who They Are. Why They Clash. How to Solve the Generational Puzzle at Work.* New York: HarperCollins, 2003.

McNulty, Barry, and Mark McNulty. *The Canadian Small Business Owner's Guide to Financial Independence.* Toronto: Insomniac Press, 2006.

The Business Plan, Alternative Module:
The Family Firm

FAMILY/BUSINESS STRUCTURE

1. Briefly describe the history of your family business, identifying those family members currently involved with the company. If necessary, attach a family tree as an appendix.

_____

_____

_____

_____

_____

_____

_____

_____

_____

_____

2. Explain the legal form and the distribution of ownership of the business.

_____

_____

_____

_____

_____

_____

_____

_____

_____

_____

3. Briefly explain the advantages and disadvantages for your family members of being in business together.

_____

_____

_____

_____

_____

_____

_____

_____

_____

4. Describe any formal company policies or informal techniques used by the family that are designed to reduce conflict among family members.

_____

_____

_____

_____

_____

_____

_____

_____

_____

THE SUCCESSOR(S)

5. Describe the response of family and employees to your declaration of intent to take over leadership of the family business.

_____

_____

_____

_____

_____

_____

_____

_____

_____

_____

6. Briefly explain your suitability to lead the business, in terms of your work experience and education.

_____

_____

_____

_____

_____

_____

_____

_____

_____

7. Describe any personal contacts, association memberships, or other techniques that you will use to stay abreast of issues related to family businesses.

_____
_____
_____
_____
_____
_____
_____
_____
_____
_____
_____

CURRENT LEADER/OWNER(S)

8. Identify specific sources of information on retirement and succession, as well as the particular advisers that the current business owner(s) will rely on for planning advice.

_____
_____
_____
_____
_____
_____
_____
_____
_____
_____
_____

9. Briefly outline the retirement plans for the current owner(s) of the business, including retirement goals, income, living arrangements, ongoing involvement in the business, and planned dates for retirement.

_____
_____
_____
_____
_____
_____
_____
_____
_____
_____
_____

10. Explain the estate planning for the current owner(s), describing major provisions of wills and powers of attorney as well as the types of insurance carried.

_____

_____

_____

_____

_____

_____

_____

_____

_____

BUSINESS SUCCESSION

11. Describe specifically the mechanism for transferring control of the business to the successor(s) and how ownership of the business will be distributed and controlled.

_____

_____

_____

_____

_____

_____

_____

_____

_____

_____

12. Describe the steps in the transition of control from the current owner(s) to the successor(s), with a clear time frame for each step.

_____

_____

_____

_____

_____

_____

_____

_____

_____

_____

13. List the major problems you expect to face as new leader(s) of the business and how you will deal with these issues.

_____

_____

_____

_____

_____

_____

_____

_____

_____

_____

14. Briefly describe your planned changes for the business and how they will avoid the typical pitfalls of second-generation owners.

_____

_____

_____

_____

_____

_____

_____

_____

_____

_____

chapter 9

Managing for Growth
How Can I Expand My Business?

LEARNING OBJECTIVES

On completion of this chapter, you should be able to:

- *Describe the business cycle and identify characteristics of each of its phases.*
- *Identify the early warning signs of decline for a small business.*
- *Explain the factors involved in SWOT analysis.*
- *Define and discuss the various strategies for increasing sales.*
- *Explain how to measure market share.*
- *Discuss the considerations for broadening or deepening the product mix.*
- *Identify methods of product development.*
- *Identify appropriate expansion markets for a small business.*
- *Discuss how growth affects the elements of the marketing mix.*
- *Compare building a chain with selling franchises.*
- *Discuss advantages and disadvantages of export markets for small firms.*
- *Identify sources of assistance for exporting.*
- *Identify types and sources of expansion capital.*

With what you know about the income statement, you can see that there are two basic ways to increase profits: either increase sales or decrease costs and expenses. The first option is about business *growth,* and the second is about managing for greater *efficiency.* Ideally, as you plan for the more distant future, you will be concerned with both. This chapter is about making more profit through business growth.

Does My Business Need to Grow?

BUSINESS CYCLE   Many businesses never really get a proper start in life and die in their infancy. Of those that survive and become established, some remain for many years pretty much the same as they were at start-up. But these are a minority. More typically, small enterprises are seen as going through a life cycle with several specific stages:

- *Start-up.* Little revenue, high expenses (therefore little or no profit), and a high failure rate are the characteristics of this stage.
- *Growth.* At this stage the business experiences increasing revenue and profits, plus a declining risk of failure.
- *Maturity.* The business levels off in this stage, with stable sales and profits, plus a low risk of failure.
- *Decline.* Here is where profits fall; this stage will ultimately lead to the failure of the business. *Ask yourself: Does this mean that my business is doomed from the start?* The length of the cycle is hugely variable depending on your services or products and your markets. It may take only months for your business to go into decline or it may take many decades.

Fortunately, another stage in the cycle counteracts decline:

- *Renewal.* This stage is where the business adapts to the changing environment: changes in customer needs, in technology, in the competition, and so on. In many ways it is similar to the start-up stage, with high expenses and very slow growth. See Figure 9.1.

Head Start Exercise

✓ Test Yourself 9.1
True or False? The growth stage of the business cycle is characterized by stable sales and profits.

9.1   Estimate where your company fits in the business cycle. Give reasons for your placement. ($\frac{1}{4}$ page maximum.). *Note:* Students who are using the Head Start Exercises as class assignments will each have to interview an entrepreneur with an existing business. Each student can use this firm as an example for the exercise assignments.

Figure 9.1   **THE BUSINESS LIFE CYCLE**

The sooner an entrepreneur recognizes (or better, anticipates) the start of decline, the sooner the process of renewal can be started so that the business may continue to grow. *Ask yourself: Does a business have to grow?* There is the old saying *grow or die,* but a truer saying for business might be *change or die.* When a real opportunity for growth presents itself, if you don't take it, your competitors will. And if your direct competitors are allowed to grow unchallenged, they will eventually be in a position to overwhelm your enterprise. But this doesn't mean that you must always meet your competition in a head-to-head battle. **Renewal** for your firm may mean a strategy of finding a new direction, a new **niche**. In fact, growth for some firms comes by selling fewer products or services to fewer types of customers—in other words, greater specialization. By becoming more of a specialist, you could be turning your direct competition into indirect competition.

> **renewal** A part of the business cycle; the process of refocusing the business, leading to a new phase of growth.

> **niche** A very small market segment that a business satisfies with specialized products or services.

INDICATORS FOR RENEWAL   The warning signs or indicators that your business needs renewal can be either internal or external to the business and include issues relating to:

- sales and profits
- employee turnover
- available capacity

SMALL BUSINESS PROFILE 9.1
Leigh & James

Leigh & James is a fashionable home décor store in Toronto's trendy Queen St. West district. The company sells high-quality, distinctive furniture, lighting, and textiles. Despite the success of this growing small business, owners Nikki Andriet and Dean Fletcher have no interest in being big-time corporate executives. Their intention is that the firm will remain pretty much the size that it is now. Yes, sales will hopefully continue upward, but there are no plans to expand beyond a point where the two of them, with occasional part-time help, can handle all of the operations themselves.

Neither of the partners (they are business and life partners) had any background in the furniture business before getting into this venture. What they did have was shared passions for travel and design. Nikki and Dean both graduated from the University of Guelph in liberal arts programs, and after working at a variety of jobs the couple set off on an extended trip to Asia. While indulging their interest in design, they encountered many unique home décor products that were not available in Canada. On returning home, they brought with them many new interior design ideas as well as contacts for suppliers. The pair sold their home in Ottawa using their equity to finance Leigh & James. (These are their own middle names.) Nikki and Dean decided to locate in the part of Toronto with the highest concentration of innovative artists and designers, and they spent weeks driving around the area before settling on the current 1850-square-foot site.

The decision to remain small is clearly not a resistance to change. "It's strictly a lifestyle issue," explains Nikki. In fact, their business is changing constantly, with new products, styles, suppliers, and services. During their four years in business, the couple has expanded their product range to include custom wood furniture and now they are offering interior design services. They have added warehouse space close to the store and currently are investigating the feasibility of adding an ecommerce capability to their website (***www.leighandjames.com***) so that customers will be able to order online. As well, they have recently tried a new method of promotion with a booth at the Interior Design Show. All this reflects the advice that Nikki offers to budding entrepreneurs: "Trust your instincts and don't be afraid to make mistakes."

- market share/market potential
- competition
- various other cues that might be particular to your own industry.

Sales and Profits: Sales forecasting for a business at start-up is both difficult and inaccurate. But for the established firm, sales are more predictable because the forecast is based on past sales. Past sales are then adjusted for your growth pattern, for known changes in the market or changes in the competition, and for any changes in your own products, services, and promotion. For example, if you know that 20 percent of sales are a direct result of customers seeing your ads, and you are going to increase your advertising budget by 50 percent, you may reasonably forecast a 10-percent increase in sales (50% of 20% = 10%). But let's say your actual sales have fallen short of the forecast for several periods in a row. This may be an early indicator that your business is going into decline. For some firms, a more immediate warning is the loss of a key customer, which could represent a substantial portion of the company's sales. In such a case, it is imperative to find out why the customer has switched suppliers in order to determine if the same cause could result in a pattern of decline.

Not reaching your expected profit, or a pattern of falling profit, should also act as a warning that strategic changes may be needed. But apart from the pure value of your *profit* is the issue of *profitability,* or relative return on investment. For example, you might have $200,000 invested in a silk weaving business. Last year, after paying yourself a reasonable salary, the business made $8,000 in net profit. This would be a 4-percent return on your investment of $200,000. Now, you may think that this is an acceptable return—but if at the time the average silk weaving business in Canada is making an 8-percent ROI, your business cannot be considered particularly profitable: another warning sign. In this case, you are comparing your profitability to the average profitability of companies in your industry, usually based on information from Statistics Canada. This sort of *ratio analysis* (see Chapter 6) is not a very accurate process since the statistics you will use may be several years out of date. Nevertheless, it can serve as an indicator of your performance pattern and where you are in the business cycle.

Employee Turnover: Losing employees and hiring replacements is normal for most businesses, and the rate at which this takes place can vary significantly from industry to industry, and from company to company. But for any firm with employees, there is usually some recognizable pattern of employee turnover. Any sudden increase in turnover is a warning sign, especially when lost employees can be seen going to the competition. And just as the loss of a key customer can be critical for a small firm, the loss of a key employee can be devastating when there is no one else available to fill the role.

Whenever an employee decides to leave your business, it is very important that you conduct an **exit interview** with the departing member of your staff. One objective in holding such a meeting is to make sure that the employee leaves on good terms, keeping the door open for return, and ensuring that the employee will have good things to say about your firm. But the most important purpose of the exit interview is to find out *why the employee is leaving.* This may take some patience and careful discussion. Employees who may be leaving because they can't stand your management style, or who feel that their future is much more secure with the competition, may be reluctant to come out and say so. On the other hand, an employee who is leaving may not feel the need to be diplomatic and could end up informing you of some critical problem in the organization. There are no

✓ Test Yourself 9.2

True or False? A *niche* refers to a very small market segment.

? Get Help 9.1

Financial ratios, including indicators of profitability, are listed by industry on the Performance Plus Internet site, at *http://sme.ic.gc.ca.* This site has a feature that allows you to input your own financial data and receive a report comparing your firm to the industry averages. When using this site, a good hint is to select the *Incorporated Businesses* option for building your profile, since more financial data is available for corporations. Your accountant is an important aid in interpreting ratio analysis information.

exit interview An interview with a departing employee intended to find out any reasons for the employee's dissatisfaction as well as to have the employee leave with positive feelings about the company.

✓ Test Yourself 9.3

True or False? Sales forecasting for established firms is easier than for start-ups.

guarantees on the outcome, but you cannot afford to let slip an opportunity to interview any employee who quits.

Available Capacity: A more subtle issue that can indicate a firm's need for a new strategy relates to the idea of *operating capacity*—**100-percent capacity** represents the highest amount of activity (sales revenue) that a business can handle in a year without buying more equipment, hiring new staff, opening another store, or in some other way increasing the capacity of the business. For example, if your business consists of you and a small excavating machine (for landscaping, or digging pools and small foundations), you may hire out yourself and the machine for, let's say, $100 per hour. Considering some downtime for maintenance of the equipment and some time for inclement weather, you could still probably work as many as 45 hours a week, or (45 × 52 =) 2,340 hours a year. At $100 per hour, this would mean that your business, under perfect conditions, could bring in (2,340 × $100 =) $234,000 in a year. This would be 100-percent capacity for your firm. To have sales in excess of $234,000, you would have to increase your capacity, likely by buying a second machine and hiring another operator.

100-percent capacity The maximum amount of sales or production that a company could generate in a year as the company currently stands in terms of space, equipment, and employees.

The concept of *100-percent capacity* can be applied to most businesses. Picture yourself owning a restaurant which seats 50 people, where the average meal price is $20 and, on average, customers spend about an hour eating. For your market, under the best possible circumstances, you could turn over each of your seats twice at lunchtime and three times in the evening. This means that all of your seats would be full between noon and 2:00 p.m. (50 × 2 = 100 meals) and between 6:00 and 9:00 p.m. (50 × 3 = 150 meals), for a total of 250 meals per day. Over a year, this would produce sales of $1,825,000 (250 meals × $20 per meal × 365 days). This represents your 100-percent capacity. Most restaurants operate at only a tiny percentage of their full capacity, while businesses like the example of the excavator often have to operate at better than 50 percent just to break even.

Like the concept of break-even, with which it can be associated, 100-percent capacity is not a very precise tool. Typical methods of estimating 100-percent capacity for a business include:
- machinery or equipment capacity (the dollar income value of everything your equipment could produce in a year).
- facilities capacity (for example, the number of seats in your theatre × the number of performances a year × the average ticket price).
- employee capacity (for example, the maximum number of customers your travel agents can serve in a day × your average commission × the number of working days per year).
- best sales period (for example, using the best day of sales your business has ever had × the number of selling days per year; or your best week or month or quarter projected to the entire year).

✔ **Test Yourself 9.4**
True or False? The break-even point is where a business can start to produce net profit.

It is usually convenient to express 100-percent capacity in dollars, but this is not always a valid measure. For example, as a freelance writer you may be capable of producing and selling 1500 words a day of quality copy. But 1500 words can represent a huge variation in revenue. You could be paid very different amounts for the same amount of work depending on whether it is for work on a children's advice column in a small local paper or an internationally best-selling novel. You may be writing as much as you are capable of each day (working at 100-percent capacity), but not necessarily bringing in as much money as you are capable of. So, instead of dollars, some firms must represent 100-percent capacity in terms of units of output (in this case, words).

Head Start Exercise

9.2   Estimate 100-percent capacity for your business, clearly explaining the method you use ($\frac{1}{4}$ page maximum).

If you know your 100-percent capacity, you can easily calculate the percentage of capacity that your business is currently operating at:

$$\frac{\text{Current sales volume}}{\text{Sales at 100\% capacity}} \times 100\% = \text{Current \% of capacity}$$

Your operating level, or *current percentage of capacity*, and your growth pattern expressed as a percentage of capacity are important inputs for strategic planning. For example, your business may be operating at 80-percent capacity. Last year, you were at 60 percent, and the year before at 45 percent. By projecting the annual growth rate (115 percent, 120 percent, 125 percent), you get a pattern of 45 percent, 60 percent, 80 percent, and for next year 105 percent: 5 percent more business than you can handle. If you don't move to either increase capacity, or, alternatively, change the focus of your business, you will be encountering problems *before* the year is out. Signs that your business is operating at close to 100 percent can include turning away new customers, turning down jobs, late deliveries, or failure to meet deadlines.

Ask yourself: Is it good to have lots of spare capacity? You may have a business that consistently operates at only a small fraction of its full capacity. Considering that *capacity* is usually reflected as *fixed expenses,* operating at a low level is not the most economical way to run—spare capacity means unrealized profits. A pattern of operating at a small percentage of capacity is a clear indicator that your renewal strategy should be to increase sales (either through better promotion or finding new markets) in order to take advantage of the spare capacity.

Market Share and Market Potential: It's possible that you are in a position where your sales and profits have been increasing by, let's say, 3 percent a year for the last three years. This might lead you to believe that your enterprise is comfortably growing. But if you are in an industry where the overall market potential (see Chapter 2) has been growing at 10 percent per year, your share of the available business has been shrinking despite your increasing sales. You will have been losing market share. Your market share is calculated as:

$$\frac{\text{Your sale of a particular product or service}}{\text{The market potential for that product or service}} \times 100\%$$

Ask yourself: Would I be able to calculate my market share? Obviously, in order to calculate your market share you must have some estimate of the entire *market potential.* Many entrepreneurs will estimate market potential as part of their start-up business plans and then carry on business for years, never giving a thought to how the market might change. However, for most industries there are convenient secondary sources an entrepreneur can use to maintain some ongoing sense of what is happening to the size of a particular market. These sources include:

Get Help 9.2
Speak to a reference librarian at your public library or community college to make sure you are familiar with all the publications related to your industry.

- *Industry publications.* Trade journals and association newsletters are often the best way to keep abreast of market trends since the publishers know that market issues are of primary interest to their readers. In fact, trade journals will often conduct their own primary research to get information about industry trends. *Ask yourself: Are you familiar with all the publications aimed specifically at your industry?*

- *Economic reports.* The federal government (mostly through Industry Canada) provides a variety of economic reports showing trends in various sectors of the economy. As well, private groups, such as the Conference Board of Canada, publish their own analyses and projections for the economy. Large banks also produce a variety of published reports based on the predictions of their own economists.
- *Business periodicals.* These days there is no shortage of daily business news, but for strategic planning it is better to look at the broader kind of analysis found in magazines such as *Canadian Business* or *Report on Business Magazine.* And because Canada so often follows American trends in business, it may be worthwhile to look at publications such as *The Economist* or *Forbes* magazine.
- *Trend newsletters.* These reports provide broad analysis of current trends (growing or declining markets, changing attitudes, new technologies, and so on), often with some expert predictions for the future. These reports are prepared from analyses of items in a broad range of media. It is even possible to have your own customized reports or even just electronic *clippings* of the current media stories on any topic you specify.

Clearly, it is important to know how the market potential—how much business is out there—is changing over time. Is it growing? Shrinking? Remaining stable? For example, the consumer market for cell phones grew at a very rapid pace for several years then fell steeply to a point where it levelled off. The big drop came when pretty much everyone who was going to get a cell phone had one. This was the market saturation point. The relatively steady business that came after the drop was from the natural growth in the population, as well as current users replacing and upgrading equipment. Markets tend to be cyclical, picking up with the introduction of new products and falling after the market is saturated. By historically tracking the market potential, you can have some idea about the future demand for your products or services. An approaching saturation point is a definite warning that you must embark on some form of renewal.

Competition—Direct: Identifying your direct and indirect competition was part of the start-up business plan. But once your business is running, you must develop ways of regularly monitoring the competition for changes. Have your competitors decided to open new locations? Where? Are they purchasing a new type of machinery? What? Are they starting new advertising campaigns? When? Are they hiring new managers? Who? Are they laying off employees? Why? You'd like to know all of this, and just about anything else of strategic value concerning changes in your competition. Techniques for keeping an eye on the direct competition include:

- Bookmarking and regularly monitoring the websites of competitors, looking for changes in their marketing mix and for any special announcements.
- Doing regular Web searches for *recent* references to competitors.
- Participating in trade associations where you can meet with other entrepreneurs in the same industry and where the natural lunchtime topic of conversation is business. It's surprising what your competitor may reveal in a social setting.
- Using clipping services to let you know what the media are saying about your competitors (see above).
- "Shopping" competitors regularly by making phone calls requesting information, or taking trips to retail sites. (Note the ethical issue of being careful not to abuse the time of commission sales people who will think you are a prospective customer.)

Get Help 9.3
Start with the Strategis website, at ***www.strategis.ic.gc.ca***, and click on *Economic Analysis, Statistics* for links to a variety of reports. For examples of bank reports, try ***www.bmo.com*** and click on *Economic Reports.*

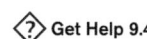
Get Help 9.4
Check the phone book or Internet for "media monitoring services" if you require clippings about your products or services, your own company, or even your competitors.

Test Yourself 9.5
True or False? Market potential is made up of your market share plus the market share of all your competitors.

- Gathering information from your own sales prospects and new customers (who presumably are or were dealing with your competition).
- Undertaking formal primary marketing research that surveys customer experiences with you and your competitors.

Competition—Indirect: It is a definite warning for renewal when competitors, perhaps many times larger than your company, invade your territory. Huge indirect competitors often strike terror into the hearts of small entrepreneurs, who complain that they cannot compete with the big box retailers or the giant **multinational** manufacturing and service companies. True, you usually cannot compete on *price* against such large buying power, but these big companies are committed to a strategy of serving the broadest possible markets. Your small-town paint store does not have to go out of business when Home Depot opens up in your area. But you may have to redefine *what* you are selling (perhaps specialize in high-end designer wallpaper) and redefine *to whom* you are selling (perhaps target the new downtown condo-dwellers and wealthy owners of older homes).

It is necessary to look carefully at your large competitors and identify goods and services that they do not provide or groups that they do not cater to. You are looking for things that are just not economical for them to get into, or areas where they cannot be flexible. Burger King will not make your favourite meal of a chicken salad sandwich on rye with a side order of beans. But the local diner where you regularly eat lunch will have no problem filling your order. The smaller firm has the advantage of flexibility.

A Note of Perspective: Theoretically, it would be nice to think of a business as continually assessing and renewing itself, constantly anticipating and smoothly responding to changes in the environment. In reality, businesses, like most other forms of human endeavour, develop in fits and starts. Rarely are major changes to a business proactive in nature. More typically, the entrepreneur is responding to problems in the enterprise or the environment. Entrepreneurs who are true visionaries are rare, and the best that the rest of us can hope for is to recognize the warning signs when it's time for change.

Head Start Exercise

9.3   Make a list of any warning signs that might indicate your business is approaching decline ($\frac{1}{4}$ page maximum).

SWOT ANALYSIS   Identifying the need for renewal in your business is only recognizing the problem. To address the need, you still have to develop a revised business plan. But before doing that, you should perform some form of **SWOT analysis**. This means a *broad* look at the internal and external advantages and disadvantages of your business: strengths, weaknesses, opportunities, and threats.

SWOT analysis is a form of marketing research that uses the kind of information described above. But SWOT is also much wider in focus. In your original feasibility research, you knew exactly what you were trying to calculate. In SWOT analysis, you start out not knowing as precisely what you are looking for. What you perceive as your greatest strength may, in fact, just be the industry average. You may have very little idea of where your opportunities and

multinational A very large company that typically has supply sources or facilities in several countries and markets their products internationally.

SWOT analysis Research and drawing conclusions about the strengths and weaknesses of a particular company, as well as about the opportunities and threats that it faces.

SWOT Analysis

	+	−
Internal	Strengths	Weaknesses
External	Opportunities	Threats

threats lie. Because of this, much of SWOT consists of **hypothesis testing**. For example, you may believe that *low pricing* is the single biggest factor that your customers use in deciding to buy from you. When this hypothesis is tested (perhaps a telephone survey conducted on a sample of your customers), it may turn out that most of them come to you simply because of your convenient location—and that they would continue to come even if your prices were higher. Your hypothesis, or assumption, was wrong.

This research is more complicated than gathering the descriptive kind of information used in your feasibility research. In addition, it requires more careful analysis and the drawing of conclusions (the creation of new hypotheses) on which you are going to base the future strategy of your business. Presumably, the research is also taking place when the value of your business is much greater than it was at start-up. This means that you have more to lose from bad strategic decisions. As a result, the likelihood of your needing professional help in performing the SWOT analysis is greater than it was for start-up research.

Strengths and Weaknesses: *Ask yourself: What could be the difficulties in identifying the strengths and weaknesses of my enterprise?* Like many entrepreneurs, you may find describing the weaknesses of your business as difficult as describing the shortcomings of your own children. It's hard to be objective. And in describing the strengths of your business, there is a tendency to list vague platitudes like saying that you have a *good reputation* or that you provide *excellent customer service*. Such comments have little meaning unless you can specifically answer the question: *Compared to what?* Even though strengths and weaknesses are internal factors of a business, the benchmarks for describing them are usually external: compared to specific competition, compared to industry averages, or compared to customer expectations.

Examples of internal issues that would be described as strengths or weaknesses include:
- *Site.* For example, if you have a retail store that gets considerably less traffic than your direct competitor gets, this would be a considerable weakness.
- *Image.* If your ice fishing business is widely recognized as the cheapest place to rent a hut (and if low price is an important issue for your market), this would be a powerful strength.
- *Product/service mix.* Your business may sell industrial filters and have the exclusive rights to distribute an improved patented filter throughout Canada—for you, a huge competitive strength.
- *People and expertise.* Let's say you have an interior design firm and your partner is the only interior designer in your town who has a certificate in feng shui (the Chinese art of creating harmony in the human environment). During a time when feng shui is wildly popular, you would have a big strength.
- *Financial position.* You may have very little equity in your company and almost no cash reserves compared to your larger competitors. This weakness makes you less likely to survive tough sales periods.

hypothesis testing Research to see whether a particular assumption can be supported by the evidence.

Get Help 9.5
See the Yellow Pages under "Marketing Research and Analysis" to identify firms near you; check their websites before approaching them for pricing information. Keep in mind that a lower-cost alternative is offered by some universities, for example, as credit for their MBA students. Check your local university websites to identify the appropriate department chair.

Contracts, intellectual property, methods, systems, and many other aspects of your business can be seen as relative strengths or weaknesses.

Head Start Exercise

9.4   List your major assumptions or beliefs about the strengths and weaknesses of your business ($\frac{1}{4}$ page maximum).

Opportunities and Threats: Opportunities and threats can arise whenever something (just about anything) in your environment changes. Just a few examples of such changes are:

- *Legislation.* A law that perhaps changes the way education is funded by giving an annual education allowance to each student would represent a great opportunity for your small aesthetics-training institute.
- *Demographics.* A rapid fall in the birth rate would be a serious threat for your baby-furniture plant.
- *Competition.* The bankruptcy of your leading direct competitor would be a wonderful opportunity for your custom bookbinding company.
- *Technology.* The invention of truly wrinkle-free, stain-free, odour-free clothing would be a serious threat to your small dry-cleaning chain.

Changes in social patterns, fashion, the economy, government foreign policy, climate, disease patterns, population, lifestyle—any of these could hold threats or opportunities for your business.

Head Start Exercise

9.5   List your major assumptions or beliefs about the opportunities and threats facing your business ($\frac{1}{4}$ page maximum).

9.6   Briefly describe research approaches you could use to test your SWOT assumptions ($\frac{1}{2}$ page maximum).

✓ **Test Yourself 9.6**
True or False? Strengths and weaknesses in SWOT analysis refer to external factors of a business.

In the SWOT analysis you investigate your hypotheses, modify them as required to fit the evidence, and so identify the real strengths, weaknesses, opportunities, and threats facing your business. Then, on the basis of this analysis, you can decide how to either expand or refocus your venture for long-term profitability.

How Will I Increase My Sales?

In many cases, the sales of a business will change because of changes in the marketplace. For example, if the population in the area of your market grows, you will likely have an increase in sales. Conversely, if four new competitors move into your stable market area, you will likely have a decrease in sales. You cannot control changes in the marketplace, but you can control your own strategy in an attempt to increase sales.

You can choose from three basic strategies to help your company grow:
- You can sell more of what you're already selling to the customer groups you're already selling to. This is **market share expansion**, since generally you are getting your new sales by taking business away from the competition.
- You can sell new things to the customer groups you're already selling to. This is called **product/service expansion.**
- You can sell what you're already selling, but to new groups of customers. In this case we are talking about **market segment expansion.**

A Note of Perspective: It is also possible to grow your business by buying other businesses in the same field and incorporating them into your firm. This *acquisition* strategy is a less common approach to growth for small firms and it involves all the complexity of buying a business (see Chapter 6) as well as the many problems of integrating the ventures or attempting to run them as separate entities. As a result, business acquisitions are not dealt with in this text.

As part of a well-managed growth strategy, you should not embark on more than one of the three basic strategies at a time. If you attempt to sell totally new products or services to totally new groups of customers, you are essentially starting a new business. You will be facing much lower risk if you attempt one strategy at a time. For example, you may own a full-service car wash that has declining sales due to the growth of mini-washes in franchise gas bars. You may decide to fight back through:
- Market share expansion, perhaps with an advertising and sales promotion campaign mailing discount coupons to consumers in your area; or
- Market segment expansion, maybe by trying to get high-volume contracts with local used-car dealers who could use your wash facilities; or
- Product/service expansion, possibly by installing your own pumps and selling gasoline.

Ask yourself: What would be the problem with attempting these three strategies simultaneously? By taking on so much change, there is a huge risk that your business—even your life—will become unmanageable. While trying to plan, execute, and measure the effectiveness of your advertising campaign, you will also be negotiating with gasoline suppliers, franchisors, construction people, auto dealers, and doubtless the bank or some other source for financing it all. With so many issues to deal with, there is the danger that you will lose your strategic focus and have your time and attention used up by the thousand small issues that will arise. Also, by employing one strategy at a time, you will be more able to measure the effectiveness of your approach.

MARKET SHARE EXPANSION   An increase in market share (selling a greater percentage of the products and services purchased by your current target groups) is usually related to changes in your price and promotion strategies. A recent study of small manufacturers indicates that the fastest route to growth is by competing on the basis of price.[1] But before lowering your price in the hope of greater market penetration, consider the effect this will have on profit. A lower price means a lower per-unit profit, so the increase in volume you are expecting will have to be more than enough to make up for lost profit: enough to actually *increase* the profit. And it is a dangerous strategy to lower your price *temporarily* to get new customers, hoping that you can later raise prices and that the customers will stay with you

market share expansion Growth by selling more of the same products and services that a business is already selling to the same customer groups that the business already targets; capturing a greater portion of the market potential.

product/service expansion Growth by selling new products and/or services to the customer groups that a business already targets.

market segment expansion Growth by selling the products and services that a business already offers to new groups of customers.

Get Help 9.6
The website for *Profit* magazine offers a number of excellent resources and links to help entrepreneurs plan a business expansion. See *www.profitguide.com* and click on *Essential Web Guide*.

Test Yourself 9.7
True or False? *Market segment expansion* means growth by selling to new groups of customers, those products and services that you already provide.

because of some other competitive advantage (such as superior products, services, location, and so on). If you are working in a price-sensitive market, the customers will tend to leave when your prices go back up.

Ask yourself: How will I know the optimum amount to lower prices to get the market share I want? Marketing research can make predictions about your future market share using techniques like surveys and even test marketing. As well, you can make financial projections by having your projected income statements on a spreadsheet where you can change sales and cost figures to see the impact on your future profit. In some cases, however, you will have to use a system of trial and error by changing your prices in slow increments and measuring the effect on your sales volume and profit.

Head Start Exercise

9.7 Estimate how low you could move your prices and still make a profit (refer to your break-even point). Speculate about how such pricing would affect your market share and how your competition would likely respond. ($\frac{1}{2}$ page maximum.)

Changes in promotion that you may consider for increasing your market share would include:
- Increased personal selling, through the hiring of more sales staff or a more aggressive sales approach that could include changing the incentives for your salespeople.
- Increased sales promotion and publicity activities, although these tend to have only a short-term effect on sales activities as opposed to a more permanent capture of market share.
- Increased advertising, through either greater frequency in currently used media or an expansion to new advertising media.

As you plan any changes in your promotion, you must also plan methods for measuring the effects of those changes. And by making one change at a time, you will more easily be able to measure the effects of your changes.

With changes in either your prices or your promotion techniques, there is the constant possibility that your competition will quickly make similar changes in response. And there is even the possibility that this could trigger an advertising war (where you and your competitors are spending an uneconomical amount to vie for the attention of customers) or worse, a price war (where neither you nor the competition can make money at the prices being charged). If the competitors decided to wage such a war indefinitely, the natural outcome would be that only the richest competitor would survive to own the entire market. Even with legislation to protect businesses against **predatory pricing** practices, the costs of getting involved in such a war (lost profit, time, legal costs) can be very high.

predatory pricing Where a company loses money on a product or service by charging prices so low as to drive competitors from the market. Then the company recoups its losses by overcharging in a market where it has no competition.

One dangerous assumption about increasing your market share is that if you are getting more of the pie, then all of your competitors must therefore be getting less. Envision that you own a remedial tutoring business that targets high-school students in your suburban area. You estimate that last year you had 20 percent of a market that you share with three other independent firms (20 percent each) and a franchise unit of a national operation (20 percent). This year, because of new advertising, your share has increased to 25 percent, and for next year you are targeting 30 percent. What you may not know is that the franchise operation this year grew to 35 percent of the market and next year is targeting 60 percent. The growth of this competitor represents a substantial threat to your business. This is an argument for why your knowledge of your market should not be a single research event at start-up, but more of an ongoing process.

A second tricky issue about increasing market share is that you must be careful not to be a victim of your own success by gaining market share beyond 100 percent of your capacity. For example, you may decide to increase market share for your gas fireplace company, which sells to consumers in your town. So you increase the commissions paid to your salespeople and step up your advertising until the orders start to pour in. But if you don't have the capacity to supply and install the volume of business you have created, you will be facing cancelled orders, an image problem with your new customers, and likely the alienation of your own sales staff, who will probably not be paid for cancelled work. Any attempt, therefore, to increase the market share should be undertaken cautiously and with consideration for your capacity to deliver.

PRODUCT/SERVICE EXPANSION   The second obvious way to increase your sales is by finding something new to sell to your existing clientele. But introducing a new product can affect other elements of the marketing mix. It is best to start by adding products/services that work with your existing promotion, distribution, and pricing strategies. If you have a high-end shoe store that is already pricey, adding the option of custom-made shoes would be well in line with your image. But if yours were a discount shoe store, adding the custom-made option would require a change in pricing strategy that won't work for your market segment.

Any products or services that you add to your mix must be perceived as logical by your customers. For example, you may have some spare floor space in your party supply store and decide to install a key-making machine. Now, you may get the odd customer who is in the store and, on seeing the machine, remembers the need to have a key duplicated. But if your customer is at home, the need to get a key made will trigger a trip to the hardware store, not your business, since long habit makes this seem the logical supplier. Giant retailers, because they generate so much traffic and have so much advertising power, are able to change customer perceptions about the logical product/service mix. So Wal-Mart can teach you pretty quickly that it's normal to get your hair styled and your oil changed at the same place you buy underwear. But with a small business you will not have this power and so must cater to the already existing perceptions of customers, making only small logical changes. For instance, your bottled water delivery service could probably add ice delivery to the mix, but adding garden supplies would make no sense to the consumer.

You also must be careful *not* to add products that will *not* bring new profit. For example, you may have an ice cream store that carries 10 flavours of ice cream, which you sell in either cones or sundaes. In an attempt to get more business you may decide to go to 20 flavours of ice cream plus 5 fresh-fruit flavours of frozen yogurt. You will now have the expense of increasing your freezer space and buying the equipment to mix the yogurt and fruit. It will also cost you money for the extra time it takes to prepare the yogurt cones—and you may find a problem with customers slowing the lineup because, with more to choose from, they are taking longer to make up their minds. It's possible that in the long run you have absolutely no increase in sales at all. Sure, the customers are happy to pick from your new

? **Get Help 9.7**

Canada's Competition Bureau administers the Competition Act, which forbids predatory pricing as a way of eliminating competition. Information about both the Act and the Bureau are available from the Strategis website, at ***www.strategis.ic.gc.ca***.

product selection, but without this expansion you might have had the same customers who would just choose from the original 10 flavours and be satisfied.

This example of adding extra flavours is an increase in the *depth* of the product mix. Adding yogurt, cakes, doughnuts, or other confection lines would be examples of increasing the *breadth* of the mix. *Ask yourself: Is it best to increase the breadth or depth?* Generally, it is easier and cheaper to increase depth, but less likely to bring new profit from existing customers. Deepening the mix is more likely to be a move in response to competition or changing trends. Offering whole new product lines (more breadth) has greater potential for new profit, but also greater risk.

Finding or Developing Products: If your business involves reselling products (you're a wholesaler or retailer) then your task is to *find* appropriate new products for your customers. If you're a manufacturer or pure service business, you are more likely to be *developing* the products or services yourself. *Ask yourself: How do I know which products or services to find or develop?* Conventional business advice would be to formally research the needs and wants of your customers before seeking or developing new offerings for them. Certainly, this is the professional marketing approach and should be used whenever economically possible. But with smaller retailers and wholesalers it is more likely that the process starts with finding a product that you then realize would be ideal for your customers. The solution may present itself before you have even identified the problem. You may, then, as a small retailer or wholesaler, see your task as staying up-to-date on what products are available. *Ask yourself: Where could I find out about new products to resell?* This task has been made easier than ever with the growing number of online product catalogues and trade directories. There are also the more traditional sources of information such as trade associations, trade shows, industry publications, and world trade centres. Many large cities have World Trade Centres, supported by various levels of government, local chambers of commerce, and other non-profit organizations. These centres offer a variety of activities and services that promote international trade.

Shopping for products that you can resell is still *shopping*, an activity that most of us enjoy. Keep in mind, however, that finding new products is a process of shopping for your customers' needs, not your personal tastes. So it shouldn't be a *seat-of-the-pants* exercise. At least some research should be carried out before any final decision on whether to carry a new product. For example, you may want to determine:

- *Customer needs and benefits.* Interviews with customers and providing samples for customers to try out will show if the new product can satisfy a true need.
- *Sales potential for the product.* This can be determined by test marketing with a representative sample of your customers and extrapolating from the sales results.
- *Profit potential for the product.* This should include an estimate of your sales as well as your direct costs plus all related overhead for promoting, storing, delivering, and servicing related to the product.
- *Length of the product life cycle.* Fashion issues or leapfrogging technologies can mean that even though a product is new, it is going to become obsolete so quickly that it's not economical for you to offer it. For some products, an estimate of the length of this cycle may be the deciding factor in whether it will be added to your product mix.

Like the business cycle, individual products tend to have their own life cycle with the stages of:
- *Introduction.* This is when the product requires high levels of promotion and high levels of monitoring (research) for future profitability.

Test Yourself 9.8
True or False? Predatory pricing usually benefits a smaller competitor.

Test Yourself 9.9
True or False? A business cannot supply products or services beyond 100 percent of its capacity.

Get Help 9.8
There are many international trade directories, which can be searched for specific product categories Search for *B2B* (business-to-business) *trade directories* or check the *Business.com* search engine for trade directories or even specific products: **www.business.com**. Other good sites include **www.bigex.com** and **www.webtrados.com**.

Get Help 9.9
You can find the World Trade Centre closest to you from the website of the *World Trade Centers Association*: **http://world.wtca.org**.

- *Growth.* During this stage, successful methods for promoting the product have been refined and sales are increasing.
- *Maturity.* In this stage, the product is widely accepted by the market, providing high profits for relatively little maintenance cost. Methods to extend the life of the successful product (improvements) should be considered at this point.
- *Decline.* This is where sales of the product drop because of market saturation, product obsolescence, or high numbers of competing products. The product should be closely monitored for profitability and considered for abandonment.

Understanding, predicting, and extending the product life cycle is particularly important in industries with short cycles, such as information technology businesses. This has given rise to the specialized study of product life-cycle management (**PLM**) and even PLM software that can organize and share information about factors that can affect the cycle. Formerly a tool of large firms, PLM is becoming increasingly important to smaller companies,[2] especially those that depend on large firm suppliers and customers.

Product/ Service Development: Finding products or services for resale may not be appropriate for your company. Your task may be to create new products and services or to improve existing ones. This means *innovation*, which is commonly associated with *entrepreneurship*. The belief that innovation by itself produces entrepreneurial success is found in the old saying:

> Build a better mousetrap and the world will beat a path to your door.
> Ralph Waldo Emerson (Popular American Writer, 1803–1882)

This belief, however, may be more myth than reality since the relationship among the growth of sales, profits, and innovation turns out to be rather more complex. In fact, over 80 percent of new products will fail to produce new profit.[3] True, the success of new products and (we can assume) services is closely connected to having superior quality or value of the product.[4] But factors such as timing, targeting, price, and promotion are also critical.

Ask yourself: How do you come up with the idea for a new product or service? There are many different routes that can be taken for the development of a new product or service. Here is one example of steps that can be followed:

- *Customer research.* As in finding new products, the first step is to identify unsatisfied needs of your customers through formal (surveys, focus groups) or informal (sales conversations, observation) methods.
- *Idea development.* This can involve creative idea-generating sessions with sales reps, end-users, outside experts, production engineers, etc., as well as the scanning of competitors, journals, and trade shows to produce a great many new ideas, many of which will be unsuitable. Ideas must then be screened and ranked to come up with the few most feasible (cost-efficient, potentially profitable) approaches. This might be accomplished with a small committee discussing each idea and using a **weighted ranking** approach to evaluate and compare the ideas.
- *Product testing.* Production of a **prototype** and/or samples of a new product can provide data about the cost and problems of producing the new item. Samples can then be tested for function, safety, durability, and so on. Testing can be done in house, with customers, through independent laboratories, or by the Canadian Standards Association (**CSA**) for safety certification.

PLM (product life-cycle management) Methods and systems for organizing and sharing product-related information that can affect the length of time a product can be viable.

✓ **Test Yourself 9.10**
True or False? It's always best to trust your instincts when looking for new products to resell.

✓ **Test Yourself 9.11**
True or False? Products in the *maturity* stage of the product life cycle require high levels of promotion.

✓ **Test Yourself 9.12**
True or False? The majority of new products fail in the marketplace.

weighted ranking A method of numerically ranking competing options on different performance dimensions (for example cost, reliability, comfort, appearance, etc.). Each dimension is rated for its relative importance (for example on a scale of 1–5, with 5 being most important). As an example, Option A might be ranked 3 on the dimension of cost, and the dimension of cost is rated as a "5" in importance. Therefore, on the dimension of cost, Option A will pick up 15 points (3 × 5). Final scores, based on a series of dimensions, determine the best option.

prototype A single working sample of a product.

• *Test marketing.* This involves promoting and providing your product or service to a limited segment of your target customers. For example, if your business is a small chain of coffee bars in the Montreal area, you may use only one of your outlets to introduce and test the new mocha-banana flavoured iced coffee that you have developed.

Product/service development does not always mean coming up with brand-new offerings. Modifying products or services that you already produce is a way of improving the product mix economically as well as a way of showing customers that you have been listening to them. Product materials, features, size, and packaging can all be changed to make the product more appealing and increase sales. This can be accomplished by following the steps, described above, for developing a brand-new product. A modification to an existing product should be a legitimate improvement, not just a minimal change so that the product can be promoted as "new and improved." So-called *changes* that the customer cannot readily appreciate can damage your credibility, your firm's image. Regardless of whether you are coming up with whole new products or services, or modifying your existing offerings, there is some evidence that *product development* is a more powerful method of improving your profits than putting the same energy into improving your efficiency.[5]

Head Start Exercise

9.8 Briefly identify any new products or services that could logically be added to your current mix ($\frac{1}{4}$ page maximum).

MARKET SEGMENT EXPANSION Remember that at start-up it is safer for your business to specialize in a very narrow group of customers (a specific age range, a particular type of institution, or a defined geographic area) rather than a broad segment. Later, when expanding your range of customers, you should ideally expand one segment at a time. The selection of the appropriate segment to start your expansion should be influenced by the need to disrupt the rest of your marketing mix as little as possible.

For example, you may be a cleaning supplies distributor that targets government institutions in the greater metropolitan area of your city. You are considering several new target segments, each of which may require some changes to your product/service, price, promotion, or distribution strategies. Right now, you carry a narrow range of products in bulk containers, your prices are a little on the high side (which your customers accept because of your reliability), you promote only by personal selling, and your distribution relies on your online ordering system and same-day delivery from your warehouse. Among your targets under consideration are:

• *Industrial cleaning services within your city.* This option would require a change in your packaging (using smaller containers since these services carry all their supplies in car trunks), and your distribution would have to include allowing the cleaners to pick up supplies at your warehouse at night.

• *Consumers in the area of your warehouse.* This option would mean changing your packaging into much smaller containers and remodelling part of your warehouse into retail space. As well, your promotion would have to include some form of local advertising and provision for dealing with cash or retail credit cards.

• *Discount retailers across the country.* With this option you have to be able to deliver nationally, since most of the discount stores are national chains. Again, you would need a change in packaging and labelling, perhaps as the house brands of the stores you will sell to.

• *Government institutions throughout the province.* For this you would need to improve your ability to deliver throughout the province.

Ask yourself: Which of the above options would require the fewest changes to the marketing mix?

✓ **Test Yourself 9.13**
True or False? An increase in your market share must mean a decrease in the market share of each of your competitors.

✓ **Test Yourself 9.14**
True or False? It is best to expand into several new market segments at one time.

Head Start Exercise

9.9 List various market segments that you could logically expand into, noting any changes to the marketing mix that each would require ($\frac{1}{2}$ page maximum).

Expanding to new markets may require changing distribution channels. For example, you may have a business packaging organically grown herbs, which you sell directly to health food stores across Canada. Upon expanding to the UK market, you deal through a British importer that sells to stores over there. Now you are dealing through two different distribution channels for customers in different locations. For larger firms that are already highly complex, dealing through multiple distribution channels may not be a problem. For example, Nike sells their products through their own retail outlets, as well as through department stores, large shoe chains, and even smaller specialty chains. For a small company, however, multiple channels may add a layer of complexity and cost that is too great to bear.

New markets may also require adding new ordering and delivery modes. For example, your business may be a store in Vancouver that sells high-end hiking equipment, which you advertise in sports magazines. When the business first opened, all sales were over-the-counter to walk-in customers. Later, you started to use the company truck to deliver items in the Vancouver area that were not in stock when customers ordered them in the store. Later still, you started to accept phone orders from regular customers, which you would deliver within the city or mail to customers outside the city. Eventually, you advertised the company number in your magazine ads and included an order form that could be mailed in with a cheque. Finally, you configured your company website for online ordering, giving customers the option of delivery by post or, at extra cost, courier. In each of these cases, distribution is still direct to the end-user but you are offering four different ordering modes (in store, phone, mail-in, online) and four different delivery modes (pick-up, truck, post, courier). And since you have a website, of course, you are now promoting to a worldwide market, inviting all of the ordering complexity (time zones, languages, exchange rates) and delivery complexity that this involves (foreign postal services, package tracking, receipts).

Ask yourself: Is it even possible to restrict your business to a narrow market segment in the age of the Internet? Not only is it possible, but it is imperative that the growing small business stick to a planned marketing strategy in a time when market forces could overwhelm the business with complexity.

✓ **Test Yourself 9.15**
True or False? It is best for a small firm to deal through as many different distribution channels as possible.

REPLICATING THE BUSINESS   Expanding to new geographic segments, especially for retail and consumer services, can mean opening new sites in new territories. This usually means copying, as closely as possible, the original successful business in increasingly distant geographic locations, thus building a network of outlets. You have a choice between two basic approaches for doing this:

1. building a chain of company-owned sites
2. selling franchises.

If you opt for building your own chain, the money needed to open the second site—or at least part of the money—will have to come from the profits of the first. Then, the profits from two sites can eventually be used to open a third, and so on. This will produce an accelerating growth (sites will open at a faster and faster rate), but it is still a slow process compared to the option of selling franchises. With the franchise option, you can initially invest your profit from the first store in setting up a system to sell franchises. Then, each new site will be set up using the money of the franchisees, who will also pay you a fee for the privilege of using your business method. This allows the chain to grow about as fast as you can sell franchises.

Ask yourself: Is franchising the best way to expand? Not all businesses are suitable for franchising. If the potential franchisee could just look at your business and do pretty much the same thing in a different location, why bother paying you a franchise fee? Your franchising operation must be providing some value to the franchisee in terms of an established name, a proven concept, training, or something else they will not have if they start up on their own. And even if your business could be replicated as franchises, the obvious drawback of franchising is that you will be sharing the company profits with the franchisees.

With your own chain, you get all the profit and everyone working in the business is an employee that you can direct, although you will have to build a management hierarchy to do so. Franchisees are not your employees, but you still have control over them, although control is only through the complex contract that the franchisees must sign. See Figure 9.2 for a brief comparison of these two expansion techniques.

In the past decades, franchising has continued to grow at a very strong rate. This has been facilitated by the growth of free trade areas, making foreign franchising and licensing much easier.[6] Exporting your franchise can mean selling large area or **master franchises**, which allows the **master franchisee** to sell individual franchises to others. Potentially a very fast way to grow, this involves a highly complex contract (and the associated legal fees) but also faster cash returns. See information on "master franchises" in Chapter 7.

✓ **Test Yourself 9.16**
True or False? Selling franchises is a faster way to expand than building your own company-owned chain.

master franchise An arrangement where a **master franchisee** buys the right to sell franchises to others within a given territory.

⟨?⟩ **Get Help 9.10**
If you consider selling franchises, an early consultation with a lawyer who specializes in franchising is a good idea. For a referral, check the website of your provincial or territorial Law Society.

Figure 9.2

BUSINESS REPLICATION COMPARISON		
	Company-Owned Chain	**Franchise Operation**
Growth rate	Slower	Faster
Cash outlay	More	Less
Profit	Your own	Shared with franchisees
Legal complexity	Minimal	Complex
Control	Direct	Via contract
Management staff	Larger	Smaller

Head Start Exercise

9.10 Briefly discuss the feasibility of opening new sites for your company ($\frac{1}{3}$ page maximum).

Should I Consider Exporting?

Moving to new, larger geographic segments ultimately leads to an *export market*. When we think of exporting, the tendency is to see this as something for manufactured products. True, there have been long-standing traditions among governments to encourage the export of manufactured products, especially those made from local raw materials. And recent history indicates that Canadian manufacturing, agriculture, and natural resource–based industries are more successful exporters than retail or service industries.[7] But export markets are a possibility for all types of business—everything from stand-up comics and jazz bands to air-conditioning consultants and graphic artists. *Ask yourself: What are the problems of becoming an exporter?*

SMALL BUSINESS PROFILE 9.2
Outer Coast Seaweeds Ltd.

Sooke, B.C. is near the southern tip of Vancouver Island about 35 km east of Victoria. It's from here that Diane Bernard runs her seaweed business: Outer Coast Seaweeds Ltd. This business started out of Bernard's home in 2001, and since then the demand for the company's products has been growing steadily.

There are many hundreds of species of seaweed, a range of fast-growing ocean plants that thrive in the swift currents from the Strait of Juan De Fuca. There are many uses for seaweed, ranging from industrial chemicals to cosmetics to just plain eating it in a variety of forms. In Japan, where seaweed is practically a staple, the industry is worth billions of dollars annually. But even in Canada, it is used as a fish wrapping, in salads and soups, or as a dried snack. When harvested properly, seaweed continues to grow, making this a totally renewable resource for which Bernard pays a licensing fee to the federal government.

Although she had some general knowledge about the product, Bernard's education (Master's degree in criminology) and previous careers (local politician) were totally unrelated to this form of marine farming. In Bernard's case, she simply saw an opportunity in her own back yard, the Pacific Ocean. The business has grown to five full-time employees plus the seasonal help she needs for harvesting. The two main uses for the seaweeds collected by Bernard are cosmetic products and gourmet foods. She ships fresh seaweed to upscale restaurants in Canada and the U.S., and she produces a range of skin products for sale to spas as well as directly to consumers via her website (**www.outercoastseaweeds.com**). In addition, tourists to Vancouver Island can book one of several Wild Seaweed Tours, where education is combined with a fun, hands-on seaweed experience.

Bernard's current growth thrust is targeting the large spa industry in California, for which she now has her own sales representative.

The decision to export is a major one, full of risks. Potential problems of exporting include complex foreign regulations; shipping costs and unreliable carriers; difficulties in getting payment; and, in some countries, corrupt systems and officials. There can be, however, significant advantages to moving into export markets. Obviously, moving to additional markets increases the sales potential for a product or service but it is also a kind of diversification that can reduce risk. For example, if the local market for your product dries up or you are losing customers to competitors, you might still have foreign customers to keep you afloat. As well, exporting can be a method of extending the product life cycle for some services or products.[8] For example, you may be selling training programs in Canada for the use of a particular flight simulator, which is now becoming obsolete as the aging aircraft it simulates are less frequently used here. The used aircraft, however, have likely been sold in developing nations where there will continue to be a demand for your training programs for many years.

SELLING ABROAD   Canada is, to a great extent, a nation of immigrants, many of whom have extensive family and business connections in their countries of origin. Recognizing the competitive advantage of a Canadian product or knowing of demand in their originating country has been the impetus for many small Canadian exporters to set up businesses using family or friends as the importers. This kind of arrangement eliminates many typical exporting problems such as dealing in foreign cultures or trust issues with importing partners. It is possible, however, to find customers and navigate these problems in countries where you have no previous contacts or experience.

All the prospecting and promotional methods that we use in Canada to find new customers can apply to looking for foreign customers. For example, you may choose to run an ad in a foreign trade journal or newspaper. Both of these would likely be accessible through websites that would tell you about their customer types and circulation numbers. When looking for foreign customers, though, a great starting place is the website of the federal ministry responsible for trade: *International Trade Canada* (ITC). This ministry sponsors several initiatives to help exporters find customers. One of these is the *Virtual Trade Commissioner*, where your company profile is matched with international business opportunities. Another ITC program is the series of Team Canada trade missions. These are visits by groups of Canadian businesspeople to countries where there are markets for Canadian products. Offshore customers can also be found using the same resources that are available for finding foreign products to import: trade fairs, world trade centres, your own listings in trade directories, and so on.

We know that selling to government, on average, carries considerably lower risk than selling to private-sector customers. This principle also holds true for export markets, and many foreign governments have been customers for Canadian goods and services. A source for finding *tenders* or *requests for proposal* from foreign governments is through the website of the Canadian Commercial Corporation (CCC). Small Canadian firms can register with the CCC and have their products, services, or capabilities listed in the database that CCC shares with Industry Canada. The firms are then notified of appropriate opportunities, and CCC offers a variety of support services for securing export contracts.

There are other excellent sources to assist small Canadian exporters. Canada's Department of Foreign Affairs and International Trade (DFAIT) provides travel, cultural, and market information for most areas of the world. As well, this department actively promotes the sale of

Canadian technology, products, and services around the world. Export Development Canada (EDC) is a federal Crown corporation with programs to help Canadian small businesses with exporting in a variety of ways. This includes credit insurance (in the event a buyer does not pay you), bonding (to protect a buyer in case the Canadian exporter fails to perform), and even loans to foreign businesses (so they can buy from Canadian exporters).

REGULATIONS   *Ask yourself: Is it still exporting if I have a contract for my personal services in a foreign country?* Exporting a service, such as consulting, training, or entertaining, is often a matter of applying for and securing a visa and or temporary work permit for the country where you will be selling your service. But the shipment of goods is usually more complicated. As a Canadian exporter, you will have both foreign and Canadian regulations to deal with. For example, you must file a Canadian *export declaration* with the Canada Border Services Agency (**CBSA**) before shipping anything to a foreign country. As well, you may need a permit, certificate, or licence for exporting any sort of goods that are controlled by legislation (for example, protected species or dangerous goods).

The import rules and documents vary for each country, but most countries have some requirements for the quality or safety of specific goods with which the exporter must comply. In recent years there has been increasing international co-operation in *standardizing* some of these requirements across many countries. Generally, as an exporter, you will have to investigate these requirements, including the need for any certification, *before* concluding any deals. A good place to start is the website of the Standards Council of Canada, which has links to several important international standards organizations.

SHIPPING AND PAYMENT SYSTEMS   As an exporter, your primary document is the contract between you and your foreign customers. This will cover information like:
- specifications of goods to be supplied
- delivery dates
- who is responsible for shipping arrangements and from what point (**F.O.B.**)
- who (the buyer or the seller) will be designated as the official **importer of record**
- who is responsible for any export licences, customs duties, and insurance charges
- who is responsible for completing all required documentation
- how much is to be paid for the goods, when, and under what circumstances.

The complexity of moving goods to other countries is the reason that most new and small exporters will use a **freight forwarder** to act as a sort of travel agent for their goods. Freight forwarders arrange shipping and packaging of your goods to comply with regulations. As well, they will complete and forward documentation, which will likely be critical to your getting paid. Some freight forwarders also function as **customs brokers,** or they may arrange for any customs broker services you need. Customs brokers are more involved in the import side of international trade, offering services like warehousing, arranging customs inspections, duty payments, and local deliveries. (These can be your responsibility as an exporter if the contract designates you as the importer of record.)

A foreign buyer will often pay for goods through using a **letter of credit**. A letter of credit is a document from a foreign bank promising to pay a certain amount of money

? **Get Help 9.13**
Check the Department of Foreign Affairs and International Trade website at ***www.dfait-maeci.gc.ca***.

? **Get Help 9.14**
Check the EDC website at ***www.edc.ca*** for a large variety of export information and services.

CBSA The Canada Border Services Agency, a federal government agency (formerly the *Customs* portion of Canada Customs and Revenue Agency) responsible for controlling the flow of goods, services, and money across Canadian borders (***www.cbsa-asfc.gc.ca***).

✓ **Test Yourself 9.17**
True or False? Governments in Canada offer many services to assist small exporters.

? **Get Help 9.15**
www.scc.ca is the website for the Standards Council of Canada, a federal Crown corporation that provides information and services related to international product requirements.

? **Get Help 9.16**
A handy U.S. resource to help decipher trade documents is the TradePort Reference Library for Global Trade. Go to ***www.tradeport.org/library*** and click on "Trade and Shipping Terms Glossary."

F.O.B. (free on board) The point in the shipping process to which the seller bears all of the costs and risks. For example, *FOB the buyer* would mean that the seller is totally responsible for the merchandise right up to the point where it is delivered to the buyer's place of business.

importer of record The party (buyer or seller) specified as being responsible for paying duties and ensuring that traded goods are in compliance with customs regulations.

✓ **Test Yourself 9.18**
True or False? "F.O.B. the seller" means that the buyer will be responsible for all shipping costs.

✓ **Test Yourself 9.19**
True or False? Customs brokers are more involved with the export side of international trade.

❓ **Get Help 9.17**
The *Export Check* service is available through the EDC website at **www.edc.ca**. Click on *Our Services* and then *Customer/Credit.*

❓ **Get Help 9.18**
The website for the Canada Business Service Centres, at **www.cbsc.org**, offers a summary of the key NAFTA provisions as well as provincial links and specific publications.

✓ **Test Yourself 9.20**
True or False? Mexico is a partner in NAFTA.

(on behalf of the buyer) on receiving documented proof that certain conditions have been met (such as the goods have been delivered as specified and on time). Here's an example of how this can work: After the goods have been delivered as promised, your freight forwarder will provide the necessary documents, as specified in your contract with the buyer, to your bank in Canada. Your bank will then contact the foreign bank to execute the letter of credit, and payment will be sent to your bank. It all sounds quite simple, but there is lots of room for problems or delays because of minor disputes or even the tiniest mistakes in the paperwork.

Ask yourself: What happens if the foreign bank refuses to honour the letter of credit because of some minor paperwork error, even though the goods have been delivered? Generally in business, when someone owes you money and doesn't pay up, you sue them. This recourse to the courts, which we take for granted here, may not be easily accessible or economically feasible in other countries—another argument for using the professional help of a freight forwarder to keep all the documentation correct.

You can reduce the risk of a foreign customer not paying for goods by checking on the past performance and creditworthiness of your customer. The EDC offers their *EXPORT Check* service through the EDC website, providing several options for obtaining financial history and credit report information about foreign companies. Always ask for credit references and make sure the wording on contracts and letters of credit does not give the buyer unreasonable options for withholding payment.

U.S. MARKET   For most Canadian small firms, the first choice in export targets is the United States because of its proximity, cultural similarity, and large wealthy markets. There is also a lot of reliable, easily accessible market research information for the U.S. Furthermore, the North American Free Trade Agreement, NAFTA (intended to reduce trade barriers between Canada, the U.S., and Mexico), makes the U.S. an even more attractive market. The vast majority of Canadian small business owners consistently express strong support for NAFTA. For many, it has reduced the red tape on U.S. imports, and for some the U.S. market has been a golden opportunity. But along with great successes, the history of Canadian business is filled with failed attempts to penetrate the U.S. market.

Ask yourself: What are the dangers of chasing U.S. business? The sheer size of the U.S. market (or even the size of its many segments) should raise concern about stimulating a market that your small firm may not be able to satisfy. There is also the risk of putting all your efforts and money into chasing the U.S. pot of gold and letting your attention slide from your local customer base. As well, there is an aggressive entrepreneurial culture in the U.S.; there are many government programs to support U.S. entrepreneurs; and there is a political system that can give great influence to protective industrial lobbies. Nevertheless, of all the nationalities exporting to the U.S., Canadians have the inside track because of the systems in place to expedite the huge trade we already share (we are the biggest trading partner of the U.S.). As well, we have a deep knowledge of the country and its culture (most of us have grown up watching more U.S. TV than Canadian). Furthermore, there is some argument against the apparent logic of saturating local or national markets first before expanding to foreign territory.[9] For many Canadian firms, **contiguous growth**, geographically, is most naturally into the U.S. since our own population tends to be concentrated in a few, separated pockets along the U.S. border.

The United States is a nation of divergent viewpoints and political influences, some that support Canadian exports, some that represent potential roadblocks. For example, many American political leaders support the expansion of NAFTA to an ultimate Free Trade of the Americas agreement that would include North, South, and Central America as well as the Caribbean. This would be the world's largest trading bloc and represent many opportunities for Canadian exporters. Recently, however, the U.S. has imposed various protectionist tariffs against several of its trading partners to protect U.S. industries, making trade more difficult. Over the years since the 9/11 attacks, U.S. Customs has attempted to implement a set of security guidelines for exporters—Customs–Trade Partnership Against Terrorism (**C–TPAT**)—that are widely expected to become firm regulations. Compliance with these guidelines has meant considerable cash outlay for some Canadian exporters. (At the time of publication, the EDC is offering substantial unsecured loans to Canadian exporters that will cover up to 85 percent of costs associated with C-TPAT.) Despite these sorts of hurdles, thousands of Canadian companies export successfully to the U.S. each year.

C–TPAT (Customs–Trade Partnership Against Terrorism) This is a set of security guidelines that U.S. Customs is requesting exporters to the U.S. to comply with, in order to maintain expeditious clearance for entry of goods to the U.S.

Get Help 9.19
If you plan on exporting to the U.S. or Mexico see the NAFTA customs website, ***www.cbp.gov/nafta/nafta_new.htm***, which offers forms and procedures common to the three countries.

Head Start Exercise

9.11 Make up a list of the advantages and disadvantages your company would face in deciding to export to the U.S. Be as specific as possible. ($\frac{1}{2}$ page maximum)

How Can I Finance Growth?

VARIETIES OF GROWTH CAPITAL   All the sources of finance previously discussed (see Chapter 5, "Where Will I Get the Money?") can be considered as sources of expansion capital, but some will be considerably more available than they were at start-up.[10] Typically, at start-up the new entrepreneur must rely on personal savings or loans from family and friends. Then, as the business becomes established, larger amounts of capital will become available from bank and government lending programs. Eventually, as the business grows, it can access very large amounts of capital from venture capitalists, or (the ultimate source of growth capital) with a public share offering. Over this cycle, the shift in the available capital has been from little or no outside capital to debt capital to equity capital. Now, there is a positive relationship between the ability of a company to grow rapidly and the use of equity capital.[11] But this requires a willingness of the entrepreneur to share ownership. Ironically, the older the entrepreneur (and presumably the longer in business), the less willing the entrepreneur is to share ownership in order to finance growth.[12] While younger (newer) entrepreneurs are very willing to share ownership, no one wants to invest with them. Reasons for this change in the attitude of entrepreneurs are not clear, but the implied warning is clear: if your business is ready for growth, re-think any reluctance you might feel toward bringing in other investors.

Once your business has become established, with a proven track record of paying your bills and making a profit, both lenders and investors are more interested in participating. Remember, however, that they want to finance a logical growth of your already successful venture, not to take a high risk on some radically new direction for your firm. Keep this in mind when writing your Strategic Growth Plan. Your plan must recognize that lenders and investors are now interested in three aspects of your finances: the past (financial history), the present (financial position), and the future (financial projections):

- *Financial history.* This includes looking at credit reports for a pattern of the business paying its bills on time and checking whether there are outstanding judgments against you or the company. Your financial sources will be looking for a consistent pattern of profit growth (income statements) as well as patterns of reducing debt and increasing equity (balance sheets). A history of good cash management (for example, your collection period) will also be important. Anything that indicates a pattern of careful financial management (Did you file and pay your taxes on time?) could be helpful.
- *Financial position.* Where your company stands right now in terms of equity and unencumbered assets that can be used for collateral is important. As well, detailed ratio analysis (see Chapter 6) will indicate the financial health of your business relative to others in the industry. Break-even analysis will indicate how safe the current sales/profit position is in case of changes in the market.
- *Financial projections.* Your projected income statements, balance sheets, and cash flow must all be conservative and backed up by research evidence (see Chapter 2). Together, they must form a realistic plan showing how the new funds will be used and how the business will provide a good return to investors or consistent loan repayment to lenders. The recently published *Survey on Financing of Small and Medium Enterprises*[13] in Canada shows that the number one reason that lenders give for turning down loans is insufficient sales or cash flow for repaying the loan.

Increasingly, financial institutions are offering new and more creative finance options to small businesses, some which blur the line between *debt* and *equity* financing. An example of this is *quasi-equity capital* or **subordinate financing**, which is offered through flexible programs that can include features like:

- temporary share ownership by the financing institution
- options for permanent equity positions
- royalties on company sales
- deferred interest and principal payments
- flexible repayments based on actual company cash flow, and possibly
- even more complex features that most business owners would need professional help in negotiating.

If your business is one of those rare companies that are clearly poised for massive growth, requiring massive capital, you will likely consider the option of going public. Such a move marks the transition from small or medium-sized business into the realm of big business, at least in terms of the capital involved. Typically, though, it also means a transition from being an entrepreneur to CEO of a publicly traded company. And even though you may effectively control the company, you will still be ultimately responsible to and under the scrutiny of the other shareholders. Going public is an expensive manoeuvre involving complex negotiations for the underwriting and floating of a share issue. It is usually designed to both provide expansion capital to the company and give the entrepreneur the opportunity to become incredibly wealthy.

Test Yourself 9.21
True or False? Banks and other lenders are more interested in helping to finance new businesses than in lending to established firms.

Get Help 9.20
A business plan looking for large amounts of expansion capital will require significant assistance from your accountant in preparing the financial projections. As well, you will need your accountant's advice in choosing the form of funding that's best suited to your needs.

subordinate financing A hybrid form of financing involving features of both debt and equity but for which the debt is usually ranked below (subordinate to) the claims of other secured creditors.

Head Start Exercise

9.12 Briefly explain the most likely source of growth capital available to your firm. Explain the reasons for this. ($\frac{1}{4}$ page maximum)

FINANCIAL ANALYSIS   Lenders look at financial projections in a business plan to see that they will be repaid as per the terms of the loan. Investors are looking to see the returns they can expect on their investment. But for an entrepreneur, choices about bringing new capital into the business are analyzed from a different viewpoint. For example, in assessing the value of borrowing a particular amount of money, the business owner may use the idea of **payback period.**

> **payback period** The length of time it takes to recoup the amount of a particular investment.

Let's say you have a refrigeration supplies business where all your customers are within a two-hour drive of your site. Currently, all customers must place their orders by phone and then pick up the orders or pay for their own courier services. A recent survey has shown that your customers have a desire for both delivery by you and for the capability of ordering from you online. You decide that you can afford to invest in only one of these new services at a time and in each case you will have to borrow money. *Ask yourself: Which of these new services should be the priority?* The cost of purchasing two trucks that you will need for delivery, including the interest over the three-year loan period, will be about $70,000. You know that by charging your customers for delivery, you will be able to increase your revenues by $180,000. The drivers' salaries and benefits and operating cost of the trucks (depreciation, fuel, repairs, etc.) will come to about $160,000 per year. So, this will give you a net increase in revenue ($180,000 − $160,000) of $20,000. The payback period for this option, then, will be:

$$\frac{\$70,000}{\$20,000 \text{ per year}} = 3.5 \text{ years}$$

The cost for an online ordering system (hardware, software, installation, training, etc.) including interest over the three-year loan period, will be about $55,000. Your annual revenue will increase by the amount of money you save on an order-taker salary and benefits; about $30,000 minus the costs of maintenance and hosting for your new system, around $5,000 per year. This will give you a net increase ($30,000 − $5,000) of $25,000 per year. For this option, the payback period will be:

$$\frac{\$55,000}{\$25,000 \text{ per year}} = 2.2 \text{ years}$$

This is an indicator that the online ordering system is your best bet as the more immediate priority.

In assessing the value of bringing new equity capital into the business, an owner might employ return on investment calculations. For example, you might have $100,000 owner's equity in a business that produced $10,000 net profit last year. For you, this is an ROI of 10 percent. You have estimated that by investing $50,000 in a new promotional program, you could double your sales and triple your profits to $30,000 annually. A friend offers to give you the $50,000 in exchange for one-third ownership of the business. It seems fair and if things work out, both you and the friend will have a 20-percent return on your investment for next year. Your friend, in fact, may feel that he or she is being generous because it is the friend's one-third investment that will result in two-thirds of the new profit. True, the $50,000 investment will result in new returns of $20,000 (a 40-percent ROI) but this is really just a **project ROI.** It is valuable to show that the project is worthwhile; however, your friend is investing in the whole business, not just the project. So, *Ask yourself: Is one-third ownership a fair exchange for the $50,000?* What if, in exchange for the $50,000, you gave your friend only 25 percent ownership in the business,

> **project ROI** The additional annual profit expected from a new investment, divided by the total cost of that particular investment (expressed as a percentage).

not the asked-for one-third? In this case, your friend would expect a return of (25 percent of the $30,000 profit) $7,500 on an investment of $50,000. This would be an ROI of 15 percent, still a healthy return. And the value of your friend's investment is not just based on the rate of return, but on many other factors (See "Valuation Concepts" in Chapter 6) that would become part of a negotiation process. Even though ROI is a valuable concept for assessing new equity investment, no single ROI calculation by itself can assess how good a particular deal to share ownership is for you.

Head Start Exercise

9.13 Describe how you will assess the value of any new debt or equity capital that your firm pursues ($\frac{1}{2}$ page maximum).

✓ Answers to Chapter 9 Test Yourself Questions

9.1 The growth stage of the business cycle is characterized by stable sales and profits. *False*

9.2 A *niche* refers to a very small market segment. *True*

9.3 Sales forecasting for established firms is easier than for start-ups. *True*

9.4 The break-even point is where a business can start to produce net profit. *True*

9.5 Market potential is made up of your market share plus the market share of all your competitors. *True*

9.6 Strengths and weaknesses in SWOT analysis refer to external factors of a business. *False*

9.7 *Market segment expansion* means growth by selling to new groups of customers those products and services that you already provide. *True*

9.8 Predatory pricing usually benefits a smaller competitor. *False*

9.9 A business cannot supply products or services beyond 100 percent of its capacity. *True*

9.10 It's always best to trust your instincts when looking for new products to resell. *False*

9.11 Products in the *maturity* stage of the product life cycle require high levels of promotion. *False*

9.12 The majority of new products fail in the marketplace. *True*

9.13 An increase in your market share must mean a decrease in the market share of each of your competitors. *False*

9.14 It is best to expand into several new market segments at one time. *False*

9.15 It is best for a small firm to deal through as many different distribution channels as possible. *False*

9.16 Selling franchises is a faster way to expand than building your own company-owned chain. *True*

9.17 Governments in Canada offer many services to assist small exporters. *True*

9.18 "F.O.B. the seller" means that the buyer will be responsible for all shipping costs. *True*

9.19 Customs brokers are more involved with the export side of international trade. *False*

9.20 Mexico is a partner in NAFTA. *True*

9.21 Banks and other lenders are more interested in helping to finance new businesses than in lending to established firms. *False*

Questions for Discussion

1. Picture yourself as a graduate of your current program looking for a job in the marketplace. Prepare a brief SWOT analysis of yourself.

2. The fastest way for most businesses to increase sales is to compete on the basis of price. Discuss why this might be true. What are the dangers of a penetration pricing strategy?

3. Discuss the benefits and drawbacks of NAFTA for Canadian small firms.

4. In recent times, the U.S. has passed protectionist legislation while simultaneously trying to negotiate a Free Trade of the Americas agreement. What are the forces involved in this apparent contradiction?

5. On average, entrepreneurs become more reluctant to share ownership in their firms as they become older, even though bringing in new investors could lead to faster growth. Explain this reluctance of older entrepreneurs.

Recommended Reading

Allen, Kathleen R. *Growing and Managing an Entrepreneurial Business.* Boston: Houghton Mifflin Company, 1999.

Fry, F.L., C.R. Stoner, and L.G. Weinzimmer. *Strategic Planning for Small Business Made Easy.* Madison, WI: Entrepreneur Media Inc., 2005.

Little, Steven S. *The 7 Irrefutable Rules of Small Business Growth.* New York: John Wiley and Sons Inc., 2006.

Mohr, Angie. *Managing Business Growth: Get a Grip on the Numbers That Count.* North Vancouver: Self-Counsel Press, 2005.

Taft, Robert. *Growing Your Business Globally.* Mason, OH: The Thompson Corporation, 2005.

Weiss, Kenneth D. *Building an Import/Export Business.* New York: John Wiley and Sons Inc., 2002.

The Strategic Growth Plan

THE NEED FOR GROWTH

1. Briefly outline the history of the business.

_____
_____
_____
_____
_____
_____
_____
_____

2. Identify any obvious *internal* indicators of the need for renewal in your business such as changes in sales, profits, employee turnover, operating capacity level, etc.

_____
_____
_____
_____
_____
_____
_____

MARKET ANALYSIS

3. Estimate the current market potential for each of your major product/target groups and explain your sources. (See Chapter 2 for assistance.) Discuss any changes in your market share.

_____
_____
_____
_____
_____
_____
_____

4. Identify any significant activity or changes in your direct and indirect competition.

_____

_____

_____

_____

_____

_____

_____

_____

_____

5. Summarize the above findings and any other relevant information about your business under the SWOT headings of strengths, weaknesses, opportunities, and threats.

_____

_____

_____

_____

_____

_____

_____

_____

_____

GROWTH STRATEGY

6. Briefly discuss the strategy that you will use to make best use of your strengths and opportunities while at the same time attempting to overcome your weaknesses and to protect against threats.

_____

_____

_____

_____

_____

_____

_____

_____

7. If your strategy involves increasing your market share, outline the specific tactics you will use for this and list the costs involved. State your new sales forecast and explain the basis for it.

    or

    If your strategy involves selling new products or services, outline the specific tactics you will use for this and list all additional costs involved. Explain how you will test any new products or services. State your new sales forecast and explain the basis for it.

    or

    If your strategy involves selling to new market segments, outline the specific tactics you will use for this and list the costs involved. State your new sales forecast and explain the basis for it.

    _____

    _____

    _____

    _____

    _____

    _____

    _____

8. If you are pursuing new market segments, briefly discuss the option of opening new sites for your business (for new market segments) and whether this would be by building your own chain or by franchising. Briefly identify and estimate the costs involved.

    _____

    _____

    _____

    _____

    _____

    _____

9. If you are pursuing new market segments abroad, explain the details of your target market and the export distribution system you will use. Describe the shipping and payment systems you will use and provide a sales forecast and the basis for it.

    _____

    _____

    _____

    _____

    _____

    _____

FINANCING GROWTH

10. Explain in detail the sources of finance you will use for your expansion program. Discuss why this is a suitable method of finance, using any appropriate comparisons of payback period or return on investment.

_____

_____

_____

_____

_____

_____

_____

_____

_____

Managing for Efficiency:
How Will I Reduce Costs and Expenses?

LEARNING OBJECTIVES

On completion of this chapter, you should be able to:

- *Discuss issues affecting the efficiency of a business.*
- *Identify several key ratio indicators of efficiency.*
- *Describe the expansion and contraction cycles of business strategy.*
- *Discuss the various renewal strategies that a small business might pursue.*
- *Explain a variety of efficiency systems and tools available to small firms.*
- *Outline recent advances in automation.*
- *Describe various small business applications for the Internet.*
- *Identify several considerations for website design.*
- *Discuss potential problems of customer relationship management systems.*
- *Outline processes for hiring, training, and motivating small business employees.*
- *Identify several techniques for controlling costs in a small firm.*
- *Prepare an operational efficiency plan for a small firm.*

Chapter 9 looked at making the business more profitable by increasing sales. This chapter is concerned with the other broad approach to improving profits: reducing costs and expenses.

Typically, with a new business, you begin with a clear focus on what you're selling and whom you're selling to. But over time, you start expanding into new products or services and new markets. Later again, marketing research and financial analysis (formal or informal) will indicate which elements of your business are most profitable and you will decide to refocus on these aspects of your venture. This refocusing is often the trigger for the *renewal* part of the business cycle discussed in Chapter 9.

How Can I Refocus the Business for Efficiency?

Refocusing the business is about becoming more profitable by managing for greater efficiency (reducing costs and expenses). It is possible, however, that your business is already highly efficient. *Ask yourself: How can I tell if my business is running efficiently?*

MEASURING EFFICIENCY Ratio analysis was discussed in Chapter 6 as a method for assessing the value of a business. This involves calculating certain key ratios (using values from your financial statements), then comparing those ratios to industry averages. Some of these ratios are indicators of how efficiently your company is operating, relative to other businesses in the same industry. Statistics Canada provides average Key Ratios for Small Businesses, classified by specific industry. For example, if you own a convenience store, you can see how efficiently your store operates compared to the industry averages for convenience stores in just your province, or for all of Canada. The broadest indicator of efficiency is the **return on sales** ratio.

return on sales The ratio of net profit to sales, usually expressed as a percentage.

$$\text{Return on sales} = \frac{\text{Net profit}}{\text{Sales}}$$

Think of two firms in the heating and air-conditioning repair business that each have sales of $500,000. One of the companies has a net profit of $20,000, while the other has a net profit of $40,000. This second company would be considered twice as efficient. This ratio does not indicate where specific inefficiencies lie within the company, just that they are there. Another important efficiency indicator is **return on assets.**

return on assets The ratio of net profit to total assets, usually expressed as a percentage.

$$\text{Return on assets} = \frac{\text{Net profit}}{\text{Total assets}}$$

If two small businesses in the same field have roughly the same value of assets, but one has a higher net profit, the more profitable one is using those assets more efficiently. Again, this doesn't tell you exactly where the problem lies but it does indicate the direction of the problem. For example, if your business is one where you have mostly *fixed assets* (machinery, equipment, buildings, tools, furniture, vehicles, etc.), the problem could lie with inefficient promotional techniques, or the fact that you have money tied up in equipment you don't need. If the assets are mostly *current* (inventory, cash, supplies, etc.) the problem could be inappropriate inventory or the fact that you have paid too much for it. To further narrow the source of your inefficiency might mean looking at other indicators, or other ratios, such as **inventory turnover.**

Get Help 10.1
Small business key ratio data is most easily accessed from Industry Canada's Performance Plus website: ***http://sme.ic.gc.ca***. See your accountant if you need advice on this topic.

inventory turnover The ratio of *cost of goods sold* to the *average inventory*.

$$\text{Inventory turnover} = \frac{\text{Cost of goods sold}}{\text{Average inventory}}$$

Generally, the higher the inventory turnover, the more profitable it is for your company. For example, two companies might have the same sales, but one has an inventory turnover of three (meaning that on average inventory is replaced three times a year) and the other has an inventory turnover of four. The company with the higher turnover will likely be more profitable. Because it is replacing its inventory more often, it can keep less inventory in stock. (It only needs 75% of the inventory carried by the first company.) This means that it has less money tied up in inventory and will save money on the associated expenses (interest, insurance, storage, display).

Another area where your business might have money unnecessarily tied up is in your accounts receivable. There are considerable costs associated with having customers owe you money, especially for bills that are past due (lost interest, re-billing, reminders, and other collection costs). It can be important to know if you are taking longer than the industry average to collect from your customers. This ratio is the average **collection period.**

collection period The ratio of *accounts receivable* to the *average sales per day.*

$$\text{Collection period} = \frac{\text{Accounts receivable}}{\text{Average sales per day}}$$

One of the most obvious ways to save money, of course, is to pay less for the inventory that you will be re-selling. You can check your relative cost of goods sold compared to the industry average with the **gross margin** ratio.

gross margin The ratio of *gross profit* to *sales*, usually expressed as a percentage.

$$\text{Gross margin} = \frac{\text{Gross profit}}{\text{Sales}}$$

Key ratios by themselves do not tell you where you are wasting money, but they are indicators that point you in the right direction of making your business operate more efficiently.

✓ **Test Yourself 10.1**
True or False? "Sales/Equity" is a key ratio indicator of efficiency.

Head Start Exercises

10.1 Using the Industry Canada Strategis website or some other source, calculate for your industry the key ratios for return on sales, return on assets, inventory turnover, collection period, and gross margin ($\frac{2}{3}$ page maximum).

10.2 Using your most recent financial statements, calculate your firm's ratios for return on sales, return on assets, inventory turnover, collection period, and gross margin. Briefly discuss the relative efficiency of your business. (1 page maximum.)

SPECIALIZATION   If you follow the business news, you will eventually notice that major announcements coming from the big public companies tend to fall into two categories: *expansion* (when the company has bought another firm or moved into new markets or new products) and *contraction* (when the company has sold part of its holdings or relinquished products or markets). When companies are announcing contractions, they will often say that this is in favour of refocusing on their **core business.** The history of business can be seen as a cycle or pendulum swing between expansion (less specialization) and contraction (greater specialization). It is during the contraction phase that the business is becoming more specialized. Naturally, there are many factors that will affect

core business The combination of products and services and the market segments that produce most of a particular company's profit.

James Anthony

James Anthony is a musician from Burlington, Ontario. In fact, he's one of the most accomplished and versatile guitar players, composers, and singers in Canada. Skilled in every form of popular music, he has played with many of the greatest entertainers in the world, everywhere from New Orleans to Budapest. Turning professional at age 17, James played in a variety of bands but really honed his skill as a guitarist with the house band at the legendary Lulu's. This was the Kitchener, Ontario, landmark that for several years was billed as *The World's Biggest Nightclub.* At Lulu's he played with over 150 of rock and roll's biggest stars, performing for thousands of fans every weekend. For the last decade, James has been celebrated for his outstanding blues compositions and guitar technique. He is recognized in the *Encyclopaedia of the Blues* for this work.

These days, James divides his time among live performances, studio session work, and working in his own fully digital studio in Burlington. It's here that he writes, arranges, produces, and records his own music as well as recording, producing, and tutoring other musicians.

James Anthony recognizes that he makes his money not by simply being a musician, but rather by running a music business: a technologically sophisticated, partly automated and complex business at that. For a start, James identifies a variety of distinct products that he has for sale:

- The James Anthony Band
- James Anthony solo act
- over 200 songs with copyright on words and music
- four CD albums
- digital sound engineering and re-mixing
- digital studio recording and arranging
- TV and commercial soundtrack and jingle composition and recording
- musical instrument promotion
- musical coaching and tutoring

He also understands the complex chain of distribution for his services and products and who the *customer* is at various levels: music distributors, advertising agencies, music retailers, entertainment venue owners, broadcasters, film and TV producers, booking agents, other musicians, and—the ultimate consumers—the fans.

At the time of writing, James Anthony is ready to release a new CD, and he is in the process of revising his overall marketing strategy. He is currently evaluating which of his main *products* he will concentrate on to use his time most efficiently and profitably. He is refocusing his business. James' main promotional tool is his website (***www.jamesanthony.ca***), which is aimed mostly at fans, who can sample CDs for sale, check James's schedule of performances, or get information about the artist and his band.

the decisions of whether to concentrate on expanding or specializing, including industry and market conditions at any given time.[1] Nevertheless, most businesses over the years will be subject to some cycle of expansion and contraction.

Ask yourself: In what way should I become more specialized? This decision is usually a case of identifying and concentrating on those particular market segments and/or product or service lines that have proven most profitable or show future promise of high profits. Greater specialization doesn't necessarily mean abandoning all products or services except the most profitable, or refusing to deal with any but the most profitable groups of customers. Better that it should be a prioritization of where your marketing resources will be allocated.[2] See the example in Table 10.1.

Refocusing or redefining the business can also mean a change of image, presenting yourself as more specialized. For example, if your business depends on supplying a *high-quality* product or service, you may have to get involved with ISO 9000 certification. The purpose of the International Standards Organization (ISO) is to set and measure quality control standards through its member organizations in 140 countries. The certification process can be long (over a year) and expensive, but many companies now demand that their suppliers be ISO 9000 registered as a way of ensuring their own quality. There are lots of consultants available who specialize in helping small firms receive ISO certification.

◇ Get Help 10.2

For information on ISO 9000 certification, take a look at the ISO's website, at **www.iso.org**. Also, the consulting service of the Business Development Bank of Canada has a program to manage a firm's ISO 9000 certification. Contact the BDC at 1–888–463–6232 for more information.

✓ Test Yourself 10.2

True or False? Most of a company's profit will come from the *core business*.

Table 10.1	**EXAMPLE REFOCUSING STRATEGY**	
Priority	**Product and or Market Segment**	**Marketing Tactics**
Highest	Fast growing market potential Growing sales	High levels of promotion Intensive research Penetration pricing Innovation in distribution methods and service levels
Medium	High stable sales Stable market share Stable market potential	Maintenance of inventories and promotional levels Competitive pricing Minimal research
Low	Low sales Unknown prospects for growth of market potential or market share (possibly new product or poorly defined segment)	Minimal promotional effort Monitoring for changes in market or product innovation
Abandon	Declining market potential Low sales	Discontinue product lines or discontinue promotion to segment Provide product or service only as a customer retention issue for customers that also puchase in other more profitable categories

Head Start Exercises

10.3 Identify any products or services that you offer that provide little or no profit. List the merits of or problems with abandoning these. ($\frac{1}{2}$ page maximum.)

10.4 Identify any unprofitable or low profitability market segments that your business promotes to. Discuss the rationale for promoting to these segments. ($\frac{1}{2}$ page maximum.)

SYSTEMIZATION   When you order a Big Mac combo at McDonald's, the person serving you will always key in your selection, then get the drink, then get the sandwich. And the french fries will be last. It's always done in this same order, because the restaurant has figured out that this is the most efficient way. French fries cool quickly and if they were to serve them first and there were some delay with your drink or sandwich, the fries would get cold and have to be replaced. This inefficiency would cost the restaurant time and money. Any task that you perform over and over in your business is an opportunity for maximizing efficiency. This means ensuring that the task involves the least possible time and effort, by using the best tools, methods, and even the best paperwork for the job.

Forms and Templates: Let's say your business is working as a bodyguard for celebrities. This doesn't sound like a business where you would have to worry very much about paperwork. But you will have to use a contract for each job. And even though each job is different, it would be extremely time-consuming and expensive to sit down and create an original, customized contract for each new client. Instead you will develop a contract template where you can just fill in the blanks to specify things like the number of operatives to cover the celebrity, the hours and places of coverage, fees, and so on.

Common document templates include proposals, contracts, and letter templates, including email. Typical forms used by businesses include invoices, purchase orders, bills of lading, estimates, work orders, receipts, and various forms of checklists. One critical issue in designing forms and templates is that the design should cover most eventualities—but not all. The more possibilities covered by a form or letter, the longer and more difficult it becomes to use. You have to try to strike a balance between simplicity and comprehensiveness that will give you maximum efficiency. Another issue is that forms and templates should be periodically checked and updated, not just continually reordered with the same old mistakes that reduce their efficiency.

Employee Handbooks and Operations Manuals: If you have a business that is growing rapidly, or if you depend on part-time or contract employees with a high turnover, you may be spending lots of time telling new employees the same information over and over. Employee handbooks and operations manuals can serve as training tools as well as part of the contract between you and the people working for you. Normally, employee handbooks cover topics like:

- company history and mission
- employee benefits
- behaviour and dress codes
- probation periods and policies
- termination policies

Get Help 10.3
Many printing firms will help you design forms, often by customizing their own computerized templates to your requirements. See "Printers" in the Yellow Pages.

Get Help 10.4
You can buy books and CDs of business legal forms and letter templates that are easy to customize for your business. See your local office supply store.

Test Yourself 10.3
True or False? Templates should be designed to cover all possible eventualities.

- work and vacation scheduling
- pay schedules.

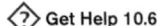 **Get Help 10.5**

Templates and software for writing employee handbooks and operations manuals can be purchased on CD or via the Internet.

Operations manuals (often called *procedure manuals*) tend to be larger and more detailed than employee handbooks. Although the two may overlap on topics such as company policies and work schedules, the operations manual is filled with the specific procedures and processes that a firm uses.

The operations manual covers much the same issues as are found in Section 4 of the business plan. While the business plan is aimed at owners, outside investors, or lenders, the operations manual is written for those who are actually performing the duties of the business. Policies and procedures for major functional areas of the business are covered, including details on topics like:

- organizational structure and job descriptions
- accounting systems and procedures
- purchasing and inventory control
- production methods and procedures
- customer service procedures and policies
- promotion methods and policies
- engineering or design process, and
- whatever else is a significant activity for the particular business.

✓ **Test Yourself 10.4**

True or False? Operations manuals tend to be larger and more detailed than employee handbooks.

The need for an operations manual is related to both the size of your company and the complexity of the activities you perform. A skydiving school consisting of yourself and four employees would be quite likely to use an operations manual, but it would be unusual in a window-cleaning company of the same size. However, as the window-cleaning company grew to 50 or more employees, the likelihood of having such a manual would increase. *Ask yourself: Is an operations manual necessary for my field?*

work design The process of finding the most efficient methods and procedures for doing particular jobs.

Work Design: Developing the most efficient procedures to use in a job is called **work design**. In manufacturing and some service industries, this can involve **time and motion studies** (where videos of someone performing a job are analyzed) as well as the setting of **job standards** (where a reasonable expectation of time to perform a job is calculated). Modern work design does not involve the dictatorial or exploitive approaches of the past. Today, we realize that the highest productivity comes when people can take satisfaction in their work and where employees are safe and comfortable. If your business uses processes involving highly repetitive activities, it may be worthwhile to hire an industrial engineer to analyze the process and find new efficiencies.

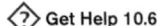 **Get Help 10.6**

To perform job analysis and design you will likely need the help of an industrial engineer. See "Engineers" in the Yellow Pages.

time and motion studies
Research to determine the most efficient way to perform particular jobs.

If this option is too expensive for you, the most obvious source of help in redesigning a job is the employee actually performing the work. You are more likely to get a significant productivity improvement if you approach the employee in a co-operative manner, explaining that you would like the employee to find ways to make the job safer, more comfortable, and less boring as well as faster. The first step, of course, is for you and the employee to measure a base line of productivity so that you can be sure that whatever changes you try are actually improving the work rate.

job standard A statement of the quality and quantity of work that can reasonably be expected from an employee performing a particular job.

Automation: The wealth produced by the Industrial Revolution came from the ability to use machines in a systematic way to produce products more cheaply than could be done by human labour alone. The second great wave of **automation**, the one we are experiencing now, has been the application of ever-faster computers to improving productivity. And increasingly, automation is being applied not just to the manufacture of products, but rather to the delivery of services, especially those related to information. For example, when you are on vacation and determined not to answer your email, your system can be programmed to provide an automatic response with no on-going labour from you. The jobs of telephone receptionists and information operators have largely been taken over by automatic prompts and customer searches. None of these service delivery mechanisms is without problems, controversy, and questions of cost-benefit. But the same inadequacies, concerns, and complaints were true of the telephone and automobile in 1900. Modern phones and cars are very reliable, and these developing technologies will continue to improve. Only a few years ago, microcomputers were expected to "crash" pretty much on a daily basis. *Ask yourself: At what point is it economical or efficient to adopt a new technology?* Adopting a new technology can certainly be risky. But there is evidence that those small firms that are more willing to adopt new technologies (especially in the manufacturing sector) are those with the greatest success.[3]

> **automation** The redesign and integration of repetitive tasks so that they can be carried out by mechanical and computerized equipment.

Automation for the small firm becomes increasingly important as the cost of labour rises and the cost of new technologies falls. Small retailers increasingly use UPC scanning at the cash register and electronic security tags. Online ordering and electronic inventory control for wholesalers and online booking for service firms are increasingly common. All provide huge efficiencies in the saving of labour costs. And small manufacturers are increasingly turning to **robotics.**

> **robotics** The use of automatic computerized mechanisms to carry out tasks previously performed by human labour.

Robotics and *automation* are terms that are pretty close in meaning and often used interchangeably, but there are some small differences in how they apply. Robots are tools of automation. Until recently, the extensive use of robots has been the domain of large manufacturers; however, robots have now become cheaper and more flexible in that they can perform a greater number of tasks and more complex tasks. At the same time, there has been improvement in robotics software, making them easier to program, and, with *learning software,* to some extent even self-programming.[4] This allows the smaller manufacturer, generally producing smaller lots of a product, to reprogram the same robot for different products. And robots are not just for manufacturers, but have uses in everything from medicine to the arts, with new applications turning up constantly.

> ✓ **Test Yourself 10.5**
> True or False? A *job standard* identifies a reasonable amount and quality of work to expect for a particular job.

Head Start Exercise

10.5 Make a brief list of the major repetitive tasks that are carried out in your business. Identify any systems, tools, or methods you do not currently use that would automate this work. ($\frac{2}{3}$ page maximum.)

Ebusiness Tools: The Internet itself is a versatile tool for efficiency in all the following categories:

- *Marketing research.* Government statistics, competitor promotions, industry journals, and university research are all secondary forms of research accessible from the Internet. But it can also be used for primary research such as customer questionnaires and specific email queries.

- *Promotion.* Direct email campaigns and website advertising are the two most obvious applications, but advertising on emagazines or links to other websites are also common. Sales promotion applications (contests, samples) and publicity (interviews on electronic media) are also possible.
- *Distribution.* For some industries, the Internet serves as a means of actually delivering the product or service or at least a part of it. Certainly when the product is information or a form of intellectual property, it can be delivered electronically. And even for physical products, online ordering is an option.
- *Finance.* Everything is available from online banking to loan rate shopping to customer billing and credit checks.

Get Help 10.7
A clear, quick read on ebusiness techniques is *Low-Budget Online Marketing for Small Business* by Holly Berkley, published by the Self-Counsel Press. It is available through most large bookstores.

At the time of writing, the majority of small businesses use the Internet for some business-related activities and almost 40 percent have their own website. But only about 12 percent actually sell any of their products or services online.[5] Most of the firms that do not have websites or do not sell online have considered these options and concluded that these ebusiness tools are unsuitable for their products or services.

Websites: The design, complexity, and cost of a website are all dependent on the purposes or goals of the site. *Ask yourself: Do I want a site merely to have a web presence and keep my company image up-to-date? Will my site be a reference tool for providing information to post-purchase customers? Or will my site be used for active sales, customer orders, and even payments?* Some general principles of web design are that sites should be:

- *Simple.* Any lack in clarity or difficulty of use will serve as a frustration for the customer.
- *Fast.* Downloading time should be short.
- *Professional.* Mistakes in grammar, spelling, and style are distractions for the reader and undermine your company image.
- *Consistent.* Choose a pattern of fonts and graphic styles and stay with it throughout, so readers do not think that they have strayed to another site.
- *Specific.* There should be a clear message about what your firm is selling and what the website will do in that regard.
- *Imperative.* Use command verbs, clearly instructing the reader to provide email or other personal information, to place an order, to phone now, and so on, specifically eliciting the behaviour you want from the customer.

A website can be an efficient, cost-effective tool only if it is being accessed by the market segment you are targeting. To ensure this, most entrepreneurs, unless they are information technology specialists themselves, will need the help of a professional web developer. Issues to be negotiated with the web developer include:

- *Host selection.* The company that will physically hold the data for your website on its computers must be identified, along with its fees.
- *A domain name.* An example of a domain name would be "*studententrepreneur.com.*" Webpages and email addresses are attached to a domain name. It's not necessary to register your own, but it projects a more successful professional image if you do. And if your domain name contains keywords relevant to your business, it makes it easier for customers to find your site with a search engine.
- *Site design.* All the details of how your site will function, how it will be updated, and how data will be gathered from it must be planned.

- *Tracking programs.* You must select the particular software that will measure the activity of your website as well as gather specific information about its users. There are lots to choose from, with a wide range in prices.
- *Search engine strategy.* Perhaps the key decisions for the success of your site. This involves the selection of the key words that search engines use to match sites up with customer queries. It can also involve paying search engines to give priority to your "sponsored" site.
- *Design contract.* The details of your deal with the web developer must be spelled out, including all fees, warranties, payment schedules, and follow-up service.

Ecommerce: Selling, delivering, and being paid for products over the Internet are all components of **ecommerce**. These activities move a website from the more passive roles of advertising and gathering limited data to the more active role as a channel of distribution. The implementation of ecommerce capabilities is considerably more complex and expensive than simple website functions. But this tool is now starting to prove itself cost-efficient and reliable, especially for things like selling intellectual property (music, photographic images, software, etc.) and time-booked services (hotel rooms, theatre tickets, limousine services).

It is possible to sell products and services on the web without having to build an expensive ecommerce capability of your own. This can be done through a third-party virtual store where your products or services are displayed on the third-party site (often along with the products of other companies) and customers can pay for your products directly to this third party. Your orders are transmitted to you via email and the third party will pay you. Drawbacks are:

- sharing revenue with the third-party intermediary
- possible delays in payments coming via the third party
- lack of control of the website promoting your products or services.

How Do I Retain Customers?

Two axioms of business that almost always hold true are:
1. Most of the profit made by most businesses comes from repeat customer purchases.
2. It is cheaper to keep an existing customer than it is to get a new one.

If you accept these two ideas, then it is not difficult to accept the notion that **customer retention** might be the most important form of efficiency that a business can practise. Often, however, we lose customers in an effort to obtain other efficiencies.

Let's say your business consists of supplying and installing inventory software for small- and medium-sized companies. When a company buys from you they have access to your customer service phone line, where they can call in to get help with their computer problems. You may find that a lot of your service person's time is spent patiently listening to customers talk about business and computer issues irrelevant to the problem that needs fixing. And, in most cases, when the problem is identified, you find that the customer could have fixed it just by spending a couple of minutes with the instruction manual. Therefore, you may find that it is much

---

✓ **Test Yourself 10.6**

True or False? A good website will use a broad variety of fonts, colours, and graphic styles.

❓ **Get Help 10.8**

To find a competent web developer, what better way than by a web search using the terms "web developer" and the name of your city, neighbourhood, or region. You can make an initial assessment by comparing the quality of the web developer's own site against the website criteria listed on this page.

✓ **Test Yourself 10.7**

True or False? An email address contains a domain name.

❓ **Get Help 10.9**

Industry Canada's *ebiz.enable* page is an excellent source for help on assessing which ebusiness tools would be of benefit to your company. From the Strategis home page (***www.strategis.ic.gc.ca***) select *Using Electronic Commerce* from the "Strategis Guides" list. Then click on *ebiz.enable*.

ecommerce The selling, ordering, payment and, at times, even the delivery of products or services over the Internet.

✓ **Test Yourself 10.8**

True or False? Robotics is a tool of ecommerce.

customer retention Maintaining the loyalty of existing customers for repeat sales.

more cost-efficient to have the phone line go directly to voice mail where the customer must clearly explain what the problem is and then wait for your service rep to call back. It could well be the case that if you wait half an hour before calling back, 90 percent of the customers will have already fixed their own problems—and those who haven't fixed them are no longer in a mood for time-consuming conversation. This may be a very efficient tactic, but *Ask yourself: What is the problem here?*

Be careful that your idea for efficiency is not just a way of downloading work to your own customers, unless that is what the customers want. At one time, virtually every gas station in Canada provided gas-filling service. Now the norm is *self-service*, because the majority of people are willing to perform this function if it's going to save them a couple of cents a litre. On the other hand, just about everyone is infuriated by telephone answering systems that make you listen to a list of options, none of which cover the reason you are calling. Beware of risking your customer relationships in the name of efficiency.

✓ **Test Yourself 10.9**
True or False? For most businesses, it's cheaper to get a new customer than it is to keep an existing one.

Head Start Exercise

10.6 Briefly estimate the percentage of your sales that comes from repeat customers. Explain your method. If this information is not readily available, describe a method you could use for estimating repeat sales. ($\frac{1}{2}$ page maximum.)

CRM Customer relationship management is a marketing information technology strategy that monitors customers and classifies them into different categories, giving special treatment to those groups of customers that provide the most profit.

MANAGING CUSTOMER RELATIONS   Businesses are increasingly taking a highly integrated approach to customer relationship management (**CRM**). The idea behind CRM systems is to have higher retention of the most profitable customers by providing them with the highest service levels. Over the past decade, the software for CRM systems has fallen in price to the point where it is affordable by many small businesses. For example, you may own a small hotel that uses a CRM system to calculate the value of each of your repeat customers. Your system may award points based on customer behaviours that are more profitable (provide higher revenue or reduce costs) for your business. Points, or in this case *stars*, would be awarded based on the actual profitability of each behaviour. For instance, your system may award:

- one star for each five bookings in the past six months
- one star for every three reservations in your dining room in the past year
- one star for each five bookings at off-peak times in the past year
- one star for every three times that room service was ordered in the past six months
- one star for using automatic check-out three or more times in the past two months
- one star for using online booking three or more times in the past two months
- one star for every $250 of laundry service in the past six months.

Each time that someone on your staff (switchboard, front desk, kitchen) deals with a customer, that customer's file is retrieved on the employee's computer screen, indicating a customer code (the number of stars.) The employee can see the rank or importance of that customer and provide the appropriate level of service. For example, the room service order of a 5-star customer would receive priority over the orders of all other customer ranks. Table 10.2 shows the kind of service levels and perks that might be received by customers at different levels.

| Table 10.2 | EXAMPLE CRM CUSTOMER SERVICE LEVELS | | | | | |

| Included Service | Customer Rank | | | | | |
	New	*	**	***	****	*****
complimentary newspaper	✓	✓	✓	✓	✓	✓
discount coupon via email		✓	✓	✓		
automatic check-in			✓	✓	✓	✓
bed turn-down service			✓	✓	✓	✓
complimentary Internet access				✓	✓	✓
complimentary fruit and nut basket				✓	✓	✓
telephone response priority					✓	✓
preferred room assignment					✓	✓
preferred room rate					✓	✓
room service order priority						✓
hotel car pick-up and delivery						✓
free valet parking						✓
live operator wake-up reminder						✓

The CRM systems can be developed using existing database, spreadsheet, and communication software. Dedicated sales management and customer tracking software has been available for a long time. And more recently software providers such as SAGE (makers of ACCPAC), which target smaller firms, are offering sophisticated integrated CRM software at prices in line with small-firm budgets. Problems with CRM systems include the fact that customer behaviour is often erratic. *Ask yourself: What happens when some customers change behaviour and drop to a lower classification, receiving service that is below what they have come to expect?*

Ask yourself: What happens when a new customer, who has the potential to be a 5-star customer, is not impressed with the 1-star service levels on his or her first stay?

Someone might earn a 5-star rating in a 2-month period and then make purchases at a 2-star level for the next year. Accounting for contingencies like this can make CRM systems increasingly complex.

SERVICES MARKETING   Many businesses offer their customers no physical product: hairdressers, consulting firms, delivery services, music schools, even babysitters. All these are **pure services**, and they differ in a number of ways from product-based businesses. In pure services:

- *Price differentiation is difficult to justify.* At different hair salons, you can pay anywhere from $20 to $100 or more for pretty much the same haircut. *Ask yourself: Why might you be willing to pay more?*
- *The customer may participate in the creation of the "product."* The quality of massage you get may depend on how clearly you tell the therapist where it hurts and how hard to massage. *Ask yourself: Then, how can a business control the service quality?*
- *Evaluation of the service quality may be difficult.* After a concert, a band gets feedback from one customer who thought the performance was brilliant, but for another it was weak. *Ask yourself: How can the band assess the quality of their work?*

✓ **Test Yourself 10.10**
True or False? CRM, customer relationship management, usually refers to a retail job title.

◇? **Get Help 10.10**
CRM Daily is a newsletter ezine published by News Factor Network. It is up-to-date on CRM issues, although heavy with software advertising (**www. crm-daily.com**).

pure services Businesses offering no, or insignificant, physical product.

services marketing An area of business study that examines the non-product elements of keeping customers satisfied.

It is by studying questions like these that the field of **services marketing** has been able to shed light on important issues of customer satisfaction and retention. These findings have implications for product-based business as well since a firm can be judged on the quality of customer service as much as the quality of the product.

Much of the understanding of customer satisfaction comes from the examination of *customer dissatisfaction*. Studies of dissatisfied customers provide evidence that:

- The vast majority of dissatisfied customers do not complain to the service provider.
- The average dissatisfied customer tells around 10 people of the problem.
- The majority of dissatisfied customers who do complain are likely to be retained as customers if their complaint is resolved.[6]

This implies that customer retention depends on actively eliciting feedback from customers about whether or not they are satisfied (most won't volunteer the information) and correcting deficiencies for unsatisfied customers as quickly as possible, so the story they will be spreading is a positive one and so you will keep them as customers.

One of the biggest areas of customer dissatisfaction is wait times. Research into customer perceptions about wait times shows that how long customers feel that they have been waiting can depend on a number of factors, most of which can be influenced by the service provider.[7]

The wait feels longer when it is:

- *Of unknown duration.* Keep customers informed about how long they can expect to wait.
- *Unoccupied.* Make sure that there are activities or reading material available or that customers are not left alone.
- *Pre-process*, compared to waits during the process. For long waits, move customers to a second area or have them fill out a questionnaire so that they will feel the service process has begun.
- *Unexplained.* Provide reasons to a customer for any delay.
- *Unfair.* Customers are willing to wait longer when the delay was their fault, but when it's your fault, be sure to apologize.

✓ **Test Yourself 10.11**
True or False? Pure services generally have no physical product.

❓ **Get Help 10.11**
The Customer Relationship Management Association, CRMA Canada, is a non-profit organization providing Canadian firms with information on CRM strategies (***driveit.clickspace.com/ webpage/1000414/1000190***). As well, this organization sets standards for and has a certification process for CRM consultants.

✓ **Test Yourself 10.12**
True or False? The wait seems longer for a waiting customer who knows how long he or she is going to have to wait.

Clearly, if a business is to be efficient, customer satisfaction cannot be handled *by default,* or only when the customer complains. Rather it must be a proactive process of anticipating customer perceptions and asking for feedback.

SATISFYING THE DIFFICULT CUSTOMER   Some customers, even when treated fairly, courteously, and promptly, will remain unsatisfied for reasons that often have more to do with the customer's personal issues and history than with the service that your business provides. These customers, however, can pose a threat by disrupting your operations and/or attacking your reputation. See Table 10.3.

Head Start Exercise

10.7 Identity specific methods you currently use, or methods that you could use, to measure customer satisfaction in your business ($\frac{1}{2}$ page maximum).

Table 10.3

PROBLEM CUSTOMER TYPES AND RESPONSES

TYPE	CHARACTERISTICS	APPROACH
Genuine	Customer is emotional, upset over a legitimate complaint of poor service or product. Perhaps this is a subsequent attempt to resolve the problem	Apologize. Resolve the complaint as fast as possible. Explain the steps you are taking to prevent repeats of the problem. Compensate the customer for any inconvenience. Thank the customer for complaining and giving you the chance to set things right.
Bullying	Customer demands unreasonable or preferential treatment, often intimidating staff and using the threat of withdrawing business unless the demanded concessions are received immediately.	Firmly remind customer that the service you provide is directly related to the prices that you charge. Inform customer that their business is highly valued and (if possible) you are willing to negotiate additional services at prices that would be profitable for you.
Abusive	Customer is likely to create a scene, shouting and using crude language, verbally attacking staff, and deriding the company and its service.	First isolate the customer from vulnerable staff and other customers. Let the customer vent, then ask for assurance that they have finished and are willing to let you respond. Inform the customer that you will immediately resolve any legitimate complaint, but now there is a second problem to deal with. The problem of the customer's behaviour puts you in an embarrassing position where you may have to use legal remedies to protect your staff from abusive behaviour and protect your company reputation, which may have been slandered. Allow the customer the opportunity for apologies or assurances of no-repeats. Document the occurrence.
Fraudulent	Customer insists on unfair or even unlawful consideration from the company such as return of customer-damaged goods or false receipts for tax purposes.	Remind customer that they deal with you because they receive fair, ethical, treatment from your company and that's the only way you operate. Take the moral high ground and "red flag" this customer for careful monitoring of all interactions.

Continued

Table 10.3	(CONTINUED)	
Needy	Customer uses exceptional amounts of staff time for social "chatting," repeated explanations, reassurances, "double-checking" of information, or just plain hanging out at your place of business. Often motivated by reasons of loneliness or poor interpersonal skills, this customer is seeking social interaction.	If this customer's social need is not being met, the behaviour should change. So, remain meticulously polite with the needy customer but encourage staff to treat the customer as abruptly and efficiently as possible, within the bounds of good manners. If this fails, a frank discussion with the customer and a request to engage less of the staff's time may be required.

How Do I Make Employees More Efficient?

HIRING THE RIGHT STAFF   When starting out as an entrepreneur, you are pretty much solely responsible for the profit that your business makes. But as your business grows, you increasingly become dependent on employees to make profit for you. That, of course, is how you become rich: by having lots of people making money for you. But some people are more willing and able to make money for you than others. The trick is to hire the ones that are *willing* and then train them properly to be *able*.

recruiting The process of informing qualified candidates that a job opening is available and encouraging them to apply.

selection The process of choosing a new employee, usually conducted by putting all the applicants through a series of screening steps until the best candidate remains.

◇ **Get Help 10.12**
Service Canada has put together a website that helps entrepreneurs with hiring, training, compensating, and even terminating employees. See the human resources management site at **www.hrmanagement.ca**.

The hiring process is really two separate activities: getting people to apply for a job (**recruiting**) and then choosing the best applicant (**selection**). When very small businesses are looking for new employees, a common practice among owners is to ask existing employees if they know anyone looking for a job. This is often followed by a selection process of offering the first candidate who shows up a *try-out*: hiring him or her for a short probation period. If the try-out is successful, the candidate is considered hired. If the try-out is not successful, the owner dismisses the candidate and starts the process over again. This hit-and-miss approach to hiring is unlikely to get you the best candidate for the job.

Recruiting: The objective in choosing a recruiting source is to try to use one that will pre-screen or attract candidates who have the kind of qualifications you need. Common recruiting sources include:

- *Walk-ins.* This refers to people who send in a résumé or who just show up and ask to apply for a job, sometimes in response to an ad in your window or sometimes on their own initiative. If the candidate is just someone looking for a job, you have no pre-screening advantage.
- *Employee referral.* One of the problems of staffing based on employee referral is that you may end up hiring people all from the same family or group of friends, in which case your employees may feel a greater sense of loyalty to their referral group than to your business.

On the other hand, if you're looking for someone who can get a reliable ride to work, this type of pre-screening is an advantage.

- *Job match.* This online service from Services Canada allows employers to submit their recruiting requirements and allows job seekers to submit their qualifications and job preferences. The database then electronically matches employers with candidates, who can submit an application. Candidates are therefore pre-screened by qualifications, but only as far as by the information they provide themselves.
- *Employment agencies.* These companies commonly specialize in a particular type of employee (office help, legal assistants, engineers, and so on). Some pre-screening and sometimes even testing will have been conducted by the agency.
- *Professional recruiters.* Sometimes referred to as "head-hunters," these consultants do not have waiting candidates. Instead they go out and find people fitting your requirements and encourage them to apply, usually getting paid only when and if you hire one of their finds.
- *Educational institutions.* Among other things, college graduates have proven that they have the ability to learn. This is a major plus if you are hiring for a position that requires you to quickly train the new hire. Post-secondary institutions have student and graduate databases and staff that can help screen for the kind of expertise you need.

 Get Help 10.13

When recruiting, it is worthwhile to look at the website for job match, at *jobbank.gc.ca*. The process takes only a few minutes and you may find some good candidates.

Selection: The selection process is usually a series of steps where you start out with a large number of applicants. The applicants go through a series of screening steps that have the purpose of eliminating candidates, so that the final selection step involves choosing the best candidate from a very small number of qualified applicants. Screening steps can include:

- *Screening from the application.* This means carefully reading résumés, letters, and application forms to eliminate all who do not have the minimum requirements you are looking for.
- *Initial interview.* Here, obviously unsuitable candidates (inadequate communication skills, poor social skills, inadequate knowledge of the field) can be eliminated.
- *Testing.* This can cover a large variety of activities including work samples, performance tests, or even aptitude testing, eliminating all but a small number of the best performers.
- *In-depth interview.* At this interview, candidates are assessed for personality and fit with the organization as well as for their expectations about the job.
- *Reference/background check.* Candidates who lied on their résumé or whose reputation is doubtful can be eliminated at this step.
- *Final selection.* This step should be relatively easy since only a very small number of candidates (and perhaps only one) will remain.

✓ Test Yourself 10.13

True or False? Professional recruiters maintain lists of candidates looking for particular kinds of jobs.

Head Start Exercise

10.8 Identify specific methods that you currently use or that you could use to measure employee productivity ($\frac{1}{2}$ page maximum).

Obviously, for high-turnover, minor jobs within your business, it would not be economical to use all of the above screening steps. But the more critical the job is to your organization, the more steps you are likely to employ in the selection process.

✓ **Test Yourself 10.14**
True or False? The *in-depth inter-view* is where candidates are assessed to see if they fit into the firm in terms of their personality.

on-the-job training Where employees learn by observation and by trial and error, usually working with someone who is already competent in the particular job.

STAFF TRAINING   The larger and more sophisticated your business becomes, the more likely you are to send employees out for training or to bring in specialized trainers from outside the company. But the majority of training that takes place in small firms is **on the job.** This usually involves partnering the trainee with someone who knows the task to be learned and who will supervise the learning process. On-the-job training is not a passive system where trainees just hang around until they absorb the information and skills to do the job. It works best when it is well planned and the trainer provides active teaching. Techniques to use for conducting any type of on-the-job training are:

- *Incentive.* Explain to trainees why they need to learn the particular skill or task and indicate how they will personally benefit from accomplishing this (pay raise, the chance to work unsupervised, a step toward permanent employment).
- *Small portions.* Plan the training by breaking whatever has to be learned into small manageable portions, allowing trainees to progress in clear steps.
- *Demonstration.* Slowly and clearly show trainees how to perform tasks, resisting the temptation to show off your own proficiency or speed as this will just discourage the novice.
- *Performance.* Allow the trainee to practise the task in safe circumstances (both physically, where the trainee or others cannot be injured, and psychologically, where the trainee's errors will not produce embarrassment).
- *Feedback.* Carefully observe trainees so that you can correct their errors, and use plenty of positive reinforcement whenever they do something right.
- *Reward.* When the trainee has completed training, provide some reward (it does not have to be monetary) as a form of recognition. Certificates, names on plaques, new job titles—all these can be powerful motivators.

◇ **Get Help 10.14**
Check the Web for your provincial Ministry of Education or Training for available courses, materials, and programs.

Training largely comes under provincial jurisdiction, and some provinces provide assortments of skills training and management training materials and courses to their business communities. Especially popular are train-the-trainer programs that can provide you with skills to be a more effective on-the-job trainer.

Many business owners are reluctant to get involved with any significant amount of training because they believe it is cheaper to find people who have been trained by another company and then lure those employees away from their current jobs by paying slightly above the going rate. Some entrepreneurs also feel that if they spend the money to train employees, they will not be able to afford competitive pay rates and so will lose their own employees to the competition. *Ask yourself: Is it better to spend money on training for the skills you need or better to spend money on higher salaries so you can hire from outside?* The truth is that it's not an either–or situation. The most successful companies tend to do more training than average, as well as pay competitively.

morale The feeling of relative enthusiasm for the business collectively held by the employees.

ORGANIZATIONAL DEVELOPMENT   The discussion of leadership in Chapter 4 is very much about how you as an entrepreneur can personally motivate those working for you to higher levels of productivity. As your business grows, however, you will have less time to spend with individual employees, possibly because you will have more of them and possibly because you will have to spend more time dealing with strategic issues rather than day-to-day operations. Because of this, employee **morale** and efficiency may slip. One option is to try to systemize the principles of good management throughout your organization by establishing a **leadership program**. Over the years many such systems have evolved, going by names like:

- management by objectives
- participative management
- management teams
- total quality management
- The Learning Organization.

At the time of writing, The Learning Organization is a widely popular leadership program based on the series of *Fifth Discipline* books written by Peter Senge. The program is adaptable to organizations of all sizes, and reports excellent improvements in organizational effectiveness.

The main advantages of such programs are that they give a common focus to all employees and formally involve everyone in decision making. In the start-up phase of a company, such systems are not required since everyone is focused on survival of the firm and everyone feels a sense of importance while there are only a few people in the organization. As the organization grows, however, individual employees may have less and less contact with the entrepreneur and may come to feel uninvolved. A formal leadership program can often help these employees become re-connected with the company.

It seems that pretty much any kind of organization-wide leadership program will produce a significant improvement in productivity for a period of time (roughly a couple of years) and then productivity will start to fall back to the baseline level (from before the introduction of the program). The implication of this trend for the business owner is that a new program or organizational focus should be planned for when the current one starts to fade.

An important motivator for employees within a growing business is the opportunity to grow personally—which means getting promotions. But before you can promote from within your company, your employees must be prepared to assume new and larger responsibilities. And they must have others ready to take over the responsibilities that they leave. For example, imagine that you are a distributor of industrial generators, ready to expand into a neighbouring province. You will need a sales manager for the new region; although several of your salespeople have indicated an interest, none of them have had any management training or experience. Besides, if you promote one of your top salespeople you will have to backfill that job. And even though one of your telephone order-takers has asked to go on the road as a salesperson, you cannot risk sending your customers someone with no experience. *Ask yourself: What will happen to morale if you do not promote from within? If you hire someone new from outside the company?* The problem here is that specific staff should have been developed for future promotion before any promotions were available. This is called **succession planning.**

Good succession planning does not necessarily identify one specific understudy for each job in the organization, but it does identify certain individuals as likely candidates for promotion in certain directions. These candidates are developed by various means, such as **mentoring** (forming an association with a senior manager who will act as an adviser), **job shadowing** (spending time observing or assisting managers in their jobs), and even

---

leadership program A formal, organization-wide system to improve morale and involve employees in the decision-making process.

◇ **Get Help 10.15**
Before starting any kind of leadership program, check the library for recent management and organizational development texts. You will likely need outside help to start such a program. Use the Yellow Pages to start your hunt for management consultants.

succession planning The identification and grooming of specific employees for future promotion to specific areas in the organization.

✓ **Test Yourself 10.15**
True or False? *Leadership programs* tend to produce a permanent increase in an organization's productivity.

mentoring An employee development technique that matches the employee with a senior manager (not necessarily in the same department) who functions as an adviser for the employee.

job shadowing An employee development technique that allows employees to observe or assist managers in their jobs.

✓ **Test Yourself 10.16**
True or False? *Succession planning* should identify one specific understudy for each senior job in the business.

formal classroom training (often through continuing education courses). Succession planning not only ensures the preparedness of employees for promotion, but also acts as a great motivator for those who can see the likelihood of their efforts being rewarded.

SMALL BUSINESS PROFILE 10.2
Wicked Rides—Speed N' Custom

Started in 2004, Wicked Rides—Speed N' Custom is already established as a leading automobile performance shop in Sudbury. The entrepreneur Vincent "Vince" Kuber, only 24 years old, recently moved to larger premises to accommodate the growth of his business. The shop specializes in customizing imported and domestic sports compacts—exactly the type of vehicle preferred by (affordable for) the younger male market targeted by Wicked Rides. Growing secondary targets are more mature vintage auto collectors who are looking for restoration work and younger do-it-yourselfers who purchase specialized parts.

After graduating from his high school automotive program, Vince was working in the parts department of a Canadian Tire store during the day, working in a body shop at night, and customizing his own low-rider trucks in his spare time. With the knowledge and skills he gained from these activities combined with a natural talent for automobile styling and a desire to be his own boss, Vince was able to access start-up funding and mentoring assistance through the Canadian Youth Business Foundation and Business Plan assistance from the Nickel Basin Regional Business Centre. These days, Vince is spending less time doing hands-on work and more time in the office, running the business. But that's not a problem since he has four competent employees—one with more than 20 years of experience in custom bodywork.

Vince has seen lots of changes as the business quickly matures. One of the problems in the old shop was the large number of young car enthusiasts just hanging out in a place of interest to them. "It was starting to disrupt the work," Vince says, "so when we moved I just had to put my foot down." These days, the biggest customer problem that Vince faces is staying in close touch with customers for the really big jobs. "You have to stay in daily contact with them," says Vince, who worries about having to redo work that has not met customer expectations.

Wicked Rides has an attractive, highly graphic website (***www.wickedrides.ca***) with lots of pictures and details of the company's work as well as links of interest to car enthusiasts. Vince admits, however, that the website is not a significant source of business. He feels that the main promotional techniques that seem to bring in new business are the visibility of the shop and sign and the company stickers on completed customer cars. And those stickers—driving everywhere, advertising his quality work—are the cheapest, most efficient form of advertising available to Vince.

How Can I Control Costs?

Careful management of costs and expenses might be a better investment of your effort than using that same effort to increase sales. For example, you could have a business that runs with a net profit of about 3 percent of sales. By spending a little time shopping around, you may find that you could save $100 on the cost of your supplies. That savings ends up as $100 more net profit for you to keep. At the 3-percent rate, you would have to increase your sales by $3,333 in order to make the same $100 net profit. Clearly, there is a point of diminishing returns when trying to reduce costs. *Ask yourself: For your business, which would be the easiest way to make $100 more net profit?*

COSTING SYSTEMS   The best approach is to develop a systematic way of reviewing your costs and expenses. This could mean something like annual or even quarterly meetings with your accountant where you compare all of your costs and expenses to the industry averages (again by using key ratios). Your system could mean setting aside a regular day to *shop* the prices of all of your suppliers, including things like insurance and any professional services that you use (such as your accountant). The system might also include a method of checking the costs on every contract or job that you undertake, to make sure that you are covering all of your costs and expenses and therefore making a profit on every job. This is often accomplished by using some sort of costing work sheet, like the one in Figure 10.1.

Direct Materials: In the *direct materials* section of the costing sheet, the purpose is to make sure you are listing and accounting for the costs of materials that will be used for the job. This doesn't mean small incidental supplies like paper or cleaning liquids or computer disks (these will be taken into consideration as part of *overhead*). But, it means the major predictable materials you will need along with any predictable wastage. For example, a ceramic tile installer may know from experience that a certain percentage of tiles will crack when being cut to fit around the edges. This wastage is part of the job material costs.

Direct Labour: The cost of direct labour is the amount you pay to people (usually calculated at an hourly rate) for the time they will actually be working on the particular project. It doesn't include things like the hours of sales time it took to get the contract. Neither does it include things like time spent with customers while they finalize details of a job nor time for incidental phone calls or paperwork related to the job. (Again, these are part of the overhead calculation.)

Get Help 10.16
Specific costs and expenses are listed by industry as a percentage of sales on the Performance Plus site, at *http://sme.ic.gc.ca*.

Overhead: An accurate measure of your *overhead* (operating expenses of the company) can really only come from the income statement, after the company has been operating for a while. Attempting this before start-up, working just with your experience and financial projections, will be much less accurate. Nevertheless, in some industries—for example, a machine shop or a cabinet-making business—a costing system like this should be necessary right from the beginning.

The worksheet uses an *overhead percentage of direct labour* to estimate the amount of overhead that should be charged for every dollar of labour that is charged. The overhead percentage of direct labour is calculated by dividing all the annual operating expenses of the business by the amount of direct labour that would have been billed to customers during that year. This is expressed as a percentage:

$$\text{OH\% of Direct Labour} = \frac{\text{Annual Operating Expenses}}{\text{Annual Direct Labour Billings}} \times 100\%$$

Let's say that the example shown in Figure 10.1 has an overhead percentage of direct labour of 290 percent. This means that for every dollar of direct labour that this company charges, it must charge $2.90 for overhead. (This figure would normally be calculated from past customer invoices and your income statement.)

| Figure 10.1 | **PATH AND PATIO COST WORKSHEET** |

Customer: _____ Skinner, 98 Brown St., Saint John 555-5987 _____

Project Description: ___ Curved interlocking patio around pool (600 sq. ft.: $8\frac{1}{4}"\times 7\frac{1}{4}"$ paver stones) __

Direct Materials

Description	# Units	×	Cost/unit	=	Material Cost	
1440 pavers (110% waste)	1584	×	$ .95	=	$ 1,505.00	
Portland cement (40-kg bag)	20 bags	×	$ 9.50	=	$ 190.00	
Sand	2 tons	×	$ 12.00	=	$ 24.00	
Edging	100 ft.	×	$ .80	=	$ 80.00	
Total Direct Materials Cost					$ 1,799.00	$ 1,799.00

Direct Labour

Employee	# Hours	×	Hourly Rate	=	Labour Cost	
Designer	4	×	$ 32.00	=	$ 128.00	
Installer	36	×	$ 22.00	=	$ 792.00	
Assistant	36	×	$ 12.50	=	$ 450.00	
Total Direct Labour Cost					$ 1,370.00	$ 1,370.00

Overhead

OH% of Direct Labour	×	Direct Labour Cost	=	Overhead Charge	
290%	×	$ 1,370.00	=	$ 3,973.00	$ 3,973.00

Pricing

Total Costs (Direct Materials + Direct Labour + Overhead)	$ 7,142.00

Total Costs	×	% Net Profit	=	Job Profit	+	Total Costs	=	Job Price
$ 7,142.00	×	4%	=	$ 286.00	+	$ 7,142.00	=	$ 7,428.00

Cost-based Pricing: The overall pricing strategy for your business should always be more of a marketing issue than a costing issue, and it should be related to your company image and market conditions. But you still have to make sure that you are making a profit on each transaction. You may need a costing worksheet to ensure that you cover all of your costs and expenses as well as make a profit on every job. And, for some businesses, this tool is the most efficient way of calculating a job price—simply applying a predetermined mark-up to your costs and expenses.

Clearly, the information shown in Figure 10.1 is not something that you would want to show to a customer. The problem is that if you are showing a 4-percent net profit, the customer will wonder why you can't get by with 2 percent, or 1 percent. Your profit is none of the customer's business. The customer should be concerned only with your final price compared to the prices of competitors. If you plan on showing your costing sheet to anyone (as in the case where you are using the same form to provide price quotations to customers), you may wish to build your profit directly into your materials and labour costs.

No job costing work sheet is perfect. The assumption that the labour cost is directly proportional to the overhead does not always hold. For example, in Figure 10.1, if the designer were able to do the work in one hour, the labour cost would be reduced by $96 and the overhead would go down by $278 (290% × $96), which is just about equal to the job profit. For this job, however, very little of the overhead is related to the work of the designer working at a computer in the office. Most of the overhead would come from transportation and machinery expense at the job site, which would remain the same regardless of how many hours the designer puts in. For some businesses, where there is a huge variation in the overhead from job to job, a more complex costing method may be required, actually calculating an amount of overhead for each job activity. This is called **activity-based costing**.

Make or Buy Decisions: The "make or buy" decision refers to the individual products that your business is selling and whether you are producing those items yourself or buying them from some other supplier for resale to your customers. For example, you might be a manufacturer of small industrial vacuum cleaners, but about half of your company income is from selling replacement filter bags for your machines. One of your options is to invest in paper and cardboard cutters as well as industrial sewing machines, purchase pre-printed filter paper and board, and then produce your own bags in your plant. Alternatively, you could go to a firm that produces paper-filtering products and give them the contract to produce all of your bags, custom-made to your specifications. *Ask yourself: Which is the better option?*

Each of the options has its own advantages:

Make	**Buy**
Direct control of quality	No investment in equipment
Direct control of delivery	Greater specialization of business
Guaranteed source of supply	Easier to redesign product (not limited by own equipment)

Generally, the fewer activities your company *specializes* in, the more efficiently you will operate, favouring the *buy* option. *Ask yourself: Could the question of "make or buy" apply to service firms that have no physical product?* Yes, although the question becomes slightly different: Do it yourself or subcontract? A garage may send out its transmission work to a specialist in this area and still make a small profit on transmission work orders, without having to invest in special tools and expertise. A generalized computer-consulting firm can subcontract web

Get Help 10.17
There are various activity-based costing software packages available (check "Computer Software" in the Yellow Pages), but most novices will need the help of an experienced consultant (see "Management Consultants" in the Yellow Pages) to set up such programs.

activity-based costing A method of apportioning overhead to a job by breaking the job down into detailed activities, each of which has a specific overhead cost.

Test Yourself 10.17
True or False? The pricing strategy of a business is primarily a marketing issue rather than a costing issue.

outsourcing The buying of products or services from outside a company, instead of producing them in house, especially when producing them yourself is a feasible option or past practice.

design work because so many small firms that specialize in web design can do this specialty work more efficiently. **Outsourcing** is a term often used to describe the buying of a product you could choose to make, or to describe the subcontracting of a service or process instead of providing it with your own staff.

Like the issue of pricing, make-or-buy is sometimes a marketing issue as opposed to a cost issue. For instance, you could have a restaurant that specializes in gourmet breakfasts. It may be cheaper, faster, and a lot less work to buy pre-made scrambled eggs in 30-portion boil-and-serve bags. The eggs wouldn't taste that much different, but how would customers react if they found out? *Ask yourself: What would it do to their perception of your restaurant—your image?*

Budgeting for Efficiency: Increasing the efficiency of your business can be costly. In other words: *You have to spend money to save money.* And in just about any business, there will be many alternatives on which you could spend money for greater efficiency. But small business owners would never have the time or money to implement all possible efficiency measures at the same time. So the logical way to manage for efficiency is to look at several of the most likely ways of saving money and then prioritize whichever would be the most profitable. The first thing you have to do is figure out the costs for any particular efficiency project being considered.

✓ **Test Yourself 10.18**
True or False? The *make or buy* decision only applies to manufacturing firms.

Project Budgeting: Identifying the costs for any efficiency project means listing any capital outlay for new equipment, machinery, software, consulting fees, subcontract work, and so on. It also means identifying the soft or hidden costs associated with a particular project. These could include putting a value on the entrepreneur's own time that would be used by the project, along with the time of involved employees (including time for training on new systems) plus any travel costs and incidentals. This process can be difficult, will involve imaginative thinking, and may not be particularly accurate (with the tendency being to underestimate costs). The next step, perhaps even less accurate but still necessary, requires estimating the annual savings that would result from the particular efficiency measures. See the Sales Forecasting techniques described in Chapter 2 for ideas on methods. *Ask yourself: How much training time would be saved in a year if new employees had a comprehensive operations manual to refer to? What would be the dollar value of that time? How much would customer retention increase with a new online ordering system? What would be the dollar value of the profit from those retained customers?*

Head Start Exercise

10.9 Briefly identify any costing methods that your business uses. Identify the average gross margin of your business. Using the *return on sales* figure from Head Start Exercise 10.1, calculate how many dollars of sales you must make for each dollar of net profit. ($\frac{1}{2}$ page maximum.)

✓ **Test Yourself 10.19**
True or False? It is easier to have a product redesigned when you outsource it, instead of making it yourself.

Return on Investment (ROI) Analysis: The cost of implementing an efficiency program is an investment that should yield savings (additional profit) for the company. But *profit* only has real meaning in the context of the investment needed to produce it. So, for each proposed efficiency program, it should be possible to calculated an estimated return on investment where:

$$\text{Projected ROI} = \frac{\text{Estimated annual savings}}{\text{Estimated implementation costs}}$$

With this calculation it will be easy to compare the relative estimated profitability of different proposed efficiency programs and prioritize them accordingly. *Ask yourself: How accurate is this comparison?* It's certainly not precise. So other considerations (changing market conditions, changing technologies, competition changes, etc.) may well be part of any decision on an approach to efficiency.

Like most decisions that an entrepreneur has to make, the choice of approaches to better efficiency (reduced costs and expenses) is one that has to be made with imperfect information and some degree of risk.

✓ **Test Yourself 10.20**
True or False? The ROI for the cost of an efficiency program can be estimated with a high degree of accuracy.

✓ Answers to Test Yourself Questions

10.1   "Sales/Equity" is key ratio indicator of efficiency. *False*

10.2   Most of a company's profit will come from the *core business*. *True*

10.3   Templates should be designed to cover all possible eventualities. *False*

10.4   Operations manuals tend to be larger and more detailed than employee handbooks. *True*

10.5   A *job standard* identifies a reasonable amount and quality of work to expect for a particular job. *True*

10.6   A good website will use a broad variety of fonts, colours, and graphic styles. *False*

10.7   An email address contains a domain name. *True*

10.8   Robotics is a tool of ecommerce. *False*

10.9   For most businesses, it's cheaper to get a new customer than it is to keep an existing one. *False*

10.10 CRM, customer relationship management, usually refers to a retail job title. *False*

10.11 Pure services generally have no physical product. *True*

10.12 The wait seems longer for a waiting customer who knows how long he or she is going to have to wait. *False*

10.13 Professional recruiters maintain lists of candidates looking for particular kinds of jobs. *False*

10.14 The *in-depth interview* is where candidates are assessed to see if they fit into the firm in terms of their personality. *True*

10.15 *Leadership programs* tend to produce a permanent increase in an organization's productivity. *False*

10.16 *Succession planning* should identify one specific understudy for each senior job in the business. *False*

10.17 The pricing strategy of a business is primarily a marketing issue rather than a costing issue. *True*

10.18 The *make or buy* decision only applies to manufacturing firms. *False*

10.19 It is easier to have a product re-designed when you outsource it, instead of making it yourself. *True*

10.20 The ROI for the cost of an efficiency program can be estimated with a high degree of accuracy. *False*

Questions for Discussion

1. Identify some automated services that you dislike and explain the reasons why. Could the automated service be corrected in a way to address your complaints? Discuss.

2. Think of some large organization where you have been a repeat customer: perhaps a bank or a college or university. How do you feel when you think of yourself calling in to this organization, knowing that the person answering the phone may have significant information about you on the computer screen? What are some of the implications of this for CRM systems?

3. Customer satisfaction does not necessarily equal customer retention. Discuss some of the reasons why this might be true.

4. For a small business that needs skilled staff, discuss the advantages of *training* vs. *hiring*.

5. "Pricing should be a marketing decision rather than a costing decision." Discuss.

Recommended Reading

Antion, Tom. *Electronic Marketing for Small Business: Low-Cost/High-Return Tools and Techniques That Really Work.* New Jersey: John Wiley & Sons Inc., 2005.

Berkley, Holly. *Low-Budget Online Marketing for Small Business.* Vancouver: Self-Counsel Press, 2003.

Hoffman, D., and J. Bateson. *Essentials of Services Marketing: Concepts, Strategies and Cases.* New York: Harcourt, 2002.

Senge, Peter M. *The Fifth Discipline: The Art and Practice of the Learning Organization.* New York: Doubleday Currency, 1990.

Stern, Carl W. *Perspectives on Strategy from the Boston Consulting Group: The Best Strategic Thinking from the Boston Consulting Group.* New York: Wiley, 1998.

Zeithaml, Valarie A., and Mary Jo Bitner. *Services Marketing: Integrating Customer Focus across the Firm.* New York: McGraw-Hill, 2003.

Operational Efficiency Plan

MEASURING EFFICIENCY

1. Briefly identify any general indications of a need for efficiency improvement in the business.

    _____

    _____

    _____

    _____

    _____

    _____

    _____

    _____

2. From the financial statements of the business, calculate key ratio indicators of efficiency and provide data comparing these to industry averages.

    _____

    _____

    _____

    _____

    _____

    _____

    _____

    _____

3. Discuss any conclusions about the relative efficiency of your firm and identify any serious examples of waste.

    _____

    _____

    _____

    _____

    _____

    _____

    _____

    _____

REFOCUSING

4. Identify any elements of the core business that you will concentrate on for greater profits.

_____

_____

_____

_____

_____

_____

_____

_____

_____

5. Identify any products or segments that you will marginally maintain or abandon.

_____

_____

_____

_____

_____

_____

_____

_____

_____

_____

SYSTEMS AND AUTOMATION

6. Identify any new systems, tools, or methods improvements that you will introduce for greater productivity.

_____

_____

_____

_____

_____

_____

_____

_____

7. Estimate the costs involved for all of the changes identified in #6.

_____

_____

_____

_____

_____

_____

_____

_____

_____

8. Estimate the productivity gain in terms of additional profit over the next three years for all of the changes identified in #6. Give a clear rationale.

_____

_____

_____

_____

_____

_____

_____

_____

_____

CUSTOMER RETENTION

9. Identify any new systems or methods you will introduce to improve customer satisfaction/retention.

_____

_____

_____

_____

_____

_____

_____

_____

10. Estimate the costs involved for all of the changes identified in #9.

   _____
   _____
   _____
   _____
   _____
   _____
   _____
   _____
   _____

11. Estimate any additional profit over the next three years expected from all of the changes identified in #9. Give a clear rationale.

   _____
   _____
   _____
   _____
   _____
   _____
   _____
   _____
   _____

EMPLOYEE PRODUCTIVITY

12. Identify any new systems or methods you will introduce to improve employee productivity.

   _____
   _____
   _____
   _____
   _____
   _____
   _____
   _____

13. Estimate the costs involved for all of the changes identified in #12.

_____

_____

_____

_____

_____

_____

_____

_____

_____

14. Estimate any additional profit over the next three years expected from all of the changes identified in #12. Give a clear rationale.

_____

_____

_____

_____

_____

_____

_____

_____

_____

_____

COST CONTROL

15. Identify any new systems or methods you will introduce to control direct costs of your business.

_____

_____

_____

_____

_____

_____

_____

_____

_____

16. Estimate the costs for all changes identified in #15.

_____

_____

_____

_____

_____

_____

_____

_____

17. Estimate any additional profit over the next three years expected from all of the changes identified in #15. Give a clear rationale.

_____

_____

_____

_____

_____

_____

_____

_____

Developing Entrepreneurship:
How Can I Build and Apply My Skills?

LEARNING OBJECTIVES

On completion of this chapter, you should be able to:

- *Describe how the focus of the entrepreneur changes as a business grows.*
- *Describe various leadership skills and techniques and identify different circumstances for their uses.*
- *Argue the importance of communication skills to the entrepreneur.*
- *Outline the organizational skills of decision making, delegating, and planning.*
- *Define ethics and morality and apply these terms to business behaviours.*
- *Explain various ways in which entrepreneurs are involved with their communities.*
- *Describe how entrepreneurs can develop personal skills of time, lifestyle, and health management to help cope with the demands of their careers.*
- *Identify some personal tax implications of entrepreneurship.*
- *Discuss the entrepreneur's need for personal financial planning.*
- *Define insolvency and bankruptcy and describe techniques for dealing with a financial crisis.*
- *Outline alternative career paths for entrepreneurs.*
- *Discuss various employment opportunities for former entrepreneurs.*
- *Prepare a Personal Development Plan*

Chapters 9 and 10 discussed strategies and techniques for developing the business. Now, Chapter 11 focuses on the entrepreneur as an individual. This chapter is about how the entrepreneur must adapt and evolve as the business changes. It looks at the kinds of choices a maturing business owner must make about the future of the company as well as about the entrepreneur's personal life.

How Will I Grow as a Manager?

As small companies grow, there is a definite shift in the management concerns of the entrepreneur from an operational focus to a strategic focus.[1] *Ask yourself: Do the entrepreneur's concerns change because of the company growth, or is it the change in the approach of the entrepreneur that leads to the growth?* It's a bit of a chicken-and-egg question. Many business professors would argue that "strategic focus produces growth," although there is, so far, little data to support this conclusion. Nevertheless, as the business grows, the common pattern is for the entrepreneur to become more focused on long-term planning and more concerned about external influences on the business. This shift is outlined in Figure 11.1.

In Chapter 4, we looked at management in terms of its broad functional areas or activities. But here, we examine management as a set of skills. For convenience, these skills are grouped into four categories (although there is considerable overlap among them): *leadership skills, communication skills, organizational skills,* and *crisis management skills.*

leadership The motivational aspects of management that encourage greater productivity from employees.

LEADERSHIP SKILLS   We have seen in previous chapters that **leadership** is about getting people to work harder. Traditionally, small business owners have leaned toward a highly directive, even dictatorial management style that can be an impediment to company growth. There is nothing wrong with a tough directive management style per se. In fact, this is a skill that many entrepreneurs develop. The problem occurs when this is the only style in the entrepreneur's leadership repertoire. These days, we tend to believe that the most productive managers are those who are skilled in a variety of leadership approaches and can switch among them, depending on what the situation calls for.[2] This requires striking a balance among *discipline, coaching, delegating,* and *team-building* leadership styles. It also means developing skills in all of these areas.

Discipline: A disciplinary leadership style means tight control of each individual subordinate, giving specific directions (orders) and close supervision to make sure that the orders are followed. It usually involves seeking little employee input, with the entrepreneur acting in a militaristic manner, as the commanding officer. Feedback to employees is frequently in the

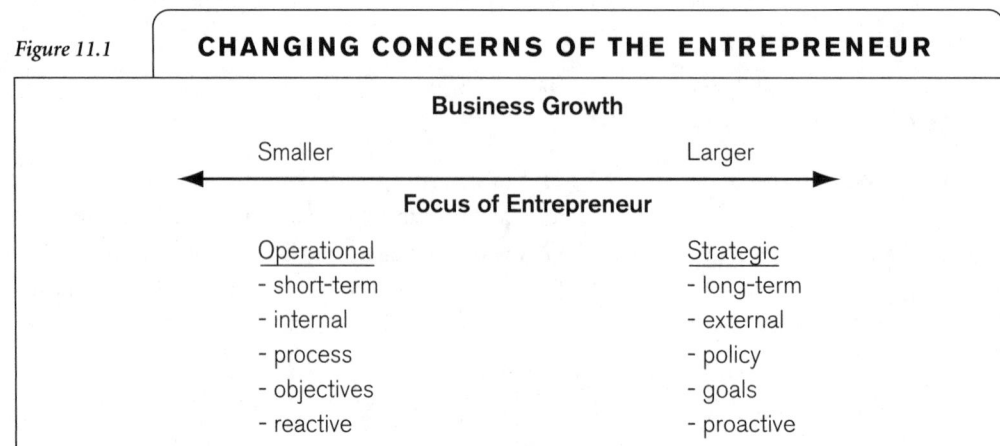

Figure 11.1   **CHANGING CONCERNS OF THE ENTREPRENEUR**

form of criticism of performance. The term *discipline* is often used interchangeably with *punishment* and of course the ultimate form of employee punishment is *termination*. *Ask yourself: Can I see myself as a disciplinarian? Could I fire someone?*

Naturally, this style of leadership is considered *old fashioned* in most settings today. Nevertheless, there are times when an entrepreneur is facing a crisis or dealing with a problem employee and disciplinary tactics must be used. Good rules for discipline include:

- *Clear warnings.* Both the expected behaviours and the consequences of not meeting expectations should be made clear to employees. Reminders should be frequent, especially to employees who fail to meet expectations.
- *A progressive approach.* The punishment should fit the crime. A minor infraction should not mean that the employee gets fired, when a lesser punishment (sent home for the rest of the shift) would be fair.
- *Documentation.* Any disciplinary attempt to influence the behaviour of an employee should be written down. This record can be used to measure the effectiveness of the entrepreneur's management approaches. It can also serve as evidence of justification (to the employee and in rare cases to a court) for any eventual firing.

These approaches help ensure that the disciplinarian boss will be considered *tough but fair* as opposed to tyrannical. Most employees are willing to accept the tough-but-fair boss. However, working for a tyrant usually means looking for a new job.

✓ **Test Yourself 11.1**
True or False? The terms *leadership* and *management* are totally interchangeable.

Coaching: As a leadership style, coaching implies working with subordinates, often in groups, in a supporting and encouraging manner, but with the coach or entrepreneur still very much in control of the process. The coach sets the objectives and then tries to shape the behaviour of the subordinates, largely with **positive reinforcement** or rewarding employee improvement. Behaviour can also be shaped by **negative reinforcement,** which is much the disciplinarian, or punishment, approach. But when applied correctly, positive reinforcement is a faster, more powerful way to change employee behaviours. The idea is to catch an employee behaving in a desired way or even just an improved way and then reward the employee. Rewarding improvement produces more improvement at an accelerating rate. Key points to remember are:

positive reinforcement Any action that makes an employee behaviour more likely to re-occur.

negative reinforcement Any action that makes an employee behaviour less likely to re-occur.

- *Rewards can be small.* When it comes to changing human behaviour, even tiny actions (a nod, a smile, the words "thank you") can be powerful reinforcers—often more powerful than fat bonus cheques.
- *Rewards must be quick.* To be effective, positive reinforcement must come immediately after the desired behaviour. If you see an employee handling a customer well, immediately tell the employee: "good job." Don't wait for the month-end sales meeting to mention the good behaviour; by then it is too late for effective reinforcement.
- *Rewards can be vicarious.* Unlike animals, human beings don't have to personally receive reinforcement for it to affect their behaviour. When Brad sees Kevil getting a pat on the back for a particular behaviour, Brad also is reinforced and more likely to behave accordingly. So don't hesitate to do your reinforcing in front of the whole team.

For good coaches and good managers, the habits of positive reinforcement are deeply ingrained.

delegating Giving subordinates responsibility and full authority for completing specific tasks.

Delegating: For many entrepreneurs, failure to acquire the skill of **delegating** is a roadblock to the growth of their companies. Business owners commonly have no problem giving orders to subordinates. But giving orders is not delegating. Proper delegation means assigning responsibilities to individuals and giving them the authority to fulfill those responsibilities however they see fit, without interference from you. To truly delegate, you have to be able to give up control to the subordinate. This takes trust and self-discipline, especially when you know that you have much more experience and knowledge than your employee has. However, delegating has many benefits including:

- freeing up the entrepreneur's time for more strategic work
- helping to develop the skills of employees
- building self-confidence in employees by showing trust in their judgment.

micro-management The overly close supervision of subordinates and the exercise of authority over minor decisions that should be left to those subordinates.

Failure to delegate properly is usually manifested as **micro-management** on the part of the entrepreneur. This is the tendency of some managers to involve themselves in extremely minor decisions, often second-guessing or overruling the decisions of subordinates. *Ask yourself: How do you feel when the boss is "breathing down your neck" or "looking over your shoulder"?* Micro-management is the fastest way to undermine the self-confidence of employees in whom you are trying to develop that very characteristic. The steps for delegating are:

1. Assign the new tasks for which the employee will be responsible.
2. Explain the authority the employee has for carrying out the tasks.
3. Ask for feedback to ensure that the new role is clear.
4. Arrange a process to monitor progress of the tasks.
5. Control your own tendency to hover or take back delegated authority.
6. Provide feedback and positive reinforcement to the employee.

Get Help 11.1
Experienced team building facilitators are readily available, and programs of any length are offered by most management consulting firms. The Centre for Collaborative Organizations at the University of North Texas has a website that offers a variety of free literature on the subject of team building: *www.workteams.unt.edu*.

Team Building: Team building is like delegating to a group. In fact, the most highly developed (and most theoretical) sorts of teams are self-managed, using goals and levels of support that have been negotiated with the entrepreneur. Leadership is shared within the team and the team is held accountable for its performance as a single unit. Most practical teamwork within small enterprises, however, falls far short of this ideal.

Test Yourself 11.2
True or False? A good manager should develop a single personal leadership style and stick with it.

A team-building leadership style is most appropriate when dealing with experienced competent specialists in a non-critical environment. For example, imagine you owned a forms-design software company with a secure niche. You have acquired the rights to Canadian distribution for a new product that must be translated for use in French. To accomplish this, you might assemble a team consisting of a software engineer, a translator, a forms designer, and a salesperson. Your intention is to negotiate what the finished product will look like, a deadline for completion, and then let them go to it, with just the occasional progress report. But first, you will likely have to set up some sort of process to ensure that the group will function as a team. This may involve:

Test Yourself 11.3
True or False? Reinforcement can affect employee behaviour even for employees who do not personally get reinforced.

- *Self-assessment tools.* There are various tests that classify personalities and then show how individuals are likely to interact with other personality types.
- *Relationship exercises.* The better people know each other, the more likely they are to build trust in one another. These exercises often involve some sort of group challenge.
- *Process definition.* The group will have to come to an agreement on who will do what, using which procedures, as well as issues of how decisions will be made and conflicts resolved.

The ultimate management skill, of course, is knowing when to use which leadership style. This choice is influenced by factors in two broad categories:

- *The development level of the employees.* This addresses whether you have mature, trained, experienced, willing employees who can be left alone; or are they marginally competent, lazy novices who have to be directed for each step of the job and checked on after each activity? Naturally, employee development is not an either–or proposition, but rather a continuum.

- *The nature of the risk.* There are two kinds of risk involved here: the risk related to the actual job the employee performs and the external risks to the business. If you have employees assembling heart pacemakers, on which lives will depend, high risk is involved, so it is expected that the control and supervision of those employees will be tight. On the other hand, if you have an employee stuffing envelopes with flyers, the job-related risk is low, requiring maybe the occasional spot-check, but not a lot of direction or control. Similarly, the risks of the business environment might be high when new competitors have entered the market or a change in the economy has killed demand and put the business into a financial crisis. The entrepreneur's assessment of risk is the combination of both the internal and external factors.

Theoretically, the most effective leadership style is the one that fits the circumstances. Figure 11.2 represents this model of leadership styles, drawing on the widely recognized theories of Hersey and Blanchard,[3] but presented here in a more entrepreneurial context.

Head Start Exercise

11.1 Describe the management style that you feel you are most likely to use most of the time. Ask several subordinates, colleagues, or even friends to describe the way you typically manage people, then re-assess your own description of your primary leadership style. ($\frac{2}{3}$ page maximum.)

✓ **Test Yourself 11.4**
True or False? Delegating means assigning both responsibility and authority.

✓ **Test Yourself 11.5**
True or False? Generally, the less risk involved, the less control needs to be exercised over employees.

Figure 11.2

SITUATION AND LEADERSHIP STYLE

Risk

High

| Discipline | Delegating |

Individual management

high ← control → low

Group management

| Coaching | Team Building |

Low

Employee Development

- Reluctant
- Untrained
- Novice
- Marginally Able

- Willing
- Educated
- Experienced
- Highly Competent

COMMUNICATION SKILLS   Think of a busy entrepreneur and *Ask yourself: How much of an entrepreneur's time is spent talking on the phone, handling emails, corresponding with customers, or talking to employees?* All of these activities are some form of communication, and as a business grows, the entrepreneur spends more and more time on this activity.

Writing: Unlike verbal communication, in written communication, there is no ongoing opportunity to test whether a message is being understood and to modify the communication accordingly. Writing is a one-way process. It is definitely too late for the author of this book to change the parts that you are not understanding. That's why writers must work to make things as clear as possible. Whether you are writing an offer of employment to an applicant, a sales flyer for prospects, or a complaint email to a supplier, the need for clarity is paramount.

Much business writing, especially in emails, is flawed by the imprecise or incorrect use of words. What you write represents your company, so your writing should be as reliable as you represent yourself to be. It is difficult to write precisely without the correct tools. Every business owner should have handy:

Get Help 11.2
Most community colleges offer short or part-time business writing courses that can be highly effective.

- A good *dictionary.* This means the actual book, not a word processor or online dictionary. A physical dictionary is a superior technology to a computer when it comes to learning about words. The dictionary should include Canadian usage.
- A *thesaurus.* By all means, use the handy synonym feature of word processors, but these have more limitations than a hard-copy thesaurus for finding a precise word.

Get Help 11.3
The most widely used style guide is *The Elements of Style* by Strunk and White. Inexpensive and in use for almost 70 years, it is now in its 4th edition.

- A *style guide.* This is a book that explains the correct use of language and punctuation. *Ask yourself: Do I know when to use "which" instead of "that"? Do I know the correct use of the semi-colon?* The answers are easy to find in a style guide.

The key to clarity is proofreading. It's hard to proofread your own work because you know what you intended to say, so it seems as if your message is clear. Try to have someone else proofread all your writing or leave some time between the writing and the proofreading to clear your mind of your writing intentions.

Test Yourself 11.6
True or False? Writing is a two-way communication process.

Presenting: Entrepreneurs are frequently called upon to make presentations ranging from the extremely casual (a short demonstration for employees on using the new printer) to the fully formal (the main speech at an awards dinner). And most of them get nervous about it. Everyone has some level of apprehension about public speaking. Just look at some of the world's leading entertainers at the Academy Awards: shaking hands, voice tremors, and forgotten lines. Part of the skill of public speaking is accepting your own nervousness and then moving forward. Tips for good business presentations include:

- Write out the entire presentation as you imagine yourself delivering it.
- Present from point-form notes so you do not end up *reading* a speech.
- Make eye contact with and speak directly to members of the audience. This keeps you in a conversational mode.
- Use visual enhancements (photos, charts, outlines, animation) but beware of *Death by PowerPoint.* Presentation software can be beneficial for organizing a presentation and as a visual assist. But reading something to an audience that they can read for themselves is insulting and boring.
- Anticipate likely questions and prepare answers.
- Practise. Practising in front of live volunteers is best and using video is also valuable. Using the mirror is cheap and handy, and at the very least you should practise in your own head.

No matter how bad your current public speaking abilities, recognize that this is just a skill that you can learn and eventually enjoy. Some of the world's greatest presenters were absolutely awful when they first started out.

Listening: When an employee, customer, child, or anyone else for that matter, comes to tell you something, your first job is to listen. It would be rare to hear an entrepreneur admit: "I'm not a good listener. I interrupt, I jump to conclusions, I misunderstand, I offer quick advice and I don't really care all that much." But we all know people who *listen* exactly like that. Now *Ask yourself: How critical am I of my own listening skills?* Chances are, like most people, you think you're already a good listener, so you don't pay much attention to the issue. However, the really good listeners understand that listening, like the other elements of communication, is a skill; and, as a skill, it must be practised. To develop your skills as an active listener, practise the following:

- *Attending to the speaker.* This means facing the speaker, not interrupting, and not doing something else like checking your email at the same time.
- *Asking for clarification.* This must be done by asking open-ended questions (*Can you explain*) rather than giving choices to the speaker that fit your preconceptions.
- *Summarizing.* Here you must paraphrase what the speaker has said, reflecting both the facts as you understand them and how the speaker feels about the situation.

It's surprising what you learn when you actually listen.

ORGANIZATIONAL SKILLS   The term *organizational skills* is one of those overused expressions that is applied in so many different ways, it risks losing all meaning. *Ask yourself: How often have I seen a job posting requiring strong organizational skills? What does it mean?* Here, we are simply using it to group together those management skills of decision making, documenting, and planning.

Decision Making: An entrepreneur can make hundreds of decisions in a day: which phone call to return next, whom to choose as a supplier, how much to charge for a new product, whether to ask for better credit terms, when to hire more help, which questions to ask in the interviews, what to have for lunch. Part of the decision-making skill is differentiating between administrative (routine or minor) decisions and strategic (unique or major) decisions. **Administrative decisions** must be made efficiently. Incorrect administrative decisions carry only minor consequences and can always be changed. **Strategic decisions,** on the other hand, carry high levels of risk and potentially permanent consequences. Nevertheless, they must be made.

Such important decisions are worthy of a more formal decision-making process using the following steps:

- Defining the issue.
- Gathering and analyzing relevant information.
- Listing and evaluating the possible alternatives.
- Selecting the best alternative based on the available evidence.

This sort of **evidence-based decision making** (as opposed to gut instinct) certainly has the advantage of making better decisions, on average. But it also provides a logical explanation

? Get Help 11.4

Toastmasters International is a non-profit organization that has helped many thousands of people develop public speaking skills cheaply and effectively. Through local clubs, business-like meetings are held where skills are practised in a non-threatening environment. Check the website (*www.toastmasters.org*) to find a local club.

✓ Test Yourself 11.7

True or False? The majority of people have apprehension about public speaking.

administrative decisions Routine, frequent, often minor decisions about the day-to-day operations of a business.

strategic decisions Broad, often one-time decisions that affect the long-term positioning of a business.

evidence-based decision making Choices based on logic and measured, documented information, as opposed to choices based on intuition.

✓ **Test Yourself 11.8**
True or False? An entrepreneur never has to explain or justify his or her decisions.

for decisions that can be given to customers, employees, suppliers, partners, or other involved parties. When you explain the logic for your decisions, it makes them more acceptable to others. It also gives other parties the opportunity to point out flaws in your logic or information, and it provides a chance to correct bad decisions. If you make decisions on instinct, or gut feeling, you cannot explain them. Those you work with will come to feel that your decisions are simply because *you're the boss* and that's the way you want it. Such an arrogant approach is unlikely to generate support.

Documenting: Documenting is the process and skill of creating written records, either on paper or electronically. The busier an entrepreneur becomes, the more important it is to stay organized and the more difficult it is to keep everything in your head: things like appointments, scheduling promises, quoted prices, new contact names, passwords, order specifications, and thousands of other bits of essential information. Recording all of these things in a precise, logical way is vital for two reasons:

1. It provides a retrievable text that can be referred to, copied to others, or even offered as evidence in a dispute.
2. The process of making and filing the document is what rehearses and strengthens the human memory. Ironically, this can make the document itself less necessary but not the process of making it.

Planning: Most of this textbook is about planning: planning for a business or planning for life as an entrepreneur. The start of this chapter outlines the changing focus of the entrepreneur from operational to strategic concerns. Similarly, as the business grows, the entrepreneur spends less time on operational planning and more on strategic. Regardless of the type of planning, the steps remain the same:

- Set goals or objectives.
- Assess the resources available (internal).
- Assess the environment (external).
- Set out the steps needed to reach the goals or objectives.

◇ **Get Help 11.5**
The Industry Canada Strategis website offers an email update service that provides excellent background information on the business climate including economic conditions, legislative changes, and many industry reports. You can sign up for the service on the Strategis home page: *www.strategis.ic.gc.ca*.

Developing better planning skills as an entrepreneur can mean better habits for staying informed. Strategic planning requires information about things that could affect the future of a business. *Ask yourself: How can a busy entrepreneur stay informed about the business environment?* Some methods are:

- Using bookmarks on your web browser and regularly checking sites of organizations and publications relevant to your industry and location.
- Signing up for email newsletter and bulletin services for your industry.
- Meeting regularly with key advisers such as your accountant.
- Joining industry associations and attending occasional conferences.
- Reading general news magazines such as *Maclean's* or *Time* for trend information.

Head Start Exercise

11.2 Rank your communication skills of writing, presenting, and listening from strongest to weakest. Identify specific problems that you would like to improve. Do the same for your skills delegating, planning, and decision making. ($\frac{2}{3}$ page maximum.)

CRISIS MANAGEMENT SKILLS   Imagine:

- Your three most valuable employees all quit on the same day to go to your direct competitor.
- Your sprinkler system failed during an electrical fire in your offices. Everything is burned to the ground.
- Rampaging political protesters trashed your store after police tried to break up a violent demonstration. Your insurance company refuses to pay, saying that this was an act of insurrection and not covered by your policy.

Each of these is a crisis that could mean the end of your business. Entrepreneurs will face many crises throughout their careers (not necessarily as serious as these) and must develop some skill in dealing with them. Crisis management is essentially about three things: planning, response, and recovery.

Crisis Planning: *Ask yourself: If I don't know what the crisis will be, how can I prepare for it?* For a start, you can outline in writing the approach you and your company will take during any crisis. This could include the values and priorities you will conduct yourselves by. You can also identify a crisis team, deciding who will provide legal advice, who will contact employees, and who will handle any media releases or interviews. A crisis contingency fund can be created and employees can be trained in first aid, CPR, and fire response. Finally, you can plan for a crisis by studying how others have handled crises: the sorts of mistakes they have made and the things they have done well.

Crisis Response: Responding to a crisis usually means making a lot of important decisions (like the strategic decisions above) but making them quickly (like the routine decisions above). So you can still follow an *evidence-based decision making* process, but recognize that there will be little time to analyze information or evaluate alternatives. It will be a best-guess situation, based on available information, predetermined principles, and the hope of buying time for making better long-term decisions. History has shown that during a crisis, best practices include:

- Honesty and openness in providing information to employees, customers, the public, or any other stakeholders in the situation.
- Documenting decisions to show that they are best guesses based on available information.
- Asking for help from appropriate sources.
- Always putting human health and security at the top of your priority list.

Crisis Recovery: The effectiveness of the recovery from a crisis depends largely on the planning and response phases. But a well-handled crisis can be seen as an opportunity for growth. Returning to the examples above, the ship-jumping employees could be giving you an opening to replace them with better workers who are not part of a clique. The electrical fire will get you out of your lease and could present the chance to move to better premises. The political protest and vandalized store might have won you media exposure that you could never afford to buy, and the publicity could well embarrass the insurance company into waiving the insurrection clause. These sorts of outcomes result from approaching the crises as an opportunity for change.

Head Start Exercise

11.3 Describe the most significant business or personal crisis you have faced and identify any ways that you could have handled it better ($\frac{1}{2}$ page maximum).

✓ **Test Yourself 11.9**
True or False? Minor administrative decisions should not involve a formal decision-making process.

✓ **Test Yourself 11.10**
True or False? As a business grows, the entrepreneur spends an increasing amount of time dealing with operational issues.

◇ **Get Help 11.6**
There are several recent, interesting books on how to handle a business crisis, including one from the Harvard Business Essentials Series: *Crisis Management— Master the Skills to Prevent Disasters.*

✓ **Test Yourself 11.11**
True or False? By definition, it is impossible to plan for a crisis.

◇ **Get Help 11.7**
Business and management associations frequently sponsor two- and three-day intensive seminars in specific skills such as business writing or delegating. Also, check with the continuing education department of your local community college for short courses or seminars on management skills.

How Will I Grow Personally?

ENTREPRENEURSHIP AND ETHICS   As you become a more successful entrepreneur, your power to affect others—for better or for worse—becomes greater. With this influence also comes greater responsibility for leadership in ethical issues. *Ask yourself: What will happen when I am faced with a choice between making more profit and doing the morally right thing?*

Everyone has some sense of *right* and *wrong*. And, not surprisingly, your beliefs about right and wrong, on most issues, are pretty similar to the beliefs held by your parents, friends, and teachers. Your values don't stand in isolation from each other, but rather tend to be part of a system of beliefs that you share with those closest to you. This is what we mean by **morality.**

morality A system of beliefs about right and wrong.

Ask yourself: Is it morally wrong to kill another human being? Is it morally wrong to lie? For most of us, after we give it some thought, the answer to these questions is: *it depends on the situation.* Killing to save your own life may be a moral necessity; lying when your aging aunt asks how you like her new outfit, a simple kindness. So morality is *situational.* It can also change over time. *Ask yourself: Is it morally wrong to operate a business?* For much of the last century in Eastern Europe, not only would it have been morally wrong, but it also would have been illegal to practise entrepreneurship. Today, throughout this area, entrepreneurship is legal and even admired. Morality can change over time.

ethics Professional rules of conduct (common usage).

Ask yourself: Do the words "ethics" and "morality" mean the same thing? Most dictionaries will tell you that **ethics** means *the branch of philosophy that studies morality.* But most dictionaries tend to be pretty conservative. And, just as morality changes over time, the meaning of words tends to change. These days, the word *ethics* is widely used to mean *professional rules of conduct.* In this sense, we commonly talk about things like *legal* ethics, *medical* ethics, *academic* ethics, and, of course, *business* ethics. So, even though they are closely connected, *morality* and *ethics* do have different meanings. It's possible, even, to have a conflict between the two. For example, a doctor may consider it morally acceptable to end the life of a suffering terminal patient. In many jurisdictions, however, the medical society would brand this as unethical (as well as illegal). A lawyer might find it morally repugnant to help a murderer escape justice, while at the same time being ethically bound to give the best possible defence to a guilty client.

Business ethics are rules to protect those whom you, as an entrepreneur, have the power to harm, including:
- *Customers* who could be harmed by misleading information or outright lies to get them to buy; by unfulfilled contracts; or by damaged goods.
- *Suppliers* who could be victim to late payments or cancellation of orders.
- *Employees* who could suffer from false promises of future opportunity, harassment, or deficient pay.
- *Competitors* who could be harmed by lies or unfair pricing practices. (*Note:* any harm to your competitors from your superior services, products, or prices is certainly *not* unethical).
- *The community* as a whole, which could suffer from unpaid taxes, lax environmental practices, or failure to follow safety regulations.

✓ **Test Yourself 11.12**
True or False? The word *ethics* is commonly used to mean "professional rules of conduct."

When rules of conduct for a particular group are written into a document, this is known as a *code of ethics*. Many professional organizations and business associations have codes of ethics, which their members promise to abide by. Violation of the code can result in expulsion from the organization or other sanctions. Most of Canada's larger cities have Better Business Bureaus (BBBs), which keep lists of complaints made against businesses in the community. Businesses that are members of the bureau agree to abide by the bureau's code of ethics and are permitted to advertise themselves as BBB members.

Fair Trade/Ethical Trade: Many small firms buy, sell, or use products from abroad, and entrepreneurs are increasingly making supplier choices based on factors that go beyond issues of price, quality, and reliability.

The **fair trade** movement evolved in response to the exploitation of agricultural labourers and small producers in developing countries. There are many commodities grown in poor countries that are sold in Canada and provide excellent profits for foreign exporters as well as Canadian importers, processors, distributors, and retailers. But all too often the small coffee farmer or tea plantation worker is surviving at a subsistence level, sometimes in near slave-labour conditions. Canadian practitioners of fair trade try to ensure that producers of agricultural products get some fair return for the costs of producing their crops.

Over the years, the fair trade movement has set off concerns about broader ethical issues in international trade. This has coincided with the movement of agricultural workers in developing nations from the land, where they can no longer produce competitively, into urban areas where they become a source of cheap labour for manufacturers. Many developing nations, including some with clear labour legislation, have such high levels of corruption that existing standards are poorly enforced and easy to circumvent. *Ask yourself: Were any of the clothes I'm wearing today made by underpaid, abused, or child labourers?* Chances are you don't know, but if you did, it might well make a difference in your choice of products. Helping you to know is one of the goals of the **ethical trade** movement. These organizations are interested in a wide range of human rights, health, and labour conditions for foreign workers. The idea behind the movement is for Western businesses to ensure that foreign suppliers, partners, and contractors adhere to some set of minimum labour standards for their employees. Some day, labelling and certification will be able to assure Western consumers that their product choices have been made by people working under reasonable conditions.

The Environment: When it comes to environmental issues, the International Organization for Standardization has gone a step beyond a code of ethics by certifying businesses that meet certain standards in environmental practices that far exceed most legal requirements. This is the ISO 14000 certification. The ISO certification process can be complex and expensive, involving the training of employees and the monitoring of company practices. But many participants hope to see at least some cost savings by introducing more environmentally friendly practices into their businesses. As well, they, hope to benefit by presenting the image of a **green business**, making the firm more appealing to customers.

? Get Help 11.8
For links to your local branch of the Better Business Bureau, go through the Canadian Council of Better Business Bureaus at *www.canadiancouncilbbb.ca*.

fair trade A movement of Western commodity processors and distributors to ensure that small producers in the developing world are adequately paid for their products.

✓ Test Yourself 11.13
True or False? The fair trade movement is broader in scope than the ethical trade movement.

ethical trade A movement of Western retail and consumer groups to ensure that manufacturing labourers in developing countries have healthy and safe working conditions.

? Get Help 11.9
For more information about fair trade, start with the website of the U.S.-based Fair Trade Federation. (*www.fairtradefederation.org*). The Ethical Trading Initiative offers an excellent U.K. site on ethical trade (*www.ethicaltrade.org*).

? Get Help 11.10
Learn more about ISO 14000 at *www.iso.org/iso/en/iso9000-14000/*. Also, the consulting service of the Business Development Bank of Canada has a program to manage a firm's ISO 14000 certification. Contact the BDC at 1-888-463-6232 for more information.

green business A company that has implemented environment-friendly practices throughout its operations.

A final word about ethics—Some entrepreneurs think of ethical behaviour as enlightened self-interest: doing the right thing *because it's good for business.* But that sort of reasoning really means doing things a certain way because it's all you can reasonably get away with. By contrast, true ethical behaviour means observing certain rules of conduct simply because *it's the right thing to do!*

✓ **Test Yourself 11.14**
True or False? A *green business* is a company that practises both fair trade and ethical trade.

Head Start Exercise

11.4 Identify several unethical practices your company could likely get away with. Identify who would be hurt by these practices. ($\frac{1}{3}$ page maximum.)

COMMUNITY INVOLVEMENT   Closely associated with the issue of ethics is the entrepreneur's influence in and responsibility to the community. *Ask yourself: What is my community?* Admittedly, you can belong to many different communities: the business community as a whole, the community of your own industry, the neighbourhood where you do business, the neighbourhood where you live, your municipality, country, and

---

SMALL BUSINESS PROFILE 11.1
Bean North

Bean North is a successful, very small coffee roasting company, located in the Yukon's beautiful, forested Takhini Valley. Michael King started this "fair trade" business in 1997, buying organically grown and certified coffee beans from farmer co-operatives all over the world. The business was started to help ensure the ethical treatment of small coffee growers in developing countries. Bean North holds membership in Cooperative Coffees Inc., an organization whose 21 members across North America establish direct relationships with the small coffee producers that they buy from.

This growing business sells about half of its product to upscale cafés throughout North America and Europe, and the rest to individuals via the Internet. King's website (**www.beannorth.com**) devotes more space to promoting fair trade than it does to promoting his own coffee. As well, the site has links related to environmental issues and offers Bean North's own online newsletter: *Coffee & You.* This entertaining and informative publication educates the reader about coffee and its production. It also journals the trips taken by Michael King (and family) to the coffee-producing areas that he buys from, and it includes descriptions of the lives, concerns, and opinions of the producers.

But fair trade is not the only agenda for Bean North. The company must make a profit. It does so by providing extremely high-quality products to carefully targeted consumers who tend to be socially, environmentally, and health conscious. Even though it is on a small scale, research, product development, and quality control are critical to this business.

So what could possibly be the advantage of roasting coffee in the Yukon? According to Michael, the secret in roasting coffee beans is that once they are roasted to the desired degree, they must be cooled as quickly as possible. For some roasters, that can mean expensive cooling and ventilation equipment. "In the Yukon," he says, "it usually means just opening the window." A significant advantage.

so on. As you become recognized for success as an entrepreneur, each of these communities will increasingly turn to you looking for involvement, leadership, and financial support.

It's possible for successful small firms to be approached by others in the same industry (complementary businesses or even competitors) with a view to forming strategic alliances. These are generally informal partnerships for achieving some goal that the involved firms could not accomplish on their own. For example, imagine you are running a three-person translation service that specializes in translating between English and several African languages. Perhaps the Canadian International Development Agency is requesting bids on a project to develop training materials for schools in Southern Africa. The project would involve preparing about 12 textbooks, each in 5 languages: a project far too large for your small firm to handle. But let's say your direct competitor (a similar-sized firm doing similar translations) approaches you to form a consortium—along with a small publisher of training materials—to bid on the project. Together you could handle it, each taking a share of the revenue based on the work you do. Despite the dangers of working so closely with your competitor, this kind of co-operation within your business community can be profitable.

There are many service organizations that seek the skills of experienced entrepreneurs to help them achieve their community and philanthropic goals. One of the great advantages of financial success is the ability to help others through charities, sponsorships, and service clubs. Such activities can provide you with a rich social life. Interestingly, self-employed Canadians give significantly more hours to volunteer organizations than employees do, even though the entrepreneurs have fewer non-work hours to spare.[4]

The ultimate community involvement, of course, is to run for political office. Canadian entrepreneurs are routinely elected to offices at all levels of government. Getting elected may require that an entrepreneur put the business in trust and have no involvement with its operations during the term of office. These rules are intended to avoid a conflict of interest while a politician makes decisions on behalf of the community. This necessity of being divorced from the business rules out the option of running for office for many business owners.

Head Start Exercise

11.5 List several ways in which you could be more involved with your community. What would be the benefits? ($\frac{1}{3}$ page maximum.)

✓ **Test Yourself 11.15**
True or False? Because they are so busy, entrepreneurs tend to give fewer volunteer hours than employees do.

TIME MANAGEMENT   The topic of *time management* could easily be seen as an organizational management skill rather than a personal life skill because it is so important to use your work time effectively. The argument for putting the topic here is that your life is merely a finite amount of time. What you make of your life is how you use that time. Time management issues apply to both business and personal time equally. In business, new entrepreneurs commonly identify their biggest problem as "insufficient time to get everything done." The problem, of course, is not a lack of time, but rather how the available time is being spent, or perhaps wasted. *Ask yourself: As a business owner, how should I be spending my time?*

Many of the "time-saving" software tools used in business are systems that keep you informed about what's going on in your company, and they tell you whether or not your plans are on track. Nowadays, it's relatively easy for firms to produce up-to-the-minute income statements, and detailed reports on sales, inventory, receivables, customer complaints, employee performance, and so on. But the reports you can produce only have value if they are used. The issue is not one of information availability, but rather one of personal time management. As a busy entrepreneur, it's all too easy to let your involvement with the work override your responsibility as manager. It's too easy to put those reports to the side until you "have more *time* to look at them": time that may never come. It is necessary, therefore, to set aside a specific, regular period to review marketing, operational, and financial information. Even if you are the only person in the business and know everything that's going on, you still need to formally set aside time for this process. This way you will know whether your business is on track, whether it is achieving the long-term goals and short-term objectives you have set.

The steps to getting control of your time are to:
• Set goals and objectives.
• Analyze time use to identify time wasters (Figure 11.3).
• Differentiate between things that are *important* and those that are *urgent* (Figure 11.4).
• Plan your time to handle urgent things first, but to devote more time to important issues.

It sounds simple, but time management is a skill and it takes practice to become good at it. Finally, a warning about *multi-tasking*, an approach that some people see as the quick-fix for time management. It is not really possible, so far, to train the human mind to focus on two separate tasks at the same time. What really happens is that we can toggle back and forth between tasks at a very high rate, never giving our full attention to either of them because we also have to think about the toggling process. Sure, it's possible to eat soup and read at the same time, but *Ask yourself: What are the chances of spilling the soup?* Busy entrepreneurs may take pride in the fact that they can handle important phone calls while driving to work, but the evidence is piling up that using a cell phone while driving is pretty similar to driving drunk. Organization of time, not multi-tasking, is the key to using time more productively.

✓ **Test Yourself 11.16**

True or False? Good time management means handling the important things first.

Head Start Exercise

11.6 Briefly outline your own method (paper-based and/or electronic) for tracking and analyzing how you spend your working time ($\frac{1}{3}$ page maximum).

LIFESTYLE MANAGEMENT   The tabloid media love to sensationalize the lives of successful people, often giving the impression that these lives are filled with failed relationships, illness, addictions, eating disorders, and despair. But, *Ask yourself: How could people coping with all these problems find the time to build thriving careers and businesses?* If you look at successful entrepreneurs you may know, you will probably see that their lives tend to

	DAILY ACTIVITY LOG	

Figure 11.3

Date: Monday, May 4

Time Start	Time End	Activity	Time Spent (hr)
0800	0847	answer emails	0.3
0847	0855	check on Bob (new-hire shipper)	0.3
0855	0910	answer call from Clockman (customer) confirming shipped	0.3
0910	0920	conversation with Bob re: his personal problems	0.3
0920	0925	start trademark application	0.1
0925	0931	phone call from Peters (customer) changing appointment	0.1
0931	0945	restart trademark application	0.2
0945	1005	call from bookkeeper calling in sick; hear medical issues	0.3
1005	1022	work on trademark application	0.3
1022	1030	call from Peters reinstating appointment	0.1
1030	1044	call Ellen (salesperson): remind about Peters lunch. Hear about problems with her new house	0.2
1044	1048	redirect phone call to sales	0.1
1048	1110	call Dunoon (supplier): place new order	0.4
1110	1130	walk order copy to receiving, check on warehouse, go to unit next door to get them to move delivery truck blocking our access	0.3
1130	1140	see Katy (receptionist/clerk): delegate trademark app.	0.2
1140	1145	see Karen: explain will go separately to Peters lunch	0.3
1145	1155	brief her on customer background	0.3
1155	1417	travel to Peters lunch and meeting	2.4
1417	1430	meet with Ellen in parking lot re: Peters order: explain to her method to write it up	0.2
1430	1505	travel back from meeting	0.6
1505	1515	discuss/supervise Katy on trademark app.	0.3
1515	1605	return customer calls	0.8
1605	1612	redirect phone calls	0.3
1612	1640	read/answer emails (30% junk or misdirected)	0.3
1640	1645	check with Katy on trademark application	0.3
1645	1705	discuss Katy's problems with daughter's school	0.3
1705	1735	complete payroll work for bookkeeper (ill)	0.5
1735	1740	order pizza	0.1
1740	1805	call home	0.4
1805	1810	delete irrelevant (junk) emails	0.1
1810	1905	plan sales meeting and new brochure	0.9
1905	1910	lock up	0.1

Figure 11.4	**WEEKLY WORK TIME ANALYSIS**				
Activity Category	**Activity Priority**	**Hours Spent**	**% of Work Week**	**Goal %**	**Goal hrs/wk**
Reading/analyzing internal reports	1	0.5	0.8	8.0	4
Reading/researching market information	1	0.1	0.2	2.0	1
Strategic planning	1	0.5	0.8	8.0	4
Operational planning	2	3.0	4.5	8.0	4
Visiting customers (including travel)	2	3.5	5.3	12.0	6
Customer phone calls	2	8.5	12.8	18.0	9
Scheduled staff meetings	2	1.3	2.0	10.0	5
Miscellaneous troubleshooting	3	3.2	5.0	5.0	2.5
Supplier phone calls	3	6.4	9.6	5.0	2.5
Administrative records	3	4.0	6.0	2.0	1
Listening to employee problems	3	5.0	7.5	4.0	2
Supervising/training employees	3	8.2	12.3	8.0	4
Answering mail/email	4	7.5	11.3	6.0	3
Miscellaneous personal (calls, breaks)	4	9.1	13.8	4.0	2
Reading junk mail/junk email	–	3.5	5.6	0	0
Answering misdirected phone calls	–	2.1	3.1	0	0
Total		66.4			50.0

be a little more stable, healthy, and planned than most. *Ask yourself: Does being a successful entrepreneur lead to a healthy lifestyle? Or, does the healthy lifestyle improve the chances of business success?* Perhaps the set of skills needed to build and manage a business are those same skills that help create a satisfying, healthy lifestyle? Keep in mind, though, that success as an entrepreneur is measured in profit. And financial success is relatively unimportant in determining overall happiness or quality of life.[5] More important are issues of personal relationships and health and fitness.

Personal Relationships: Various studies have identified family life and friendships as the first and second most important factors for a sense of well-being.[6] For some entrepreneurs there is no compartmentalization of work life, family life, and social life, since family members work in the businesses and those considered friends tend to be customers, suppliers, employees, partners, and so on. But even for those with strict lines between these groups, each set of relationships has the potential to affect the others.

Over the past decade or so, a great deal has been written about the importance of striking a healthy balance between work life and home life. And since women in Canada today still carry a greater share of responsibility for the home and family, women entrepreneurs are more concerned about striking this balance. One study of female entrepreneurs in Illinois and California found a strong relationship between business success and satisfaction with home life and, conversely, trouble in one area likely meant dissatisfaction in the other.[7] The study does not compare results for male entrepreneurs, which may well be similar, nor does it offer solutions for striking a balance between home and business demands. Nevertheless, it is valuable for entrepreneurs to be conscious of the interaction between home and business relationships.

The primary personal relationship, of course, is with a spouse. One interesting Australian study offers evidence that those with the greatest life satisfaction are people in long-term formal marriages[8] (not just cohabitation). The reasons for this are not known, although the issues of commitment and a sense of security are likely involved. Some keys to healthy personal relationships are:

- actively listening to the other party (see "Communication Skills" above)
- openly expressing your own feelings and concerns
- taking the other party's concerns seriously
- avoiding blame, criticism, or name-calling
- a commitment to fairness and sharing.

✓ **Test Yourself 11.17**
True or False? Research shows a strong relationship between wealth and ultimate happiness.

Success in relationships with family and friends, like success in anything else, takes time and effort.

Health and Fitness: **Health** and **fitness** are not the same thing. Health is about coping with disease processes. Fitness is about the body's strength, endurance flexibility, and fat content. Health and fitness are closely connected but it is possible to have one without the other. For example, you could be totally healthy (no diseases, no injuries, not even a hint of a cold) and, at the same time, totally unfit (40 kilograms overweight and not able to do a single push-up or sit-up). Or conversely you could be physically fit (trim and able to run a kilometre in four minutes) but taking daily medication to control a potentially fatal heart disorder: fit, but not healthy.

health The absence of or control over disease processes.

fitness The body's ability to cope with stress; often indicated by strength, flexibility, endurance, heart rate, and proportion of fat.

In many countries, unlike Canada, personal health care decisions are largely economic in nature. With our medicare system, however, many decisions, such as whether to consult with your doctor, are mere personal preferences. So the entrepreneur has few excuses for not taking advantage of every option for preventive health care. *Ask yourself: Is "too busy running a business" a valid reason for avoiding a check-up?* It's a poor excuse when you realize that an investment in your own health and the health of your employees can pay off on your bottom line.

Obesity can be seen as both a *health* and a *fitness* issue. Much of the disease in the developed world is related to diet and exercise (the lack of it). As a group, we're too fat and we worry about it. Just look at the size of the weight-loss industry. There are hundreds of programs, supplements, drugs, and diets for sale and many of them work quite effectively. But the problem for most busy people is not losing weight, it's keeping it off. Success rates for long-term weight maintenance are becoming better as the research in this area expands. It seems that formerly obese people who maintain a normal weight (regardless of how they lost the weight) have several habits in common.[9] They generally tend to:

- Control their diets primarily for fat (as opposed to carbohydrates or calories).
- Eat regularly, including breakfast.

- Get at least one hour of physical activity per day. (It doesn't have to be all at once, and includes walking.)

Physically fit entrepreneurs are more likely to achieve their business and personal goals.[10] In fact, small business owners with higher cardiovascular fitness (runners) on average have higher sales.[11] Again, this is an issue where the causality cannot be demonstrated: it is possible that having higher sales gives you more time to get physically fit. But in all likelihood it is the fitness that allows you to function better as an entrepreneur. *Ask yourself: How can you know for sure if fitness will improve your business performance?* Go and get in shape then see how you feel and how you perform in all aspects of your life. When just starting on a physical fitness program, tips to remember include:

- Start slowly. Always run a much shorter distance or lift much less weight than you think you're capable of at the beginning. This will help avoid injury or exhaustion and let you stick with the program.
- Measure progress. Fitness and strength levels, especially at the beginning of a program, increase quickly. It is important to see these increases for encouragement.
- Build slowly and regularly. Set realistic goals for improvement and have a regular scheduled time for your activity.
- After each session, when you're feeling good from the **endorphin effect** of exercise, notice your sense of pride and mentally reward yourself for having stuck to your program.

Stress: There is no compelling evidence that entrepreneurs are any more, or any less, stressed than employees;[12] however, environmental stress is a factor in everyone's life. And the health issue is less about your stressors and more about how you deal with them. Commonly used techniques for dealing with life stress include:

- *Becoming aware of your physical self.* This often involves short time-outs where you run through your five senses, making yourself conscious of what you're seeing, touching, smelling, tasting, and hearing.
- *Controlling your breathing.* Here you must replace the short panting breaths of the stressed individual with the deep, slow breaths of relaxation.
- *Relaxing your muscles.* This is accomplished by repeatedly tightening and releasing groups of muscles progressively throughout the body.
- *Meditating.* No big mystical trick, this simply means focusing on a simple word or object in a way that will temporarily clear your mind of nagging worries.

These techniques work, but they require practice to the point where they become ingrained habits.

Head Start Exercise

11.7 Using specific examples, identify which of the following areas you are best at: maintaining strong personal relationships; managing your health; maintaining physical fitness; eating a healthy diet; and coping with stress. Again, using examples, identify your problem areas. ($\frac{1}{2}$ page maximum.)

endorphin effect The euphoric feeling produced by vigorous exercise that results from particular hormones (endorphins) being released in the brain.

? Get Help 11.11
Alberta's Steadward Centre for Personal & Physical Achievement offers a site with excellent tips for fitness training: ***www.steadward centre.org.***

? Get Help 11.12
The Public Health Agency of Canada offers an excellent website with articles on active living, diet, safety, sexuality, violence, and workplace safety. This Canadian Health Network website can be found at ***www.canadian-health-network.ca.***

✓ Test Yourself 11.18
True or False? It is possible to be fit and unhealthy or to be healthy and unfit.

How Can I Gain Personal Financial Security?

Students or young entrepreneurs in their twenties have little interest in discussing, reading, or thinking about retirement, although most would admit that retiring wealthy or at least well-to-do is among their expectations. Ironically, the most likely way that you are going to retire wealthy is by thinking about it and making plans while you are young. Building wealth or equity is the same process either inside or outside a business. It requires generating income (through an active business or investments) and managing expenses so that there is a surplus (profit) available to reinvest. In this process, one of the most important expenses to manage is your taxes.

MINIMIZING TAXES   Tax evasion is an illegal activity. It is the false reporting of tax information in order to avoid paying taxes owed. Don't do it. You could end up being prosecuted in criminal court. **Tax avoidance**, on the other hand, is something most accountants and entrepreneurs would simply see as good business. It means adopting business practices that legally take advantage of the tax rules in order to pay as little taxes as possible. Unfortunately, these issues are not nearly as simple as they sound. Part of the problem is that Canada's tax collector, the Canada Revenue Agency, uses the term *tax avoidance* somewhat differently from mainstream use. The CRA uses it to describe tax practices that are, at the very least, unethical:

> *Tax avoidance* results when actions are taken to minimize tax, while within the letter of the law, those actions contravene the object and spirit of the law.[13]

Ask yourself: Does this mean I could end up in a dispute with CRA, or even in court, by using a tax practice that is within the letter of the law? The answer, of course, is yes, largely because tax law is so complicated and has so many grey areas. This is why it is prudent to get tax advice from an experienced professional accountant, someone who is up-to-date on CRA rulings and the outcomes of taxation court cases.

Effective and ethical tax avoidance usually results from good planning. Sitting down with an accountant to do tax planning for the upcoming year is an excellent investment of your time and money. Here are some examples of techniques for minimizing taxes:

Income Sharing: In the area of income tax, Canada has what's known as a **progressive tax rate** as opposed to a **flat tax rate**. This means that those with higher incomes not only pay more taxes, but also are taxed at a higher percentage rate. Since spouses and children of entrepreneurs often help out in a family business, it is a good idea to formally pay them for this assistance, especially if they will be taxed at a lower rate than the entrepreneur would. In fact, at the time of writing, the first $8,148 of income for Canadians is tax exempt, with plans in the current budget for the basic personal exemption to eventually increase to $10,000.[14] So a child who provides unpaid help to the business but receives an allowance paid out of household funds could be costing the entrepreneur thousands of dollars in unnecessary taxes.

Time Income and Expenses: Knowing the tax rules and your own financial position can have great benefits when you are in business for yourself. In sole proprietorships and general partnerships, business and personal finances follow the same rules, so there are fewer opportunities

tax evasion False reporting of tax information in an attempt to avoid paying taxes legally owed.

tax avoidance Minimizing the amount of taxes an individual or business pays by careful planning and the use of exemptions, deductions, and tax shelters.

progressive tax rate A tax system where as incomes increase, the percentage of tax paid increases up to some maximum tax rate.

flat tax rate A system where all income is taxed at the same percentage rate, regardless of the amount of income an individual has.

to use the tax system to full advantage. However, options are still available. For example, you might be a sole proprietor of a firm supplying portable toilets to outdoor events. Your year-end is December 31, and let's say it is near the end of a year that has been particularly profitable for you. This means that you will be paying tax at a higher rate. Your last major event of the year is for a festival running through the holidays at the end of December and into the New Year. Normally you would receive a large portion of your payment in December, but this year, by contracting for payment in early January, you can reduce your income and your tax rate for the current year. As well, your company may have an advertising program planned for February that requires several thousand flyers to be printed. By getting the printing done and paying for it in December, you are increasing your expenses and therefore reducing your profit and taxes for the current year.

Incorporation: Once a business is profitable and growing, incorporation can offer some big tax saving opportunities. There are differences in the tax rules from year to year and from province to province. But overall, the corporate tax rate is significantly lower than the personal income tax rate. This means that if your business was making a large profit and you intended to retain much of the profit in the business to help it grow, it would be better to have the profit taxed at the lower corporate rate, rather than the personal rate that you would pay as a sole proprietorship or partnership.

When your corporation makes a profit, taxes are paid on the profit at the corporate rate. If you then decide to pay the profit out to yourself in the form of a dividend, you must pay personal income tax on that dividend, so it's true that you could end up paying tax on the same profit twice. Nevertheless, with dividend tax reductions and some flexibility to juggle how you pay yourself (salary, bonuses, dividends), incorporation is usually, though not always, the lower tax bet.

Head Start Exercise

11.8 Make a list of tax-saving opportunities that apply to you and your company. Identify those that you currently use. ($\frac{1}{2}$ page maximum.)

Savings and Investments: As you start to accumulate some personal wealth, the question becomes what to do with it. Reinvesting it in your own business is great during periods when the business requires capital for growth but this also means putting all of your financial eggs in the one basket. Long-term personal financial security is more likely to come from spreading the risk across a variety of investments. And your choice in investments will probably be influenced by the tax laws. This is because the government uses tax laws to implement financial policies. For example, government economists know that Canada's growing population of seniors cannot all rely on government programs for support in old age. As a result, tax incentives are given to Canadians who save and invest for their own senior years. A portion of personal income (up to a set maximum) that is invested in a Registered Retirement Savings Plan (**RRSP**) is tax-free. Furthermore, the investment income produced by the RRSP remains untaxed within the plan. The money is not taxed until individuals remove it from the plan, presumably when they are retired, making less money and therefore paying a lower tax rate than when they earned the money.

RRSP (Registered Retirement Savings Plan) A federal government program that allows tax deferral or avoidance on a portion of the money individuals save for retirement on behalf of themselves or their life partners.

Younger entrepreneurs are likely to see RRSPs as something they intend to invest in *sometime in the future.* But you don't necessarily have to wait until retirement to reap some of the benefits of these programs. For example, some untaxed income can be borrowed from your RRSP for the specific purposes of buying your first home or for going back to school. The Home Buyers' Plan (**HBP**) lets you borrow up to $20,000 from your RRSP to buy or build a home and repay the amount over a 20-year period. That means that life partners buying their first home together could use up to $40,000 of untaxed income for this purpose. Business owners or employees wishing to go back to college or university can also borrow RRSP money under the Lifelong Learning Plan (**LLP**). This means you could withdraw up to $20,000 (a maximum of $10,000 in any one year) for a qualifying program and pay the money back over a 10-year period. After repaying the money, the program can be used again and it can also be used for the education of a life partner. For example, you may continue running your business while your spouse goes to college to study accounting.

You wouldn't think of running a business without a detailed record of your business expenses. *Ask yourself: Do I know where almost every penny of my personal money goes?* Just like managing time, the first step in managing money is finding out where you spend it. This can be as simple as writing down every expenditure in a notebook and then grouping your expenses into categories. Seeing how you spend your money makes it easier to plan a better way for spending. This plan is called a **budget**, and sticking to it is the first rule of personal financial management. Other tips include:

- *Negotiate prices on all consumer items and services.* Asking for a discount is not impolite and frequently pays off.
- *Control interest expenses.* Avoid carrying credit card balances that incur high-rate interest expenses. Don't allow bills to become overdue, incurring interest and penalties.
- *Invest in your own home.* This asset appreciates, but you pay no capital gain when you sell it. The interest you pay on a mortgage is not deductible, but you can use your equity as security when you borrow for investments where the interest is deductible.
- *Spread your investment risks.* As you build a personal portfolio of investments, it is wise to vary the type of investment as well as the investment sector. When one area of the economy is in trouble, another may be buoyant.

Head Start Exercise

11.9 Explain any systems you use or will use to keep track of how you personally spend money. Create a realistic monthly budget for your personal and household expenses. (1 page maximum.)

Ask yourself: Should I use a financial planner? The decision on whether to use a **financial planner** depends on your own knowledge of investment tools and tax issues as well as the clarity of your financial goals. There are many people who designate themselves as financial planners, with a range of educational backgrounds, certifications, and affiliations. There are over 40 different designations that can promote themselves as qualified financial planners in Canada. Before approaching one, it's a good idea to hit the library or bookstore so you will have some background on what financial planners do and how they are compensated.

HBP (Home Buyers' Plan) A federal government program that allows first-time buyers to withdraw money from their RRSPs to buy or build a home.

LLP (Lifelong Learning Plan) A federal government program that allows individuals to withdraw money from their RRSPs for continuing education or retraining.

✓ **Test Yourself 11.19**
True or False? Other than for certain special exceptions, income tax must be paid on money withdrawn from an RRSP.

budget A plan for how money will be disbursed.

? **Get Help 11.13**
Go to the Canada Revenue Agency website at ***www.cra.gc.ca*** and under the *Individual* column, click on *RRSP*. The page that comes up will give you choices for information on RRSPs, HBPs, and LLPs. Banks and other financial institutions offer brochures and website information on their particular RRSP plans and options.

? **Get Help 11.14**
Self-Counsel Press publishes a *Personal Budgeting Kit* by Sylvia S. Lim. The kit includes a booklet and CD with worksheets for tracking spending and budgeting for financial goals.

financial planner Someone holding one of a great variety of designations, usually working on commission, helping individuals to build personal investment portfolios of mutual funds and other investment instruments.

Get Help 11.15
To see a list of acronyms and
designations for Canadian financial
planners, go to the site of the
Financial Planners Standards
Council, which promotes its own
CFP designation (*www.cfp-ca.org*)
and search for Acronyms and
Designations.

Test Yourself 11.20
True or False? The capital gain on
an owner-occupied family home in
Canada is tax-free when the home
is sold.

Test Yourself 11.21
True or False? There is a single,
national certification process that
allows someone to call themselves
a *Qualified Financial Planner* in
Canada.

insolvent The condition of an individual or company that does not
have sufficient assets or income in
order to pay the debts that are due.

bankrupt The state, declared by a
court, of an insolvent individual or
company whereby the assets of the
bankrupt person or firm are taken
over by a trustee for distribution to
creditors.

proposal to creditors A formal
attempt to avoid bankruptcy by
having creditors agree to accept a
portion of debt as settlement in full.

Test Yourself 11.22
True or False? The majority of
financial planners work on commission rather than an hourly
fee-for-service basis.

Get Help 11.16
For information on dealing with a
personal or business financial crisis,
go to the website for the Office of
the Superintendent of Bankruptcy
Canada (*osb-bsf.ic.gc.ca*) and
click on *Debtors*.

You are paying for the time of the financial planner, even though you may be doing this indi-rectly. Some financial planners work on a strict, hourly fee-for-service rate, but the vast majority make their money from commissions on the investment instruments they sell you. The commissions can be hidden from the investor, paid by the fund you are investing into, or by the financial institution that holds your investment. In some cases, a portion of manage-ment fees charged by an institution are paid to the adviser on an annual basis. Be cautious when planners describe their service as completely free, or are vague about how they will be compensated. Full disclosure is the first sign of an adviser in whom you can place trust. And by keeping in mind that different investments will pay different levels of commission to your planner, you will be reminding yourself that even the most ethical commissioned advisers can never be totally objective in the advice they give you. Take all the investment advice you can get, but final investment decisions are always yours.

HANDLING A FINANCIAL CRISIS   Sometimes a business or the entrepreneur personally can get into serious financial trouble. The sales for a business can unexpectedly dry up because of changes in market conditions. Or, as we saw in Chapter 5, a business may be profitable, but still get into a position where it does not have sufficient cash flow to be able to pay debts that are due. For an individual, easy access to unsecured personal credit and mismanagement of per-sonal finances can leave an entrepreneur in a position where the business cannot provide enough income to make the payments on personal debts. Whether it is the business or the entrepreneur personally that is in financial crisis, the options for resolving the crisis are pretty much the same.

INSOLVENCY AND BANKRUPTCY   An individual or a business that does not have suffi-cient assets or income to be able to pay its debts is said to be **insolvent**. This does not auto-matically make an individual or a corporation **bankrupt**; there are other options. These options are set out under the federal *Bankruptcy and Insolvency Act*. An insolvent individual (including a sole proprietor of a business), a partnership, or a corporation all have the option of making a **proposal to creditors** offering to pay the creditors some portion of what they are owed, while allowing the debtor to avoid many of the consequences of bankruptcy.

If you offer a formal proposal to your creditors, the creditors must suspend any legal action against you, and interest stops accumulating on the debt from the date that the proposal is filed. This gives you time to reorganize your personal or business finances. If a majority of your creditors agree to your proposal, then all will have to abide by it and you should be able to make manageable payments. This does not mean (despite the implication of many newspaper and Internet ads) that you can escape business or personal debts without any consequences. Your future ability to obtain credit will certainly be impaired, but it is preferable to settle insolvency by negotiating with your creditors than by going out of business. In the past decade, this method of dealing with insolvency for businesses has gone from about 5 percent of cases to about 20 percent, and the trend is upward.[15]

If your debts cannot be restructured or renegotiated there may be no alternative but to file for bankruptcy. Even if a small business is a corporation (theoretically protecting the personal assets of the owner), a business bankruptcy can also mean a personal bankruptcy for the entrepreneur. This is especially true in the early stages of the business where the entrepreneur has been required to personally guarantee debts of the business. But bankruptcy is not the end of the world, nor even the end of a business career. The ability of the bankrupt to secure credit is certainly impaired for up to several years, but the law is specifically designed to ensure that the punishment for financial failure does not last forever. In fact, there are many cases of former bankrupts rising to great financial success.

Get Help 11.17
For advice on dealing with a financial crisis, you should contact a licensed *trustee in bankruptcy.* See the phone book under "bankruptcies—trustees". Usually, initial consultations are free.

Head Start Exercise

11.10 Outline some possible scenarios that could create a business or personal financial crisis for you ($\frac{1}{2}$ page maximum).

Test Yourself 11.23
True or False? An insolvent business will ultimately be declared bankrupt.

What Are My Career Alternatives?

A **career** is really all the jobs held by an individual in his or her lifetime. So, very few people have had careers of pure entrepreneurship. Most Canadians have careers of pure employment. Many move at some point between entrepreneurship and employment. Some do both at the same time.

career An individual's entire history of jobs.

MULTIPLE ENTREPRENEURSHIP   For the past decade, a number of researchers have been classifying entrepreneurs into three different categories for their studies:
- *Novice.* **Novice entrepreneurs** are people who have started, bought, or inherited a single business of which they are still owner or part-owner. These entrepreneurs are classified as "novice," regardless of how long they have owned the business or their years of experience in the industry.
- *Serial.* **Serial entrepreneurs** are currently owners (or part-owners) of a single business and in the past have been owners or part-owners of at least one previous business (now sold or closed).
- *Portfolio.* **Portfolio entrepreneurs** currently own all or part of at least two and maybe more independent businesses. The firms may or may not be part of the same industry cluster or supply chain.

novice entrepreneurs Own all or part of a single business, which is the only firm they have ever had ownership in.

serial entrepreneurs Own all or part of a single business, but have been an owner of at least one other business in the past.

portfolio entrepreneurs Currently own all or part of at least two independent firms.

These categories can be seen as different entrepreneurial career paths, generally associated with different skills and aspirations of the entrepreneur. Serial and portfolio firms are often referred to together as **multiple entrepreneurship**. These firms tend to be characterized by higher growth, clearer goals, broader research, and more complex distribution chains.[16] Portfolio entrepreneurs tend to start out with more resources and produce the highest growth.[17] In some ways, these categories can be seen as levels or degrees of entrepreneurship, with portfolio as the highest degree. So, *Ask yourself: What category of entrepreneurship do I aspire to?*

multiple entrepreneurship A broad category of entrepreneurs including both those who have owned previous businesses and those who own two or more firms.

If you envision yourself in a specific role, in a very specific company (for example owning a particular antique store in your home town or as a potter in your ceramics studio) chances are the single business approach of the novice will satisfy your aspirations. If it is important to you to be in business for yourself (perhaps within a particular industry or area of expertise) but if one business fails you would happily try another, then you may find your career following the serial track. And finally, if you are the type that is fascinated by the concepts and processes of entrepreneurship, regardless of the industry, you may be a candidate for portfolio entrepreneurship, applying your knowledge to a number of firms simultaneously.

LEAVING THE BUSINESS   The life pattern of starting a business, making a living from it, and then retiring in your mid-60s is becoming more of a rarity in today's fast-changing world. In fact, many of our paradigms about retirement are no longer valid. *Ask yourself: When is the normal time to retire?*

For many years, in Canada, pretty much everyone retired around age 65. But a number of factors are disrupting this pattern, including the overall aging of the population and the low birth rate in Canada. At the time of writing, about half of the provinces and territories have abolished mandatory retirement ages as the courts increasingly see this as unfair age discrimination. Before this change, entrepreneurs were among the few groups that could work as long as they felt like it. Nevertheless, until recently there were an increasing number of people in their 50s opting for early retirement. Already, in Western Europe, only two-fifths of 55- to 64-year-olds are still working.[18] In Canada, the mean retirement age in 1997 was 60.6 years but the downward trend has started to reverse, making the median retirement age now closer to 62.[19] This is likely because some are now choosing to work longer, implying that the range of retirement ages is expanding. In short, people now have more choice about whether and when to retire.

Not everyone who chooses to retire ends up happy with the choice. There is some evidence that the biggest predictor of satisfaction with retired life is having realistic expectations about one's lifestyle in retirement.[20] This means understanding your own needs as well as researching and planning for retirement. Chapter 8 discusses the retirement planning tools for someone leaving a family business. Some of the issues for retirement decisions include needs of a spouse, living arrangements, income requirements, and so on. But ultimately the decision to retire must be based on personal needs. Some entrepreneurs choose to work for as long as they are able, not because of a need for more money, but because of a need to stay busy, or to be the boss, or to have a sense of purpose.

Retirement is not the only reason for leaving a business. The reasons for parting from a business include:
- *Intent from start-up.* Some entrepreneurs are really in the business of "start-ups." For example, you might be a restaurateur who specializes in starting new restaurants, getting them up and running profitably, and then selling them quickly so you can move on to start other new restaurants. In such a case, parting company with your business has little emotional cost, since this was your intention from the beginning.
- *Failure of the business.* If the business is just not making money, but still solvent, you have the opportunity to close the business, pay off any outstanding debts, and keep whatever is left of your investment. In the case of a bankruptcy, however, you have no investment and your personal assets may be at risk unless you have protected yourself by incorporation.
- *Ejection by partners.* If you are in a partnership, depending on the provisions of the partnership agreement, you could be bought out of your share of the business, even if this is not your wish. And even though your agreement will likely ensure that you are financially compensated, you will not be compensated for your sense of loss.

- *Sale of the business.* If you accept an enticing offer to sell your business, be sure that the price is enough to compensate you for your lost way of life. Remember that many buy/sell agreements will include a non-competition provision, where you are effectively excluded from your entire business community after the sale.
- *Family succession.* You may have planned to cede your business to family members at some point and stay on in an advisory capacity. Just be sure that if you do this, you are ready to relinquish the authority you have held by long habit. Both the business and family will suffer if you try to hold on to control.

Businesses, just like people, are born and die. Their end need not be tragic to the entrepreneur. Just like the end of a long human life that has been well lived, it may be sad, but it is not tragic. If the business was profitable and engaging for the entrepreneur during most of its life, then it was a success. And if the entrepreneur makes a gracious exit to a well-planned retirement, so much the better.

Head Start Exercise

11.11 Discuss your level of commitment to entrepreneurship and whether you see yourself going into another venture (subsequent to or concurrent with this business), retiring, or leaving entrepreneurship for employment ($\frac{1}{2}$ page maximum).

✓ **Test Yourself 11.24**
True or False? The current trend is for governments to lower mandatory retirement ages.

CAREERS RELATED TO ENTREPRENEURSHIP   Experience as an entrepreneur helps develop skills that are valuable in many other roles including management, teaching entrepreneurship, international development, and small business consulting and counselling.

Management: *Ask yourself: Do former entrepreneurs make good managers in companies that they work for but have no ownership in?* There is no significant research data to answer this question, but entrepreneurs who have run businesses with employees should presumably have developed some skill in managing people. On the other hand, there may well be concerns on the part of employers about hiring former entrepreneurs as managers. For example:

- Concern that the reason the applicant is a *former* entrepreneur could be a lack of management skills. This might have been the reason for a business failure.
- Concern that the former entrepreneur may retain the habits of having full authority over personnel and other decisions. Every manager who is not the business owner will have considerable limitations on authority, and former business owners will likely need at least some period of adjustment to these limitations.
- Concern that any former business owner will want to return to entrepreneurship, maybe even in competition with the new employer.

So, any decision to leave entrepreneurship in favour of seeking employment should consider these possible perceptions on the part of employers, and the job seeker should prepare to deal with them.

COMMISSION SALES   The life of a salesperson working on commission can be appealing to former entrepreneurs in that salespeople are employees (usually with the security of benefit packages) but operate largely independently in terms of how they use their time or deal with their own customers. So the sales role provides some advantages of both employment and entrepreneurship. Again, some employers may feel cautious about exposing their customer lists and techniques to a potential future competitor, but well-written employment contracts can overcome these concerns.

TEACHING ENTREPRENEURSHIP   Over the past few years there has been a huge growth in the teaching of entrepreneurship,[21] and who better to teach this subject than former entrepreneurs? But, *Ask yourself: Can entrepreneurship really be taught?* In a word, yes. It may be that some people are "born entrepreneurs," but there is good evidence that the skills of business planning and operation can be learned and entrepreneurial attitudes can certainly be fostered in the classroom.[22]

Ask yourself: Do former entrepreneurs make good teachers? How about unsuccessful former entrepreneurs? The most annoying saying for teachers is "those who can't do teach." This outrageous insult to the teaching profession, however, carries a grain of truth in the sense that you don't have to be a wildly successful entrepreneur yourself in order to help develop the skills of entrepreneurship in others. Nevertheless, some entrepreneurial experience is a great asset when it comes to providing your students with concrete examples of business principles. Some teachers, the author of this text included, have spent most of their careers teaching entrepreneurship. For others, teaching is a capstone coming at the end of a long business career; it is the opportunity to share their skills and experience. Teaching entrepreneurship is both challenging (constantly demanding new, creative approaches[23]) and highly rewarding (especially when you see a brand-new business in operation and profitable).

The majority of entrepreneurship training takes place in business schools and is designed for business students. However, there are many programs in non-business areas that lead to some form of self-employment. Typically, students in these programs develop high levels of technical skills but will be poorly trained in the skills of starting and running a business. Currently, this is the growth area for new entrepreneurial courses. As well, various levels of government provide short programs to help individuals with specific technical skills become self-employed.

consulting The providing of professional advice including specific courses of action that a client should follow.

counselling The process of informing, questioning, and guiding a client to their own decisions on a course of action.

SME CONSULTING AND COUNSELLING   Consulting is the process of providing professional advice. Business consulting is much like medical consulting in that it involves problem identification, diagnosis, and a prescription for treatment. **Counselling**, by comparison, is more of a facilitation process, providing information and an exchange of ideas. Counselling does not provide specific advice. Rather, entrepreneurs are assisted in making their own decisions.

Experienced former entrepreneurs commonly consider working for someone else or starting their own firms as small business management consultants. The feasibility of this idea is usually questionable, simply because very small firms can rarely afford non-critical consulting, and most small entrepreneurs are not interested in paying someone else to tell them how to run their companies. Consulting services that small firms do buy are more likely to be technical in nature. So the target market for general management consulting has to be considered medium-sized firms, or at the very least the SME (small and medium enterprises) market. The most likely purchasers of small business training, consulting, and counselling are in the public sector (government and government agencies) as well as NGOs (non-governmental organizations) that are receiving public funds for this purpose.

INTERNATIONAL DEVELOPMENT AND ENTREPRENEURSHIP An interesting and growing segment of entrepreneurship training and consulting is in the area of international development. The problems of the world's poorest countries are many and the solutions are difficult. However, over the past few years, economists and others working in this field have come to see small-scale entrepreneurship and improved micro-credit as parts of the solution. The poorest of the poor often have valuable technical and manual skills but

SMALL BUSINESS PROFILE 11.2
The Entrepreneurial Edge Inc.

Sandie Heirwegh is an entrepreneur who makes her living by training and coaching new entrepreneurs as well as teaching others to train and coach new entrepreneurs. The name of her business is The Entrepreneurial Edge Inc. (***www.theentrepreneurialedge.com***).

Starting this company brought Heirwegh's varied career in a full circle from entrepreneur to employee back to entrepreneur. Married at 19, she started out as a tobacco farmer and partner (with her husband) in a haulage firm. After a downturn in the tobacco industry, Sandie secured employment first as an accounting technician with a large national accounting firm; then she became a director of operations for a national franchisor before moving on to a series of government and community jobs assisting new businesses. Along the way she picked up credentials as a Certified International Trade Professional (Forum for International Trade Training) and as a Certified Business Counselor (Asia Pacific Economic Corporation).

The Entrepreneurial Edge is basically a one-woman company, although Heirwegh at times hires or subcontracts work to specialists in law, accounting, marketing, project management, and so on. At the time of writing, Heirwegh's company is partnered with the Hamilton, Ontario branch of the YWCA to deliver a federal Self-Employment Benefits program to new business owners in her area. Managing this program allows Heirwegh to use her wide range of skills including delivering workshops, mentoring entrepreneurs, and managing program staff.

As an entrepreneurship consultant, Sandie has designed and managed 13 programs that have supported over 3,000 new businesses. For seven years she wrote a regular column on small business issues for the *Hamilton Spectator*. She has designed entrepreneurship curricula for numerous colleges and government programs. Sandie has helped to create business support centres in Zimbabwe, China, and South Africa and helped to train visiting delegates from Hungary, Poland, Bangladesh, Tanzania, Japan, Pakistan, Egypt, Barbados, and other parts of the world. "The international projects are some of the most satisfying work I have ever done," says Heirwegh. "In Canada, we have so much expertise to share with those in developing countries who desperately need our help and sincerely appreciate it."

lack entrepreneurial approaches to use these skills profitably. In some areas, this is because of complex historical and cultural paradigms that make the competitive nature of entrepreneurship difficult to accept. Developing approaches to selling and teaching entrepreneurship in these areas can be difficult, but the outcomes can be profound and far-reaching. Most of the Canadian-based projects trying to foster entrepreneurship in developing countries are sponsored by the Canadian International Development Agency, which typically partners with private and public-sector organizations for the delivery of the programs.

Another increasingly important issue for economic development in poor countries is that of **microfinance**. Entrepreneurs the world over complain about lack of access to capital. In developing countries, however, this problem is immeasurably greater than in Canada, even though the loans sought by entrepreneurs are tiny by comparison to ours. There are many reasons for this situation, but three of the most important are:

1. *Lack of collateral infrastructure.* Entrepreneurs in developing countries often have collateral—for example, they may own land or machinery but cannot borrow against it for business purposes because there are none of the systems required to secure this collateral. For example, there may be no proper land-titles system to secure a mortgage, or no legislation that allows for putting a lien against a truck.

2. *Loan size.* On average, these entrepreneurs are borrowing tiny amounts, but the lenders' administrative costs are proportionally high. (For example, some micro-loans require weekly travel to the borrower for collection of loan payment.) As a result, it is impossible to lend at reasonable interest rates.

3. *Mismanagement and corruption within the micro-lenders.* A high proportion of microfinance institutes lack their own business plan, have untrained managers, and are subject to embezzlement.

These sorts of challenges are what make a career applying entrepreneurial expertise to international development so challenging. Interestingly, many of the problems faced by entrepreneurs in developing nations are similar to those faced by Aboriginal entrepreneurs in Canada. Despite this, there are a growing number of success stories for Aboriginal business in Canada and these are helping to build Canadian expertise in this area.

Get Help 11.18
The Canadian International Development Agency website (*www.cida.gc.ca*) provides details on many of the programs where your foreign aid tax dollars are spent.

microfinance The lending, borrowing, and management of small amounts of money in small enterprises.

Get Help 11.19
Anyone wishing to learn about microfinance in the developing world should start with the book published by the World Bank and written by Joanna Ledgerwood: *Sustainable Banking with the Poor, Microfinance Handbook, an Institutional and Financial Perspective.* As well, the World Bank website (*www.worldbank.org*) offers many articles on entrepreneurship in developing countries.

Get Help 11.20
For more information on Aboriginal business and government programs see the Aboriginal Business Canada website: *strategis.ic.gc.ca/epic/internet/inabc-eac.nsf/en/home.*

✓ Answers to Chapter 11 Test Yourself Questions

11.1 The terms *leadership* and *management* are totally interchangeable. *False*

11.2 A good manager should develop a single personal leadership style and stick with it. *False*

11.3 Reinforcement can affect employee behaviour even for employees who do not personally get reinforced. *True*

11.4 Delegating means assigning both responsibility and authority. *True*

11.5 Generally, the less risk involved, the less control needs to be exercised over employees. *True*

11.6 Writing is a two-way communication process. *False*

11.7 The majority of people have apprehension about public speaking. *True*

11.8 An entrepreneur never has to explain or justify his or her decisions. *False*

11.9 Minor administrative decisions should not involve a formal decision-making process. *True*

11.10 As a business grows, the entrepreneur spends an increasing amount of time dealing with operational issues. *False*

11.11 By definition, it is impossible to plan for a crisis. *False*

11.12 The word *ethics* is commonly used to mean "professional rules of conduct." *True*

11.13 The fair trade movement is broader in scope than the ethical trade movement. *False*

11.14 A *green business* is a company that practises both fair trade and ethical trade. *False*

11.15 Because they are so busy, entrepreneurs tend to give fewer volunteer hours than employees do. *False*

11.16 Good time management means handling the important things first. *False*

11.17 Research shows a strong relationship between wealth and ultimate happiness. *False*

11.18 It is possible to be fit and unhealthy or to be healthy and unfit. *True*

11.19 Other than for certain special exceptions, income tax must be paid on money withdrawn from an RRSP. *True*

11.20 The capital gain on an owner-occupied family home in Canada is tax-free when the home is sold. *True*

11.21 There is a single, national certification process that allows someone to call themselves a *Qualified Financial Planner* in Canada. *False*

11.22 The majority of financial planners work on commission rather than an hourly fee-for-service basis. *True*

11.23 An insolvent business will ultimately be declared bankrupt. *False*

11.24 The current trend is for governments to lower mandatory retirement ages. *False*

Questions for Discussion

1. There is good evidence that owners of successful growing businesses are more strategic in their thinking than owners of newer smaller businesses. Is this because entrepreneurs who manage strategically have faster growing businesses? Or is it because entrepreneurs change their approach in response to the growth of the business?

2. From recent news reports, identify a major crisis that a business has suffered. Discuss how the crisis could have been avoided and the pros and cons of the way the media has been handled in this event.

3. Argue whether *tax avoidance* is an ethical practice. Take the viewpoint of an entrepreneur trying to make money or the viewpoint of a Canada Revenue Agency auditor whose job is to make sure that every individual and company pays a fair share of taxes. (Hint: Search *tax avoidance* on the Internet. Look at the website for CRA as well as those for some accounting firms).

4. Discuss the best approaches to teaching future entrepreneurs.

Recommended Reading

Foran, Pat. *The Smart Canadian's Guide to Building Wealth.* Mississauga: John Wiley & Sons Canada Ltd., 2006.

Fritzsche, David J. *Business Ethics: A Global and Managerial Perspective.* New York: McGraw-Hill Higher Education, 2005.

Jackson, Jacky (ed.). *Essential Managers (series) Writing Skills.* New York: DK Publishing Inc., 2002.

McWaters, Graham, and Winthrop Sheldon. *The Canadian Student Financial Survival Guide.* Toronto: Insomniac Press, 2005.

Morley, Mike. *The Complete Guide to Credit and Credit Repair for Canadians.* Toronto: Nixon-Carre, 2005.

Powell, Trevor. *Free Yourself from Harmful Stress.* Montreal: Reader's Digest Association Inc., 1997.

Various. *Taking Control of Your Time.* Boston: Harvard Business School Press, 2005.

The Personal Development Plan

MANAGEMENT DEVELOPMENT

1. Describe the management style that you tend to use by default. Base this on your own opinion
    and the opinions of others you work with or have personal relationships with. Use specific
    behavioural examples.

    _____

    _____

    _____

    _____

    _____

    _____

    _____

    _____

2. Referring to Figure 11.2 in the text, assess the circumstances under which you commonly
    work and discuss the suitability of, or need for, change in your leadership approaches.

    _____

    _____

    _____

    _____

    _____

    _____

    _____

    _____

3. Describe your communication strengths and weaknesses under the categories of writing,
    presenting, and listening. Use specific examples.

    _____

    _____

    _____

    _____

    _____

    _____

    _____

4. Describe your organizational strengths and weaknesses under the categories of decision making, documenting, and planning.

_____

_____

_____

_____

_____

_____

_____

_____

5. List ways in which you are both prepared and unprepared to handle a crisis.

_____

_____

_____

_____

_____

_____

_____

_____

_____

6. Considering the above analysis of your management skills, identify two to three priority areas for development and prepare a chart showing specific readings, exercises, courses, consulting, memberships, or other means you will use for remediation (see Figure 11.5).

Figure 11.5 **DEVELOPMENT CHART**

Development need	Remediation technique	Start date	Completion date

PERSONAL DEVELOPMENT

7. Outline any company policies you will implement regarding ethics or community involvement.

_____

_____

_____

_____

_____

_____

_____

_____

_____

8. Briefly explain the paper or electronic systems you use for scheduling your time and indicate specific times you have set aside for reviewing strategic information and for planning.

_____

_____

_____

_____

_____

_____

_____

_____

_____

9. Outline a specific regimen you have, or will implement, for maintaining strong personal relationships and a fit and healthy body. Describe your personal practices for coping with stress.

_____

_____

_____

_____

_____

_____

_____

_____

10. Create a monthly analysis and budget for all of your personal, family, household, and savings/investment disbursements (see Figure 11.6).

Figure 11.6

FAMILY MONTHLY INCOME $_____

Disbursement	Current	Budget
Debt Payment	$	$
loans		
credit cards		
mortgage		
car lease/loan		
Household Expenses		
taxes		
water		
electricity		
gas		
telephone		
cable/ISP		
insurance		
food		
furnishings		
home repair		
car fuel and maintenance		
Personal Expenses		
cell phones		
entertainment		
education		
fitness		
health and beauty		
clothing		
vacation		
Miscellaneous Expenses		
gifts		
Savings and Investments		
registered pension plans		
registered retirement saving plan		
personal investment portfolio		
Total Disbursement	$_____	$_____

PERSONAL FINANCIAL PLAN

11. Identify any tax saving techniques that you currently use. Explain how you will implement any opportunities you have not taken advantage of. Identify your sources of advice in this area.

_____

_____

_____

_____

_____

_____

_____

12. Outline your long-term financial goals and your overall investment strategy. Identify any advisers you use for financial planning.

_____

_____

_____

_____

_____

_____

_____

_____

_____

_____

_____

13. Explain the factors that would be most likely to precipitate a financial crisis for your company. Discuss the dangers and likelihood of your having a personal financial crisis.

_____

_____

_____

_____

_____

_____

_____

CAREER PLAN

14. Estimate how long you expect to remain in your current role with this business and any future roles you see yourself in as an entrepreneur.

_____

_____

_____

_____

_____

_____

_____

_____

15. Identify any employment opportunities you will pursue in the future and explain your interest and suitability.

_____

_____

_____

_____

_____

_____

_____

_____

Endnotes

Chapter 1

1. United States Small Business Administration, *Guide to SBA's Definition of Small Business*, Washington, www.sba.gov/size/indexguide.html.

2. Industry Canada, *Key Small Business Statistics*, July 2005, http://strategis.gc.ca/sbstatistics.

3. Statistics Canada, *Survey on Financing of Small and Medium Enterprises*, 2001.

4. Developed for the Business School, *Humber Institute of Technology and Advanced Learning*. Used by permission.

5. Sjoerd Beugelsdijk and Niels Noorderhaven, "Personality Characteristics of Self-Employed: An Empirical Study," *Small Business Economics*, 24 (Tilburg, The Netherlands: Spring 2005): 159–167.

6. Jamal Muhammed, "Job Stress, Satisfaction and Mental Health: An Empirical Examination of Self-Employed and Non-Self-Employed Canadians," *Journal of Small Business Management*, 35, 4 (October 1997): 48–58.

7. Industry Canada, *Key Small Business Statistics*, July 2005, op. cit.

8. Hyungrae Jo and Jinjoo Lee, "The Relationship between an Entrepreneur's Background and Performance in a New Venture," *Technovation*, 16, 4 (Amsterdam: April 1996): 161.

9. John R. Baldwin, Lin Bian, Richard Dupuy, and Guy Gellatly, *Failure Rates for New Canadian Firms: New Perspectives on Entry and Exit* (Statistics Canada, 2000).

10. Statistics Canada, "Study: Business Dynamics in Canada," *The Daily*, Tuesday, February 15, 2005.

11. Industry Canada, *Micro-Economic Monitor*, Third Quarter (Ottawa: Micro-Economic Directorate, Industry & Science Policy Sector, 1998).

12. Conference Board of Canada, "Canada's Underground Economy," *Canadian Business Review*, 21 (Ottawa: Summer 1994): 26.

13. John A. Gromala and David F. Gage, "Mediating Personality Differences behind Internal Business Disputes," *The CPA Journal*, 72, 3 (New York: March 2002): 68.

14. Robert E. Staub, "The Primacy of Courage in Partnering with Others," *The Journal for Quality and Participation*, 23, 3 (Cincinnati: May/June 2000): 16.

15. Ray A. Knight and Lee G. Knight, "Planning: The Key to Small Business Survival," *Management Accounting*, 74, 8 (February 1993): 33.

Chapter 2

1. Ho Yeon Kim, "The Locational and Functional Behavior of U.S. Autoparts Suppliers," *Small Business Economics*, 24 (Spring 2005): 79–95.

2. Peter Lindelof and Hans Lofsten, "Proximity as a Resource Base for Competitive Advantage: University–Industry Links for Technology Transfer," *Journal of Technology Transfer*, 29, 3–4 (August 2004): 311–326

3. Saul Sands, "Improved Pedestrian Traffic Counts for Better Retail Site Location," *Journal of Small Business Management*, 10 (January 1972): 27–31.

4. Carol Kerns, "Making the Right Impression: How Fastsigns Uses Site Selection as a Marketing Tool," *Franchising World*, 24, 4 (July/August 1992): 15–17.

5. Michael D. Geurts and David B. Whitlark, "Six Ways to Make Sales Forecasts More Accurate," *Journal of Business Forecasting Methods and Systems*, 18, 4 (Winter 1999/2000): 21–23.

6. Mike Jakeman, "Small Business Coverages: Cost-Effective Delivery," *Canadian Underwriter*, 72, 4 (April 2005): 40–42.

7. Gary Tryon and Brian H. Kleiner, "How to Investigate Alleged Employee Theft Properly," *Managerial Auditing Journal*, 12, 1 (1997): 19–25.

8. Michele Tonglet, "Consumer Misbehaviour: An Exploratory Study of Shoplifting," *Journal of Consumer Behaviour*, 1, 4, (June 2002): 336–355.

9. Christopher Heer, "Employees and Trade Secrets: How the Concept of Inevitable Disclosure May Fit Into Canadian Law," *Intellectual Property Journal*, 19, 2 (April 2006): 323–350.

Chapter 3

1. Ali Kara, John E. Spillan, and Oscar W. DeShields Jr., "The Effect of a Market Orientation on Business Performance: A Study of Small-Sized Service Retailers Using MARKOR Scale," *Journal of Small Business Management*, 43, 2 (April 2005): 105–119.

2. Julia Chang, "How Service Impacts Your Brand," *Incentive*, 180, 7 (July 2006): 12.

3. Kate Maddox, "Small Firms' Web Spending Lags," *B to B*, 91, 7 (June 12, 2006): 16.

4. Grigorios Zontanos and Alistair R. Anderson, "Relationships, Marketing and Small Business: An Exploration of Links in Theory and Practice," *Qualitative Market Research*, 17, 3 (2004): 228–239.

5. Shuba Srinivasan, Koen Pauwels, Dominique M. Hanssens, and Marnik G. Dekimpe, "Do Promotions Benefit Manufacturers, Retailers or Both?" *Management Science*, 50, 5 (May 2004): 617–630.

6. John M. Browning and Ronald J. Adams, "Trade Shows: An Effective Promotional Tool for the Small Industrial Business," *Journal of Small Business Management*, 26, 4 (October 1988): 31–36.

Chapter 4

1. Randolph P. Johnston, "High Tech for the Small Office," *Journal of Accountancy*, 200, 6 (December 2005): 41–45.

2. Eward A. Metzger, "Adjustable Seating Promotes Lab Productivity," *Laboratory Product News*, 36, 4 (June 2006): 6–7.

3. John Davies and Nicolas Tilley, "Interior Design: Using the Management Services Approach in Retail Premises," *Management Services*, 48, 7 (July 2004): 10–16.

4. Adil Baykasoglu, Turkay Dereli, and Ibrahim Sabuncu, "An Ant Colony Algorithm for Solving Budget Constrained and Unconstrained Dynamic Facility Layout Problems," *Omega*, 34, 4 (August 2006): 385.

5. Tony Polito and Devin Watson, "Just-in-Time Under Fire: The Five Major Constraints Upon JIT Practices," *Journal of American Academy of Business*, 9, 1 (March 2006): 8–14.

6. Réne Gélinas and Yvon Bigras, "The Characteristics and Features of SMEs: Favorable or Unfavorable to Logistics Integration?" *Journal of Small Business Management*, 42, 3 (July 2004): 263–279.

7. Stephen C. Jones, Tami L. Knotts, and Karen L. Brown, "Selected Quality Practices of Small Manufacturers," *The Quality Management Journal*, 12, 1 (2005): 41–54.

8. J. Carlton Collins, "Small Business Software Grows Up," *Journal of Accountancy*, 201, 3 (March 2006): 50–57.

9. Joris Jeijaard, Maryse J. Brand, and Marco Mosselman, "Organizational Structure and Performance in Dutch Small Firms," *Small Business Economics*, 25, 1 (August 2005): 83–93.

10. Barbara Ettorre, "Is Salary a Motivator?" *Management Review*, 88, 1 (January1999): 8–9.

Chapter 5

1. Anthony J. Berry, Robert Sweeting, and Jitsu Goto, "The Effect of Business Advisers on the Performance of SMEs," *Journal of Small Business and Enterprise Development*, 13, 1 (2006): 33–48.

2. Suzanne Gaspar, "Managing Technology Turnover," *Network World*, 19, 42 (October 21, 2002): 56–57.

3. Anuradha Basu and Eser Altinay, "The Interaction between Culture and Entrepreneurship in London's Immigration Businesses," *International Small Business Journal*, 20, 4 (November 2002): 371–382.

4. Stephen Prowse, "Angel Investors and the Market for Angel Investments," *Journal of Banking & Finance*, 22, 6–8 (August 1998): 785–793.

Chapter 6

1. Mark Bruno, "Private Equity Powers More MBOs among Larger Firms," *Pensions and Investments*, 34, 12 (June 12, 2006): 1–4.

2. Gene H. Johnson, Rudolph S. Lindbeck, and Winston N. McVea Jr., "Traps to Avoid When Purchasing a Business," *Journal of Financial Planning*, 7, 1 (January 1994): 38–42.

3. Howard Levitt, "Competition Is Hard to Restrict, in Most Cases," *National Post* (November 30, 2005).

4. Margaret D. Nowicki, Eric E. Lewis, and Jeffrey W. Lippitt, "Preparing Your Business for Valuation," *New England Journal of Entrepreneurship*, 8, 1 (Spring 2005): 59–64.

5. S. Alan Aycock, "The Impact of Fairness, Reference Points, and Human Decision Processing on Negotiations," *Journal of Financial Service Professionals*, 54, 2 (March 2000): 26–82.

6. Peggy A. Lambing and Charles R. Kuehl, *Entrepreneurship*, 4th ed. (New Jersey: Pearson Education Inc., 2007), 52–54.

Chapter 7

1. Richard C. Hoffman and John F. Preble, "Convert to Compete: Competitive Advantage through Conversion Franchising," *Journal of Small Business Management*, 41, 2 (April 2003): 187–205.

2. Gregory Pang, "Multi-level Marketing," *Edmonton Journal* (February 21, 2004).

3. Patrick J. Daufmann and Rajiv P. Dant, "Multi-unit Franchising: Growth and Management Issues," *Journal of Business Venturing*, 11, 5 (September 1996): 343–359.

4. See the Competition Act on the Department of Justice website at *http://laws.justice.gc.ca/en/c-34/text.html*.

5. Dick Rennick, "Focus on the Brand," *Franchising World*, 37, 12 (December 2005): 8–9.

6. Ram C. Rao and Shuba Srinivasan, "An Analysis of Advertising Payments in Franchise Contracts," *Journal of Marketing Channels*, 8, 3–4 (2001): 85.

7. Kimberley A. Morrison, "How Franchise Job Satisfaction and Personality Affects Performance, Organizational Commitment, Franchisor Relations and Intention to Remain," *Journal of Small Business Management*, 35, 3 (July 1997): 39–68.

8. Flenn Withiam, "Who's the Customer? The Franchisee," *Cornell Hotel and Restaurant Administration Quarterly*, 41, 3 (June 2000): 12–13.

9. Scott Shane, Venkatesh Shankar, and Ashwin Aravindakshan, "The Effects of New Franchisor Partnering Strategies on Franchise System Size," *Management Science*, 52, 5 (May 2006): 773–788.

Chapter 8

1. Tammi S. Feltham, Glenn Feltham, and James J. Barnett, "The Dependence of Family Business on a Single Decision-Maker," *Journal of Small Business Management*, 43, 1 (January 2005): 1–15.

2. Jess H. Chua, James J. Chrisman, and Pramodita Sharma, "Defining the Family Business by Behaviour," *Entrepreneurship Theory and Practice*, 23, 4 (Summer 1999): 19–40.

3. Michael G. Stevens, "Passing the Family Business Mantle," *The Practical Accountant*, 31, 7 (July 1998): 20–25.

4. Byrne Fergal, "Keeping the Squabbles out of Succession: Family Businesses" (Part One), *Financial Times* (October 12, 2000).

5. Doug Bruce and Derek Picard, "Making Succession a Success: Perspectives from Canadian Small and Medium-Sized Enterprises," *Journal of Small Business Management*, 44, 2 (April 2006): 306–309.

6. Robert Napoli, "Selling Out," *CA Magazine*, 139, 4 (May 2006): 43–46.

7. Daniel H. Markstein III, "Business Succession Planning That Meets the Owner's Needs," *Estate Planning*, 33, 7 (July 2006): 20–27.

8. James P. Marshall, Ritch Sorenson, Keith Brighamm, Elizabeth Wieling, et al., "The Paradox for the Family Firm CEO: Owner Age Relationship to Succession-Related Processes and Plans," *Journal of Business Venturing*, 21, 3 (May 2006): 348.

9. William S. White, Timothy D. Drinke, and David L. Geller, "Family Business Succession Planning: Devising an Overall Strategy," *Journal of Financial Service Professionals*, 58, 3 (May 2004): 67–87.

10. Glenn Feltham, Tammi S. Feltham, and Robert Mathieu, "The Use of Estate Freezes by Family-Owned Businesses," *Canadian Tax Journal*, 51, 4 (2003): 1570–1588.

Chapter 9

1. Nicholas O'Regan, Abby Ghobadian, and David Gallear, "In Search of the Drivers of High Growth in Manufacturing SMEs," *Technovation*, 26, 1 (January 2006): 30.

2. Anonymous, "Innovations: PLM for the SME," *Strategic Direction*, 20, 11 (November/December 2004): 31–34.

3. Bruce Tait, "The Failure of Marketing 'Science'," *Brandweek*, 43, 14 (April 8, 2002): 20.

4. Peggy A. Lambing and Charles R. Kuehl, *Entrepreneurship,* 4th ed. (New Jersey: Prentice Hall Inc., 2007), p.107.

5. James A. Wolf and Timothy L. Pett, "Small-Firm Performance: Modeling the Role of Product and Process Improvements," *Journal of Small Business Management*, 44, 2 (April 2006): 268–288.

6. Chad Rubel, "Franchising Fellowship," *Marketing Management*, 4, 2 (Fall 1995): 4.

7. Jean Bosco Sabuhoro, Bruno Larue, and Yvan Gervais, "Factors Determining the Success or Failure of Canadian Establishments on Foreign Markets: A Survival Analysis Approach," *The International Trade Journal*, 20, 1, (Spring 2006): 33.

8. G. Hilton, "Knocking Down Export Barriers to Smaller Firms," *Business and Economic Review*, 51, 4 (July–September 2005): 18.

9. Michael Tobin, "Debunking the Five Myths of Global Expansion," *Financial Executive*, 22, 2 (March 2006): 57–60.

10. Brian T. Gregory, Matthew W. Rutherford, Sharon Oswald, and Lorraine Gardiner, "An Empirical Investigation of the Growth Cycle Theory of Small Firm Financing," *Journal of Small Business Management*, 43, 4 (October 2005): 382.

11. Tze-Wei Fu and Mei-Chu Ke, "Capital Growth, Financing Source and Profitability of Small Business: Evidence from Taiwan Small Enterprises," *Small Business and Economics*, 18, 4 (June 2002): 257.

12. Statistics Canada, *Survey on Financing of Small and Medium Enterprises, 2004* (February 2006), Table 31.

13. Ibid., see Table 10.

Chapter 10

1. Glenn R. Carroll, "The Specialist Strategy," *California Management Review*, 26 (Spring 1984): 126–137.

2. Carl W. Stern, *Perspectives on Strategy from the Boston Consulting Group: The Best Strategic Thinking from the Boston Consulting Group* (New York: Wiley, 1998).

3. Michael P. Steiner and Olaf Solem, "Factors for Success in Small Manufacturing Firms," *Journal of Small Business Management*, 26, 1 (January 1988): 51–56.

4. Roger H. Michell and Vincent A. Mabert, "Robotics for Smaller Manufacturers: Myths and Realities," *Business Horizons*, 29, 4 (July/August 1986): 9–17.

5. Sumaria Mohan-Neill, "An Analysis of Factors which Influence Small Businesses: Decision to Have a Website and to Conduct Online Selling," *Journal of American Academy of Business*, 8, 2 (March 2006): 204–210. (*Note*: U.S. data.)

6. K. Douglas Hoffman and John Bateson, *Essentials of Services Marketing: Concepts, Strategies and Cases* (New York: Harcourt, 2002), p. 297.

7. Ibid. pp. 276–280.

Chapter 11

1. Gary Packham, David Brooksbank, Christopher Miller, and Brychan Thomas, "Climbing the Mountain: Management Practice Adoption in Growth Oriented Firms in Wales," *Journal of Small Business and Enterprise Development*, 12, 4 (2005): 482–498.

2. O.M. Irgens, "Situational Leadership: A Modification of Hersey and Blanchard," *Leadership and Organization Development Journal*, 16, 2 (1995): 34–40.

3. See: Paul Hersey and Kenneth H. Blanchard, *Management of Organizational Behaviour: Utilizing Human Resources* (New Jersey: Prentice Hall, 1977).

4. Muhammad Jamal, "JobStress, Satisfaction and Mental Health: An Empirical Examination of Self-Employed and Non-Self-Employed Canadians," *Journal of Small Business Management*, 35, 4 (October 1997): 48–58.

5. Soren Ventegodt, Trine Flensborg-Madsen, Niels Anderson, Michael

Nielsen, Morad Mohammed, and Jov Merrick, "Global Quality of Life (QOL), Health and Ability are Primarily Determined by our Consciousness. Research Finding from Denmark 1991–2004," *Social Indicators Research*, 7 (2005): 87–221.

6. Robert E. Lane, "Does Money Buy Happiness?" *Public Interest*, 113 (Fall 1993): 56–66.

7. Charles R. Stoner, Richard Hartman, and Raj Arora, "Work-Home Role Conflict in Female Owners of Small Businesses: An Exploratory Study," *Journal of Small Business Management*, 28, 1 (January 1990): 30.

8. M.D.R. Evans and Jonathan Kelley, "Effect of Family Structure on Life Satisfaction," *Social Indicators Research*, 69 (2004): 303–349.

9. James Hill and Rena Wing, "The National Weight Control Registry," *The Permanente Journal*, 7, 3 (Summer 2003): 34–37.

10. Michael G. Goldsby, Donald F. Kuratko, and James W. Bishop, "Entrepreneurship and Fitness, An Examination of Rigorous Exercise and Goal Attainment Among Small Business Owners," *Journal of Small Business Management*, 43, 1 (January 2005): 78–92.

11. Ibid.

12. Muhammad Jamal, "Job Stress, Satisfaction and Mental Health: An Empirical Examination of Self-Employed and Non-Self-Employed Canadians," *Journal of Small Business Management*, 35, 4 (October1997): 48–58.

13. Canada Revenue Agency website, www.cra-arc.gc.ca/agency/ alert/avoiview-e.html, posted as of May 29, 2005.

14. CBCNews/INDEPTH, April 28, 2006. Federal Budget Announcement, April 27, 2006, Finance Minister Ralph Goodale.

15. Industry Canada, Office of the Superintendent of Bankruptcy of Canada, *An Overview of Canadian Insolvency Statistics*, Up to 2004, 38–41.

16. Mika Pasanen, "Multiple Entrepreneurship Among Successful SMEs in Peripheral Locations," *Journal of Small Business and Enterprise*, 10, 4 (2003): 418–426.

17. Paul Westhead, Deniz Ucbasaran, and Mike Wright, "Decisions, Actions and Performance: Do Novice, Serial,

and Portfolio Entrepreneurs Differ?"
*Journal of Small Business
Management*, 43, 4 (October 2005):
393–418.

18. Anonymous, "Leaders: Geronto-
capitalism; Entrepreneurship," *The
Economist*, London: 377, 8458
(December 24, 2005): 14.

19. Hadzipetros, Peter, "Indepth:
Retirement," CBC News Online,
February 11, 2005.

20. T.L. Gall and D.R. Evans,
"Preretirement Expectations and the
Quality of Life of Male Retirees in
Later Retirement," *Canadian Journal
of Behavioural Science*, Ottawa: 32, 3
(July 2000): 87.

21. Kyleen K. Myrah and Russell R. Currie,
"Examining Undergraduate
Entrepreneurship Education," *Journal of
Small Business and Entrepreneurship*,
19, 3 (July 2006): 233–253.

22. G. Gorman, D. Hanlon, and W. King,
"Some Research Perspectives on
Entrepreneurship Education and
Education for Small Business
Management: A Ten-Year Review,"
International Small Business Journal,
8, 4 (April/June 1997): 56–77.

23. Gary L. Benson, "Teaching
Entrepreneurship through the
Classics," *Journal of Applied Business
Research*, 8, 4 (Fall 1992): 135–141.

Index